Robert Main

Practical and spherical astronomy, for the use chiefly of students in the universities

Robert Main

Practical and spherical astronomy, for the use chiefly of students in the universities

ISBN/EAN: 9783337214968

Printed in Europe, USA, Canada, Australia, Japan

Cover: Foto ©Paul-Georg Meister /pixelio.de

More available books at **www.hansebooks.com**

PRACTICAL AND SPHERICAL ASTRONOMY,

FOR THE USE CHIEFLY OF STUDENTS IN THE UNIVERSITIES.

BY THE

REV. ROBERT MAIN, M.A., F.R.S., F.R.A.S.

RADCLIFFE OBSERVER AT OXFORD.

CAMBRIDGE:
DEIGHTON, BELL, AND CO.
LONDON: BELL AND DALDY.
1863.

Cambridge:
PRINTED BY C. J. CLAY, M.A.
AT THE UNIVERSITY PRESS.

PREFACE.

THE want of a text-book on Astronomy adapted to the requirements of our Universities, and embodying the practice and the theories of the present time, has long been severely felt. It was hoped that the author's partial translation of Brünnow's *Spherical Astronomy* would have helped materially to supply this want, or would at least have given to College and private tutors an excellent model which they might have used with proper modifications as the basis of their lectures. Whether this has been the case or not the author has had no opportunity of determining, but, on the urgent representations of several scientific friends, that a book was still wanting which should embody the methods of modern Astronomy as practised in England, and be put into a shape fit for the immediate use of students of the Universities, he has been induced to undertake the treatise which is now offered to the public.

The principal object of the writer has been to include, both in the practical and theoretical portions of the volume, all the mathematical processes which will enable the reader to understand the operations of a modern Observatory furnished with the ordinary meridional and extrameridional instruments, so that he might readily acquire, if called upon to do so, by actual practice in an observatory, the additional and more minute details which occur in the making and reducing of observations. It has not been attempted therefore, in the description of the instruments, to enter minutely into the details of the construction of their separate parts farther than is necessary to give with accuracy the mathematical theory of their use. In fact, the study of such details is only to be accomplished satisfactorily by the familiar inspection and actual use of the instruments, and will be very speedily mastered by any one who has previously gained a good knowledge of the general principles of their construction. On the other hand, it is hoped that there is scarcely a process which is used at Greenwich, or our other great English Observatories, which is left unexplained, and that a student will be enabled, by the help of this treatise, and by suitable tables, to reduce every class of observations which will be found in their annals, or to examine the accuracy of their results.

With regard to arrangement, that has been followed which appeared the most logical, and which would suggest itself most naturally to a person desirous of pursuing the study of Practical Astronomy. After the elementary notions of the planes of reference, as deduced from diurnal and annual phenomena, and a statement of the principal terms or definitions of the science, the next step would obviously be to explain the methods and to describe the instruments by means of which the positions of celestial objects can be observed with reference to these planes; and then to investigate the method of transforming from any system of co-ordinates or planes of reference to any others. Next in order would come the consideration of the most obvious of the phenomena arising from the earth's diurnal rotation and annual motion; and that of the sensible measures of time as fundamentally connected with these phenomena. After this would follow the various corrections which are necessary to determine for ultimate use the places of the heavenly bodies as freed from all the errors (including those arising from the variations of the planes of reference) which would make their observed places different as observed at different stations and at different times. And, lastly, would follow the consideration of the orbits described by the planets, as deduced from observation, with such specific notices of the peculiarities of particular planets as admit of mathematical treatment, and as belong to the subject of Practical Astronomy.

It has been thought advisable not to overload the book with examples of actual computation, for fear of giving it a repulsive appearance in the eyes of the mathematical student. It is hoped, however, that a sufficient number has been given to exhibit the way in which the mathematical formulæ are reduced to numbers in particular cases, and choice has generally been made of those formulæ which are either necessary for the use of the astronomer, or which serve to develope some peculiarity in the mode of computation.

The mathematical processes by which the various formulæ have been deduced, are always those which appeared to give the result in the simplest way by geometrical considerations, and without any regard to the severe symmetry which is aimed at in Brünnow's *Astronomy;* but, in all cases of the variation of elements, the Differential Calculus has been freely used wherever it could be employed advantageously. Occasionally there may be a little novelty in some of the methods, though in general those in ordinary use have been employed, unless a shorter or more convenient process occurred to the author for effecting particular operations. It is believed, for example, that the direct method proposed for finding the "Geocentric Position of the Corresponding Point" in the treatment of occultations of stars by the Moon, does away with the necessity for the indirect method used at Greenwich, and an example is given to shew the facility of use of the formula employed.

The author is happy to acknowledge his obligations to his son, Mr P. T. Main, B.A., of St John's College, Cambridge, for his assistance during the progress of the work. In addition to the chapter on "Precession and Nutation," which was written entirely by him, he has examined carefully every sheet before it has been finally committed for press. The examples at the end of the volume were also collected by him.

Mr A. Freeman, Fellow of St John's College, also kindly undertook a separate reading of the proof-sheets, for which the author takes this opportunity of expressing his thanks.

In conclusion, it is hoped that the book will prove sufficiently useful to recompense the author for the labour which has been bestowed upon it,—a labour which he would willingly have avoided if any other competent person had been likely to undertake the task.

RADCLIFFE OBSERVATORY, OXFORD,
August 13, 1863.

CONTENTS.

CHAPTER I.

DEFINITIONS AND FIRST PRINCIPLES.

	PAGE
Systems of Spherical Co-ordinates	2
Apparent Diurnal Motion	3
Equator and Ecliptic; Right Ascension and Declination; Longitude and Latitude; Obliquity of the Ecliptic, &c.	4
Horizon and Meridian	5
Latitude of the Place of Observation	6
Hour-Angle; Sidereal Time, &c.	7
Clock-Time and Clock-Rate	8
Method of determining R.A. and N.P.D.	ib.
Zenith-Point	9
Transit-Circle and Equatorial Instrument	10
Altitude and Azimuth Instrument or Altazimuth	11

CHAPTER II.

INSTRUMENTS.

The TRANSIT-INSTRUMENT, its Eye-Piece, and System of Wires	13
Its Construction and Mounting	14
Illumination of the Field of the Telescope	15
Appearance of the System of Wires	ib.
Errors of Collimation, of Level, and of Azimuth	16
The Micrometer	17
Method of determining the Error of Collimation	18
Mean of Wires	ib.

	PAGE
Correction to Collimation for Diurnal Aberration	18
Determination of the Intervals of the Wires	19—20
Factors for Planets and the Moon	21—22
Correction to time of transit for Error of Collimation	22
Error of Level	ib.
Description of the Spirit-Level	23—24
Determination of the Error of Level	25
Correction for Inequality of Pivots	25—27
Correction to time of transit for Error of Level	27
Error of Azimuth and correction to time of transit	28
True time of transit over the Meridian	29
Methods of determining the Error of Azimuth	29—30
Determination of Clock Error	31
„ Absolute Right Ascension	32
Transit-Instrument in the Prime Vertical	ib.
Its Instrumental Errors	33—35
Effect of Error of Level on Colatitude and Declinations of Stars	37
Struve's method of determining N.P.D. or Colatitude	37—39
The TRANSIT-CIRCLE	39
Its Collimators	40—41
Determination of Errors of Collimation and Level	42—43
Description of the Carrington Transit-Circle used at Oxford	44
The Microscope-Micrometers and their Error of Runs	45—46
Correction for Error of Excentricity of the Circle	46—47
Concluded Circle-Reading	48
Correction for Curvature	49
„ Motion of a Planet	50
Nadir-Point by Bohnenberger's Eye-Piece	51
Zenith-Point by Reflexion-observations of Stars	51—52
The EQUATORIAL	53
Its Instrumental Errors	54—57
The ALTAZIMUTH	57
Its Instrumental Errors	59—63

CHAPTER III.

TRANSFORMATION OF CO-ORDINATES.

To determine R.A. and N.P.D. from Azimuth and Zenith-Distance	64—66
To determine Azimuth and Zenith-Distance from the Hour-Angle and N.P.D.	66—67
To find the Errors of R.A. and N.P.D. in terms of the Errors of Tabular Azimuth and Z.D.	67—70

To find the Geocentric Longitude and Latitude of an object from the observed R.A. and N.P.D.	70—74
To find the R.A. and N.P.D. from the Geocentric Longitude and Latitude	74
To find the Errors of Geocentric Longitude and Latitude in terms of the Errors of R.A. and N.P.D. and *vice versâ*	74—76
Effect of the Error of Obliquity	77
On the Motion of the Sun in the Ecliptic	78
Determination of the Equinox	78—79
Determination of the Obliquity by observations of the Sun's Declination made near the Solstices	79—81
Determination of the Obliquity and of the R.A. of a Star, by two observations of difference of R.A. of the Star and the Sun, and of the Sun's Declination	83
Obliquity deduced from Greenwich Observations of 1859	84—85
Equinox similarly determined	86—87
General Formulæ for the Transformation of Co-ordinates	88—89

CHAPTER IV.

ON THE PHENOMENA ARISING FROM THE DIURNAL ROTATION OF THE EARTH ON ITS AXIS, AND ITS ANNUAL REVOLUTION ROUND THE SUN.

Signs of the Zodiac	90
The Seasons of the Year	91
Semi-Diurnal Arc	92
Tropics of Cancer and Capricorn	93
Greatest Altitude of a Planet	94
Time of Greatest Change of Altitude of a Star	95—97
Problems	97

CHAPTER V.

ON TIME.

Sidereal Time	98
Mean Solar Time	99
Lengths of the Tropical and the Sidereal Year	*ib.*
Equation of Time	100—101
Relations of Mean Solar and Sidereal Time	102—103

x   CONTENTS.

	PAGE
Computation of Sidereal and Mean Solar Time	103—104
Greenwich Table for computation of Mean Solar Time	105
Length of the Sidereal Year	106
On the Calendar	107
Determination of Time by observation	108
Comparison of Clocks	109
Error in time produced by a given error in Z.D.	110
Determination of local time by equal altitudes of the Sun or a Star before and after the meridian passage	110—112
Time and Colatitude by two observed altitudes of the Sun or a Star	112—114
Errors of deduced Colatitude and Hour-Angle in terms of the Errors of observed Z.D.	115
Determination of Time by observing when two known Stars have the same altitude	116
To find the Time by observing when two known Stars are in the same vertical	117
Graphical explanation of the Equation of Time	118

CHAPTER VI. (Part 1.)

ON THE CORRECTIONS TO BE APPLIED TO THE OBSERVED PLACES OF THE HEAVENLY BODIES, ON ACCOUNT OF THE POSITION OF THE OBSERVER ON THE SURFACE OF THE EARTH, AND OF THE PROPERTIES OF LIGHT.

On Refraction	119
Law of Vertical Refraction	121
General Differential Equation for Refraction	121—126
Simpson's Investigation	126—129
Effect of Variations of Pressure and Density	130—131
Determination of the Constant of Refraction	132
Refraction in R.A. and N.P.D. for extra-meridional observations	132—135
Expression for the Refraction on the supposition of a uniform density of the atmosphere	135—136
Effect of Refraction on the rising and setting of a Star	136—137
Effect of Refraction on the apparent Diameter of the Moon	137—138
On Twilight	139—141

CHAPTER VI. (Part 2.)

ON ABERRATION.

Illustrations of Aberration	143
Law of Aberration	144—145
Value of the Coefficient of Aberration	145—146
Aberration of a Star with reference to a given plane	146—147
Aberration of a Star in longitude and latitude	147—148
Aberration in R.A. and N.P.D.	149—150
Bessel's investigation of Aberration	151—157
Value of the Diurnal Aberration	158—159
Planetary Aberration	160
Bradley's observations of γ Draconis	160—162

CHAPTER VI. (Part 3.)

ON PARALLAX.

Magnitude and Figure of the Earth	164
Method of Eratosthenes	164—165
Measure of an Arc of Meridian	166
Formula for Radius of Curvature	167
Determination of the Ellipticity	168
Measure of Transverse Arc	169
Principal Measures of Arcs of Meridian	169—170
Angle of the Vertical	171—172
Value of Angle of the Vertical for Oxford	173
Determination of Earth's Radius-vector in terms of Astronomical and Geocentric Latitude	174—179
Law of Parallax in Altitude	180
Parallax of the Moon in Altitude	181—184
Expression for Parallax in terms of Geocentric Zenith-Distance	185
Value for Oxford	186
Parallax in R.A. and N.P.D. for Extra-meridional Observations	187—189
Constant of Parallax in terms of Solar Parallax	190
Method of finding the value of the Lunar Parallax	190—192
Observations of N.P.D. of Mars for Parallax	193—196
Recent Discussions tending to increase the received value of the Parallax of the Sun	196—198
Solar Parallax as found by the Transit of Venus	199—200

CHAPTER X.

ON THE DETERMINATION OF GEOGRAPHICAL LATITUDE AND LONGITUDE . 285

	PAGE
Method of finding the Colatitude in fixed Observatories .	285—287
Colatitude of the Radcliffe Observatory, Oxford, deduced from the observations of circumpolar stars in 1861. . .	288
Determination of Colatitude by comparison of observed Zenith Distances of Stars with their Tabular N.P.D's. . .	289—290
Determination of Latitude by the observed Altitude of the Sun	291
,, by observed Altitudes of a Star near the Meridian . . .	291—293
,, by observed Altitudes of Polaris .	293—298
,, by two observed Altitudes of a Star	298—300
,, by two observed Altitudes of the Sun	300—301
DETERMINATION OF GEOGRAPHICAL LONGITUDE . . .	301
Enumeration of the different methods in use for finding Longitude	302
The Method of Signals	303
History of the application of Galvanism to effect the self-registration of Transits of Stars	ib.
Description of the Galvanic Apparatus used at Greenwich .	304—305
Method of determining Longitude by the Transmission of Chronometers	306
Determination of the Longitude of Valentia . .	306—308
,, ,, of Pulkowa .	309
Method by the Eclipses of Jupiter's Satellites . .	ib.
Method by the Culmination of the Moon and neighbouring Stars	310—311
Effect of observing several Stars	312—313
Determination of the Longitudes of Sydney and Washington .	313—316
Method by Sextant Observations of the Moon's Greatest Altitude	316—319
Method of Lunar Distances	319
Raper's Method of clearing the Lunar Distance for Parallax	320—322
Method of finding the Greenwich Mean Solar Time corresponding to the cleared Lunar Distance . . .	322—324
Other methods of clearing the Distance . . .	324—326
Method of finding Longitude by Eclipses of the Sun and Moon, and by Occultations of Fixed Stars by the Moon . .	326—327

CHAPTER XI.

ON ECLIPSES OF THE SUN AND MOON; AND ON OCCULTATIONS OF STARS OR PLANETS BY THE MOON.

	PAGE
On Eclipses of the Moon	328
Angular values of the Umbra and Penumbra	330
Length of Shadow	331
Lunar Ecliptic Limit	331—332
Calculation of the Time, Magnitude, and Duration of a Lunar Eclipse	332—334
Numerical Computation of the Eclipse of 1863, June 1	334—337
Effect of the Earth's Atmosphere	337—338
ON ECLIPSES OF THE SUN	338
Calculation of the Length of the Moon's Shadow	339—341
Annular and Total Eclipses	341—342
Calculation of a Solar Eclipse for a particular place	342
Calculation of the effects of Parallax in Hour-Angle and N.P.D.	342—346
Parallax in Hour-Angle in terms of Apparent Hour-Angle and N.P.D.	346
Example of the application of the formulæ, from the *Greenwich Observations* for 1860	347—349
Augmentation of the Moon's Semi-diameter	349—351
Further processes of calculation	351
Calculation of the times of First and Last Contact of the Limbs of the Sun and Moon	351—352
Calculation of the Positions of the Points of First and Last Contact	352—353
Observations of Cusps and Limbs of the Sun and Moon during a Solar Eclipse	353—357
Method of Normal-centric Co-ordinates	358
Variation of Moon's Parallax in Hour-Angle and N.P.D.	359—360
On Occultation of Stars by the Moon	361
Method used at Greenwich	361—363
Equation between the Error of Elements	363—365
Determination of Longitude by observation of a Solar Eclipse or of the Occultation of a Star by the Moon	365—368
Bessel's method of treating Occultations	368—371

CONTENTS.

	PAGE
APPENDIX	372
On the Annual Parallax of the Fixed Stars . . .	372—374
Parallax-Factor for γ Draconis	374—375
Parallax of 61 Cygni	376—378
On Third and Fourth Differences	378—379
EXAMPLES AND PROBLEMS	380—392

ERRATUM.

Page 221, line 12, *for* enumerated *read* enunciated.

ASTRONOMY.

CHAPTER I.

DEFINITIONS AND FIRST PRINCIPLES.

1. SPHERICAL ASTRONOMY may be defined to be the science which teaches how to determine for any given instant the position in space of any given heavenly body. It therefore naturally divides itself into two distinct parts, speculative and practical. The speculative portion of the science admits of being considered quite independently of the practical, and shews how by Mathematical treatment the positions of bodies in the visible sphere of the heavens may be expressed with reference to certain assumed systems of spherical co-ordinates, and how their positions may be transferred from one system of co-ordinates to another. The practical portion of the science shews by what means and by what instruments the positions of the bodies are *really* determined with reference to *one* assumed system of co-ordinates, chosen on account of the facilities which it affords in connexion with diurnal phenomena. It would matter little, therefore, in what order these two divisions of the subject are treated, but it will perhaps conduce to clearness if the practical portion of the subject be taken first, because that would be the order in which a practical astronomer must really consider the two parts of the subject.

2. DEFINITIONS. In defining the position of any object considered as a point, it is usual to refer it either to a system of *rectangular* co-ordinates, or to the intersections of three planes

mutually at right angles, and intersecting at a point called the origin of co-ordinates. But, for the purposes of astronomy it is in general (though not always) more convenient to refer positions to *spherical* co-ordinates. Imagine a sphere with its centre arbitrarily chosen, but passing through the object whose position is required. Through the centre of the sphere let any great circle be drawn, and another great circle passing through the object and the poles of the first great circle, and therefore at right angles to it. If a point be taken arbitrarily on the first of these circles, then the angular distance between it and the point at which this circle is intersected by the second will determine the plane in which the object lies, and the arc of the second circle intercepted between the object and the first circle will determine its position in that plane. These two arcs or angles are the two spherical co-ordinates of the object, and are manifestly all that are requisite for determining its position. The connexion between the two systems of co-ordinates here treated of (namely, rectangular and spherical) is of great importance for the advanced student of astronomy, and is given in a most masterly way in the Introduction to Brünnow's *Spherical Astronomy*[*].

The position of the object thus determined ought rather to be called the *direction* of the object, since the reference to the two co-ordinate planes is only angular and leaves the distance quite indeterminate. With regard to the fixed stars, of which the distances are immeasurably great, these angular measures are all which are necessary to determine what are called their places; for the planets, of which the distances from the earth are comparable with the earth's distance from the sun (which is usually taken as the unit of linear measure), these distances must be determined by other considerations.

3. The first point then for consideration is the choice of an origin of co-ordinates and of a system of co-ordinate planes to which the places of celestial objects are to be referred, and this is by no means arbitrary, but is determined for us by the pheno-

---

[*] *Brünnow's Spherical Astronomy* translated by the Rev. R. Main. Deighton and Bell, 1860.

mena of the daily motions of all the heavenly bodies. The point of reference for all objects external to the earth is evidently the earth itself, and primarily that point of its surface at which the observer is situated. Ultimately all observed phenomena relating to the planets must be referred to the *centre* of the earth; but as observations can be made only on the surface, the position of the observer on it must primarily be assumed as the centre of his visible sphere of the heavens or origin of co-ordinates.

4. The phenomena of the daily motion of the sphere of the heavens offer the most convenient planes of reference passing through the observer's position, that is, the centre of this sphere. These phenomena are of the following nature.

5. Imagine a person to stand in a position in which he can have an uninterrupted view of the sky. Then, after he has made himself familiar with the positions of the stars which are visible to him, he will find, on directing his eyes towards the western horizon, that the stars in that direction successively disappear or set, while, on looking towards the east, new ones successively appear above the horizon, and those which were at first very close to the horizon rise at successive instants higher above it. A little closer observation will shew him that *all* the stars obey this law of motion from east to west, and that all apparently move in parallel planes. Again, if the same star be watched on successive nights, it will be found that the interval of time taken by any one of them in departing from any point of the heavens and returning to it again, is sensibly constant. A continuation of such observations made with greater accuracy, will shew that all the stars apparently move uniformly about an axis passing through the observer's position, and the nicest or most refined observations would fail to detect any deviation from the law of uniform rotation.

Now there are but two ways of accounting for this apparent and uniform rotation of the heavens. Either the whole heaven does really revolve from east to west, carrying with it the stars in such a way as to preserve their relative positions unaltered; or the earth moves round an axis in the contrary direction, that is, from west to east, with a velocity sensibly uniform. The first hypothesis is evidently attended with such enormous difficulties as to be rejected at once; and it therefore follows that the apparent diurnal motions of the heavenly bodies are produced by a real rotation of the earth round an axis, always remaining sensibly parallel to itself and with a uniform velocity.

6. The points at which this axis of rotation meets the visible sphere of the heavens are called the *North and South Poles* of the heavens; and the plane perpendicular to it passing through the centre of the earth (*assumed* for the present to be spherical) is called the *Celestial Equator*.

This gives us at once one system of spherical co-ordinates, by means of which the positions of all bodies can be assigned in the sphere of the heavens; the two co-ordinates of the place of any object being its angular distance from the equator (called its *Declination*, North or South, accordingly as it is North or South of the Equator), and its angular distance, (when referred to the Equator by a great circle perpendicular to that plane,) from a point chosen arbitrarily on it.

When this point is so chosen as to be coincident with the position of the sun, when on the equator, or at the vernal equinox, this latter co-ordinate is called the *Right Ascension* of the object.

7. If the course of the sun were attentively watched throughout the year, there would be no difficulty (without the consideration of any theory of his motion) in discovering that his centre describes a great circle in the heavens. This circle is called the *Ecliptic;* the two points at which it cuts the equator are called the *Vernal and Autumnal Equinoxes;* and the inclination of the ecliptic to the equator is called the *Obliquity of the Ecliptic*.

The plane of the ecliptic furnishes of course another system of co-ordinates; the angular distance of an object above or below this plane being called its *North or South Geocentric Latitude;* and its distance (when referred by a perpendicular arc to the ecliptic) from the vernal equinox being called its *Geocentric Longitude*.

HORIZON AND MERIDIAN.

8. There is still another system of co-ordinates arising from the observer's position on the surface of the earth. Assuming the earth to be a sphere (either exactly or approximately), the tangent plane to its surface at the point forming the position of the observer is called the *Horizon;* and the points at which a perpendicular to this plane would cut the sphere of the heavens, are called respectively the *Zenith* and *Nadir* of the place of observation, the zenith being the point over head, and the nadir the opposite point. This plane, the horizon, is another, though a local plane of reference; and the angular distance of an object above it is called its *Altitude*, while the angular distance from the zenith is called its *Zenith distance*.

It is plain also that the altitude is the complement of the zenith distance, or

$$\text{altitude} + \text{zenith distance} = 90°.$$

9. The great circle passing through the zenith of the observer's position and the poles is called the *Meridian* of the place; and it cuts the horizon in two points called the *North* and *South* points of the horizon. If also we draw through the place of observation a line on the horizon perpendicular to the trace of the meridian on it, it will meet the heavens in two other points, called the *East and West points* of the horizon. These four points of the horizon are called the *Cardinal Points*.

The angular distance of an object (referred to the horizon by an arc perpendicular to it) from the south or north point is called its *Azimuth*, and is the second co-ordinate in this system.

10. The whole of the preceding account of the three systems of co-ordinates will be rendered more intelligible by the accompanying diagram.

C is the position of the observer, or the centre of the visible sphere of the heavens. ZCN is the vertical line passing through C, coincident with the direction of the plumb-line or of the force of gravity at C; and the plane HO at right angles to ZC, and parallel to the plane of a fluid at rest, is the horizon.

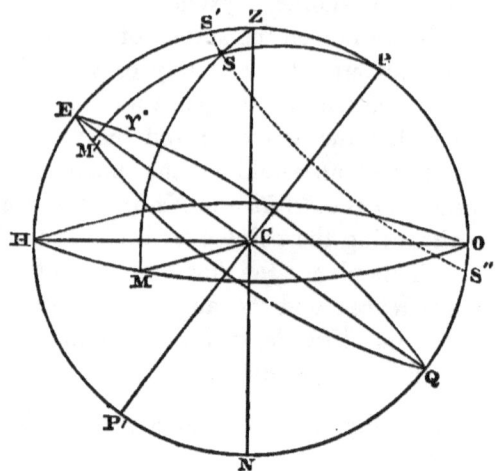

ZCN cuts the visible sphere of the heavens at the zenith, Z, and at the nadir, N.

PP' is the direction of the axis of rotation of the earth, and P and P' the north and south poles.

EQ is the plane of the celestial equator at right angles to PP'.

Thus the plane PZP', passing through the poles and the zenith, is the plane of the meridian; cutting the horizon in H the south point, and O the north point.

One of the first important consequences which we derive from the preceding considerations is this, that *the altitude of the pole is equal to the latitude of the place of observation.*

This is almost self-evident, since the latitude of the place is represented by the angle ZCE, and this is equal to PCO or to the elevation of the pole.

Hence PCZ is equal to the complement of the latitude of the place or to the *colatitude*.

11. Let now S be the apparent position, at any hour of the day, of an object describing in its diurnal course the small circle $S''SS'$, parallel to the equator. Draw through it the great

circles PSM', ZSM, meeting the equator in M' and the horizon in M.

Then is ZS the zenith distance of the object and SM is its altitude, and if these quantities be denoted by z and a, $z + a = 90°$.

Again, PS is the north polar distance (Δ), and SM' is the north declination (δ); and $\Delta + \delta = 90°$.

Also, if we join CM, then the angle HCM will be the azimuth (A) of the body measured from the south point towards the east. But it is usual to consider azimuths from the south point of the horizon positively towards the west, and therefore the azimuth of the object thus measured will be $360° - \angle HCM$.

Again, if Υ be the position of the first point of Aries or the Vernal Equinox on the equator, then is the arc $\Upsilon EM'$ the right ascension (a) of the object.

Finally, the angle ZPS which measures the time which must elapse before the object arrives at the point S' on the meridian is called the *Hour-Angle* (h).

If now we imagine the object to be on the meridian at E, then its right ascension will be denoted by ΥE. But ΥE represents the hour-angle of the first point of Aries; and therefore the hour-angle of the first point of Aries is equal to the right ascension of any object when on the meridian.

12. DEFINITION. If a clock be so regulated as to exhibit on its dial the hour-angles of the first point of Aries at successive times, or, which is the same thing, if its reading is $0^h. 0^m. 0^s$ when that point passes the meridian, and it is so regulated as to go exactly 24 hours in the interval which elapses between the time of a fixed star leaving the meridian and returning to it again, it is said to keep *sidereal time*.

Hence the right ascension of an object is determined by the sidereal time at which it comes to the meridian.

REMARK. The First Point of Aries is an imaginary point, and therefore its transits across the meridian cannot be observed, but, supposing the fixed stars to have no proper motion (or a known proper motion for which a correction can be made), the transits of the same star on successive days, if the times can by any means be observed in *clock-time*, will give the daily rate of the clock, or its loss or gain in the interval of 24 sidereal hours.

Such transits are observed by an instrument called the *Transit-Instrument*, and from observations made with this instrument are the Right Ascensions of all objects ultimately deduced.

13. The method of determining the other co-ordinate of the position of an object, namely its North Polar Distance or its Declination, by meridian observations, will be readily understood from what has preceded.

Imagine that the transit instrument, by which the right ascensions of objects are determined, is provided with a horizontal wire as well as with vertical wires in the focus of its telescope, and that it carries on its axis a graduated circle whose plane is parallel to that of the meridian. If this circle be provided with microscopes or verniers for *reading off* its divisions, it is plain that it will give immediately differences of polar distances of objects observed on the horizontal wire of the telescope by the simple difference of its readings. But if we could by any means find the reading of the circle corresponding to the pole (technically called the *Polar-point*), then we should obtain immediately the absolute North Polar Distances of all objects by the subtraction of the *Polar-point* from all other readings. By observations of North Polar Distance of Polaris, above and below the pole, we might do this, but there would be various difficulties in the way which make it far preferable to endeavour to find the reading of the circle corresponding to the *zenith* (called technically the zenith-point) instead of that corresponding to the pole. As the zenith is a point in the vertical line, or the line at right angles to the plane assumed by the surface of a fluid at rest, the use of a mercurial horizon is sufficiently obvious for determining its position, and we need at present only indicate the nature of the observations which must be made with it for this purpose, namely, those of the reflected images of stars.

ZENITH-POINT.

Let *AB* represent the horizontal surface of a quantity of mercury in a trough, and let the rays from a star *S*, reflected from the surface at *I*, proceed up the tube of a telescope *TE*, to which is solidly attached a vertical graduated circle whose cen-

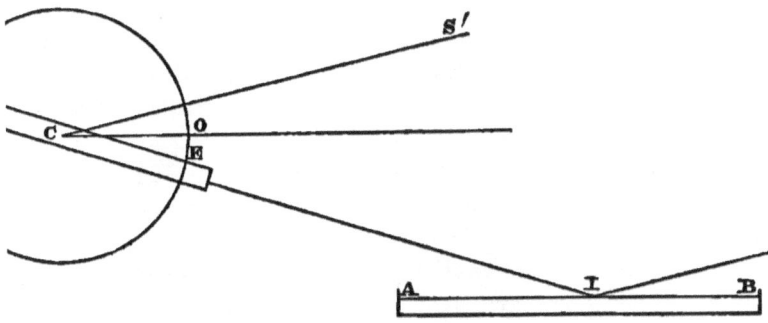

tre is *C*. The reflected image will be seen by the observer in the field of the telescope almost as distinctly (under good circumstances) as the image when viewed directly, and the star can be observed on the horizontal wire, and the circle can be read. Draw now the horizontal line *CO*, and *CS'* parallel to *SI*. Then the angle *OCI* is equal to the angle *CIA*, and the angle *S'CO* is equal to the angle *SIB*. But *SIB* is equal to *CIA*; therefore *S'CO* is equal to *OCI*. We have therefore the reading of the circle for a position corresponding to a star situated beneath the horizon, by an angle equal to the star's apparent altitude. If then we can, at the same transit of the star, or before it has gone far from the centre of the field of the telescope, observe it again by direct vision and read the circle a second time, we have the reading corresponding to the apparent altitude of the star, or to a point as much above the horizon as the other was below it. Hence half the sum of these two readings will be the reading corresponding to the horizon, or the *horizontal point*, and if this be increased or diminished by 90°, the result will give the *zenith-point*.

It is usual in the course of a night's work to observe several stars in this manner, and the mean result for the zenith-point (generally combined with the results for other nights) will give the zenith-point with much greater accuracy than a single result.

It is plain that, after the zenith-point has been found, the *apparent zenith distances* of all objects will be found by subtracting its value from the corresponding circle-readings.

14. The instrument which enables us in this way to observe both Right Ascensions and Zenith Distances is called a *Transit-Circle*. Till recently however two separate instruments, requiring two observers, have been used in England for this purpose, namely, the Transit Instrument and the Mural Circle; and, in what follows, it must be observed that all the explanation which is given of the mode of use of the Transit Circle for observation of zenith-distance, will apply generally to the Mural Circle, though we shall not refer more distinctly to this latter instrument, which may be considered to be getting into disuse.

15. Before closing this chapter it will be necessary to allude to another very important instrument used in astronomy, namely the *Equatorial Instrument*. Though the right ascensions and the declinations of objects can be observed with very great precision by the use of the Transit Circle, or of the Transit Instrument and Mural Circle used as separate instruments, yet there is this disadvantage, that they can be observed only in one portion of the heavens, namely, on the meridian of the place of observation, and therefore any given object can be observed only for a small portion of the year, and the observations on any given day will be prevented by the smallest cloud in that portion of the heavens, or by any trifling accident or want of care or prudence in the observer.

It is plain then that an instrument which would enable us to follow an object in the heavens, and to observe it at any time of the night as long as it is above the horizon, is almost indispensable for certain classes of objects, such as recently discovered planets and comets, even though the observations may not be of the same degree of accuracy as those made with the meridian instruments, and the daily motion of the heavens or the rotation of the earth on its axis furnishes us with the means of constructing such an instrument.

Imagine a telescope capable of turning freely on an axis passing through a rod or support which is itself parallel to the earth's axis of rotation, and which turns freely round two fixed pivots, the two axes of rotation being at right angles to each other. Then, if a star be seen in the telescope, it may be followed in its diurnal course by simply turning the *polar axis*, and if a circle be firmly attached to the telescope and its plane be parallel to its optical axis, and it be furnished with microscopes or verniers for reading its graduations, it may easily be made to furnish approximately the polar distances of objects. For the observation of right ascensions it is necessary that another graduated circle be firmly attached to the polar axis, and that it be read by one or more microscopes or verniers. If this circle be divided into 24 equal spaces so as to represent hours of time, and subdivided so as to represent minutes, and if one of the microscopes read 0^h. 0^m. 0^s for objects on the meridian, then the readings for any other object will represent its angular distance from the meridian, or its hour-angle. Supposing now that the eye-piece of the telescope is furnished with wires as in the case of the transit instrument, the sidereal time of transit of this object can be observed by a clock, and the difference between this time of transit and the hour-angle will be the right ascension of the object. An instrument thus constructed is called an *Equatorial*.

16. There is still another way of determining the position of an object, namely, by referring it to the meridian and horizon of the place of observation, and this requires still another instrument called the *Altitude and Azimuth Instrument*, or the *Altazimuth*.

This instrument in its simplest form consists of a fixed, horizontal, divided circle, called the *Azimuth Circle*, and of a vertical-divided circle, firmly attached to the telescope of the instrument, called the *Vertical Circle*. The frame which carries the telescope and vertical circle revolves on a vertical axis, and carries the microscopes or verniers for reading both circles, while the telescope itself revolves on a horizontal axis, the pivots resting in Y's, carried by the same frame.

In the next chapter a fuller account will be given of the mode of use of these and the other instruments referred to in this chapter, and they have been introduced in this place, that the student may have a clear notion of the need and use of them in connexion with two of the systems of co-ordinates previously mentioned.

CHAPTER II.

INSTRUMENTS.

THE TRANSIT-INSTRUMENT.

1. IT will be assumed in this chapter that the reader is acquainted with the construction of an astronomical telescope; but it will be useful to mention the peculiarities of such telescopes as are required in connexion with astronomical instruments.

For a telescope used as a transit instrument the object-glass should be achromatic, and well corrected for spherical aberration. The available diameter of the object-glass is called its *aperture*, and its focal length is the distance from the object-glass at which the inverted image of an object is formed. At this distance, or in this section of the tube of the telescope, is placed a frame across which very thin wires (usually formed of spider's webs) are stretched at sensibly equal distances. This is called the wire-frame, and usually carries five or seven vertical wires (but always an odd number, so that one of them shall be the *centre wire*). The eye-piece used for viewing the image of the object observed and the wires, is a *Ramsden's, or positive eye-piece* of two lenses, and is fixed in a small tube attached to a slider which passes across the end of the large tube of the telescope, for the purpose of observing the object as it passes the side wires (that is, as seen by oblique pencils) in the middle of the field of view*. In addition to the fixed wires there is usually one parallel to them, moveable by a micrometer, and nearly in the same plane, so as just to pass them without actual contact, for the purpose of observing the amount of the error of collimation. There are also two parallel horizontal wires, at a small

---

* This improvement was introduced by Dr Maskelyne in the last century.

distance from each other, for the purpose of defining the middle of the field of view.

The preceding description applies generally to the astronomical telescope as it is used in connexion with instruments; but in the transit instrument it is made to turn on a horizontal axis consisting generally of two cones of metal firmly fastened to opposite sides of the middle of its tube, and terminating in two accurately cylindrical steel pivots whose axes must be in the same straight line. The excellence of the instrument consists chiefly in the stiffness of the telescope and the axis, as, if there should be sensible flexure in either, arising from the weight, it would be comparatively worthless for refined observations. It is also necessary that the pivots be accurately cylindrical with their axes in the same straight line.

2. For the mounting of the telescope thus constructed as a transit instrument, two massive piers are provided* sunk deep in the earth, and resting either upon hard gravel or, if the foundation be not sufficiently firm, upon a bed of concrete. The horizontal section of each is nearly a square, two of the sides being pretty accurately parallel to the plane of the meridian. On the inner surfaces, opposed to each other, are fixed frames of metal, carrying what are called the Y's for the supports of the pivots, the pivots lying in them, as seen in section in the accompanying diagram. The Y's should be exactly equal and similar, and their forks should be in the same horizontal line. They are generally made capable of being moved, both vertically and horizontally, by means of screws working in the frames that carry them; but, after the instrument has been once well adjusted, they should rarely, if ever, be touched. Sometimes counterpoises are employed to take off part of the pressure of the instrument from the Y's, and consequently to diminish the friction.

For observations of objects at night it is necessary that the field of the telescope should be illuminated to render the wires visible. For this purpose one of the pivots is perforated, and

---

* In all that follows we must be understood to refer to the instruments of fixed observatories, where the instruments are of considerable size and weight.

the light of a lamp, or gas flame, is made to pass through it to a ring-reflector placed obliquely at the centre of the axis inside the tube of the telescope. This reflector can be acted upon by means of a rod by the observer at the eye end of the telescope, so as to have greater or less inclination to the axis of the tube. If the inclination to the axis be 45°, nearly the whole of the light will be reflected down the tube of the telescope; but if the reflector be at right angles to the axis, none will be reflected, or the field will be dark. The observer can therefore accommodate the light to the degree of brightness or faintness of the object to be observed.

On looking into the eye-piece of the telescope when it is adjusted to distinct vision the field of view will have the following appearance, supposing that there are seven vertical fixed wires, and two parallel wires at right angles to the others for defining the middle of the field of view.

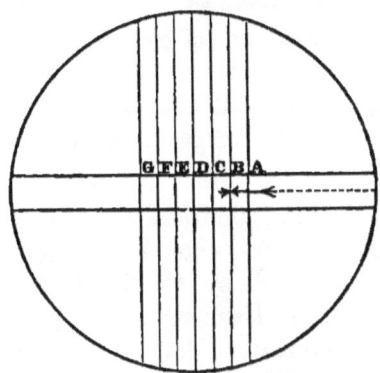

Since the telescope inverts objects, a star (unless it be on the meridian below the pole) will appear to pass by the diurnal motion from right to left in the direction of the arrow, and therefore will pass the wires marked in the figure in the direction A, B, C, D, E, F, G. If, however, the telescope be taken out from the Y's and then replaced with the pivots in the reversed positions, that is, with the previously eastern pivot west, &c., then the wires also would be reversed, so that G would take the place of A, F of B, &c. It is therefore necessary to note for distinction the position of the illuminated pivot, whether east or west, before commencing a series of observations, and to name the wires *A, B, C*, &c. in the order in which stars cross them, for that position of the telescope.

3. *On the Errors of Adjustment of the Transit-Instrument.* From the preceding description it will be evident that, when a transit instrument is in perfect adjustment, if the transits of all objects be referred to a point in the field of view (generally either a point of the central wire, or of the line corresponding to the mean of wires), then the line joining this point and the optical centre of the object-glass, which we may call the line of sight (*gesichts linie*), must, in the rotation of the telescope round its axis, trace out the plane of the meridian of the place of observation.

This will imply the three following conditions:

1. The line of sight must describe a great circle, and must therefore be at right angles to the axis of rotation; and the angle made by the actual line of sight and a line perpendicular to the axis of rotation is called the *Error of Collimation*; while the plane passing through the optical centre of the object-glass perpendicular to the axis of rotation is called the *Plane of Collimation*.

2. The axes of the cylindrical pivots must be in the same straight line, and this line must be horizontal, the *Error of Level* being the angle made by it with the horizontal line, when the axis is not perfectly levelled. When the axis is perfectly level, the line of collimation describes a great circle passing through the Zenith and Nadir, but not necessarily through the poles.

3. Supposing the instrument to have been adjusted for errors of collimation and level, then the line of collimation must be made to move in a plane passing through the poles, and the angle made by the plane of the great circle in which it actually moves, with the meridian, is called the *Azimuthal Error*.

We will consider these errors in their order.

4. ERROR OF COLLIMATION. For determination of the error of collimation of the central wire there is used either a

fixed mark or a collimating telescope, the latter being generally a small transit-instrument with a wire-cross in its principal focus, serving as a mark at an infinite distance. When fixed marks are used, it is necessary to have two, one on the north and the other on the south side, to eliminate the effects of a possible shift in the position of the axis caused by the process of reversion.

As frequent mention will be made of micrometers in the whole of the descriptions of instruments which follow, this will be the proper place for introducing such an account of their construction as will enable the student to understand their mode of use. The kind of micrometer which is most commonly used is that called the wire-micrometer. It consists of a frame across which is stretched a system of wires, the frame being so placed when applied to a telescope or reading microscope that the wires shall be in the plane passing through the common focus of the object-glass and eye-piece. When it is applied to a reading microscope the wires consist of two which form a cross, and, in use, a division of the circle, of which the reading is required under the microscope, is made to bisect this cross. Sometimes, however, two parallel wires are used in reading microscopes instead of a *cross*-wire. When the micrometer is applied to a transit-instrument there is only a single wire, which moves parallel to the vertical or transit wires. An equable motion is given to the frame carrying the wires by means of a screw, and of course the goodness of the micrometer will depend chiefly on the uniformity of the thread of the screw. On the prolongation of the axis of the screw is placed a divided circle, or *head*, which serves to measure the angle or the fractional part of a revolution through which the screw has been turned, while there is generally an index, or *comb*, for determining the number of whole revolutions which have been made from the assumed zero of the micrometer. In a treatise like the present, it would be useless to enter into the practical details of construction of various kinds of micrometers. It is sufficient for the theoretical student to understand that its measuring wire can be moved forward uniformly by means of the screw, and that the angular space through which it has been moved can be accurately deduced from the reading of the divided head.

Imagine now that in one position of the axis of the instrument (with illuminated pivot east for example) the micrometer-wire has been made to bisect the mark or wire-cross, and let the reading be r, expressed in revolutions and parts of the micrometer. Then let the instrument be lifted out of its Y's, and the axis reversed. Now, the line joining the centres of the pivots being at right angles to the *line of collimation*, the point of reference, or selected point, of the micrometer-wire will, in the rotation of the telescope, describe a circle round this imaginary line, and therefore, after reversion, the mark and the micrometer-wire will be at equal distances on opposite sides of it; hence, if the micrometer-wire be again placed upon the mark, and the reading be r', it is plain that the reading for the line of collimation will be $\frac{r+r'}{2}$. If this should be also the reading of the micrometer-wire when it is brought into coincidence with the central wire, then the central wire coincides with the line of collimation; but if the reading be R, then is the error of collimation $\frac{r+r'}{2} \sim R$, expressed in revolutions and parts of the micrometer, and this can be reduced to arc when the value of a revolution of the micrometer is known.

In some observatories it is usual to reduce all transits to what is called the "mean of the wires;" that is, to the transits over an imaginary line very near to but not necessarily coinciding with the centre wire, and such that the time of a star's transit over it is the mean of the times of transit over the wires. If this be done in the reduction of the observations, the error of collimation must also be estimated with respect to this imaginary line, and the preceding value of the error will require correction for the difference between the position of the central wire and the position of the mean of wires. This will necessitate the discussion of the methods for finding the intervals of the wires before proceeding to the Errors of Level and Azimuth.

There is also another trifling correction to be applied to the error of collimation, arising from *diurnal aberration;* but this can be understood only after the general theory of the aberration of light has been discussed.

5. *To determine the Intervals of the Wires of a Transit Instrument.*

A skilful optician will insert a system of wires at very nearly equal distances from each other, but it is always necessary to determine by observations the actual intervals. This is done, when it is practicable, by combination of several observations of Polaris, or some other stars near the pole, the transits being observed over each of the wires, and the mean of the wires calculated in each instance.

By subtracting the transits over the separate wires successively from this mean, we shall obtain for each observation of Polaris the intervals in time by which the transit over each wire precedes or follows the transit over the mean of wires; and any number of such transits can be combined by taking the mean of the separate observation of each interval.

But, as these intervals depend on the apparent North Polar Distance of the star, and as this varies several seconds in the course of a year on account of precession, nutation, and aberration, it is necessary also to take the mean of the North Polar Distances, for the times of observation, and to consider that the mean of the intervals deduced from all the observations corresponds to this mean North Polar Distance.

From these results it is very easy to deduce the angular distance in space of each wire from the mean of all. Let us take for example the wire A, (fig. on p. 15). It will be sufficiently correct to suppose that the mean of the wires coincides with the meridian.

Let S be the star on the wire AS, and PN the meridian represented by the mean of wires, (P being the Pole). Draw the perpendicular arc MS on PM. Then if t be the interval in seconds of time from wire AS to the mean of wires, the angle MPS, or the hour-angle, in seconds of space $= 15t$, corresponding to the North Polar Distance of the star, $PS (= \Delta)$.

Also MS is the angular distance of the wire AS from mean of wires.

Hence we have

$$\sin MS = \sin 15t \times \sin \Delta \quad \ldots\ldots\ldots\ldots (a),$$

whence MS can be found.

If $\Delta = 90°$ in the above equation,

$$MS = 15t,$$

$$\text{or } t = \frac{MS}{15}.$$

Hence, if the values of MS for the different wires be divided by 15, we have the intervals of transit, for an equatorial object, between each wire and the mean of wires.

Having thus found the equatorial intervals, we may conversely find the intervals for any star by the use of the equation (a).

For example, if the star be at a considerable distance from the pole (10° is a safe limit), we may put the arcs for the sines in the equation, and we have

$$t = \frac{MS}{15} \times \frac{1}{\sin \Delta},$$

$$= \frac{\text{equatorial interval}}{\sin \Delta}.$$

If the star is too near to the pole to allow of this, we have

$$\sin 15t = 15t \times \sin 1'' = \frac{\sin MS}{\sin \Delta},$$

and therefore

$$t = \frac{\sin MS}{15 \sin \Delta \times \sin 1''}.$$

The preceding results for the time occupied by a star in passing by the diurnal motion from any wire of a transit-instrument to the centre wire or the mean of wires, are true only for objects which have no proper motion, such as the fixed stars. For planets, and in particular for the moon, the formulæ above given require to be modified by the introduction of another factor.

FACTORS FOR PLANETS AND THE MOON.

For a planet, or for the sun, let I be the number of seconds of increase of Right Ascension in the time during which the planet is carried by the diurnal motion from one meridian to another, differing by one hour of terrestrial longitude*. Then, in t seconds, the increase of Right Ascension will be $\dfrac{t}{3600} \times I$, and therefore the interval of transit is increased by this quantity, and the interval itself becomes

$$t + \frac{I}{3600} \times t = \left(1 + \frac{I}{3600}\right) t,$$
$$= \left(\frac{3600 + I}{3600}\right) t.$$

And it is usual to prepare a table of values of the factor $\dfrac{3600 + I}{3600}$, and of its logarithm, for limiting values of I.

For the moon another factor is necessary on account of the difference of her distance from the centre of the earth, and from the position of the observer on the surface.

Thus, let A be the position of the observer on the earth's surface; Z the geocentric zenith; M the moon. Then, to the

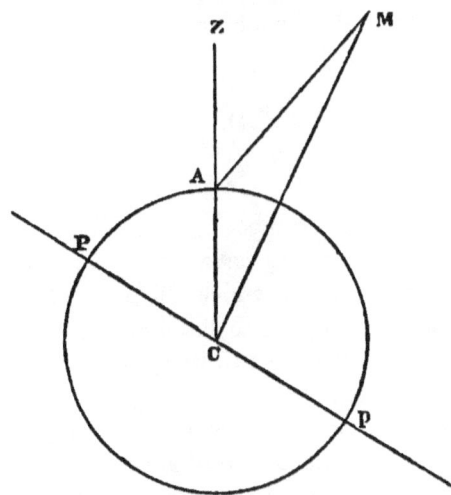

---

* The student will readily see that this is not the same as the motion in an hour of time.

observer at A, the velocity of the apparent motion of the moon arising from diurnal rotation will be greater than at the centre C, in the proportion of CM to AM, or of $\sin ZAM$ to $\sin ZCM$, or of sin geocentric zenith distance to sin apparent zenith distance, and therefore the time in which the moon describes a given angle in coming to the meridian, will be *diminished* in the same proportion. Hence, in reducing imperfect transits, we shall have to apply the additional factor $\dfrac{\sin \text{Geoc. Z.D.}}{\sin \text{App. Z.D.}}$; and the whole correction will become in the case of the moon,

$$\frac{\text{Equat. Interval}}{\sin \text{N.P.D.}} \times \frac{3600 + I}{3600} \times \frac{\sin \text{Geoc. Z.D.}}{\sin \text{App. Z.D.}}.$$

6. *Effect of Error of Collimation upon the time of transit of an object over the mean of wires.*

From what has preceded it is evident that if the error of collimation (estimated positive in seconds of space when it is to be added to the time of transit, that is, when the object passes the mean of wires sooner than it passes the line of collimation) be c, the correction to the time of transit, will be

$$\frac{c}{15 \sin \text{N.P.D.}} \dots\dots\dots\dots (\beta).$$

7. *Error of Level.* Supposing the imaginary line representing the mean of wires to have been made to coincide with the line of collimation, or, which is better, that the transits have been corrected according to the preceding methods for the difference, the mean of wires will now, in the revolution of the telescope round its axis, trace out a great circle in the heavens. If however the axis (that is, the line forming the cylindrical axis of the pivots) be not horizontal, this great circle will not pass through the zenith, and the next consideration is to make it do this, either by destroying the *error of level* of the axis, or by correcting it.

The amount of the error of level (always estimated in seconds of space, and positively when it makes stars pass the wires too soon, that is, when the western pivot is too high) is generally determined for the transit-instrument by a spirit-level. This instrument consists of a hollow tube of glass slightly curved and nearly filled with a fluid, the space which is unoccupied with fluid when the tube is held horizontal with its convex side upwards, being called the *bubble*. It is evident then that the slightest tilt of the tube will cause the bubble to be displaced in the tube, and to run *towards* that end of it which is *elevated*. For measuring the amount of this tilt, the tube is set in a frame to which is attached an ivory divided scale placed immediately above the bubble, and the values of the divisions of the scale corresponding to elevation or depression of the end of the level are determined for each instrument either by an instrument called a *level prover*, or by some other means. It is usual to make the *zero* (or 0 degrees) of the scale correspond to a point near the centre of the bubble, so that the divisions increase towards each end; and this we shall assume to be the case in what follows. Levels applied to transit-instruments are either *hanging levels* or *striding levels*. In the former case they are provided with arms above the level terminating in hooks, by which they can be hung on to the pivots of the transit-instrument, in the latter case they are furnished with legs terminating in a kind of foot, by which they are made to stand upon the pivots of the instrument. In both cases they are provided with a *cross level*, or small level of moderate sensibility placed near one end at right angles to the length of the glass tube, to insure that the level itself shall always take up the same position relatively to verticality. It must be understood that the process of levelling is one of the utmost importance and delicacy, as even the observer's breath or the warmth of his body will tend to alter the length of the bubble, and therefore to vitiate the result. The two kinds of level here described are pictured accurately enough in the accompanying diagrams.

In what follows we will confine ourselves to the consideration of the *striding* level, as this is generally adopted for modern instruments.

Imagine it to be placed upon the pivots of the transit-instrument, and, for the present, suppose the pivots to be exactly cylindrical and equal.

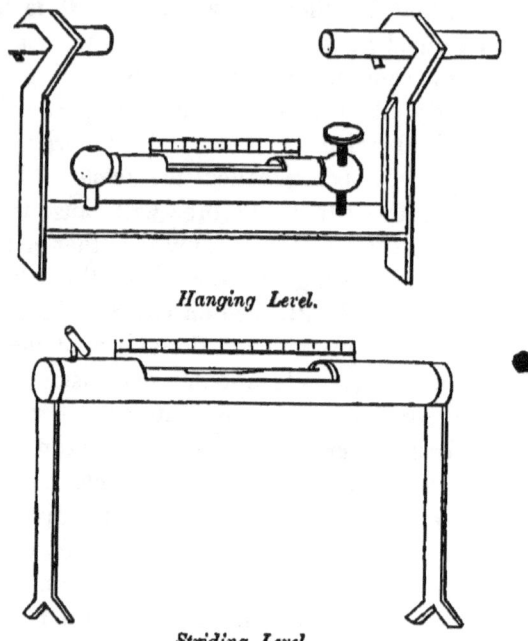

Hanging Level.

Striding Level.

If the level be accurately adjusted, the centre of the bubble, which corresponds to the highest point of the curvature of the glass tube, if it be accurately made, should be made to correspond to the zero of the scale (or origin of co-ordinates) when the level is placed upon a perfectly horizontal surface. If this were the case, it is evident that, on being placed on a surface not quite horizontal, the distance of the middle point of the bubble from the zero would give the error of level of the surface in terms of scale divisions.

This, however, is not generally the case, and must not be assumed. Generally then suppose that, with cross level west, the reading of the west end of scale is w_1, and that of the east end is e_1. Then it is plain that the distance of the centre of the bubble from the zero of the scale measured towards the west, is $\frac{w_1 - e_1}{2}$. Let now the zero of the scale be farther west than the true zero by a, measured in scale-divisions. Then the distance of the centre of the bubble from the true zero will be $\frac{w_1 - e_1}{2} + \alpha$, and this will represent the elevation of the west end of the axis to which the level is applied. Let this be l, measured in scale divisions;

$$\therefore \frac{w_1 - e_1}{2} + \alpha = l \dots\dots\dots\dots(1).$$

Let now the level be reversed end for end, and let w_2 and e_2 be the readings of the west and east end of the bubble.

We have, therefore,

$$\frac{w_2 - e_2}{2} - \alpha = l \dots\dots\dots\dots(2);$$

and $\therefore 2l = \frac{w_1 - e_1}{2} + \frac{w_2 - e_2}{2}$,

and $l = \frac{w_1 + w_2 - (e_1 + e_2)}{4}$,

or, *elevation of west end of axis = sum of west readings diminished by sum of east readings divided by 4.*

If we were to take another complete observation of the level, that is, two observations in reversed positions, we should obtain a similar result, and any number of such might be combined together and the mean taken.

Therefore generally, if n be the number of complete observations of the level in reversed positions, we shall have

$$l = \frac{\Sigma w - \Sigma e}{4n}.$$

If one division of the scale be equivalent to n seconds, then the errors of level expressed in seconds of space will be ln.

8. *To determine by the spirit-level the inequality of the pivots of a transit-instrument.*

If the process of levelling explained above were applied to a line or plane it would give accurately the inclination of the line or plane to the horizon; but it is evident that the process explained above will give the inclination of the line forming the axis of the cylindrical pivots of the transit-instrument correctly only in the case in which the pivots are equal.

If the pivots be not equal, let the radius of the eastern one, which we will assume to be the unilluminated or unperforated, be called r, and of the western or illuminated pivot $r+a$. Let also the angle formed by the forks of the level be $2i$, and that of the Y's of the transit-instrument $2i'$. Let, finally, the angle of the western Y be higher than that of the eastern Y by b. Then the height of the angle of the eastern fork of the level above the angle of the eastern Y of the instrument will be

$$r(\operatorname{cosec} i + \operatorname{cosec} i''),$$

and the height of the western fork above the western Y will be

$$b + (r+a)(\operatorname{cosec} i + \operatorname{cosec} i'').$$

The difference of these quantities is

$$b + a(\operatorname{cosec} i + \operatorname{cosec} i''),$$

and, if the distance between the pivots, or the length of the axis, be taken as the unit of distance, this expression will give the angular elevation of the western fork of the level above the eastern fork, or the quantity which is measured by reading the level in reversed positions.

Let this level result be c.

Then $b + a(\operatorname{cosec} i + \operatorname{cosec} i'') = c$.

Let now the transit-instrument be reversed, so that the illuminated pivot becomes east. Then we shall by levelling again have a similar equation,

$$b - a(\operatorname{cosec} i + \operatorname{cosec} i'') = c',$$

and $\therefore a = \dfrac{c-c'}{2(\operatorname{cosec} i + \operatorname{cosec} i'')}$.

Also the real difference in the heights of the centres of the pivots, when the illuminated end is west, is

EFFECT OF LEVEL-ERROR ON TIME OF TRANSIT.

$$b + a \operatorname{cosec} i'' = \frac{c+c'}{2} + \frac{(c-c')}{2} \cdot \frac{\operatorname{cosec} i''}{\operatorname{cosec} i + \operatorname{cosec} i''}$$

$$= c - \frac{c-c'}{2} \cdot \frac{\operatorname{cosec} i}{\operatorname{cosec} i + \operatorname{cosec} i''};$$

and, when the illuminated end of the axis is east, the difference of height will be

$$b - a \operatorname{cosec} i'' = \frac{c+c'}{2} - \frac{c-c'}{2} \cdot \frac{\operatorname{cosec} i''}{\operatorname{cosec} i + \operatorname{cosec} i''}$$

$$= c' + \frac{c-c'}{2} \cdot \frac{\operatorname{cosec} i}{\operatorname{cosec} i + \operatorname{cosec} i''}.$$

9. *To determine the effect of the error of level on the time of transit of an object.*

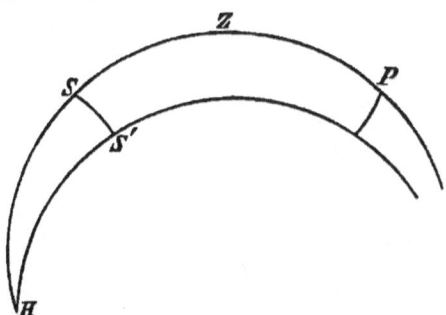

Let the western pivot be high by l seconds, and, in the accompanying diagram, let P, Z, H be respectively the pole, the zenith, and the horizontal point in the meridian PZH. It is plain that the line of collimation of the telescope will describe a great circle meeting the horizon in the meridian, but with an inclination of l'' to the east of it. Let HS' be this great circle, and S' the place of a star on it. Draw $S'S$ at right angles to HZ.

Then $\qquad SS' = l \times \sin HS = l \cos ZS$;
and time of describing SS'

$$= \frac{1}{15 \sin PS} \times SS'$$

$$= \frac{l}{15} \cdot \frac{\cos ZS}{\sin PS} = \frac{l}{15} \cdot \frac{\cos \text{Z.D. south}}{\sin \text{N.P.D.}}.$$

10. *Error of Azimuth.* The effect of the application of the errors of collimation and level is to make the line of collimation trace out a great circle of the heavens passing through the zenith. It is, lastly, necessary to make it pass through the pole, or to find what is the deviation from the meridian in azimuth.

Let the eastern pivot be too far north so as to make the telescope deviate to the east of the meridian by a seconds. Let, as before, PZS be the meridian, and ZS' the great circle traced out by the line of collimation, and transited by a star at S''. Draw $S'S$ perpendicular to PZS.

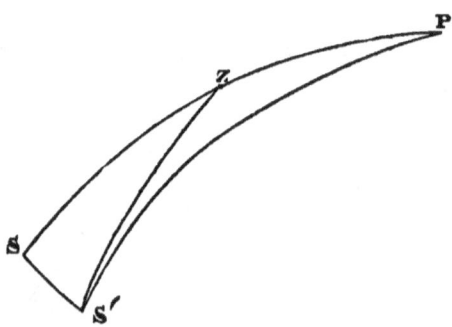

Then angle $SZS' = a$,

$$SS' = a \sin ZS,$$

and time of describing $SS' = \dfrac{a}{15} \cdot \dfrac{\sin ZS}{\sin \text{N.P.D.}}.$

This is the effect on the time of transit of a star whose zenith distance south is ZS.

11. It will be well, before going farther, to collect the preceding results in one formula.

Let a star pass the mean of wires at clock-time t, and let its zenith distance be Z, and its N.P.D. be Δ. Let also the error of the clock on sidereal time be δt (seconds) slow.

Then if the errors of collimation, level, and azimuth be respectively c, l, and a, the true sidereal time of transit over the meridian is

$$T = t + \delta t + \frac{c}{15} \cdot \frac{1}{\sin \Delta} + \frac{l}{15} \cdot \frac{\cos z}{\sin \Delta} + \frac{a}{15} \cdot \frac{\sin z}{\sin \Delta};$$

or, if γ be the co-latitude, since $z = \Delta - \gamma$,

$$T = t + \delta t + \frac{c}{15} \cdot \frac{1}{\sin \Delta} + \frac{l}{15} \cdot \frac{\cos (\Delta - \gamma)}{\sin \Delta} + \frac{a}{15} \frac{\sin (\Delta - \gamma)}{\sin \Delta}.$$

We have shewn how the errors of collimation and level are found by purely mechanical means, and it remains now to shew how the Error of Azimuth is found by observations of stars.

In the first place the factors of the respective errors, namely, $\dfrac{1}{15 \sin \Delta}$, $\dfrac{\cos (\Delta - \gamma)}{15 \sin \Delta}$, and $\dfrac{\sin (\Delta - \gamma)}{15 \sin \Delta}$ can be easily tabulated, since they are merely functions of the latitude of the place, and of the polar distances of the stars. Imagine then that a table has been made of the factors of the azimuthal errors for small intervals of N.P.D, so that for any star it may be readily taken out at sight. Let the factor of azimuthal error be generally called Z, or let

$$Z = \frac{\sin (\Delta - \gamma)}{15 \sin \Delta}.$$

12. The best mode of determining the value of the azimuthal error is by consecutive transits of a star near the pole, and there are three stars which for northern latitudes are particularly valuable for this purpose; namely, Polaris, δ Ursæ Minoris, and λ Ursæ Minoris. Polaris being a star of little lower than the second magnitude can be well seen in the daylight, and therefore its consecutive transits above and below the pole can be observed all the year round.

Let now t be the clock-time of transit of Polaris above the pole corrected for collimation and level, and $t' + 12^h$ of the next consecutive transit below the pole;

a, the required error of azimuth,

$\delta t'$, the clock's loss in 12^h,

δa, the increase of RA of Polaris in 12^h, through precession, &c.

Z_1 and Z_2, the factors of azimuthal error for Polaris above and below the pole.

Then since $Z = \dfrac{\sin(\Delta - \gamma)}{15 \sin \Delta}$, it will evidently ($\Delta$ being less than γ) be negative for Polaris above the pole, and positive for the same star below.

Therefore the correction to t will be $-Z_1 a$, and the correction to t' will be $+Z_2 a$.

Hence we shall have the equation

$$12^h + t' + \delta t' - \delta \alpha + Z_2 \times a - \{t - Z_1 \times a\} = 12^h,$$

or $(Z_1 + Z_2) \times a = t - t' - \delta t' + \delta \alpha,$

and $a = \dfrac{t - t' - \delta t' + \delta \alpha}{Z_1 + Z_2}.$

The method explained above requires no knowledge of the right ascension of the star, and is therefore preferable to all other methods, since, when the azimuthal error is thus independently determined, it can be used for the determination of the R. A. of Polaris fundamentally, that is without reference to any catalogued place.

When consecutive transits of Polaris cannot be observed, the best method is by observation of two stars near the pole, one at its transit above the pole and the other below, the transits being nearly simultaneous.

If α and $12^h + \alpha'$ be the right ascensions of two such stars, t and t' their times of transit, and Z_1 and Z_2 the factors for azimuthal errors; then, the corrected times of transit being $t - Z_1 \times a$, and $t' + Z_2 \times a$, the clock-error given by the first star will be

$$\alpha - t + Z_1 \times a,$$

and that given by the second will be

$$\alpha' - t' - Z_2 \times a,$$

and these must be equal (neglecting the rate).

Hence $a = \dfrac{\alpha' - t' - (\alpha - t)}{Z_1 + Z_2}.$

If a second circumpolar star cannot be obtained, a south star whose right ascension is well determined will do nearly as well.

The former method is followed at Oxford, the latter at Greenwich, when consecutive observations of Polaris have not been made.

13. The three instrumental errors of the transit-instrument having thus been found, and the corresponding corrections in time having been applied to the transits (which can be done for large numbers of observations very expeditiously by means of sliding-scales properly prepared), we obtain the true *clock-times* of transit of all objects over the meridian.

Now in the Nautical Almanac are given, for intervals of ten days, the Apparent Right Ascensions and Declinations of about 150 stars, derived chiefly from the Greenwich Observations, and receiving from time to time minute corrections from the increased number of observations and the more refined methods of making and reducing them, so that at the present time the places of these *fundamental* stars are given with an accuracy which scarcely admits of increase. A certain number of these *fundamental* stars are observed with the transit-instrument, together with the other objects requiring observation, and the comparison of the corrected clock-time of transit across the meridian of each of these stars with its tabular right ascension gives an error of the clock on sidereal time (see page 7). If there were no errors of observation these clock-errors should be precisely equal, or should differ only by the amount of the clock-rate (loss or gain) in the interval. But since all observations are liable to error, partly due to the temperament of the observer and partly to atmospheric circumstances, it is usual, as in all other similar determinations, to take the mean of the individual clock-errors as representing the errors at the time corresponding to the mean of the sidereal times of transit of the separate stars. If these *normal* clock-errors be compared on successive nights, the daily rate of the clock will be obtained.

14. Conversely, the error for a given time and the daily rate of the transit-clock being known, the errors can be calculated for the times of transit of all other objects and applied to them, by which means the apparent right ascensions of all these objects will be determined.

15. It will be seen from the preceding account of the transit-instrument that it has two distinct uses, namely, 1st for the determination of time; and, 2ndly, for the determination of the right ascensions of celestial objects. It gives sidereal time by determining the error of the clock adjusted approximately to sidereal time, by comparison of the clock-times of transit of fundamental stars with their tabular right ascensions; and from the sidereal times it is plain that mean solar times can be calculated, because there is a fixed relation between the two, though this relation remains to be discussed in a following chapter. Again, it gives the right ascensions of all observed objects by enabling us to compare their right ascensions with those of the fundamental stars by the method previously explained.

16. In concluding this account of the transit-instrument, there is one important remark to be made. The instrument, correctly speaking, determines only *differences* of right ascension of celestial objects, by enabling us to observe accurately the differences of their times of transit by the clock. If, however, we could discover accurately the absolute right ascension of one of the observed objects, then the right ascensions of all the rest would become known; and this was the method employed in the last century by Dr Maskelyne. He used α Aquilæ as his fundamental star, and compared all others with it. But the consideration of the method of deducing absolute right ascensions, or of settling the place of the equinox, must be left to a succeeding chapter.

17. We must not omit another important use which can be made of the transit-instrument for the determination of the latitude of an observatory, by placing it so that the line of collimation of its telescope shall move in the plane of the prime-vertical instead of the meridian.

Let P be the pole, Z the zenith, and S the position of a known star on the prime-vertical ZS. Then is the angle PZS a right angle. If the tabular right ascension of the star be α, and t the time of its transit across ZS before the meridian passage; then the hour-angle

$$ZPS = a - t.$$

Also since $\cos ZPS = \tan PZ \cot PS,$

$$\tan PZ = \cos ZPS \tan PS,$$

or $\tan$ colatitude =
$\cos$ star's hour-angle $\times \tan$ N.P.D.

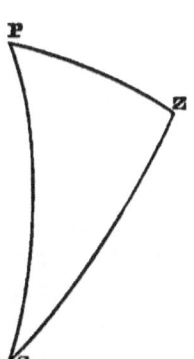

We will now proceed to discuss the errors to which a transit-instrument placed in the prime-vertical is subject.

These are precisely similar to those which require correction when the instrument is in the plane of the meridian, namely, *error of collimation, error of level of horizontal axis*, and *error of azimuth*.

The first two of these can be determined precisely in the same manner as for the transit-instrument in the plane of the meridian, and we will proceed to estimate the effect of them on the time of a star's transit over the prime-vertical.

Let the line of collimation describe the small circle $Z'S'$ parallel to ZSM, then is $S'L$, perpendicular to ZM, the error of collimation, $= c$ (suppose).

Let also $S'S$ be a portion of the small circle described by the star round the pole. Then is angle $S'PS$ fifteen times the error of time of transit $(= 15\delta t)$.

Hence $15\delta t = \dfrac{SS'}{\sin PS}$; and $SS' = \dfrac{SL}{\cos PSZ}$

$$= \frac{c}{\sin P \cos PZ}, \text{ (since } PZM \text{ is a right angle);}$$

$$\therefore \delta t = \frac{c}{15 \sin P \sin PS \cos PZ}$$

$$= \frac{c}{15 \sin ZS \cos PZ}$$

$$= \frac{c}{15 \sin \text{Z.D.} \times \cos \text{colatitude}}.$$

Again, for error of level $(= l)$; let the line of collimation describe the great circle $Z'H$, coinciding with ZSH at the horizontal point H. Let as before SS' be the small arc described by the star, and $S'L$ perpendicular to ZH. Then $Z'Z = l$;

and $S'L = l \cos ZS$.

Hence $SS' = \dfrac{S'L}{\cos SS'L}$

$$= \frac{l \cos ZS}{\cos PSZ},$$

and angle

$S'PS = 15\delta t = \dfrac{S'S}{\sin PS}$

$$= \frac{l \cos ZS}{\sin PS \cos PSZ}$$

$$= \frac{l \cos ZS}{\sin PS \tan ZS \cot PS}$$

$$= \frac{l \cos ZS}{\tan ZS \cos PS}$$

$$= \frac{l}{\tan ZS \cos PZ},$$

or $\delta t = \dfrac{1}{15} \dfrac{l}{\tan \text{Z.D.} \times \cos \text{colat.}}$.

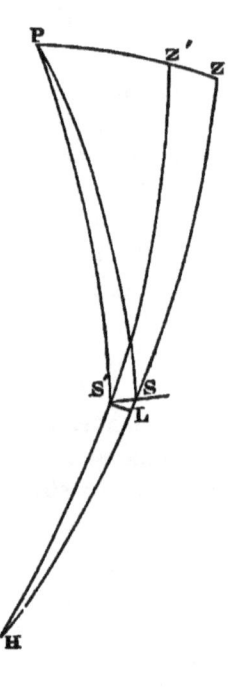

Finally, for error of azimuth, let the line of collimation describe the vertical circle ZH' near to the prime-vertical ZH; H' and H being points in the horizon; let a be the error of azimuth = angle $H'ZH$.

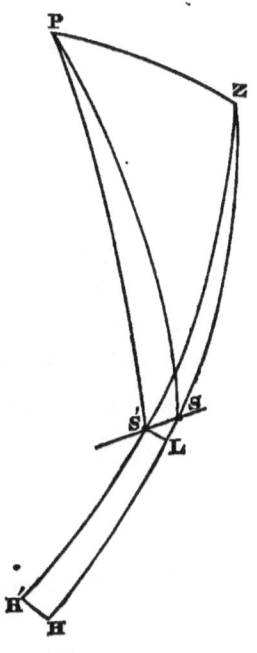

Then $S'L = a \sin ZS$,

and $S'S = \dfrac{a \sin ZS}{\cos PSZ}$,

and $15\delta t = \dfrac{a \sin ZS}{\sin PS \cos PSZ}$

$= \dfrac{a \sin ZS}{\sin PS \tan ZS \cot PS}$

$= \dfrac{a \cos ZS}{\cos PS}$

$= \dfrac{a}{\cos PZ}$,

or $\delta t = \dfrac{1}{15} \cdot \dfrac{a}{\cos \text{colat.}}$.

Let now a star be observed with the illuminated end of the axis of the telescope pointing towards the north, and let the axis point to the west of north by the quantity a''; let also the north pivot be high by l'', so as to bring western stars too early on the wires; finally let the central wire or the mean of wires lie too far south, so as to bring stars too early on the wires. Then if T be clock-time of transit over mean of wires, ΔT the amount of clock-error (additive); and t the true sidereal time of transit of a star over the west prime-vertical, we shall have (using the suffix w to denote this prime-vertical, and z to denote the zenith-distance)

$$t_w = T_w + \Delta T_w + \dfrac{c}{15 \sin z \cos \text{colat.}} + \dfrac{l}{15 \tan z \cos \text{colat.}}$$
$$+ \dfrac{a}{15 \cos \text{colat.}},$$

and, for a star on the east prime-vertical,

$$t_e = T_e + \Delta T_e - \frac{c}{15 \sin z \cos \text{colat.}} - \frac{l}{15 \tan z \cos \text{colat.}} + \frac{a}{15 \cos \text{colat.}}.$$

If now the instrument be reversed, so that the illuminated pivot be south, then it will be easily seen that the effect of error of collimation will be to make stars come too late on the wire, or that its sign must be changed; but that the effects of the error of level and of azimuth are in the same direction as before, namely, that stars pass too early.

Hence the equation will become

$$t_w' = T_w' + \Delta T_w' - \frac{c}{15 \sin z \cos \text{colat.}} + \frac{l'}{15 \tan z \cos \text{colat.}} + \frac{a}{15 \cos \text{colat.}},$$

for a star on the west prime-vertical,

and $$t_e' = T_e' + \Delta T_e' + \frac{c}{15 \sin z \cos \text{colat.}} - \frac{l'}{15 \tan z \cos \text{colat.}} + \frac{a}{15 \cos \text{colat.}},$$

for a star on the east prime-vertical, l' denoting the result of the levelling after reversion.

To find the effect of error of level on the colatitude, and on the declination of a star observed with the transit-instrument in the prime-vertical.

If l be the error of level (the south pivot being too high), the telescope when pointed upwards to the meridian will be directed to a point between the pole and the zenith, and distant from the latter by the quantity l'' (l seconds). This point we may call the instrumental zenith; and, if we subtract l'' from the true colatitude (γ), the quantity $\gamma - l''$ must be used in the equation for determining the N.P.D. of a star, namely in the equation

$$\tan \text{N.P.D.} = \frac{\tan \text{colat.}}{\cos \text{hour-angle}}.$$

But, if the true colatitude has been used in this equation, the effect of the error l'' on the N.P.D. may be thus investigated.

Let γ = colatitude,

P = hour-angle,

N.P.D. = Δ,

then $\tan \gamma = \cos P \tan \Delta$;

and, differentiating,

$$\frac{\delta \gamma}{\cos^2 \gamma} = \frac{\cos P}{\cos^2 \Delta} \delta \Delta,$$

$$\text{or } \delta \Delta = \frac{\cos^2 \Delta}{\cos^2 \gamma} \cdot \frac{\tan \Delta}{\tan \gamma} \delta \gamma$$

$$= \frac{\sin 2\Delta}{\sin 2\gamma} \delta \gamma$$

$$= \frac{\sin 2\Delta}{\sin 2\gamma} \times l''.$$

18. But the most practically useful way of using the Transit Instrument in the prime-vertical for determining the north polar distances of stars is that adopted by Professor Struve for the large instrument established at Pulkowa. This instrument is provided with an apparatus for rapidly reversing it during the progress of a series of observations, and his method is as follows.

Having determined the error of level of the axis, the telescope is directed to a star while it is yet north of the eastern prime-vertical, and the transit is observed over each vertical wire preceding the central wire. When the star has passed the last of these wires, the axis of the telescope is reversed, and the transits over the *same wires* are observed again, but of course in the reverse order. On the star approaching the western prime-vertical the same process is repeated, the transits being observed over the *same wires*, in the last preceding position of the axis, and then with the axis reversed. From these observations the north polar distance of the star is deduced by the following process, the observations over each wire being taken separately.

Let Δ be the north polar distance of the star,

h and h' the hour-angles at the transits of the star over the same wire in the two positions of the axis,

c the angular distance of the wire from the line of collimation.

Then, if N be the north point of the horizon, P the pole, Z the zenith, and S the star on the wire,

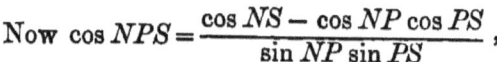

$NS = 90° - c$,
$PS = \Delta$,
$NP = 90° - \text{colat.}$
$\quad = 90° - \gamma$,

and $h =$ hour-angle $=$ angle ZPS.

Now $\cos NPS = \dfrac{\cos NS - \cos NP \cos PS}{\sin NP \sin PS}$,

or $\cos(90° - c) = \sin c = -\cos h \cos \gamma \sin \Delta + \sin \gamma \cos \Delta$.

Similarly, for the observation with axis reversed,

$\cos(90° + c) = -\sin c = -\cos h' \cos \gamma \sin \Delta + \sin \gamma \cos \Delta$;

$\therefore 0 = 2 \sin \gamma \cos \Delta - \cos \gamma \sin \Delta (\cos h + \cos h')$

$\quad = 2 \sin \gamma \cos \Delta - 2 \cos \gamma \sin \Delta \cos \dfrac{h'+h}{2} \cos \dfrac{h'-h}{2}$,

or $\tan \gamma \cot \Delta = \cos \dfrac{h'+h}{2} \cos \dfrac{h'-h}{2}$.

This equation will give Δ, when γ is known, or will serve to find γ or the colatitude, when Δ is known.

If the right ascension of the star is assumed to be known, an observation in reversed positions over one prime-vertical will be sufficient, because hour-angle = sidereal time − right ascension; but the observations over the other prime-vertical make the knowledge of the right ascension unnecessary, since it is evident that h' represents half the interval between the first transit east and the second transit west; and h half the interval between the second transit east and the first transit west.

After each reversion of the axis it is necessary to redetermine the error of level of the axis, and corrections will be necessary for the difference of the errors in the different positions; but it is not desirable to enter into minute details. If the errors do not differ much, the mean error of level may be applied to γ, or, computing with an uncorrected value of γ, we may apply the suitable corrections for error of level to Δ.

19. It is necessary that the instrument be accurately adjusted to the prime-vertical. If this be not the case the error can be found by taking half the sum of the transits east and west over the same wire, which will manifestly give the time of transit over the vertical in which the axis of rotation lies. This time (corrected for clock-error), when compared with the known right ascension of the stars, will give the angle at the pole subtended by the amount of azimuthal error. If this angle be δP, then we have seen (page 35) that

$$\delta P = \frac{a}{\cos \text{colat.}},$$

and therefore $a = \cos \text{colat.} \times \delta P$.

The Transit-Circle.

20. In the preceding part of this chapter we have treated of the transit-instrument as a separate instrument, and not as forming a portion of the transit-circle, an instrument now coming into general use. This was necessary, since the transit-instrument must for many purposes remain a separate instrument, and some of its adjustments when thus used are essentially different from those of the telescope of the transit-circle.

For the transit-instrument, for example, it is the general practice to determine the error of collimation by observations of a fixed mark or of the wires in another telescope in reversed positions of the axis of the transit-telescope, and it is also usual to determine the error of level by a spirit-level[1].

But these methods of determining the collimation and level-errors would not be practicable with the transit-circle, because the instrument is generally not capable of being reversed on its axis; and the axis is not convenient for the application of a spirit-level. It is therefore necessary to use other methods, which we will proceed to describe.

21. First for *collimation*.

This is determined by means of two smaller telescopes (called collimating telescopes) placed with their optical axes very nearly in the same line with that of the telescope of the transit-circle, one to the north and the other to the south of it. The object-glasses of the telescopes are turned towards each other, and therefore towards the instrument; and in their principal foci are placed systems of wires, one moveable laterally, and the other vertically, by means of micrometer-screws. The systems of wires are so arranged that the image of a definite point of one of the wires in one system can be easily and accurately brought into coincidence with that of a similar point of

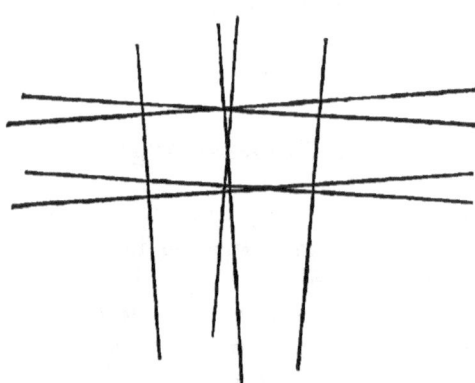

the other system, when the wires of one telescope are viewed through the other, and then this point may be easily observed

[1] Professor Challis has however been in the habit for many years of determining the error of level by means of a collimating eye-piece.

with the central vertical wire of the transit-circle. In the Greenwich and Oxford transit-circles the wires consist of two pairs of parallel spider-lines at equal distances from each other, the one pair being nearly vertical and the other pair nearly horizontal. These cross each other so as to form a square, as in the diagram, the one nearly vertical wire being rather thicker than the other, for the sake of distinction. And one of the nearly vertical sides of the square formed by the system of wires in the other collimating telescope is made to bisect the corresponding side of the square in the first system, so as to form two small acute right-angled triangles of the equality of which the eye can judge exceedingly well. To serve as a fixed mark in the meridian for certain other purposes there is another wire in each system parallel to the nearly horizontal wires, and placed at such a distance that when the squares are correctly placed on each other the middle point of the part of it intercepted by the two nearly vertical wires is in the same vertical with the middle of one of the nearly vertical sides of the square. The object of the arrangement is to secure unmistakeable points of reference in each collimating telescope, which shall admit of very accurate observation with the central vertical and the horizontal wires of the telescope of the transit-circle. It may also be mentioned that, in the use of the telescope of the transit-circle, it is found that it is most convenient that the whole system of vertical or transit-wires should be moved together by means of a micrometer-screw acting on the wire frame, instead of having, as in the transit-instrument, the wires fixed, and reference to collimators made by a separate micrometer-wire.

Let now NS represent the common axis of the two pencils by which the point N (representing the point of reference of the collimating telescopes before referred to) is visible in the field of the south collimating telescope, in contact with the similar point S, visible in the field of the north collimating telescope.

Let also AOB represent a line parallel to the axis of the telescope through the optical centre O of the object-glass, and aOb the direction of the line of collimation. Then, with the telescope pointing north, let the central wire, by means of the micrometer-screw, be brought into coincidence with the point N; and afterwards let the telescope be turned round till it points southward, so as to view the wires in the south collimator. The micrometer-wire (or rather the point of it which was in coincidence with N) will now occupy the position N', determined by making the angle $N'Ob$ equal to the angle NOa, that is, to the angle bOS. If then the reading of the micrometer be taken for coincidence with N, and the screw be turned till it is afterwards in coincidence with S, it is plain that the mean of the two readings will bring it into coincidence with b, that is, with the line of collimation.

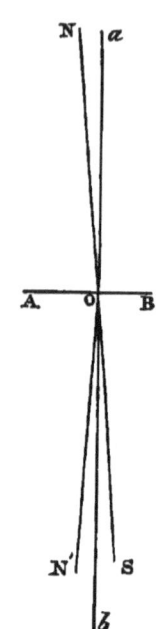

22. The position of the line of collimation (or the micrometer-reading for coincidence of the central wire with this line) being thus determined, the level-error can be determined by means of the observation of the image of this wire reflected in a trough of mercury, in the following manner:

The ordinary positive eye-piece used for observation is replaced by another called Bohnenberger's eye-piece. This is an eye-piece with three lenses, arranged in a tube which is perforated to allow the light from a gas-flame or lamp to fall upon an inclined reflector placed between the field-lens and the second lens so as to illuminate the field and to render the wires visible. If the telescope be now placed vertical with its object-glass downwards and directed to a surface of mercury, the reflected images of the wires will be seen nearly in contact with their images as seen directly in the field of the telescope. If, indeed, the central wire be made to coincide with the line of collimation of the telescope, and the axis be accurately level, the direct and reflected wires will plainly be in coincidence; but if there be any error of level, the central vertical wire and its reflected image will be seen near each other, and the amount of the separation will determine the magnitude of the error of level.

ERROR OF LEVEL OF THE TRANSIT-CIRCLE.

Let, for instance, O represent a point in the wire put into coincidence with the line of collimation; OC the axis of the pencil of rays proceeding from O to meet the surface of mercury

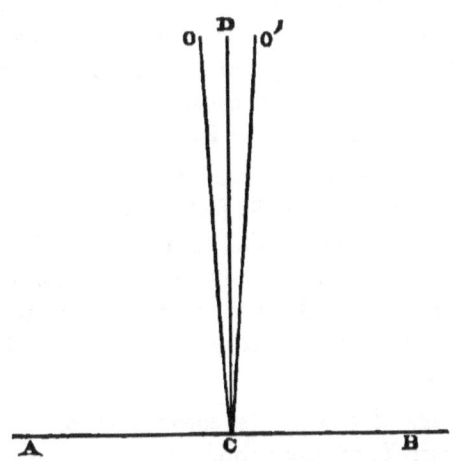

ACB in C. Then, if CD be a vertical line, and CO' the axis of the reflected pencil, the reflected image of the point O of the wire will be visible at a point O' in the field of the telescope, and the angular separation of O and O' will be the double of the angle OCD, which plainly is the error of level of the axis; the plane of the paper being the vertical east and west plane. But practically the position of the point D can be readily found by moving the micrometer-screw (and therefore the point O) till it coincides with O', the coincidence evidently taking place at D. If, for instance, the reading of the micrometer for coincidence be r', and that for the position of the line of collimation be r, and if one revolution of the micrometer be equivalent to n'', then the error of level will be $(r'-r) \times n$ seconds.

The method which has just been explained for determining the errors of collimation and level are equally applicable to the transit-instrument and to the transit-circle, but it is not generally applied to the former because it would necessitate the erection of two fixed telescopes on firm piers, and would therefore make the instrument much more expensive.

23. We will now proceed to give a more detailed account of the transit-circle in its modern form; and, to fix the ideas, we will confine ourselves in general description to that of the Radcliffe Observatory of Oxford, which was purchased from Mr Carrington, who caused it to be constructed on the model of the celebrated instrument at Greenwich. The instrument is much smaller and less complicated than that at Greenwich, and is therefore more proper for illustration of the general use of such instruments than the latter is.

The transit-circle now erected at the Radcliffe Observatory of Oxford has a telescope of $5\frac{1}{2}$ feet focal length, with an object-glass of 5 inches aperture. The axis, which, with the exception of the pivots, was cast in one flow of metal, consists of a central cube 9 inches in the side, and of two cones with which the pivots are mechanically connected. The pivots themselves are of $3\frac{1}{2}$ inches diameter.

The bearings of the pivots, constructed of brass, are of the form of the letter Y, of great solidity, and each capable of screw adjustment in level, but not in azimuth when once fixed.

The horizontal axis carries two gun-metal circles, each cast in a single flow, of 42 inches diameter. The west circle, on its west face, carries a band of gold on its surface, on which the fine divisions were laid off at intervals of 5' by Mr Simons's dividing engine. The microscopes (four in number) are, at their micrometer ends, that is, on the outsides of the piers, so far brought together that the two eye-pieces of a diametral pair are 24 inches apart. To relieve the bearings and pivots of the greater part of the dead weight, friction counterpoises are employed.

The above description of the instrument itself may be sufficient, but it is necessary to mention its collimating telescopes. These are each of 33 inches focal length and of $2\frac{3}{4}$ inches aperture, placed horizontal on separate piers of great solidity, on a level with the centre of the cube of the axis of the transit-circle, the south one pointing northwards and the north one southwards, nearly in the meridian. The webs, or systems of wires in their foci, are of the same pattern as those already described in page 41.

24. In what has preceded, the use of the transit-circle for observing time and the right-ascensions of objects has been sufficiently dwelt upon, the error of collimation being determined by means of the two collimating telescopes, and the error of level by the observation of the coincidence of the central vertical wire, with its image reflected in a trough of mercury, by the use of Bohnenberger's eye-piece. The reduction of the observations will differ in no important degree from that which has been already explained in the case of the transit-instrument.

25. It remains now only to explain the use of the instrument for obtaining by observation the other element necessary for the determination of the place of a body, namely its north polar distance, or its declination.

It has been explained that one of the circles carried on the horizontal axis of the instrument is divided into degrees and 5-minute spaces, and that four reading microscopes are directed to it by which these spaces can be subdivided into seconds and fractional parts of seconds. The circular heads of the micrometers are divided into 60 equal parts, and an index projects from the fixed body of the microscope to denote the particular second and decimal part of the second for any particular reading. They are so adjusted that five complete turns or revolutions of the screw of the micrometer will carry the wire of the microscope from one division of the circle to the next division. This however can never be accomplished with perfect accuracy, and in practice is not attempted; but the exact number of revolutions and fractions of revolutions corresponding to a space of 5' on the circle is called the *run* of the micrometer-microscope, and the difference between this run and 5 exact revolutions is called the *error of runs*, and the mean error for the four microscopes is applied to the mean of the readings as a correction.

Thus in reducing circle observations we should proceed thus. Suppose the case of a single microscope-micrometer. Let its reading, when its wire bisects one division, be x'', and, for bisection of the next division, y'' (y being greater than x). Then, remembering that one revolution corresponds approximately to 60'', it is plain that, $\left(5 + \dfrac{y-x}{60}\right)$ revolutions are equivalent to 5'.

Hence one revolution

$$= \frac{5'}{5 + \frac{y-x}{60}} = \frac{1}{1 + \frac{e}{300}} = 1 - \frac{e}{300},$$

very nearly, if $e = y - x$.

Therefore, one revolution being a nominal minute and one division of the head a nominal second we should have to subtract the $\frac{e}{300}$ th part of a revolution from each revolution, or $\frac{e''}{5}$ from each nominal minute, or e'' from each $5'$ space as measured by the microscope.

If then the reading of the microscope-micrometer be r minutes, we shall take the proportional part of the *error of runs* as applicable to this reading; and this will plainly be $\frac{re}{5}$.

26. It has been said that the microscopes are placed *diametrically* opposite to each other. The effect of this, even when only a single pair of opposite microscopes is used, is to obviate *errors of excentricity* of the circle.

The centre of the circle is, properly speaking, the centre of its divided rim, but it turns on an axis which may not be and commonly is not coincident with this centre.

Thus, in the accompanying diagram let C be the centre of the circle, and C' the centre of rotation. Join CC' and produce it to AA'. Let now the circle rotate round C' through the angle $AC'N$, the centre C describing the dotted arc CC'', and coming into the position C''. Then it is plain that the points of the circle which would, if it were accurately centred, have come under the microscopes at B and B', will have come to the points b and b', found by drawing Bb and Bb' equal and parallel to the line joining CC''.

Consider now the points under the two reading microscopes at B and B'. The small spaces Bb and $B'b'$ (each equal and parallel to CC'') may each be resolved into two, one in the direction of the limb of the circle and the other at right angles to it. With respect to the first resolved equal parts the effect will be that one microscope will read a greater arc and the other an arc less by the same quantity than they would have read if the circle were centrically placed, and therefore that

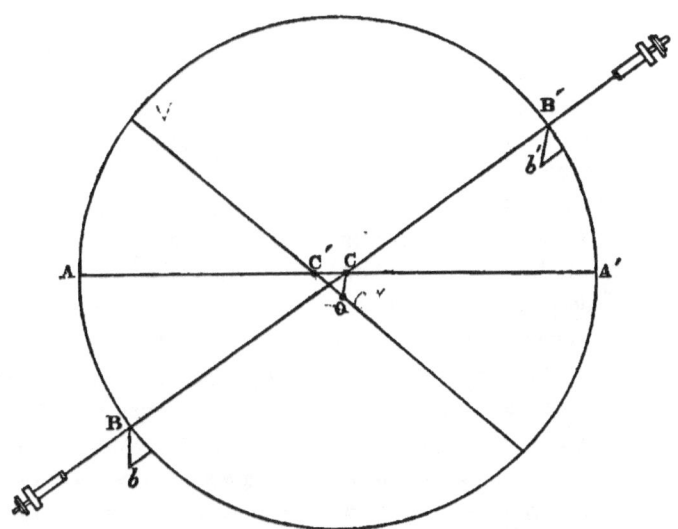

the mean of their readings will be the same as if there were no excentricity. The effect of the second resolved motion will be that the point B will be brought nearer to the microscope at B, and the point B' carried farther from the microscope at B' by the same quantity, so that the mean error of runs will not be altered. Hence the angle through which the circle has been turned round the point C' will be as accurately measured as if there were no excentricity, or the effect of excentricity is eliminated by taking the mean of the readings of two opposite microscopes.

27. Another important consideration in the treatment of observations made with the circle is the correctness of the divisions. Formerly the dividing was performed by hand, and the errors were far less reducible to law than those in which the dividing has been performed by a dividing-engine, which is the case with many of the best circles of the present day. It must never however be assumed that the divisions are

faultless, and the examination is one of the most laborious operations which an astronomer has to perform. The discussion is however of too technical a character and not sufficiently elementary for a treatise like the present.

28. ZENITH-DISTANCE OBSERVATIONS. It has been mentioned that the telescope of the transit-circle has generally in the plane passing through its focus a wire-frame with a system of fixed vertical wires at equal intervals, moveable by a micrometer-screw, and another wire horizontal and moveable by another micrometer; sometimes there is also another and fixed horizontal wire, but this is not necessary. In making the zenith-distance observation of a star, the instrument is set previously to the place of the star by means of the pointer connected with its divided circle, and, as the star is seen crossing the field of view, it is bisected with the horizontal wire by turning the head of the micrometer, at the instant (or nearly so) of its passage across the central vertical wire which represents the meridian. Care is always taken in fixing the eye-piece on the telescope that the telescope micrometer readings when reduced to arc are always additive to the readings of the microscope-micrometers. The *concluded circle reading* will then be: pointer-reading + mean of microscope-readings + correction for runs + telescope micrometer reading, where the pointer-reading includes the degrees and multiples of five minutes (such as 5′, 10′, 15′,...45′, 50′, 55′), and the microscope readings include the odd minutes and seconds, by which (the mean being taken) the crosses of the micrometer-microscopes, when placed upon the proper divisions of the circles, are distant from the zeros of the micrometers.

29. It however frequently happens that the star or other object cannot be observed exactly on the meridian, but is bisected at an interval of a certain number of seconds of time either before or after passing the meridian. This introduces another correction technically called the *Correction for Curvature*, arising from the deflection of the small circle in which the star or object, if not on the equator, is moving, and the great circle of which the horizontal wire forms a part.

To estimate the amount of this correction, let the star be observed t seconds before or after its passage over the meridian, and let its north polar distance be Δ. Let, in the annexed figure, P be the north pole, and S the place of the star near the meridian PNS'. Draw NS an arc of great circle perpendicular to PS', and let the arc SS' represent the path of the star. Then is the hour-angle $NPS = 15t$, and the arc NS represents the wire by which the star is bisected at S, while S' represents the point on the meridian where it should have been bisected. Hence NS' is the correction for curvature: let this be x.

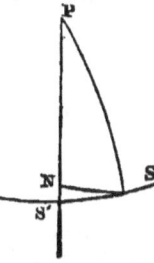

Now
$$\cos P = \tan PN \cot PS,$$
$$= \frac{\tan PN}{\tan \Delta} = \frac{\tan (\Delta - x)}{\tan \Delta},$$

or $\cos (15t) = \dfrac{\tan \Delta - \tan x}{1 + \tan \Delta \tan x} \cdot \dfrac{1}{\tan \Delta}$,

or $1 - \dfrac{(15t)^2}{2} \sin^2 1'' = \left(1 - \dfrac{\tan x}{\tan \Delta}\right) \times (1 - \tan \Delta \tan x)$,

neglecting higher powers,
$$= 1 - \frac{\tan x}{\sin \Delta \cos \Delta},$$
$$= 1 - \frac{2 \tan x}{\sin 2\Delta}.$$

Hence $\tan x = \left(\dfrac{15t}{2}\right)^2 \sin 2\Delta \times \sin^2 1''$,

or x (in seconds of arc) $= \dfrac{225}{4} \sin 2\Delta \times t^2 \times \sin 1''$,

since we may put the arc for the tangent, the quantities being generally very small.

The preceding formula is applicable to the case wherein the clock-time has been noted at which the bisection has been made. Frequently however it is more convenient, without regard to the clock-beats, to bisect the object as it passes one of the side vertical wires.

Let the time taken by an equatorial star in passing from this wire to the central wire be nT. Then, for a star whose north polar distance is Δ, the time will be $\dfrac{nT}{\sin \Delta}$, and this must be put for t in the preceding formula.

Hence
$$x = \frac{225}{4} \sin 1'' \times \frac{n^2 T^2}{\sin^2 \Delta} \times \sin 2\Delta$$
$$= \frac{225}{2} T^2 \sin 1'' \times n^2 \cotan \Delta,$$

where $\dfrac{225}{2} T^2 \sin 1''$ is a known constant, and its numerical value must be calculated.

30. In the case of a planet, or of the Sun and Moon, when observed off the meridian, there is another correction to be applied, namely, that for the motion in north polar distance between the time of bisection and that of meridian transit. In the cases of the Sun and planets, the motion for one hour is given in the Nautical Almanac in the Ephemerides of their motions, and the proportional part corresponding to the time t must be calculated, and is the correction required. Thus, if the hourly motion be m, the correction will be $\dfrac{t}{3600} \times m$.

In the case of the Moon, the *motion during the passage of the Moon over one hour of geographical longitude* is given in the section of *Moon-culminating stars* of the Nautical Almanac, and if this be m, the factor given above for the planets must be multiplied by $\dfrac{\sin \text{Geo. Z.D.}}{\sin \text{App. Z.D.}}$, for the same reason as in the case of reduction of imperfect transits of the Moon.

31. Supposing all the preceding corrections (for runs, curvature, and motion) to have been applied, we have the correct *Concluded Circle Reading*, that is, the value of the mean reading of the microscopes, for an object at its bisection on the meridian, supposing that five revolutions of each microscope-micrometer are exactly equivalent to 5'. Hence, if two or more objects be thus observed at their meridian passages, we can obtain immediately the differences of their north polar distances or

north or south zenith distances, which are plainly the same as the differences of the circle readings. If then we could obtain for any one object its absolute apparent zenith distance, we should obtain the apparent zenith distances of all other objects.

Now as the zenith is the point of the heavens marked by the direction of gravity at the observer's station on the surface of the earth, it is plain that there are only two ways of observing its position, namely, by means of a plumb-line, which gives immediately the direction in which gravity acts, or by means of the surface of a fluid at rest (mercury, for example) which gives the position of the horizon. The former method was formerly employed with the old quadrants in use before the introduction of the mural-circle; but the latter method is now invariably employed.

There are two ways of observing the circle reading corresponding to the position of the circle when the telescope is directed to the zenith, namely, either by observation of the images of stars both by direct vision and by reflexion in a trough of mercury, or by observing the coincidence of the direct and reflected images of the horizontal wire by means of a Bohnenberger's eye-piece (as previously explained for error of level of the axis).

First, for the method by stars. A skilful observer will be able with sufficient ease to observe a star at the same transit both by reflexion and by direct vision, in the following manner. He will, a few minutes before the transit, point the telescope to the direction in which the rays coming from the star will enter the telescope after reflexion, and arrange the mercury trough. He will then wait till the star is near one of the side wires before meridian passage, and will bisect it and take the reading of the telescope-micrometer, having previously read the circle, which is supposed to be clamped. Unclamping the circle, he will then rapidly turn it round till the star is visible by direct vision (generally near one of the side wires after the transit), and, after clamping the circle again, he will bisect and read the telescope-micrometer and microscope-micrometers a second time, having thus made two complete observations of the star.

From what has been explained in Chapter I. p. 9, it will be plain that if Z be the concluded circle reading for the direct observation, and Z' for the observation by reflexion, then the reading for the *horizontal point* will be $\dfrac{Z+Z'}{2}$, and for the *zenith-point*, $\dfrac{Z+Z'}{2} \pm 90°$.

It is usual to observe several stars in different parts of the heavens for determining the zenith-point, and it is especially desirable that an equal number should be observed north and south of the zenith, to eliminate any errors that may arise from flexure of the telescope or unknown errors of divisions of the circle, or any thing else that may vitiate a single observation.

But in addition to star observations, the determination of the *nadir-point* by observing the coincidence of direct and reflected images of the wire by means of Bohnenberger's eye-piece is of great importance, since this is an observation which is independent of the weather and the state of the sky, and can be made at all times whenever it is considered desirable.

Having, by combination of star-observations and wire-observations, determined the *zero of zenith distance* or the *zenith-point* with sufficient accuracy, (an accuracy which in first class instruments may be equal to, or even smaller than, a quarter of a second of space), the *apparent zenith distances* of all objects will be obtained by simply subtracting the zenith point from the circle readings; and as this element, the apparent zenith distance, that is, the zenith distance of an object as affected by refraction, is that which alone is determined primarily by the instrument, we will for the present assume that the account already given of the processes of observation and calculation are sufficient. The deduction of the co-latitude of the place of observation and of the north polar distances of objects involves the application of refraction, and therefore cannot properly be treated of till the theory of refraction has been explained.

32. THE EQUATORIAL. The Transit Instrument, and the Mural or Meridian Circle, produce observations of the greatest

possible accuracy, chiefly through the nature of the construction of the instruments, which are symmetrical with respect to the direction of gravity, and of which therefore the errors of adjustment can be easily determined and remain without much fluctuation. But, if equal accuracy could be obtained, it is evident that an instrument which would enable the observer to follow an object in its diurnal course, and give, by direct observation, its right ascension and polar distance, would be much more natural and convenient.

Such an instrument is the *Equatorial*.

In its simplest form it consists of an axis capable of free rotation, supposed to be parallel to the earth's axis, that is, to pass if produced through the poles of the heavens, and of a telescope connected with this axis in such a manner as to admit of being pointed at any star and then fixed, so that, when the axis is turned round, it will follow the star in its diurnal course. For the purpose of measuring the angle which the line of collimation of the telescope makes with the axis, a circle is fixed to it either in its own plane or parallel to it; and for the purpose of measuring the angle through which the polar axis has carried the telescope out of the plane of the meridian, which is considered to be the zero-plane, another circle is attached to the polar axis with its plane perpendicular to it, and revolving with it.

These circles are read in the usual way by micrometer-microscopes fixed to some part of the pier carrying the instrument, or to some part of the fixed frame.

In the English mode of mounting equatorials the telescope is in the plane of the polar axis, which consists of a framework of rods or hollow metallic columns forming a kind of open cylinder, and connected with the pivots which rest in Y's at the upper and lower ends. In the German, or Frauenhofer's, mode of mounting, the telescope is at one extremity of the *declination axis*, that is, of the axis on which the telescope turns; and its weight is counterbalanced by heavy weights at the other extremity of the declination axis. This necessity of counterbalancing the telescope is of itself a disadvantage, since it increases the pressure on the Y's, and therefore the friction which resists the turning of the instrument. The great telescope at Greenwich, of nearly 18 feet focal length and 13 inches aperture, is mounted in the English fashion, and the Heliometer at Oxford is an excellent specimen of the German mounting.

To the general description given above it needs only to be added, that the circle which moves with the telescope and which serves to measure *declinations* or *polar distances* of objects is called the *declination circle*, while that which is attached to the polar axis is called the *hour-circle*, since it serves to measure the angular distance from the meridian of the circle in which the star is at the time of observation.

33. The student will readily see, from the preceding account, that it is necessary for the perfect adjustment of the instrument that the following conditions should be fulfilled:

1. The polar-axis must point to the true pole of the heavens, or, in other words, its elevation must be equal to the latitude of the observatory; and the vertical plane passing through it must also be the plane of the meridian.

2. The line of collimation of the telescope must be perpendicular to the declination-axis.

3. The declination-axis must be perpendicular to the polar-axis.

4. The index of the hour-circle should point to zero when the line of collimation of the telescope is directed to an object in the meridian of the place of observation.

5. The index of the declination-circle should point to zero or to $90°$ when the line of collimation of the telescope is directed to the equator.

We will discuss these errors in their order:

1. To find the errors of elevation and azimuth of the polar-axis.

ERROR OF POSITION OF THE POLAR AXIS.

Let P be the pole of the heavens, and P' the pole of the instrument, that is, the point towards which the polar-axis is directed. Join PP' by an arc of a great circle, and draw a perpendicular arc $P'N$ on PQ the meridian. Then is PN the error of elevation of the axis, and $P'N$ is the azimuthal deviation. Let S be a star, whose N. P. D. is Δ, and hour-angle $SPQ = \theta$. Draw $P'ML$ and NO perpendicular to SP, and NL parallel to it. Then, the small triangles $P'PN$, $P'MO$, &c. being considered as rectilinear, MP will be the error of observed N. P. D. of the star, or $\delta\Delta$.

Now
$$MP = MO + OP$$
$$= LN + OP$$
$$= P'N \sin SPQ + PN \cos SPQ;$$

or, if azimuthal deviation $= x$, and error of elevation $= y$,
$$x \sin \theta + y \cos \theta = \delta\Delta.$$

It follows from the above, that if the hour-angle $= 0$, or if the star be on the meridian, $y = \delta\Delta$;

and if the hour-angle $= 90°$ or 6^h, $x = \delta\Delta$.

Hence, to find this error of elevation, a star should be observed in reversed positions of the instrument, on or near the meridian; and, to find the azimuthal deviation, a star should be observed nearly six hours before or after its meridian passage.

2. To find the error of collimation of the central wire of the telescope.

Let the transit of an equatorial star be observed in reversed positions of the instrument, that is, with the declination-circle first east and then west, or *vice versâ*. Then it is plain that any error in the position of the declination-axis will have no effect. Let also the hour-circle be read for each observation. Then, if t and t' be the times of transit, and H and H' the readings of the hour-circle, the right-ascension of the star will be from the two observations $t-H$ and $t'-H' \mp 12^h$. If there is no error of collimation these should be equal, but if otherwise the error of collimation will be equal to

$$\frac{15}{2} \times \{t - H - (t' - H') \pm 12^h\}.$$

It is plain also that the index error of the hour-circle will be eliminated in taking the difference of the observed right-ascensions.

3. To find the error of position of the declination-axis.

With declination-circle west, suppose that the west end of the axis is too high when the telescope is in the meridian. Let the inclination of the axis to the horizon in this position be i. Imagine now the transit of a star whose N.P.D. is Δ to be observed at any hour-angle. The line of collimation of the telescope will now describe a great circle $P'Q$ lying to the east of the corresponding circle of declination PQ, and passing east of the pole by the quantity i, the two circles intersecting on the equator at Q. Let P be the pole of the heavens, S' the star on the wire describing the small circle $S'S$; $PP' = i$, at right angles to QP'.

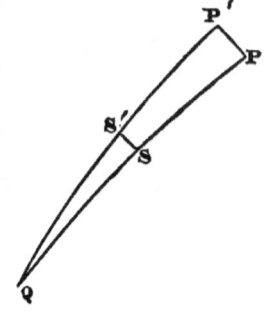

Then $\qquad SS' = PP' \sin QS'$
$$= i \cos \Delta,$$
and the time of describing SS'
$$= \frac{i \cos \Delta}{15 \sin \Delta}$$
$$= \frac{i}{15} \cotan \Delta.$$

This then is the error in time caused by the error i of declination-axis, by which the star will come too early on the central wire. Let the right ascension of the star be determined thus by the time of transit of the star and the reading of the hour-circle, and let this be A, subject to index-error e, and to clock-error c.

Then the true right ascension, $\alpha = A + e + c + \dfrac{i}{15} \cotan \Delta$.
Let now the instrument be reversed, so that the declination-circle may be east; then a similar observation will give the equation

$$\alpha = A' + e + c - \dfrac{i}{15} \cotan \Delta;$$

$$\therefore A + e + c + \dfrac{i}{15} \cotan \Delta = A' + e + c - \dfrac{i}{15} \cotan \Delta,$$

$$\text{and} \therefore \dfrac{2i}{15} \cotan \Delta = A' - A,$$

$$\text{and} \quad i = \dfrac{15}{2} \dfrac{A' - A}{\cotan \Delta}.$$

4. When the errors of collimation and declination-axis have been corrected, the index-error of the hour-circle can be immediately found by observing the transit of a star and reading the hour-circle. The difference between the observed right ascension and the tabular right ascension will be the index-error.

Similarly, for the index-error of the declination-circle, let the N.P.D. of a star be observed in reversed positions of the instrument and the mean taken. The difference between the resulting and the tabular N.P.D. will be the index-error.

34. The Altitude and Azimuth Instrument, or the Altazimuth.

A brief description of the Altitude and Azimuth Instrument is necessary, because of the importance which it has recently acquired amongst the instruments of a fixed observatory by the admirable use which has been made of that erected at Greenwich in observations of the moon.

This instrument, like the equatorial, has two principal axes, namely, a vertical axis, the axis of azimuthal rotation, moving on an upper and a lower pivot, round which the whole instrument revolves, and a horizontal axis, carried by the frame of the instrument, round which the telescope revolves. Firmly connected with the telescope, and parallel to it is a vertical divided circle, with which are connected two microscope-micrometers for reading off zenith distances of objects, while a fixed horizontal circle, read by microscope-micrometers carried by the revolving frame of the instrument, serves to determine the azimuths of objects.

This instrument is subject to the same classes of errors as the transit-instrument, meridian-circle, and equatorial, but its errors are precisely analogous to those of the equatorial if we bear in mind that the fundamental plane of reference is the horizon instead of the equator.

Thus the error of collimation may be found by observing the azimuth of a distant object, or a collimating mark in the direction of the horizon in reversed position of the vertical circle, half the difference of the readings of the azimuth-circle being the error of collimation of the vertical wire with which the observation is made. Again, the instrument is supposed to rotate round an axis accurately vertical, that is, which would pass through the zenith if produced, while the horizontal axis, which carries the telescope and the vertical circle, is supposed to be exactly at right angles to the azimuthal axis of rotation; and defects in these adjustments will introduce errors in the observed azimuths and zenith distances precisely analogous to those arising from the want of adjustment of the polar-axis and declination-axis of the equatorial. Still there are circumstances in the construction of each individual instrument which render necessary a specific mode of treatment of the observations, and, to fix the ideas, we shall confine ourselves to the mode of treatment applied to the observations made with the Altazimuth at the Observatory of Greenwich, as the whole theory of this class of instruments has been best worked out with it.

35. Of this instrument, which is remarkable as being the first of a class which combines the ordinary facility of use with extraordinary solidity and firmness, the frame revolving in azimuth, consists of a top and bottom connected by two vertical cheeks all of cast iron, while the azimuthal circle upon which rests the lower pivot for azimuthal rotation rests upon a solid

cylindrical pier, which is built upon a much larger structure, or three-rayed pier, carried up from the foundation. The upper pivot for azimuthal rotation is supported by a framework of iron triangles, carried by the three-rayed pier; three radial bars, supported on the angles of the upper horizontal triangle, carrying at their point of junction the Y in which the upper pivot of the vertical axis turns. Of the four parts constituting the rotating frame of the instrument, the top and bottom pieces carry four levels parallel to the horizontal axis, the bottom carrying also in the same flow of metal the tubes for the microscopes which read the horizontal circle; while, of the two vertical cheeks, the one carries in one flow of metal the microscopes for viewing the vertical circle, and the supports of the levels parallel to the plane of that circle.

Of the other parts, the side of the vertical circle which carries the graduated limb, the ends of the telescope, and one of the pivots, is cast in one flow of metal, and the other side of the circle and its pivot are cast in another flow.

The numbers of the level-scales increase from one end to the other, so that the sum of east and west readings must be taken in the reduction of the observations.

We will take the observations of azimuth and zenith distance separately.

For azimuth let the error of collimation be c'', estimated positive when the graduated face of the vertical circle is right. Let (in Fig. 1) Z be the zenith, S the position of a star at an observed time t, on crossing the line corresponding to the mean of the vertical wires. S' the position on crossing the line of collimation. Then $SS' = c$; if then ZA and ZM be each 90°, and $AM = \delta A$ = error of azimuth, it is plain that

$$c = \delta A \sin ZS$$
$$= \delta A \sin z;$$
or $\delta A = c \cdot \operatorname{cosec} z,$

if z be the zenith distance.

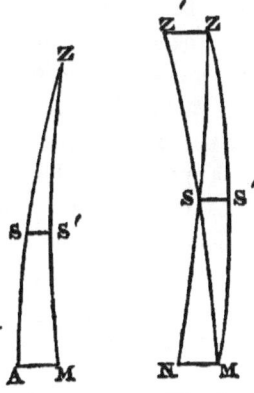

Fig. 1.   Fig. 2.

Again, the inclination of the horizontal axis being l, let the line of collimation of the telescope describe the great circle $Z'M$ (Fig. 2), ($Z'M$ being $= 90°$, Z the true zenith, and M a point in the horizon). Thus ZM is a vertical circle. Let a star cross the mean of wires at time t at S, S' being the corresponding position on the vertical circle. Then

$$SS' = \angle SMS' \cos z$$
$$= l \cos z;$$

and, if ZS be drawn and produced to meet the horizon at N ($NM = \delta A$ being the corresponding error of azimuth), then

$$SS = MN \sin z,$$
$$\text{or } \delta A = \frac{SS'}{\sin z} = \frac{l \cos z}{\sin z}$$
$$= l \cot z.$$

Hence, for given errors of collimation and level, the resulting errors of azimuth vary respectively as the cosecant and the cotangent of the zenith distance.

36. *To find by observations of stars the error of collimation and the error of level of the horizontal axis.*

Let the graduated face of the vertical circle be right, and let a star be observed at the time t, of which the azimuth computed from the right ascension and declination is A_r. Let also C_r be the concluded reading of the azimuthal-circle, and α the zero of azimuth; x the error of collimation with sign corresponding to this position of graduated circle; y the level-indication for horizontal position of horizontal axis (that is, mean of east and west scales, or reading for centre of the bubble), and L_r the actual level-indication from the reading of the level at the observation; also let Z_r be the star's zenith-distance. Then will $L_r - y$ represent the error of level, and therefore, assuming the star's place to be correct, we shall have the equation

$$C_r - \alpha + x \operatorname{cosec} Z_r + (L_r - y) \cotan Z_r = A_r.$$

Similarly, using l for the suffix when the graduated circle is left, and remembering that the errors of collimation and level change their signs, we shall have the following equation

$$C_l - \alpha - x \operatorname{cosec} Z_l - (L_l - y) \cotan Z_l = A_l;$$

and, by subtraction,

$$x (\operatorname{cosec} Z_r + \operatorname{cosec} Z_l) - y (\cotan Z_r + \cotan Z_l)$$
$$= C_l - C_r - (A_l - A_r) - (L_r \cotan Z_r + L_l \cotan Z_l)$$
$$= (C_l - L_l \cotan Z_l - A_l) - (C_r + L_r \cotan Z_r - A_r),$$

or
$$x \frac{\operatorname{cosec} Z_r + \operatorname{cosec} Z_l}{\cotan Z_r + \cotan Z_l} - y$$
$$= \frac{(C_l - L_l \cotan Z_l - A_l) - (C_r + L_r \cot Z_r - A_r)}{\cotan Z_r + \cotan Z_l} \quad \ldots\ldots (\alpha).$$

If we denote by small letters the values of A, C, L, and Z occurring in the similar equation arising from the observation of another star, we shall have

$$x \frac{\operatorname{cosec} z_r + \operatorname{cosec} z_l}{\cotan z_r + \cotan z_l} - y$$
$$= \frac{(c_l - l_l \cotan z_l - a_l) - (c_r + l_r \cotan z_r - a_r)}{\cotan z_r + \cotan z_l} \quad \ldots\ldots (\beta),$$

and these two equations, of which the coefficients may be calculated numerically for each observation, will by an easy elimination give the values of x and y.

It may be remarked, that it is necessary that a high and a low star be used in the two observations, that the differences in the coefficients and constants of the equations may be as great as possible.

If a collimator or a fixed mark be used instead of the second star, the equation (β) becomes simpler. Since $z_r = z_l = z$ (suppose); and $a_r = a_l = a$ (suppose), the equation becomes

$$\frac{x}{\cos z} - y = \frac{c_l - l_l \cotan z - (c_r + l_r \cotan z)}{2 \cotan z}$$
$$= \frac{c_l - c_r - (l_l + l_r) \cotan z}{2 \cotan z}$$
$$= \frac{1}{2} \left\{ \frac{c_l - c_r}{\cotan z} - (l_l + l_r) \right\}.$$

As the error of collimation in general is not subject to change, when its value has been well determined, its numerical value may be substituted in the equations given above, and the value of y only will have to be determined. Thus, in equation (α), let accented letters denote the circle-readings corrected for error of collimation. Then we shall have

$$y = \frac{(C_r' + L_r \cot Z_r - A_r) - (C_l' - L_l \cotan Z_l - A_l)}{\cotan Z_r + \cotan Z_l}.$$

When the values of both x and y have been well determined, they may be applied to all the observations which have been made, and the circle readings thus corrected and compared with the computed azimuths of stars whose positions are accurately known, will give the *zero of azimuth*. Finally, by the application of the zero of azimuth to all the concluded circle readings, the observed azimuths will be determined.

In the observation of zenith distances, the only correction to be applied is the error of level corresponding to the want of verticality of the axis of azimuthal rotation. For the estimation of this error two levels are provided parallel to the plane of the vertical circle, and carried by one of the side cheeks of the revolving frame; but in theory it is only necessary to consider one.

The only instrumental constant to be determined by observation is the zenith-point, and the process is the following:

Let the same well-known star be observed in reverse positions of the vertical circle, and let C_r and C_l be the circle readings including the level-indications (that is, the sum of readings of east and west scales), and let α be the zenith-point including that part of the level-indication which corresponds to the vertical position of the axis of rotation. Let also Z_r and Z_l be the computed zenith distances subject to a small error e.

Then true zenith distance, face right,

$$= C_r - \alpha = Z_r + e,$$

and true zenith distance, face left,

$$= \alpha - C_l = Z_l + e.$$

Hence
$$2\alpha - (C_r + C_l) = Z_l - Z_r,$$
and
$$\alpha = \tfrac{1}{2}(C_r + C_l) + \tfrac{1}{2}(Z_l - Z_r).$$

USE OF COLLIMATING MARK.

Cor. If a collimator mark be used, $Z_l = Z_r$,

and $\alpha = \frac{1}{2}(C_r + C_l)$.

When the zenith-point has been accurately found and applied to the concluded circle readings of all objects observed, their apparent zenith distances will then be known, or the other element which it is the object of this instrument to observe.

In a following section it will be shewn how these observed azimuths and zenith distances are to be converted into right ascensions and declinations.

CHAPTER III.

ON THE TRANSFORMATION FROM ONE SYSTEM OF CO-ORDINATES DETERMINING THE POSITION OF AN OBJECT TO ANOTHER SYSTEM; AND ON ITS APPLICATION TO THE EQUATOR AND ECLIPTIC.

1. IN the preceding chapter it has been shewn by what instruments and by what methods the position of a body on the sphere of the heavens is determined. These instruments are chiefly the meridian-circle (or its equivalents, the transit-instrument and mural-circle), the equatorial, and the altazimuth. The transit-circle determines with great accuracy the Right Ascension and North Polar Distance (or declination) of the object by observations made in the plane of the meridian, while the equatorial determines the same elements with less accuracy. These instruments therefore give elements referred to the equator as the fundamental plane. On the contrary, the altazimuth, or altitude and azimuth instrument, refers the positions of celestial objects to the horizon as the fundamental plane. It is plainly necessary therefore to be able to transform from one of these systems of co-ordinates to another.

We will proceed therefore to shew how this transformation can be conveniently effected, premising that the inclination of the two fundamental planes, namely the equator and the observer's horizon, is equal to the colatitude of the place of observation.

2. *Having given the zenith distance and azimuth of a star, to find its hour-angle and north polar distance or declination.*

AZIMUTH AND ZENITH-DISTANCE.

Let Z be the zenith of the place of observation; P the north pole of the heavens; and S the star, joined by arcs of great circles. Then is PZS its azimuth measured from the north point of the horizon $(= Z)$; ZPS is the hour-angle (h); ZP is the co-latitude $= \gamma$; $ZS =$ the zenith distance $= z$; and finally PS is the N.P.D. $= \Delta$.

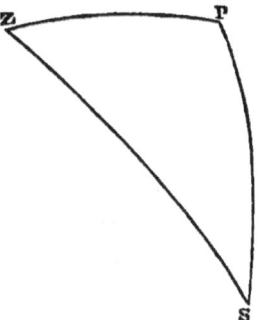

We may mention that the angle at S is called the *parallactic angle*, and its calculation is frequently required.

We have now $ZP = \gamma$, angle $PZS = Z$; and $ZS = z$ given, to find $ZPS = h$ (the hour-angle), and $PS = \Delta$.

First, we have, by a well-known property of spherical triangles,

$$\cot h = \sin \gamma \cot z \operatorname{cosec} Z - \cos \gamma \cot Z.$$

This gives the hour-angle immediately in terms of the azimuth (Z) and zenith-distance (z).

To adapt the formula to logarithmic computation, let $\cos Z = \tan \phi \cot z$, which equation is always possible,

$$\therefore \cot h = \frac{1}{\sin Z} (\sin \gamma \cot z - \cos \gamma \tan \phi \cot z)$$

$$= \frac{\cot z}{\sin Z} \frac{\sin (\gamma - \phi)}{\cos \phi},$$

where ϕ is determined by the equation

$$\tan \phi = \cos Z \tan z.$$

Having determined the hour-angle (h), the N.P.D. (Δ) may be found from the equation

$$\sin \Delta = \frac{\sin z \sin Z}{\sin h},$$

but, in cases where Δ is nearly equal to $90°$, this equation would not give a correct result because the variation of the sine of an arc near $90°$ is so small. We must then use another equation; or we may divide the spherical triangle into two right-angled triangles by means of a perpendicular arc drawn from one of the angles on the opposite side, which is generally the most convenient method in practice.

Thus, in the spherical triangle ZPS, draw SM perpendicular to ZP.

Then $\cos Z = \tan ZM \cot z$,

or $\tan ZM = \cos Z \tan z$,

which gives the value of ZM.

Also, $MP = \gamma - ZM$,

and $\cos MS = \dfrac{\cos z}{\cos ZM}$,

which gives MS.

Finally, $\cos \Delta = \cos MP \cos MS$,

and $\cot P = \sin MP \cot MS$,

which give Δ and the hour-angle (h).

It needs scarcely be mentioned that if α be the Right Ascension of the object, t the Sidereal Time of observation, and h the hour-angle, $\alpha = 15t - h$.

3. *Having given the N.P.D. and Hour-angle, to find the azimuth and zenith-distance.*

This can be done by the preceding formulæ *mutatis mutandis*.

Thus we have

$$\cot Z = \sin \gamma \cot \Delta \operatorname{cosec} h - \cos \gamma \cot h,$$

which can be adapted to logarithmic computation as before, by means of the auxiliary angle ϕ, by the equations

$$\tan \phi = \cos h \tan \Delta,$$

$$\cot Z = \frac{\cot \Delta}{\sin h} \frac{\sin (\gamma - \phi)}{\cos \phi}.$$

Also by dividing the triangle ZPS into two right-angled triangles as before, we have

$$\cos P = \tan MP \cot \Delta,$$

or

$$\tan MP = \cos P \tan \Delta,$$

$$ZM = \gamma - MP,$$

$$\sin ZM = \tan MS \cot Z,$$

$$\sin MP = \tan MS \cot P,$$

whence

$$\tan Z = \frac{\sin MP}{\sin ZM} \tan P,$$

and finally,

$$\cot z = \cos Z \cot ZM.$$

These are the formulæ used at Greenwich for the calculation of the Tabular Azimuths and Zenith-distances from the Right Ascensions and North Polar Distances.

4. *Having given the errors of Tabular Azimuth and Zenith-distance, to find the corresponding errors of Right Ascension and North Polar Distance.*

Let the observed values of Azimuth and Zenith-distance at the time t be Z and z, and the Tabular values be $Z + \delta Z$ and $z + \delta z$, then are δZ and δz the errors of Tabular Azimuth and Zenith-distance; and it is required to find the values of δa and $\delta \Delta$ in terms of them.

Let the hour-angle be measured positively towards the west. Then h being the hour-angle, a the right ascension, and t the sidereal time of observation, and the other notation as before, $a = 15t - h$, and $\therefore \delta a = - \delta h$. It will conduce to clearness if we consider the variations of the elements separately. First then, let the hour-angle at P be increased by SPS', ($= \delta a = - \delta h$) in the accompanying figure. PS being equal to PS', draw $S'M$ perpendicular to ZS produced. Then the zenith distance $ZS (= z)$ is increased by $SM = \delta z$,

5—2

and
$$SM = \delta z = SS' \sin SS'M$$
$$= - \delta h \sin \Delta \sin ZSP$$
$$= + \delta \alpha \sin \Delta \sin S.$$

Again, the Azimuth measured towards the west is increased by the angle SZS'

$$= \frac{MS'}{\sin z} = \frac{SS' \cos S}{\sin z}$$

$$= + \frac{\delta \alpha \sin \Delta \cos S}{\sin z},$$

or
$$\delta Z = - \frac{\delta \alpha \cos S \sin \Delta}{\sin z},$$

where the parallactic angle S is given by the equation

$$\sin S = \frac{\sin \gamma \sin h}{\sin z}.$$

Secondly, let the N.P.D. alone vary, the hour-angle remaining the same, and let it be increased by $\delta \Delta$; then in the accompanying figure

(SM being perpendicular to ZS', and $SS' = \delta \Delta$)

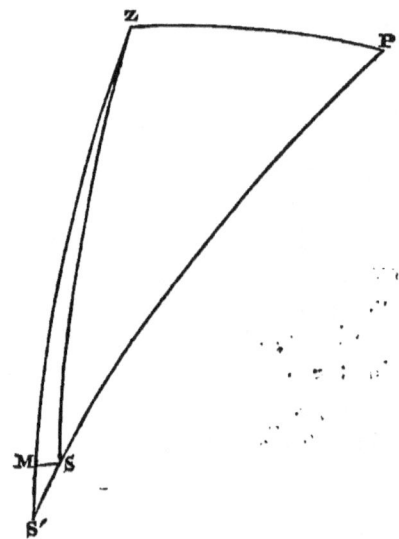

$$S'M = \delta z = SS' \cos S$$
$$= \delta\Delta \cos S.$$

Finally, angle $S'ZS = -\delta Z$.
$$= \frac{SM}{\sin z}$$
$$= \frac{SS' \sin S}{\sin z}$$
$$= \frac{\delta\Delta \sin S}{\sin z},$$

or the azimuth is diminished by
$$\frac{\delta\Delta \sin S}{\sin z},$$
corresponding to the increase of N.P.D., $\delta\Delta$.

Hence, if δz and δZ denote the whole increase of zenith distance and azimuth, arising from the increase $\delta\alpha$ of right ascension and the increase $\delta\Delta$ of N.P.D., we have

$$\delta z = -\sin S \sin\Delta \, \delta\alpha + \cos S \, \delta\Delta,$$
and
$$\delta Z = -\frac{\cos S \sin\Delta}{\sin z}\delta\alpha - \frac{\sin S}{\sin z}\delta\Delta.$$

For the reduction of a large series of observations it is necessary to form tables for the coefficients of the variations, or for such parts of them as admit of being tabulated. Let then

$$\sin S = p, \quad \cos S = q, \quad \frac{\cos S}{\sin z} = r, \text{ and } \frac{\sin S}{\sin z} = s.$$

Then
$$\delta z = -p \sin\Delta \, \delta\alpha + q\, \delta\Delta,$$
and
$$\delta Z = -r \sin\Delta \, \delta\alpha - s\, \delta\Delta.$$

Imagine now that, in the course of an evening, several observations have been made giving distinct values of δz and δZ, then these values will differ from each other considerably, being functions of the position of the object with respect to the horizon of the place, while $\delta\alpha$ and $\delta\Delta$ will, even for the Moon, remain sensibly constant. Hence by addition we shall have the two following final equations:

$$\Sigma (dz) = - \Sigma (p) \sin \Delta \, \delta\alpha + \Sigma (q) \, \delta\Delta,$$

and
$$\Sigma (\delta Z) = - \Sigma (r) \sin \Delta \, \delta\alpha - \Sigma (s) \, \delta\Delta;$$

and their solution will give

$$\delta\alpha = \frac{\Sigma (s) \, \Sigma (\delta z) + \Sigma (q) \, \Sigma (\delta Z)}{- \sin \Delta \, \{\Sigma (p) \, \Sigma (s) + \Sigma (q) \, \Sigma (r)\}},$$

and
$$\delta\Delta = \frac{\Sigma (r) \, \Sigma (\delta z) - \Sigma (p) \, \Sigma (\delta Z)}{\Sigma (p) \, \Sigma (s) + \Sigma (q) \, \Sigma (r)}.$$

This is the mode of treatment applied to the observations of Zenith-distance and Azimuth of the Moon, made at Greenwich.

5. Having given the Right Ascension and North Polar Distance of a star or other heavenly body, to find its geocentric latitude and longitude.

Without entering into any theory of the motion of the Sun (or rather of the earth round the Sun), the reader may take for granted, as has been previously stated at page 4, that his apparent motion is performed in a great circle (the Ecliptic) cutting the celestial equator at two points, named the vernal and autumnal equinoxes, distant from each other by 180°.

We may repeat here that the inclination of the Ecliptic to the Equator is called the *obliquity of the Ecliptic*, and that the Great Circle passing through the poles of the Ecliptic and Equator is called the *Solstitial Colure*.

The obliquity of the Ecliptic is not quite constant, but has a small secular inequality arising from the action of the planets, amounting to a diminution of about 50" in a century. It is also affected by a periodical inequality, *Nutation*, to be treated of hereafter. Its values are tabulated for every ten days in the Nautical Almanac.

Let ΥM and ΥN be portions of the ecliptic and equator projected on the sphere of the heavens, and intersecting each other at the vernal equinox or *First Point of Aries* (Υ).

INTO GEOCENTRIC LONGITUDE AND LATITUDE.

Let S be the position of a star referred to the equator and ecliptic by the great circles SM and SN perpendicular to them.

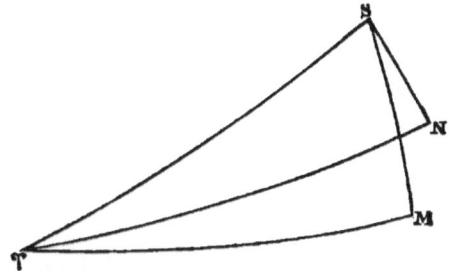

Then ΥN is the longitude (l) of the star, and $SN(\lambda)$ is its latitude. In like manner $\Upsilon M (= \alpha)$ is its right ascension and $SM (= \delta)$ is its declination. Also the angle $N\Upsilon M$ is the obliquity of the ecliptic (ω).

Let angle $S\Upsilon N = \phi$, and angle $S\Upsilon M = \theta$.

Then in the triangle $S\Upsilon M$ we have

$$\sin \Upsilon M = \tan SM \cot S\Upsilon M,$$

or $\tan \theta = \dfrac{\tan \delta}{\sin \alpha}$, which determines θ;

also $\phi = \theta - \omega$,

and $\cos \Upsilon S = \cos \alpha \cos \delta$.

Finally, $\tan \Upsilon N = \cos S\Upsilon N \tan \Upsilon S$,

or $\tan l = \cos \phi \tan \Upsilon S$ .... (α),

and $\sin \lambda = \sin \phi \sin \Upsilon S$ .... (β).

Or, we may obtain l, in terms of α, δ, and ω, immediately, as follows:

$$\tan l = \tan \Upsilon S \cos S\Upsilon N$$

$$= \tan \Upsilon S \cos (S\Upsilon M - \omega)$$

$$= \frac{\tan \alpha}{\cos S\Upsilon M}(\cos S\Upsilon M \cos \omega + \sin S\Upsilon M \sin \omega)$$

$$= \tan \alpha \cos \omega + \tan S\Upsilon M \sin \omega \tan \alpha$$

$$= \tan \alpha \cos \omega + \frac{\tan \delta}{\sin \alpha} \sin \omega \tan \alpha$$

$$= \tan \alpha \cos \omega + \tan \delta \sin \omega \sec \alpha.$$

Thus may as usual be easily adapted for logarithmic computation.

Thus let, $\tan \delta = \sin \alpha \tan \psi$;

$$\therefore \tan l = \tan \alpha \cos \omega + \tan \alpha \sin \omega \tan \psi$$

$$= \tan \alpha \left(\frac{\cos \omega \cos \psi + \sin \omega \sin \psi}{\cos \psi} \right)$$

$$= \tan \alpha \, \frac{\cos (\omega - \psi)}{\cos \psi}.$$

It will be still more convenient and analogical to consider, instead of the triangles given above, the triangle formed by the great circles joining the star and the poles of the equator and

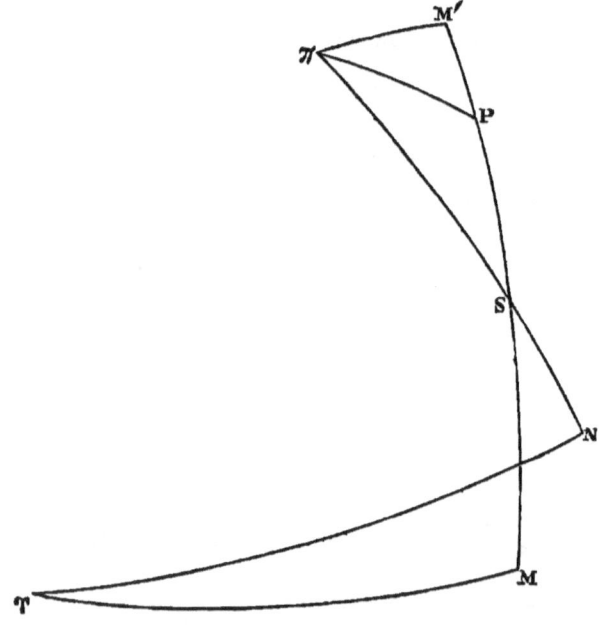

ecliptic. If, for instance, NS and MS be produced to π and P, so that each become $90°$, then π and P are the poles of the ecliptic and equator. Join πP, which is evidently equal to the obliquity (ω).

Also $PS = $ N.P.D. of the star $= \Delta = 90° - \delta$,

$\pi S = $ ecliptic polar distance of the star $= \epsilon = 90° - \lambda$.

Angle $P\pi S = 90° - l = l'$,

and angle $\pi PS = 90° + a = a'$.

Hence immediately $\dfrac{\sin P}{\sin \pi} = \dfrac{\sin \pi S}{\sin PS}$,

or $\dfrac{\cos a}{\cos l} = \dfrac{\sin \epsilon}{\sin \Delta}$ .... (1).

Again, draw $\pi M'$ perpendicular to SP produced,

then $\tan PM' = \tan \pi P \cos \pi PM'$

$= \tan \omega \cos (180° - \pi PS)$

$= \tan \omega \sin a$,

which gives the value PM' ($= \beta$),

and $\sin \pi M' = \sin \pi P \sin P$,

which gives $\pi M'$.

Also $SM = \Delta + \beta$.

Hence $\cos \pi S = \cos \pi M' \cos (\Delta + \beta)$,

or $\cos \epsilon = \cos \pi M' \cos (\Delta + \beta)$,

which gives the ecliptic polar distance, and the latitude $\lambda = 90° - \epsilon$.

Finally, $\cos l = \cos a \dfrac{\sin \Delta}{\sin \epsilon}$, by (1),

which gives the longitude. Or, we may obtain the longitude in terms of the Right Ascension, North Polar Distance, and the obliquity immediately by a process similar to that used on page (65), and we shall have

$\cot l' = \cot \Delta \sin \omega \csc a' - \cos \omega \cot a'$,

or $\tan l = \tan \delta \sin \omega \sec a + \cos \omega \tan a$, as before.

Of all the formulæ here given for determining the longitude and latitude from the Right Ascension and Declination, those given on page 71, and marked (α) and (β), are the most generally useful for planetary computations.

6. Having given the longitude and latitude of a heavenly body, to find the Right Ascension and Declination.

It is evident that the preceding formulæ will apply to this problem by making ω negative, and by replacing α and δ by l and λ, and *vice versâ*.

Thus, from the formulæ on page 71, we shall get

$$\tan \theta = \frac{\tan \lambda}{\sin l},$$

$$\phi = \theta + \omega,$$

$$\cos \Upsilon S = \cos l \cos \lambda,$$

$$\tan \alpha = \cos \phi \tan \Upsilon S \quad \ldots\ldots\ldots\ldots\ldots (\gamma),$$

and $\quad \sin \delta = \sin \phi \sin \Upsilon S \quad \ldots\ldots\ldots\ldots\ldots (\delta).$

It is not necessary to give the modifications of all the other formulæ, as they will be useful exercises for the student.

7. Having given the errors of tabular Right Ascension and Declination, to find the corresponding errors of longitude and latitude.

This is precisely similar to the problem for finding the errors of Right Ascension and Declination from the errors of azimuth and zenith distance, but on account of the danger of having wrong signs in the formulæ it will be desirable to discuss them separately.

In the triangle πPS let P and π be, as before, the poles of the equator and ecliptic, and S the place of the body observed at the sidereal time t. Then, as before, $\pi P = \omega$,

$$\text{angle } P\pi S = 90° - l,$$

$$\text{angle } \pi P S = 90° + \alpha.$$

INTO ERRORS OF GEOCENTRIC LONG. AND LAT. 75

Let $\alpha + d\alpha$, $\Delta + d\Delta$ be the tabular R.A. and N.P.D., and $l + \delta l$, $\epsilon + \delta\epsilon$ the corresponding computed longitude and ecliptic polar distance; while α and Δ are the observed R.A. and N.P.D., corresponding to the computed longitude and ecliptic polar distance l and ϵ.

First, to find the increments of l and ϵ, corresponding to the increment ($\delta\alpha$) of α, taken alone.

In the figure let angle $SPS' = \delta\alpha$,

and $PS' = PS$.

Draw $S'M$ perpendicular to πS produced.

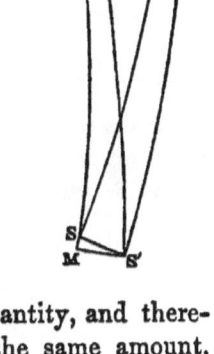

Then angle $S\pi S' = \dfrac{S'M}{\sin \epsilon}$

$$= \dfrac{SS' \cos S}{\sin \epsilon}$$

$$= \dfrac{\sin \Delta \cos S}{\sin \epsilon} \delta\alpha,$$

and the angle $P\pi S$ is diminished by this quantity, and therefore, since $P\pi S = 90° - l$, l is increased by the same amount, that is

$$\delta l = \dfrac{\sin \Delta \cos S}{\sin \epsilon} \delta\alpha.$$

Also $\quad SM = \delta\epsilon = SS' \sin S$

$$= \sin \Delta \sin S \delta\alpha.$$

Again, to find the increments of l and ϵ, corresponding to the increment ($\delta\Delta$) of Δ, taken alone.

Let SS', in the adjoining figure, $= \delta\Delta$.

Draw SM perpendicular to $\pi S'$.

Then $MS' = \delta\epsilon = \cos S\, \delta\Delta$,

and angle $M\pi S = \delta l$

$$= \frac{MS}{\sin \epsilon}$$

$$= \frac{\sin S}{\sin \epsilon}\, \delta\Delta.$$

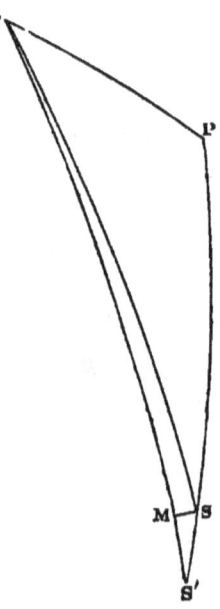

And it is plain that the longitude l is diminished by this quantity, since the angle $P\pi S = 90° - l$ is increased.

Hence on the whole,

$$\delta l = \frac{\sin \Delta \cos S}{\sin \epsilon}\, \delta\alpha - \frac{\sin S}{\sin \epsilon}\, \delta\Delta,$$

and $\delta\epsilon = \sin \Delta \sin S\, \delta\alpha + \cos S\, \delta\Delta.$

If we were to find the values of $\delta\alpha$ and $\delta\Delta$ from the equations above in terms of δl and $\delta\epsilon$, we should obtain

$$\delta\alpha = \frac{\sin \epsilon \cos S}{\sin \Delta}\, \delta l + \frac{\sin S}{\sin \Delta}\, \delta\epsilon,$$

and $\qquad \delta\Delta = -\sin \epsilon \sin S\, \delta l + \cos S\, \delta\epsilon.$

In the preceding expressions for δl and $\delta\epsilon$, if it be required to incorporate the effect produced by an error $\delta\omega$ of the obliquity of the ecliptic, this may be done as follows.

Let $P\pi$ be the true obliquity $= \omega$ (Fig. on next page)

and $P\pi'$ the tabular obliquity $= \omega + \delta\omega.$

Draw πM perpendicular to $\pi'S$.

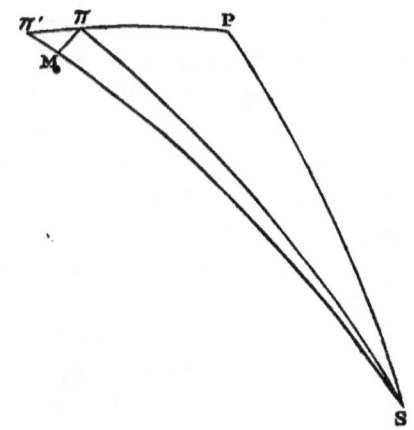

Then $\pi' M = \delta\epsilon = \delta\omega \cos P\pi' S$

$\qquad = \delta\omega \cos P\pi S$ nearly

$\qquad = \cos l' \, \delta\omega$

$\qquad = \sin l \, \delta\omega.$

Again, $\quad \dfrac{\sin P\pi' S}{\sin P\pi S} = \dfrac{\sin(l' + \delta l')}{\sin l'} = \dfrac{\sin \epsilon}{\sin(\epsilon + \delta\epsilon)},$

or, developing to the first powers,

$$1 + \cot l' \, \delta l' = 1 - \cot \epsilon \, \delta\epsilon,$$

or $\tan l \, \delta l = + \cot \epsilon \times \sin l \, \delta\omega;$

$$\therefore \delta l = + \cot \epsilon \cos l \, d\omega.$$

Hence on the whole we have

$$\delta l = \frac{\sin \Delta \cos S}{\sin \epsilon} \delta a - \frac{\sin S}{\sin \epsilon} \delta\Delta + \cot \epsilon \cos l \, \delta\omega,$$

and $\quad \delta\epsilon = \sin \Delta \sin S \, \delta a + \cos S \, \delta\Delta + \sin l \, \delta\omega.$

Similarly, we should easily find

$$\delta a = \frac{\sin \epsilon \cos S}{\sin \Delta} \delta l + \frac{\sin S}{\sin \Delta} \delta\epsilon - \cot \Delta \cos a \, \delta\omega,$$

$$\delta\Delta = -\sin \epsilon \sin S \, \delta l + \cos S \, \delta\epsilon - \sin a \, \delta\omega.$$

8. *On the motion of the Sun in the Ecliptic.*

As the ecliptic is the great circle in the heavens traced out by the sun's apparent path, and as the position of this fundamental plane is therefore defined by his motion, it will be proper in this place to shew how the observations of the sun are applied to determine this position.

In the preceding chapters it has been shewn how the transit-circle, (or the transit-instrument and mural circle) is applied to determine the Right Ascensions and North Polar Distances or declinations of the heavenly bodies; the right ascensions being measured from an assumed equinox (or which is the same thing, the stars used for determining the clock-errors being referred to an assumed equinox), and the North Polar Distances being deduced from the observed zenith-distances by the application of an assumed colatitude. In this way the Right Ascensions and North Polar Distances of the centre of the sun can be deduced from the observations of transit of the first and second limbs, and the observations of zenith-distance of the upper and lower limbs, and his right ascensions thus deduced will be referred to the same equinox as that assumed for all other objects. But since this equinox is the point of the equator at which the centre of the sun is when his declination vanishes, it is evident that, observations of his declination at the time of the equinoxes, both vernal and autumnal, will furnish us with the means of accurately determining what error has been made in the assumption of the longitude of this point. Again, since the sun's solstitial declination is equal to the obliquity of the ecliptic, it is plain that observations of the sun's declination at the time of the summer and winter solstices will determine the error of the assumed obliquity.

First, then, to determine the correction of right ascensions.

Let S be the Sun near the vernal equinox Υ, ΥM the equator,

$SM = \delta$, the declination,

$\Upsilon M = \alpha$, the right ascension,

angle $S\Upsilon M = \omega$, the obliquity.

Then $\sin \alpha = \tan \delta \cot \omega$.

Let the observed values of δ on successive days be substituted in this equation, using an assumed value of ω moderately correct, and let the corresponding values of α be calculated. Then a series of values of α will be obtained referred to the true equinox which can be immediately compared with the observed values of α, and the error of the assumed equinox will thus be known.

Suppose now that either on account of a constant error in the instrumental zeros or of the refraction applied to the observed zenith distances the observed values of δ should be in error, then to find the effect of this error on the computed right ascensions, we have only to differentiate the preceding equation.

Thus $\cos \alpha \, d\alpha = \sec^2 \delta \cot \omega \, d\delta - \csc^2 \omega \tan \delta \, d\omega$,

and $d\alpha = \dfrac{\cot \omega}{\cos^2 \delta \cos \alpha} d\delta - \dfrac{\tan \delta}{\cos^2 \omega \cos \alpha} d\omega$

= (near the vernal equinox) $\cot \omega \, d\delta$ very nearly.

Let now observations be made near the autumnal equinox, when the right ascension is $180° - \alpha$. Then the error of $180° - \alpha$, or $- d\alpha = \cot \omega \, d\delta$, where the mean or average value of $d\delta$ will remain sensibly the same as at the vernal equinox, because the meridian zenith distance is sensibly the same. Hence the errors of the computed right ascension near the autumnal equinox will be sensibly equal to the errors near the vernal equinox, but with a contrary sign, and therefore the mean of the errors will be very correctly the quantity which is to be used in correcting the place of the assumed equinox. This is the method which was used by Dr Maskelyne*.

9. *To find the obliquity of the Ecliptic.*

This must be done by observations of the Sun's declination at the summer and winter solstice.

At the transit over the meridian on any day very near the solstice, let the R.A. of Sun's centre = $90° - \alpha'$, and let the corresponding declination be δ.

* See Maskelyne's *Star Ledgers* (forming the Second Appendix to the Greenwich Observations for 1851) edited by the author.

Then we shall have

$$\sin(90° - \alpha') = \frac{\tan \delta}{\tan \omega},$$

$$\text{or } \cos \alpha' = \frac{\tan \delta}{\tan \omega},$$

and therefore
$$\frac{1 - \cos \alpha'}{1 + \cos \alpha'} = \tan^2 \frac{\alpha'}{2} = \frac{\tan \omega - \tan \delta}{\tan \omega + \tan \delta}$$

$$= \frac{\sin(\omega - \delta)}{\sin(\omega + \delta)}$$

$$= \frac{\sin x}{\sin(\omega + \delta)} \text{ suppose.}$$

Hence $\sin x = x \sin 1''$ (since x is supposed to be small,)

$$= \tan^2 \frac{\alpha'}{2} \sin(\omega + \delta),$$

and
$$x = \frac{\tan^2 \frac{\alpha'}{2} \sin(\omega + \delta)}{\sin 1''},$$

where an approximate value of ω must be used in determining the value of x.

If however the value of ω were not known with any approach to accuracy, a very few successive approximations would enable us to deduce its value very accurately from the same formula.

We may however expand ω in a series of sines of multiples of δ without resorting to a solution depending on successive approximations.

Thus we have $\tan \omega = \dfrac{\tan \delta}{\cos \alpha'}$,

or
$$\frac{e^{2\omega\sqrt{-1}} - 1}{e^{2\omega\sqrt{-1}} + 1} = \frac{1}{\cos \alpha'} \cdot \frac{e^{2\delta\sqrt{-1}} - 1}{e^{2\delta\sqrt{-1}} + 1};$$

$$\therefore e^{2\omega\sqrt{-1}} = \frac{(1 + \cos \alpha') e^{2\delta\sqrt{-1}} - (1 - \cos \alpha')}{1 + \cos \alpha' - (1 - \cos \alpha') e^{2\delta\sqrt{-1}}}$$

POSITION OF THE ECLIPTIC. 81

$$= e^{2\delta\sqrt{-1}} \times \frac{1 - \dfrac{1-\cos\alpha'}{1+\cos\alpha'} e^{-2\delta\sqrt{-1}}}{1 - \dfrac{1-\cos\alpha'}{1+\cos\alpha'} e^{2\delta\sqrt{-1}}}$$

$$= e^{2\delta\sqrt{-1}} \times \frac{1 - \tan^2\dfrac{\alpha'}{2} e^{-2\delta\sqrt{-1}}}{1 - \tan^2\dfrac{\alpha'}{2} e^{2\delta\sqrt{-1}}};$$

or, taking the logarithms,

$$2\omega\sqrt{-1} = 2\delta\sqrt{-1} - (\tan^2\tfrac{\alpha'}{2} e^{-2\delta\sqrt{-1}} + \tfrac{1}{2}\tan^4\tfrac{\alpha'}{2} e^{-4\delta\sqrt{-1}} + \&c.)$$
$$+ (\tan^2\tfrac{\alpha'}{2} e^{2\delta\sqrt{-1}} + \tfrac{1}{2}\tan^4\tfrac{\alpha'}{2} e^{4\delta\sqrt{-1}} + \&c.,$$

or $\omega = \delta + \tan^2\dfrac{\alpha'}{2} \cdot \dfrac{e^{2\delta\sqrt{-1}} - e^{-2\delta\sqrt{-1}}}{2\sqrt{-1}} + \tfrac{1}{2}\tan^4\dfrac{\alpha'}{2} \dfrac{e^{4\delta\sqrt{-1}} - e^{-4\delta\sqrt{-1}}}{2\sqrt{-1}} + \&c.$

$$= \delta + \tan^2\tfrac{\alpha'}{2} \sin 2\delta + \tfrac{1}{2}\tan^4\tfrac{\alpha'}{2} \sin 4\delta + \&c.$$

10. In the operations of a fixed observatory it is however desirable to apply to the correction of the equinox and of the obliquity of the ecliptic all the observations of the sun which have been made in the course of the year. For this purpose it is necessary to calculate the errors of ecliptic polar distance corresponding to the errors of R.A. and N.P.D. of each observation by the equation $\delta\epsilon = \sin\Delta\sin S\,\delta\alpha + \cos S\,\delta\Delta$ given in page 76, since it is evident that these errors applied to the assumed ecliptic will enable us immediately to trace out the true ecliptic.

Let S be the sun on the true ecliptic; SS' perpendicular to ΥSM: then SS' is the error ($\delta\epsilon$) in ecliptic polar distance of the sun.

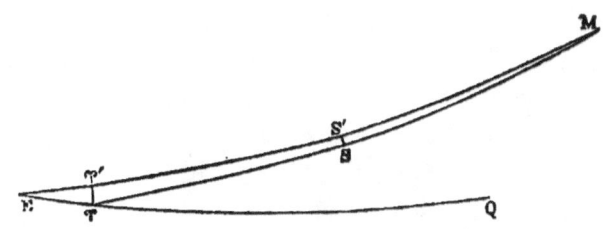

M. A.

Let $\Upsilon\Upsilon'$, perpendicular to EM, $= x$; and let y be the difference between the inclinations of EM and ΥM to the equator EQ, or the error of the obliquity.

The error $\delta\epsilon$ may be found by adding the errors due to x and y separately; thus, if the obliquity does not vary, in which case (as is easily seen on examining the polar triangle of $E\Upsilon M$), $\Upsilon M = 90°$ nearly,
$$SS' = x \cos \Upsilon S = x \cos l.$$

Similarly, if x were equal to 0, or obliquity only varied, we should find
$$SS' = y \sin l.$$
Hence, $\delta\epsilon = x \cos l + y \sin l$.

Since now the errors of the solar tables are very small, and the errors of R.A. and N.P.D. change but little throughout the year, it is usual to group their values for convenient intervals (generally in monthly groups) throughout the year, and then to compute the values of $\delta\epsilon$ which correspond to the mean day of each of these groups. The equations thence resulting are then solved either by the method of minimum squares or by some other method which will give values of x and y most in accordance with the truth, or least affected by the inevitable errors of the observations.

There is, however, another circumstance to be regarded, namely, that on account of the imperfection of the best refraction tables used in the reduction of the observations and other causes, the value of the obliquity deduced from the summer solstice can never be made to agree with that deduced from the winter solstice, and, that this difference may not affect the values of x and y, it is necessary to introduce it as an unknown quantity into the above equations.

We must then generally make the equation above take the form of
$$\delta\epsilon = x \cos l + y \sin l + z,$$
and the value of z must be found simultaneously with those of x and y by the method of minimum squares.

If we put now $l = 90°$ and $l = 270°$, the values of $\delta\epsilon$ which depend solely on the error of obliquity will be
$$y + z \text{ and } -y + z,$$

POSITION OF THE ECLIPTIC.

and, since increase of obliquity decreases the values of ϵ at the northern solstice and increases them at the southern, the corresponding errors of obliquity will be

$$-(y+z) \text{ and } -(y-z),$$

and the difference of these quantities is $2z$, by which the obliquity deduced from the northern solstice is greater than that deduced from the southern solstice.

11. The following problems may be useful to the student.

(1) To determine the obliquity of the ecliptic, and the absolute R.A. of a star, by two observations of difference of R.A. of sun and star, and of the sun's declination.

Let a and a' be the observed differences of R.A. of sun and star; δ and δ' the corresponding declinations of the sun's centre; α the R.A. of the star.

Then $\alpha + a$ and $\alpha + a'$ are the true right ascensions of the sun; and we have

$$\sin(a+\alpha)\tan\omega = \tan\delta,$$

and $$\sin(a'+\alpha)\tan\omega = \tan\delta',$$

or $$(\sin a \cos \alpha + \cos a \sin \alpha)\tan\omega = \tan\delta,$$

and $$(\sin a' \cos \alpha + \cos a' \sin \alpha)\tan\omega = \tan\delta'.$$

Multiply 1st equation by $\sin a'$, and 2nd by $\sin a$, and subtract; then

$$\sin(a'-a)\tan\omega \sin\alpha = \tan\delta \sin a' - \tan\delta' \sin a,$$

or $$\tan\omega \sin\alpha = \frac{\tan\delta \sin a' - \tan\delta' \sin a}{\sin(a'-a)}.$$

Similarly we easily get

$$\tan\omega \cos\alpha = \frac{\tan\delta' \cos a - \tan\delta \cos a'}{\sin(a'-a)},$$

and therefore

$$\tan\omega = \frac{1}{\sin(a'-a)}\sqrt{(\tan\delta\sin a' - \tan\delta'\sin a)^2 + (\tan\delta'\cos a - \tan\delta\cos a')^2}$$

$$= \frac{1}{\sin(a'-a)}\sqrt{\tan^2\delta + \tan^2\delta' - 2\tan\delta\tan\delta'\cos(a'-a)}.$$

84 NUMERICAL COMPUTATION OF THE

(2) To determine the value of the obliquity of the ecliptic by the following results of observations of the sun made at Greenwich on the meridian:

1859, June 17, R.A. = $\overset{h.\ m.\ s.}{5.41.18\cdot 35}$; N.P.D. = $\overset{\circ\ \ '\ \ ''}{66.36.37\cdot 38}$
.... 18, ...   5.45.27·75;   ...   34.56·63
.... 21, ...   5.57.56·34;   ...   32.29·83
.... 22, ...   6. 2. 5·90;   ...   32.27·89
.... 25, ...   6.14.34·38;   ...   34.58·14

Referring to the formula on page 80,

$$x = \tan^2 \frac{\alpha'}{2} \frac{\sin(\omega + \delta)}{\sin 1''};$$

assume $\omega = 23^\circ . 27' . 30''$.

The calculations may be arranged as follows:

$\delta =$	23.23.22·62	23.25. 3·37	23.27.30·17	23.27.32·11	23.25. 1·36
$\omega =$	23.27.30	23.27.30	23.27.30	23.27.30	23.27.30
$\delta + \omega =$	46.50.52·62	46.52.33·37	46.55. 0·17	46.55. 2·11	46.52.31·86
$\alpha' =$	h. m. s. +0.18.41·65	h. m. s. 0.14.32·25	h. m. s. 0. 2. 3·66	h. m. s. −0. 2. 5·90	h. m. −s. −0.14.34·38
$\dfrac{\alpha'}{2} =$	+0. 9.20·83	0. 7.16·13	0. 1. 1·83	−0. 1. 2·95	−0. 7.17·19
=	2.20.12·45	1.49. 1·95	0.15.27·45	−0.15.44·25	−1.49.17·85
Log sin $(\omega + \delta)$	9·86305	9·86325	9·86354	9·86354	9·86325
Log tan $\dfrac{\alpha'}{2}$	8·61074	8·50143	7·65287	−7·66066	−8·50248
Again	8·61074	8·50143	7·65287	−7·66066	−8·50248
Ar. co. log sin 1″	5·31443	5·31443	5·31443	5·31443	5·31443
Sum	2·39896	2·18054	0·48371	0·49929	2·18264
$x =$	$\overset{\circ}{+}4.10\overset{''}{\cdot}59$	$\overset{\circ}{+}2.31\overset{''}{\cdot}55$	$\overset{\circ}{+}0. 3\overset{''}{\cdot}05$	$\overset{\circ}{+}0. 3\overset{''}{\cdot}16$	$\overset{\circ}{+}2.32\overset{''}{\cdot}28$
$\delta =$	23.23.22·62	23.25. 3·37	23.27.30·17	23.27.32·11	23.25. 1·86
$\omega =$	23.27.33·21	23.27.34·92	23.27.33·22	23.27.35·27	23.27.34·14

The mean of the values of ω is $23^\circ . 27' . 34'' \cdot 15$.

OBLIQUITY OF THE ECLIPTIC.

It will be desirable to compute also the obliquity as deduced from the observations of the sun at the winter solstice. The Greenwich observations for 1859 give the following results:

$$
\begin{array}{llll}
 & \text{h. m. s.} & & \text{° ′ ″} \\
\text{Dec. 15, R.A.} = & 17.29.39\cdot60\,; & \text{N.P.D.} = & -23.16.35\cdot18 \\
\ldots\ 21,\ \ldots & 17.56.17\cdot29\,; & \ldots & -23.27.26\cdot37 \\
\ldots\ 22,\ \ldots & 18.\ 0.44\cdot16\,; & \ldots & -23.27.34\cdot19 \\
\ldots\ 27,\ \ldots & 18.22.57\cdot52\,; & \ldots & -23.21.15\cdot01
\end{array}
$$

The calculations are as follow:

$\delta =$	$-23.16.35$	$-23.27.26$	$-23.27.34$	$-23.27.15$
$\omega =$	$-23.27.34$	$-23.27.34$	$-23.27.34$	$-23.27.34$
$\omega + \delta =$	$-46.44.\ 9$	$-46.55.\ 0$	$-46.55.\ 8$	$-46.54.49$
$a - 18^h = a' =$	m. s. $-30.20\cdot40$	m. s. $-\ 3.42\cdot71$	m. s. $+\ 0.44\cdot16$	m. s. $+22.57\cdot52$
$\dfrac{a'}{2} =$	$-15.10\cdot20$	$-\ 1.51\cdot35$	$+\ 0.22\cdot08$	$+11.28\cdot76$
$=$	$-\ 3.47.33\cdot0$	$-\ 0.27.50\cdot25$	$+\ 0.\ 5.31\cdot2$	$+\ 2.52.11\cdot4$
Log sin $(\omega + \delta)$	$-9\cdot86225$	$-9\cdot86354$	$-9\cdot86355$	$-9\cdot86352$
Log tan $\dfrac{a'}{2}$	$-8\cdot82144$	$-7\cdot90837$	$+7\cdot20566$	$+8\cdot70008$
Again	$-8\cdot82144$	$-7\cdot90837$	$+7\cdot20566$	$+8\cdot70008$
Ar. co. log sin $1''$	$5\cdot31443$	$5\cdot31443$	$5\cdot31443$	$5\cdot31443$
Sum	$-2\cdot81956$	$-0\cdot99471$	$-9\cdot58930$	$-2\cdot57811$
$x =$	$-\ 11.\ 0\cdot03$	$-\ 0.\ 9\cdot88$	$-\ 0.\ 0\cdot39$	$-\ 6.18\cdot54$
$\delta =$	$-23.16.35\cdot18$	$-23.27.26\cdot37$	$-23.27.34\cdot19$	$-23.21.15\cdot01$
$\delta + x = \omega =$	$-23.27.35\cdot21$	$-23.27.36\cdot25$	$-23.27.34\cdot58$	$-23.27.33\cdot55$

Hence the mean value of ω is $23°.27'.34''\cdot90$, which is greater than that given by the summer solstice by $0''\cdot75$.

If now the reader will refer to the Greenwich Observations for 1859, page 51, he will find that, by the discussion of the observations of the whole year in the way which has been previously explained, the excess of the result of the southern solstice above the northern, is $1''\cdot366$.

86   NUMERICAL COMPUTATION OF THE

(3) To determine the error of the equinox assumed in the reduction of the Greenwich transit-observations of 1859, by observations of the sun after the vernal equinox and before the autumnal equinox.

Take the following observations:

	h. m. s.		° ′ ″
March 22, R.A. =	0. 4.58·54;	Declination =	+ 0.32.21·17
... 25, ...	0.15.52·86;	....	1.43.14·40
... 29, ...	0.30.24·78;	....	3.17.10·14
... 31, ...	0.37.41·18;	....	4. 3.47·03
Sept. 12, R.A. =	11.20.10·34;	....	+ 4.17.29·42
... 13, ...	11.23.45·50;	....	3.54.34·14
... 20, ...	11.48.53·13;	....	1.12.15·79
... 22, ...	11.56. 4·11;	....	0.25.34·78

Computing now by the equation $\sin \alpha = \tan \delta \cot \omega$, we may arrange the computations as follows, making $\omega = 23°.27'.34''$.

For Vernal Equinox.

$\delta =$	$+ 0.32.21''17$	$+ 1.43.14''40$	$+ 3.17.10''14$	$+ 4. 3.47''03$
Log tan $\delta =$	+ 7·9736512	+ 8·4777047	+ 8·7590414	+ 8·8514600
Log cot $\omega =$	0·3625393	0·3625393	0·3625393	0·3625393
Log sin $\alpha =$	+ 8·3361905	+ 8·8402440	+ 9·1215807	+ 9·2139993
$\alpha =$	1.14.33''52	3.58. 9''48	7.36.10''40	9.25.14''31
=	h. m. s. 0. 4.58·23	h. m. s. 0.15.52·63	h. m. s. 0.30.24·69	h. m. s. 0.37.40·95
Observed value =	0. 4.58·54	0.15.52·86	0.30.24·78	0.37.41·18
Error of observed value....	+ 0·31	+ 0·23	+ 0·09	+ 0·23

And the mean of the errors is $+ 0^s\!\cdot\!21$.

For Autumnal Equinox.

$\delta =$	$+ 4°.17'.29''.42$	$+ 3°.54'.34''.14$	$+ 1°.12'.15''.79$	$+ 0°.25'.34''.78$
Log tan $\delta =$	$+ 8·8753002$	$+ 8·8346714$	$+ 8·3227071$	$+ 7·8716290$
Log cot $\omega =$	$0·3625393$	$0·3625393$	$0·3625393$	$0·3625393$
Log sin $a =$	$+ 9·2378395$	$+ 9·1972107$	$+ 8·6852464$	$+ 8·2341683$
$a' = 180° - a =$	$9°.57'.27''.02$	$9°. 3'.37''.25$	$2°.46'.36''.35$	$0°.58'.56''.84$
$a =$	h. m. s. 11.20.10·20	h. m. s. 11.23.45·52	h. m. s. 11.48.53·58	h. m. s. 11.56. 4·21
Observed value =	11.20.10·34	11.23.45·50	11.48.53·13	11.56. 4·11
Error of observed value....	$+ 0·14$	$- 0·02$	$- 0·45$	$- 0·10$

And the mean of the errors is $- 0^s·11$.

Then, taking the mean of the resulting errors for the vernal and the autumnal equinoxes, we get for the true error of the equinox by which the assumed right ascensions of all the Greenwich clock stars are too large, $+ 0^s·05$; or the right ascensions of all objects observed with the transit instrument must be diminished by $0^s·05$.

ADDENDUM TO CHAPTER III.

There are many cases in which it is necessary to find relations connecting the angles which determine a star's place with reference to one plane, with those which determine it with reference to another: for instance, to connect the right-ascension and declination of a star with its latitude and longitude; or its right-ascension and declination with reference to the position of the equator at a given time, with the same referred to the position of the equator at a subsequent time (as in Precession and Nutation, Chapter VII).

The following is a systematic method of finding such relations, which will often be found very useful.

Let O be the centre of the celestial sphere; xy, xy' the two planes of reference: Ox being their line of intersection: and let z, z' be the poles of these planes, and the great circle $z'zy'y$ meet them in y, y'; then Ox, Oy, Oz; Ox, Oy', Oz' are two rectangular systems.

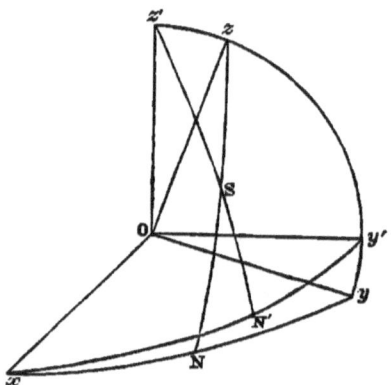

Let S be any star; zSN, $z'SN'$ arcs through S perpendicular to xy, xy': $SN = \theta$, $xN = \phi$; $SN' = \theta'$, $xN' = \phi'$; and let the angle between the planes xy, $xy' = \omega$.

Then the co-ordinates of S referred to the two sets of axes are, if we put the radius of the imaginary celestial sphere equal to unity,

$$\left.\begin{aligned} x &= \cos\theta \cdot \cos\phi \\ y &= \cos\theta \cdot \sin\phi \\ z &= \sin\theta \end{aligned}\right\} \quad \text{and} \quad \left\{\begin{aligned} x' &= \cos\theta' \cdot \cos\phi' \\ y' &= \cos\theta' \cdot \sin\phi' \\ z' &= \sin\theta'. \end{aligned}\right.$$

If, now, we wish to transform from the lower plane to the upper, we have by transformation in the plane yz,

$$y = y' \cos\omega - z' \sin\omega,$$
$$z = y' \sin\omega + z' \cos\omega,$$

hence, we have the system of equations,

$$\cos\theta \cdot \cos\phi = \cos\theta' \cdot \cos\phi',$$
$$\cos\theta \cdot \sin\phi = \cos\theta' \cdot \sin\phi' \cos\omega - \sin\theta' \cdot \sin\omega,$$
$$\sin\theta = \cos\theta' \cdot \sin\phi' \sin\omega + \sin\theta' \cdot \cos\omega.$$

· Only two of these three equations are independent, for if we square and add, we get an identity; they give θ and ϕ in terms of θ', ϕ': if we wish to get θ' and ϕ' in terms of θ, ϕ, we find by the same process

$$\cos\theta' \cdot \cos\phi' = \cos\theta \cdot \cos\phi,$$
$$\cos\theta' \cdot \sin\phi' = \cos\theta \cdot \sin\phi \cdot \cos\omega + \sin\theta \cdot \sin\omega,$$
$$\sin\theta' = -\cos\theta \cdot \sin\phi \cdot \sin\omega + \sin\theta \cdot \cos\omega,$$

derivable from the other set by changing the sign of ω; this last set serves to transform from the *upper* plane to the *lower*.

The student will have no difficulty in applying the above method to any particular case.

CHAPTER IV.

ON THE PHENOMENA ARISING FROM THE DIURNAL ROTATION OF THE EARTH ON ITS AXIS, AND ITS ANNUAL REVOLUTION ROUND THE SUN.

It has been sufficiently explained that the Sun appears to describe in the heavens a great circle called the ecliptic, and that the inclination of this great circle to the celestial equator is called the *Obliquity of the Ecliptic;* and also that the shifting points of intersection of this ecliptic with the Equator are called the *First Points of Aries and Libra,* or the *Vernal and Autumnal Equinoxes.*

1. It may in addition be mentioned that ancient astronomers supposed the Ecliptic or Sun's apparent path to be divided into twelve equal parts called *Signs of the Zodiac,* named in the order of the Sun's course, *Aries, Taurus, Gemini, Cancer, Leo, Virgo, Libra, Scorpio, Sagittarius, Capricornus, Aquarius, Pisces.*

The great circle also which is drawn through the poles of the Ecliptic and Equator, and is therefore perpendicular to each of them, is called the *Solstitial Colure* (see page 70); and the seasons at which the Sun in his annual circuit passes this great circle are called the Summer and Winter Solstices. This is usually expressed by saying that the Sun has entered Cancer and Capricornus.

2. The most important astronomical fact which has its origin in the Sun's motion in the Ecliptic, is the succession of

the different *Seasons of the Year.* These we will take in their order, commencing with Spring. This season is defined by the passage of the Sun through the *first point of* Aries, or the Vernal Equinox. At this time, therefore, the Sun is in the equator, or his North Polar Distance is equal to 90°.

To find the effect of this on the length of the day, let, generally, z be the zenith distance of the Sun on any day at the time t before or after the meridian passage, γ the colatitude, and Δ his North Polar Distance.

Then we shall have

$$\cos 15 t = \frac{\cos z - \cos \gamma \cos \Delta}{\sin \gamma \sin \Delta}.$$

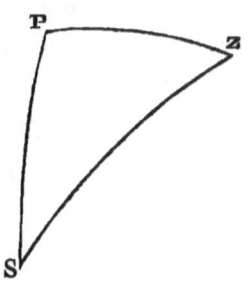

If therefore $z = 90°$,

$$\cos t = - \cot \gamma \cot \Delta,$$

which gives the hour-angle of the Sun or other body at rising or setting, when the Polar Distance is Δ and the colatitude is γ.

If now $\Delta = 90°$, or $\cot \Delta = 0$, then $\cos t = 0$, or $t = 6$ hours. That is, for all places on the earth, at the Vernal Equinox, the length of the day, measured from sunrise to sunset, is twelve hours; and is therefore equal to the length of the night. Hence the origin of the term Equinox. The same is evidently true of the Autumnal Equinox, when the Sun enters Capricorn.

3. Again, referring to the equation

$$\cos 15 t = - \cot \gamma \cot \Delta,$$

we see that $\cos 15 t$ will be negative, when γ and Δ are both greater or both less than 90°, and positive, when one of them is greater and the other less than 90°.

First then, let γ be less than 90°, which is the case for all places having north latitude, then $\cos 15 t$ will be negative when $\cot \Delta$ is positive, or when Δ is less than 90°. That is, the time between sunrise and noon, or between noon and sunset is greater than six hours, or the whole length of the day is greater than twelve hours, that is, the days are longer than the nights. This corresponds to the half year commencing with the vernal and ending with the autumnal equinox. Similarly, it may be proved that for the remaining half year, that is, from the autumnal to the vernal equinox, the nights are longer than the days. It may be proved in like manner that, for places having south latitude, the days are shorter than the nights between spring and autumn, and longer than the nights between autumn and spring.

4. The hour-angle, at rising and setting, of any celestial object is called the *Semi-Diurnal Arc*, and the same reasoning which has been used with respect to the Sun may be applied to the stars, excepting that their semi-diurnal arcs are constant and have no relation to the seasons of the year.

EXAMPLE. For the Oxford Observatory find the length of time during which α Aquila is above the horizon on Dec. 17, 1861.

Here $\Delta = 81°.29'·5$, and $\gamma = 38°.14'·5$,

$$\therefore \log \cot \Delta = + 9·17493$$
$$\log \cot \gamma = + 0·10342$$
$$-\log \cos 15t = + 9·27835$$
$$15t \text{ (in arc)} = 100°.56'·5$$
$$t \text{ in time} = 6^{h}.43^{m}·8$$
$$2t = 13^{h}.27^{m}·6$$

5. Recurring again to the equation

$$\cos 15t = -\cot \gamma \cot \Delta,$$

we see that, since the limiting value of $\cos 15t$ is unity, the limiting value of $\cot \gamma \cot \Delta$ is unity. That is, $\cot \gamma = \tan \Delta$, or $\Delta = 90° - \gamma$. If Δ be less than this value, the star or other object will not set at all. Applying this to the Sun, since the least value of Δ occurs at the summer solstice (for North latitudes) and is equal to $66\frac{1}{2}°$, nearly, the value of γ, for which at the summer solstice the Sun just grazes the horizon, is $23\frac{1}{2}°$; and if with this radius a small circle be described round the

North Pole on the earth's surface, it is called the *Arctic Circle*. For places within this circle there will be a portion of the year on each side of the summer solstice when the Sun does not set, and a portion on each side of the winter solstice when he does not rise.

Similarly, a circle drawn round the South Pole of the earth with the same radius, $23\frac{1}{2}°$, is called the Antarctic Circle, and, for places within this circle, the Sun does not set for some time near our midwinter, and does not rise for some time near our midsummer.

6. Again, since on the meridian we have generally $z = \Delta - \gamma$ (z being reckoned towards the South), the Sun will always be south of the zenith on passing the meridian as long as Δ is greater than γ, Δ and γ being always reckoned from the North Pole, and north of the zenith as long as Δ is less than γ. Now for the Sun the smallest value of Δ is $66\frac{1}{2}°$, and therefore for all places in North latitudes greater than $23\frac{1}{2}°$ (that is, for which γ is less than $66\frac{1}{2}°$) the Sun passes the meridian at midsummer South of the zenith, and for all places in North latitudes less than $23\frac{1}{2}°$ (that is, within the *Tropics*) the Sun passes North of the zenith. If $\gamma = \Delta = 66\frac{1}{2}°$, or the latitude be $23\frac{1}{2}°$, the Sun is vertical at midsummer, and if a small circle be drawn through a point having this latitude parallel to the equator, it is called the *Tropic of Cancer*. Similarly, a circle drawn parallel to the equator, and South of it, at the same distance, is called the *Tropic of Capricorn*, because the Sun having been vertical over these circles at midsummer and midwinter respectively, then *turns* or goes back again.

7. Since generally

$$\cos z = \sin \gamma \sin \Delta \cos h + \cos \gamma \cos \Delta$$

(h being the hour-angle), $\cos z$ will have its greatest or maximum value when $\cos h = 1$, that is, when $h = 0$, or the object is on the meridian, and therefore z will have its minimum or least value. This however is true only on the supposition that the N.P.D. is sensibly constant, as in the case of the stars. If the object observed be on the contrary a planet, this is not strictly true, and, to find the minimum value of z we must differentiate the preceding equation, considering Δ as variable as well as h and z.

Thus we have
$$-\sin z \frac{dz}{dh} = -\sin \gamma \sin \Delta \sin h$$
$$+ \sin \gamma \cos \Delta \cos h \frac{d\Delta}{dh}$$
$$- \cos \gamma \sin \Delta \frac{d\Delta}{dh}$$
$$= 0 \text{ (since } z \text{ is a minimum),}$$

and therefore
$$\sin h = -(\cotan \gamma - \cotan \Delta \cos h)\frac{d\Delta}{dh};$$

where $\frac{d\Delta}{dh}$ is the change of N.P.D. corresponding to the change of hour-angle dh. Thus dh being expressed in arc, if it represent a second of space, then $\frac{d\Delta}{dh}$ is the change of N.P.D. in one-fifteenth of a second of time. Now, since $\frac{d\Delta}{dh}$, even in the case of the moon, is a small quantity, we may in this equation replace $\sin h$ by $h \sin 1''$, and $\cos h$ by unity, and we then get

$$h \sin 1'' = -(\cot \gamma - \cot \Delta)\frac{d\Delta}{dh},$$

or t, expressed in seconds of time,
$$= -\frac{1}{15 \sin 1''}(\cot \gamma - \cot \Delta)\frac{d\Delta}{dh}.$$

EXAMPLE. Take the case of the meridian transit of the moon at Greenwich, on Dec. 17, 1861.

From the Section of *Moon Culminating Stars* in the Nautical Almanac, we get
$$\Delta = 66°.33',$$
also $\quad \gamma = 38°.31',$ and $\therefore \Delta - \gamma = 28°.2'.$

MAXIMUM CHANGE OF ALTITUDE.

Also variation of N.P.D. in an hour of longitude $= +229''\cdot 9$; and hence, very approximately,

$$\frac{d\Delta}{dh} = +\frac{229''\cdot 9}{15 \times 60 \times 60} = +0''\cdot 003702.$$

Again, $\cot\gamma - \cot\Delta = \dfrac{\sin\Delta\cos\gamma - \cos\Delta\sin\gamma}{\sin\gamma\sin A}$

$$= \frac{\sin(\Delta - \gamma)}{\sin\gamma\sin A}.$$

Hence

$$\begin{array}{ll}
\text{Log}\sin(\Delta-\gamma) = & 9\cdot 67208 \\
\text{Ar. co. log}\sin\gamma = & 0\cdot 20569 \\
\text{Ar. co. log}\sin\Delta = & 0\cdot 03744 \\
-\text{Ar. co. log } 15 = & -8\cdot 82391 \\
\text{Ar. co. log}\sin 1'' = & 5\cdot 31443 \\
\text{Log } \cdot 003702 = & 7\cdot 56844 \\
\hline
-\text{Log } 41^{s}\cdot 9 = & -1\cdot 62199
\end{array}$$

Hence the moon's altitude is greatest at $41^{s}\cdot 9$ before the transit over the meridian.

8. To find the azimuth when the change of altitude of a star in a given time is a maximum.

As before, taking the equation

$$\cos z = \sin\gamma\sin\Delta\cos h + \cos\gamma\cos\Delta,$$

and differentiating with respect to h, z and h being the only variables, we have

$$\sin z\,\frac{dz}{dh} = \sin\gamma\sin\Delta\sin h,$$

or, if the angle $ZSP = p$, since

$$\sin z\sin p = \sin h\sin\gamma,$$

$$\sin z\,\frac{dz}{dh} = \sin\Delta\sin z\sin p,$$

or

$$\frac{dz}{dh} = \sin\Delta\sin p;$$

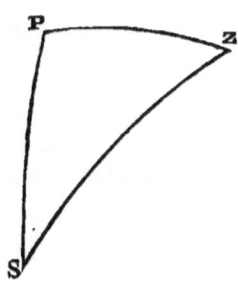

$$\therefore \frac{d^2z}{dh^2} = \sin \Delta \cos p \frac{dp}{dh};$$

but, since
$$\cos \gamma = \cos z \cos \Delta + \sin z \sin \Delta \cos p,$$
we have by differentiation
$$0 = (\cos z \sin \Delta \cos p - \sin z \cos \Delta) \frac{dz}{dh}$$
$$- \sin z \sin \Delta \sin p \frac{dp}{dh},$$
or, if A = the azimuth of the star or angle PZS,
$$0 = -\sin \gamma \cos A \frac{dz}{dh} - \sin z \sin \Delta \sin p \frac{dp}{dh},$$
or
$$\frac{dp}{dh} = -\frac{\sin \gamma \cos A}{\sin z \sin \Delta \sin p} \cdot \frac{dz}{dh}$$
$$= -\frac{\sin \gamma \cos A}{\sin z}.$$

Substituting this in the equation
$$\frac{d^2z}{dh^2} = \sin \Delta \cos p \frac{dp}{dh},$$
we get
$$\frac{d^2z}{dh^2} = -\sin \Delta \cos p \frac{\sin \gamma \cos A}{\sin z};$$
therefore, when $\frac{dz}{dh}$ is a maximum or a minimum,
$$\sin \Delta \cos p \frac{\sin \gamma \cos A}{\sin z} = 0,$$
or $\cos A = 0$, which gives $A = 90°$ or $270°$.

The change of altitude is therefore greatest on the prime vertical.

Or, the value of $\frac{d^2z}{dh^2}$ may be deduced immediately in terms of A in the following manner:
$$\frac{dz}{dh} = \sin \Delta \sin p \text{ (as before)}$$
$$= \sin \gamma \sin A;$$

$$\therefore \frac{d^2z}{dh^2} = \sin\gamma \cos A \frac{dA}{dh},$$

but, since
$$\cos A = \frac{\cos\Delta - \cos\gamma \cos z}{\sin\gamma \sin z};$$

$$\therefore -\sin A \frac{dA}{dh} = \frac{\cot\gamma}{\sin^2 z} \cdot \frac{dz}{dh} - \frac{\cos\Delta \cos z}{\sin^2 z \sin\gamma} \cdot \frac{dz}{dh}$$

$$= \frac{\cos\gamma - \cos\Delta \cos z}{\sin^2 z \sin\gamma} \cdot \frac{dz}{dh}$$

$$= \frac{\cos p \sin z \sin\Delta}{\sin^2 z \sin\gamma} \cdot \frac{dz}{dh}$$

$$= \frac{\cos p \sin\Delta}{\sin z \sin\gamma} \cdot \frac{dz}{dh},$$

or
$$\frac{dA}{dh} = -\frac{\cos p \sin\Delta}{\sin A \sin z \sin\gamma} \frac{dz}{dh}$$

$$= -\frac{\cos p \sin\Delta}{\sin z};$$

$$\therefore \frac{d^2z}{dh^2} = \sin\gamma \cos A \frac{dA}{dh}$$

$$= -\sin\gamma \cos A \frac{\cos p \sin\Delta}{\sin z}, \text{ as before.}$$

9. Several problems might be given relating to the diurnal motion, but, as they are of very little importance in the theory or practice of astronomy, it will be sufficient to enunciate them, referring to Maddy's *Astronomy* for the solution, or leaving them to the ingenuity of the student.

(1) To find the difference between the length of the morning and of the afternoon at any time of the year, that is, of the time from sunrise to noon, and from noon to sunset.

(2) To find the hour-angle of a heavenly body at which the azimuth increases fastest.

(3) To find the hour at which the sun is due east or west on a given day.

(4) To find the hour-angle when a star's motion is vertical.

(5) To find the time when two known stars are in the same vertical.

CHAPTER V.

ON TIME.

---

1. IN the preceding chapters we had occasion to speak of and to define sidereal time (page 7), and to employ the notion of it freely in all problems relating to the diurnal motion. It is however desirable that, before proceeding farther, a chapter should be devoted to a more correct and detailed consideration of time in general. We will, therefore, recapitulate what has been already said on the subject, and give such other definitions of the sensible measures of time and of its subdivisions as are necessary.

Time, without regard to any sensible measures of it, is called duration. It is difficult, however, to obtain practically any distinct notion of it without defining it by the successive epochs of events or phenomena, and, of the latter, celestial phenomena are the only ones which are adapted to our daily wants. The first and most important measure of time is that immediately derived from the rotation of the earth on its axis, or the apparent revolution of the sphere of the heavens. The time of one such revolution is called a *Sidereal Day*, as has been before mentioned (page 7). The second unit or measure is derived from the revolution of the earth in its orbit, and the time of one such complete revolution, measured from the epoch of its leaving a fixed point in the heavens and returning to it again, is called a *Sidereal Year*. The natural units of time, therefore, are a Sidereal Day and a Sidereal Year.

2. But, for all civil purposes, the apparent motion of the sun in the heavens gives much better units for the measure of time, and it will be necessary to find the relation between these units and those before defined, or between *Solar Time* and *Sidereal Time*.

Let then a solar day be defined to be the interval which elapses between two transits of the sun over the meridian or over any other declination circle. Then, since by his *apparent* orbital motion from west to east (arising from the earth's real orbital motion), that is, in the direction contrary to the diurnal motion, he describes in the course of one yearly revolution the whole circuit of the heavens, namely $360°$, it is plain that if n be the number of sidereal days in a sidereal year, the number of solar days will be $n-1$; or, the length of a *mean* solar day will be to the length of a sidereal day as $n : n-1$; a mean solar day being defined to be the mean of the intervals between the sun's leaving any meridian and returning to it again.

Since, however, the recurrence of the seasons of the year, spring, summer, autumn, and winter, depends on the time which elapses between the passage of the sun through the *vernal equinox* and his return to it again, and since this time (measured either in sidereal or mean solar intervals) is, as we have seen in Chapter III, most easily observed, this interval of time, which is called the *Tropical Year*, is used as the basis of all reckoning of time. If now the Vernal Equinox, or the first point of Aries were a fixed point, the *Sidereal Year* and the *Tropical Year* would be of precisely equal length, but, since this is not the case, the equinox moving contrary to the order of the signs along the equator at a mean rate of $50''\cdot 224$ per year (called the annual precessional motion), it is plain that the tropical year will be shorter than the sidereal year by the time taken by the sun to describe the precessional arc $50'''\cdot 224$.

By the best and most recent discussions it has been found that the length of the tropical year, that is, the time which elapses between two successive transits of the sun through the vernal equinox, is $366\cdot 24222$ sidereal days. Measured in mean solar days therefore, the length of the tropical year is $365\cdot 24222$ days, or $365^d.5^h.48^m.47^s\cdot 808$.

For the purpose of reasoning more accurately on solar time, it is usual and convenient to compare the sun's motion with that of a fictitious sun, which is supposed to move with a uniform velocity in the equator, with the real sun's mean motion in right ascension or longitude.

Let L be the right ascension or longitude of the fictitious sun at the commencement of the time t, and μ its mean daily motion; then its right ascension α at the time t will be

$$\alpha = L + \mu t,$$

where
$$\mu = \frac{360°}{365.24222} = 59'.8''\cdot 33.$$

The mean day begins for any place when this fictitious sun is on the meridian, or when the sidereal time is equal to its longitude, or to the mean longitude of the real sun, and is reckoned astronomically from 0^h to 24^h, or from mean noon to mean noon.

Let now α' be the right ascension of the real sun at the time t, l its longitude, and ω the obliquity of the ecliptic. We have thus

$$\tan \alpha' = \cos \omega \cdot \tan l.$$

And, by trigonometrical expansion,

$$\alpha' = l - \tan^2 \frac{\omega}{2} \sin 2l + \frac{1}{2} \tan^4 \frac{\omega}{2} \sin 4l - \&c.,$$

where l is of the form

$$l = L + \mu t + \zeta,$$

ζ being a periodical function of the sun's longitude, and therefore

$$\alpha' - \alpha = \zeta - \tan^2 \frac{\omega}{2} \sin 2l + \frac{1}{2} \tan^4 \frac{\omega}{2} \sin 4l - \&c.$$

This quantity is called the *Equation of Time*, and, if it is positive, then the mean sun precedes the true, or mean noon is in advance of apparent noon; but, if it is negative, mean noon follows apparent noon.

The Equation of Time vanishes four times in the year, namely, on April 14, June 14, August 31, and December 23,

equation of time = mean time − apparent time

or on the day following these days. In the first period, or from April 14 to June 14, mean time is after apparent time; and the same is true in the third interval, or from August 31 to December 23. In the other two intervals, namely, from June 14 to August 31, and from December 23 to April 14, mean time precedes apparent time. The Equation of Time is given primarily in the Nautical Almanac, and generally in common almanacs for every apparent noon.

3. The proof of the proposition that the Equation of Time vanishes four times in the year must be deferred till we consider the theory of the Sun's motion, but that part of the equation which depends upon the obliquity of the ecliptic may be discussed here.

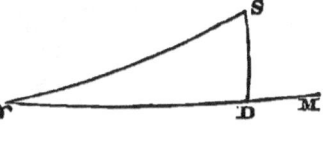

Let S be the sun, supposed to move uniformly in the ecliptic, and D its plane referred to the equator by the perpendicular arc SD.

Take $\Upsilon M = \Upsilon S$; then ΥM is the right ascension of the fictitious sun and ΥD of the real sun, and DM is the part of the Equation of Time resulting from the obliquity.

Now $\sin \Upsilon D = \sin \Upsilon SD \cdot \sin \Upsilon S$; thus, $\sin \Upsilon D$ is generally less than $\sin \Upsilon S$.

Hence, in the first quadrant, or from the spring equinox to the summer solstice, since ΥS and ΥD are both less than 90°, ΥD will be less than ΥS or ΥM, or the mean sun's R.A. is greater than that of the real sun; that is, the true sun precedes the mean sun. At the summer solstice ΥS or $\Upsilon M = 90°$, and therefore $\Upsilon D = 90°$, and the equation vanishes. In the second quadrant ΥS and ΥD are both between 90° and 180°, and hence ΥD will be greater than ΥS or ΥM, and the mean sun will precede the true sun. At the autumnal equinox $\Upsilon S = 180°$, and the mean and true suns coincide again. Similarly, it may be proved that from the autumnal equinox to the winter solstice, the true sun precedes the mean; that they coincide at the winter solstice; and finally, that from this time to the vernal equinox, when they again coincide, the mean sun precedes the true.

4. *To transform Mean Time into Sidereal Time, and vice versa.*

Since 365·24222 mean solar days are equal to 366·24222 sidereal days;

one sidereal day $= \dfrac{365 \cdot 24222}{366 \cdot 24222}$ mean solar day

$=$ a mean solar day $- \dfrac{1}{366 \cdot 24222}$ of a mean solar day

$=$ a mean solar day $- 3^{m}.55^{s}\cdot 909$ mean solar time.

And a mean solar day $= \dfrac{366 \cdot 24222}{365 \cdot 24222}$ sidereal day

$=$ a sidereal day $+ \dfrac{1}{365 \cdot 24222}$ of a sidereal day

$=$ a sidereal day $+ 3^{m}.56^{s}\cdot 555$ sidereal time.

Let then, for any given instant at a given place, t be the sidereal time, and m the mean solar time, and let T be the value of t when $m = 0$, that is, for mean noon. Then $t - T$ is the sidereal interval corresponding to the mean solar interval m.

Hence $m = (t - T) \times \dfrac{24^{h} - 3^{m}.55^{s}\cdot 909}{24^{h}}$,

and $\quad t = T + m \times \dfrac{24^{h} + 3^{m}.56^{s}\cdot 555}{24^{h}}$.

The value of $\dfrac{24^{h} - 3^{m}.55^{s}\cdot 909}{24^{h}}$ is 0·9972695,

and that of $\dfrac{24^{h} + 3^{m}.56^{s}\cdot 555}{24^{h}}$ is 1·0027379.

And, in the Nautical Almanac are given tables of the values of $0 \cdot 9972695 \times t$ and $1 \cdot 0027379 \times t$ for every hour, minute, and second in the day. There is also given in page i of each month of the Nautical Almanac the mean sun's right ascension at mean noon of each day, or the sidereal time at mean noon;

that is, the values of T can be taken out immediately from the Nautical Almanac*.

If μ and s be corresponding mean solar and sidereal equivalents for the same interval of time, it follows from what has preceded, that

$$\mu = s \times 0.9972695,$$

and

$$s = m \times 1.0027379.$$

It is however usual to find the mean time corresponding to a given sidereal time in the following manner.

Let M be the Mean Time of Transit of the First Point of Aries (tabulated for every day at page xx of each month in the Nautical Almanac);

t the sidereal time, that is, the hour-angle (west) of the first point of Aries;

m the corresponding mean solar time.

Then $m = M +$ mean solar interval corresponding to sidereal interval t,

$$= M + 0\cdot9972695 \times t.$$

Practically this would be expressed thus,

$m = M +$ mean solar interval for hours,

$+ \ldots\ldots\ldots\ldots\ldots$ for minutes,

$+ \ldots\ldots\ldots\ldots\ldots$ for seconds.

EXAMPLES. To find the Sidereal Time corresponding to 1862, January 1, $5^h.17^m.16^s\cdot92$ Greenwich mean solar time.

Here from page i of the month January in the Nautical Almanac, we find

---

* A student of Practical Astronomy cannot do better than to make himself acquainted with the contents of the Nautical Almanac, and especially with the excellent "Explanation" given at the end of it.

104 COMPUTATION OF SID. AND MEAN SOLAR TIME.

	h. m. s.
Sidereal Time at Greenwich mean noon	= 18.43.31·12
Sidereal equivalent for 5ʰ (page 502 of N.A.)	= 5. 0.49·28
.... for 17ᵐ	= 17. 2·79
.... for 16ˢ	= 16·04
.... for ·92	= ·92
Sidereal Time required	= 0. 1.40·15

To find the Mean Solar Time corresponding to the Sidereal Time 13ʰ.7ᵐ.14ˢ·94 on February 4, 1862.

Here, on page xx of the month February, we find

Preceding Mean Time of Transit of the First Point of Aries	= 3. 1.56·06
Mean Solar equivalent for 13ʰ (page 504)	= 12.57.52·22
.... for 7ᵐ	= 6.58·85
.... for 14ˢ	= 13·96
.... for ·94	= ·94
Mean Solar Time required	= 16. 7. 2·03

The computation of Mean Solar Time can, however, be made rather easier, by putting the equivalents in the following shape:

Mean time = (1) sidereal time

(2)   + 3ᵐ.47ˢ·00 − hours of sidereal time + solar equivalent for hours

(3)   +   10ˢ·00 − minutes of sidereal time + solar equivalent for minutes

(4)   +   3ˢ·00 − seconds of sidereal time + solar equivalent for seconds

(5)   + Mean Time of Transit of First Point of Aries diminished by 4ᵐ.

TABLE FOR COMPUTATION OF MEAN SOLAR TIME.

The following table gives the values of (2), (3) and (4), and the computation then becomes very easy.

TABLE I.		TABLE II.				TABLE III.			
Correction for Hours.		Correction for Minutes.				Correction for Seconds.			
Sidereal Hours.	Correction.	Sidereal Minutes.	Correction.	Sidereal Minutes.	Correction.	Sidereal Seconds.	Correction.	Sidereal Seconds.	Correction.
	m. s.		s.		s.		s.		s.
0	3.47·00	0	10·00	30	5·09	0	3·00	30	2·92
1	3.37·17	1	9·84	31	4·92	1	3·00	31	2·91
2	3.27·34	2	9·67	32	4·76	2	2·99	32	2·91
3	3.17·51	3	9·51	33	4·59	3	2·99	33	2·91
4	3. 7·68	4	9·34	34	4·43	4	2·99	34	2·91
5	2.57·85	5	9·18	35	4·27	5	2·98	35	2·90
6	2.48·02	6	9·02	36	4·10	6	2·98	36	2·90
7	2.38·19	7	8·85	37	3·94	7	2·98	37	2·90
8	2.28·36	8	8·69	38	3·77	8	2·98	38	2·90
9	2.18·53	9	8·53	39	3·61	9	2·97	39	2·89
10	2. 8·70	10	8·36	40	3·45	10	2·97	40	2·89
11	1.58·87	11	8·20	41	3·28	11	2·97	41	2·89
12	1.49·05	12	8·03	42	3·12	12	2·96	42	2·89
13	1.39·22	13	7·87	43	2·96	13	2·96	43	2·88
14	1.29·39	14	7·71	44	2·79	14	2·96	44	2·88
15	1.19·56	15	7·54	45	2·63	15	2·96	45	2·88
16	1. 9·73	16	7·38	46	2·46	16	2·95	46	2·87
17	0.59·90	17	7·22	47	2·30	17	2·95	47	2·87
18	0.50·07	18	7·05	48	2·14	18	2·95	48	2·87
19	0.40·24	19	6·89	49	1·97	19	2·95	49	2·87
20	0.30·41	20	6·72	50	1·81	20	2·94	50	2·86
21	0.20·58	21	6·56	51	1·64	21	2·94	51	2·86
22	0.10·75	22	6·40	52	1·48	22	2·94	52	2·86
23	0. 0·92	23	6·23	53	1·32	23	2·94	53	2·85
		24	6·07	54	1·15	24	2·93	54	2·85
		25	5·90	55	0·99	25	2·93	55	2·85
		26	5·74	56	0·83	26	2·93	56	2·85
		27	5·58	57	0·66	27	2·92	57	2·84
		28	5·41	58	0·50	28	2·92	58	2·84
		29	5·25	59	0·33	29	2·92	59	2·84

As an example we will take that which was previously proposed, namely, to find the Mean Solar Time corresponding to the Sidereal Time, $13^h.7^m.14^s\cdot94$ on February 4, 1862.

	h. m. s.
Sidereal time .... =	13. 7.14·94
Correction for hours .... =	1.39·22
„ „ minutes .... =	8·85
„ „ seconds .... =	2·96
Mean Time of Transit of First Point of Aries $- 4^m$. } =	2.57.56·06
Mean Solar Time .... =	16. 7. 2·03 as before.

The reader will observe that this computation requires fewer figures than the preceding, and is, on the whole, more convenient. It was devised by the Astronomer Royal, Mr Airy, and is used at Greenwich*.

5. To find the length of the sidereal year.

The sidereal year will be longer than the tropical year by the time taken by the sun to describe the precessional arc $50''\cdot224$ (page 99). Now the sun describes in a mean solar day $59'.8''\cdot33$, and, in a sidereal day, $58'.58''\cdot64$, or $3548''\cdot33$ and $3538''\cdot64$ respectively. Hence the sidereal year expressed in mean solar days is $365^d.5^h.48^m.47^s\cdot81 + \dfrac{50\cdot224}{3548\cdot33} \times 24 \times 60^m$

$= 365^d.5^h.48^m.47^s\cdot81 + 20^m.22^s\cdot90$

$= 365^d.6^h.9^m.10^s\cdot71$ mean solar days.

And, expressed in sidereal days, the length is

$366^d.5^h.48^m.47^s\cdot81 + \dfrac{50\cdot224}{3538\cdot64} \times 24 \times 60^m$

$= 366^d.5^h.48^m.47^s\cdot81 + 20^m.26^s\cdot28$

$= 366^d.6^h.9^m.14^s\cdot09$ sidereal days.

* In Schumacher's *Hülfstafeln* there is also a set of Tables, which I have found very convenient for the rapid computation of Mean Solar Time. From these Tables there can be taken out at sight the reduction to be applied to any interval of Sidereal Time to produce the corresponding interval of Mean Solar Time, from 0^h to 24^h.

6. On the Calendar.

We have seen that the tropical year consists of 365·24222 mean solar days. As this involves a fraction of a day it is not convenient for civil purposes, which requires that the year should consist of an integral number of days or assumed units. But, since the fraction 0·24222 is very nearly 0·25, or one quarter of a day, if three successive years be assumed to be of the length of 365 days, and the fourth year of the length of 366 days, the reckoning will come nearly right every fourth year. This was the correction of the calendar made in the time of Julius Cæsar, and was therefore called the *Julian Correction*. By this reckoning, however, the assumed tropical year was too long on the average by $0^d \cdot 00778$, so that in the course of 1000 years the accumulated error would amount to nearly 8 days, by which, at the *assumed* equinox, the sun would have really passed it. To correct this error, Pope Gregory the Thirteenth, after consulting with eminent astronomers of his epoch, published a bull in the year 1582, ordering that for civil purposes the nominal 5th of October of that year should be called the 15th of October, and that for the future three bissextiles or leap-years (that is, years consisting of 366 days) should be omitted in every 400 years. The leap-years or bissextiles are those which are divisible by 4, and the Gregorian correction consists in considering all years completing centuries as common years, excepting those for which the century itself is divisible by 4. Thus the years 1700, 1800, and 1900 are common years of 365 days, but the year 2000 will be a bissextile or leap-year. Thus, instead of intercalating 100 days in 400 years, Pope Gregory intercalated 97 days in 400 years, or the year consisted of $365\frac{97}{400} = 365 \cdot 2425$ days. The true length, therefore, being 365·24222 days, the error is only 0·00028 days per year, and will amount to rather more than a day in 4000 years.

It is almost needless to add that the intercalation of the day for keeping the calendar right is made in February, this month in ordinary years having 28 days, but, in leap-years, 29 days. The Gregorian Correction is adopted in almost all Christian countries (though Russia still uses the old as well as the new

108   DETERMINATION OF LOCAL TIME.

style), but it was not adopted in this country till the middle of the last century.

7. *On the determination of sidereal or mean time by observation.*

In a fixed observatory, furnished with a transit-instrument, the determination of time is effected immediately (as has been explained at page 31) by the comparison of the clock-time of transit of certain well-known stars or of the sun with their tabular right ascensions, these right ascensions being equal to the sidereal times of their transit across the meridian. The error of the clock at any instant is therefore the difference of the clock-time of transit of the object observed at that instant, and of the right ascension of the object. The rate of the clock, or its loss or gain in 24 hours, will also be found by comparing its errors thus found on successive days or other intervals of time.

When the errors and rate of the transit-clock have been thus determined, the errors of all the other clocks in the observatory, whether they be sidereal or mean solar clocks, can be found by comparing them together by the intervention of a mean solar or sidereal chronometer.

EXAMPLE. At Oxford on June 9, 1862, 10^h M.T., the transit-clock and the heliometer-clock were compared by means of a mean solar chronometer. The simultaneous readings of each clock and the chronometer were as follows:

$$
\begin{array}{ll}
 & \text{h. m. s.} \\
\{\text{Time by transit-clock} & 15.41.35 \cdot 0 \\
\phantom{\{}\text{Corresponding time by chronometer} & 10.29.0 \cdot 0 \\
\{\text{Time by heliometer-clock} & 15.43.21 \cdot 8 \\
\phantom{\{}\text{Time by chronometer} & 10.31.0 \cdot 0 \\
\end{array}
$$

The transit-clock was at this time $2^s \cdot 00$ fast.

DETERMINATION OF LOCAL TIME.

Then the computation will stand thus:

	h. m. s.
Time by chronometer (1st comparison)	10.29. 0·0
,, ,, (2nd ,,)	10.31. 0·0
Mean solar interval..........................	2. 0·0
Correction to sidereal interval...........	0·33
Sidereal interval............................	2. 0·33
Time by transit-clock.....................	15.41.35·00
Sum..	15.43.35·33
Transit-clock fast	2·00
Sidereal time at comparison of heliometer-clock	15.43.33·33
Time by heliometer-clock	15.43.21·80
Heliometer-clock slow.....................	11·53

Sometimes, even in a fixed observatory, a succession of cloudy days may prevent objects suitable for the determination of time from being observed on the meridian. If (as at Greenwich) there be an altitude and azimuth-instrument, the time can be determined by means of the observed zenith-distance of a known star with very great accuracy.

Thus, as usual let P be the pole, Z the zenith, and S the star, PZ (the colatitude) $= \gamma$, $ZS = z$, and $PS = \Delta$.

Then we have

$$\sin \frac{P}{2} = \sqrt{\frac{\sin \frac{z + \Delta - \gamma}{2} \sin \frac{z - \Delta + \gamma}{2}}{\sin \gamma \sin \Delta}},$$

which will give the hour-angle P (supposed west) expressed in arc, and the corresponding angle $\frac{P}{15}$ expressed in time. Hence, if t be the sidereal time, and α the assumed or tabular right ascension of the star, $15t = P + \alpha$, and this, compared with the clock-time of observation, gives the error of the clock.

8. To find the error in time produced by a given error in the observed zenith-distance.

Here we have $\cos P = \dfrac{\cos z - \cos \gamma \cos \Delta}{\sin \gamma \sin \Delta}$;

$$\therefore \sin P\, \delta P = \dfrac{\sin z\, \delta z}{\sin \gamma \sin \Delta},$$

or $\delta P = 15 \delta t = \dfrac{\sin z\, \delta z}{\sin \gamma \sin \Delta \sin P}$

$$= \dfrac{\sin z\, \delta z}{\sin \gamma \sin Z \sin z}$$

$$= \dfrac{\delta z}{\sin \gamma \sin Z},$$

or $\delta t = \dfrac{\delta z}{15} \dfrac{1}{\sin \gamma \sin Z}.$

Hence the error in time is the least when $\sin Z$ is greatest, or when $Z = 90°$, that is, when the object is on or very near the prime vertical.

9. The time may also be found, when the latitude is known, by equal altitudes of the sun or of a star, taken with a sextant or an altitude and azimuth-instrument before and after the meridian passage.

If the object observed be a star, whose declination does not change between the observations, half the sum of the observed clock or chronometer times will be the time of the star's transit across the meridian. If the clock or chronometer keep sidereal time, the difference between this mean and the star's right ascension will be its error. If it keep mean solar time, the sidereal time of the star's transit, that is its right ascension, must be converted into mean time, and this, compared with the mean of the observed times, will give the error.

In general the chronometer will not keep exactly either mean or sidereal time, or it will have a rate. Supposing this rate to be approximately known, it will be necessary to apply it to the interval between the first and the second observation to

TIME BY EQUAL ALTITUDES OF THE SUN. 111

obtain the true interval in sidereal or in mean time; or, to increase or diminish the second observation by the amount of the losing or gaining rate in the interval, before taking the mean, to obtain the time of meridian passage.

If the object be the sun, it will change its declination in the interval between the morning and evening observations. To correct for this, let z be the zenith-distance observed morning and evening, h the sun's morning hour-angle, and h' the evening hour-angle, corresponding to z; Δ the N.P.D. in the morning, Δ' in the evening, and γ the colatitude.

Then $\cos z = \sin \gamma \sin \Delta \cos h + \cos \gamma \cos \Delta$,

and $\cos z = \sin \gamma \sin \Delta' \cos h' + \cos \gamma \cos \Delta'$;

$\therefore 0 = \sin \gamma (\sin \Delta \cos h - \sin \Delta' \cos h') + \cos \gamma (\cos \Delta - \cos \Delta')$.

Let $h' = h + \delta h$,

and $\Delta' = \Delta + \delta \Delta$,

then, neglecting second powers,

$0 = \sin \gamma \{\sin \Delta \cos h - (\sin \Delta + \cos \Delta \, \delta \Delta)(\cos h - \sin h \, \delta h)\}$
$\qquad + \cos \gamma \{\cos \Delta - (\cos \Delta - \sin \Delta \, \delta \Delta)\}$,

or

$0 = \sin \gamma \{\sin \Delta \sin h \, \delta h - \cos \Delta \cos h \, \delta \Delta\} + \cos \gamma \sin \Delta \, \delta \Delta$;

$\therefore \delta h = \dfrac{\delta \Delta}{\sin \gamma \sin \Delta \sin h}(\sin \gamma \cos \Delta \cos h - \cos \gamma \sin \Delta)$,

or, if δt be, in time, the correction to the afternoon hour-angle,

$$\delta t = \dfrac{\delta \Delta}{15 \sin h}(\cot \Delta \cos h - \cot \gamma).$$

Let now T and T' be the chronometer-times of observation,

α and α' the corresponding right ascensions of the sun,

x the error of chronometer (slow) supposed without rate.

Let also
$$t = \frac{h}{15},$$
and
$$t' = \frac{h'}{15}.$$

Then
$$T + x = \alpha - t,$$
and
$$T' + x = \alpha' + t' = \alpha' + t + \delta t;$$
$$\therefore T' + T + 2x = \alpha' + \alpha + \delta t;$$
$$\therefore x = \frac{\alpha' + \alpha}{2} - \frac{T' + T}{2} + \frac{\delta t}{2}$$
$$= \frac{\alpha' + \alpha}{2} - \frac{T' + T}{2} + \frac{\delta \Delta}{30 \sin h} (\cot \Delta \cos h - \cot \gamma).$$

If the chronometer has a losing rate, we must add the proportional part of it corresponding to the interval $T' - T$ to the value of x for the afternoon observation. Let this be r, then we shall have
$$T' + T + 2x + r = \alpha' + \alpha + \delta t,$$
or
$$x = \frac{\alpha' + \alpha}{2} - \frac{T' + T}{2} - \frac{r}{2} + \frac{\delta t}{2}.$$

If *equal* altitudes of the sun or a known star cannot be obtained, the time (or the error of the chronometer) may be deduced from any two observed altitudes of a known fixed star. Thus, using the same notation as before, let z and z' be the zenith-distances observed at the times t and t'. Let also α be the R.A. of the star observed, and let the observations be made after the meridian passage.

Then, if h and h' be the hour-angles,
$$h = t - \alpha, \quad h' = t' - \alpha,$$
$$\cos h = \frac{\cos z - \cos \gamma \cos \Delta}{\sin \gamma \sin \Delta},$$
and
$$\cos h' = \frac{\cos z' - \cos \gamma \cos \Delta}{\sin \gamma \sin \Delta}.$$

TIME BY TWO OBSERVED ALTITUDES OF A STAR.

Hence $\cos h \sin \gamma \sin \Delta - \cos z = \cos h' \sin \gamma \sin \Delta - \cos z'$,

or $\cos h \sin \gamma \sin \Delta - \cos z = \cos (h + \beta) \sin \gamma \sin \Delta - \cos z'$,

where $\beta = h' - h$,

and $\{\cos h - \cos (h + \beta)\} \sin \gamma \sin \Delta = \cos z - \cos z'$,

or $\sin \dfrac{\beta}{2} \sin \left(h + \dfrac{\beta}{2} \right) \sin \gamma \sin \Delta = \sin \dfrac{z'-z}{2} \sin \dfrac{z'+z}{2}$ ...(1).

Again, $\dfrac{\cos h}{\cos (h+\beta)} = \dfrac{\cos z - \cos \gamma \cos \Delta}{\cos z' - \cos \gamma \cos \Delta}$,

or $\tan \dfrac{\beta}{2} \tan \left(h + \dfrac{\beta}{2} \right) = \dfrac{\sin \dfrac{z'-z}{2} \sin \dfrac{z'+z}{2}}{\cos \dfrac{z'-z}{2} \cos \dfrac{z'+z}{2} - \cos \gamma \cos \Delta}$ ...(2).

Hence we have,

$\left(\text{calling } \sin \dfrac{z'-z}{2} \sin \dfrac{z'+z}{2} = \epsilon, \right.$

and $\left. \cos \dfrac{z'-z}{2} \cos \dfrac{z'+z}{2} = \iota \right);$

$\sin \dfrac{\beta}{2} \sin \left(h + \dfrac{\beta}{2} \right) = \dfrac{\epsilon}{\sin \gamma \sin \Delta}$,

and $\tan \dfrac{\beta}{2} \tan \left(h + \dfrac{\beta}{2} \right) = \dfrac{\epsilon}{\iota - \cos \gamma \cos \Delta}$,

or $\sin \dfrac{\beta}{2} \sin \left(h + \dfrac{\beta}{2} \right) = \dfrac{\epsilon}{\sin \gamma \sin \Delta}$,

and $\cos \dfrac{\beta}{2} \cos \left(h + \dfrac{\beta}{2} \right) = \dfrac{\iota - \cos \gamma \cos \Delta}{\sin \gamma \sin \Delta}$,

whence $1 = \dfrac{1}{\sin^2 \dfrac{\beta}{2}} \cdot \dfrac{\epsilon^2}{\sin^2 \gamma \sin^2 \Delta} + \dfrac{1}{\cos^2 \dfrac{\beta}{2}} \cdot \dfrac{(\iota - \cos \gamma \cos \Delta)^2}{\sin^2 \gamma \sin^2 \Delta}$,

or $\sin^2 \Delta (1 - \cos^2 \gamma) = \epsilon^2 \operatorname{cosec}^2 \dfrac{\beta}{2} + \sec^2 \dfrac{\beta}{2} (\iota - \cos \gamma \cos \Delta)^2$,

a quadratic equation which determines γ, or the colatitude.

114 TIME BY TWO OBSERVED ALTITUDES OF A STAR.

Hence
$$\sin\left(h + \frac{\beta}{2}\right) = \frac{\epsilon}{\sin\frac{\beta}{2}\sin\gamma\sin\Delta},$$

and $h + \frac{\beta}{2}$, and therefore h, is determined.

Therefore, the time of the first observation or $t\left(= a + \frac{h}{15}\right)$ is known, and can be compared with the time shewn by the chronometer.

The solution given above, though it is direct and elegant, can scarcely be considered to be a practical solution of the problem. We need only give a sketch of the practical solution, which is as follows.

In the subjoined triangle SZS' we have $ZS = z$, $ZS' = z'$, and angle $SPS' = 15t$ ($= 2\beta$ suppose) all given quantities; also $PS = PS' = \Delta$ a known quantity; to find $ZP = \gamma$, and $ZPS = h$.

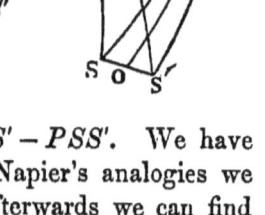

Napier's analogies immediately give us the angles ZSS' and $ZS'S$; and we can therefore find SS'. Then, knowing PS we easily find in the isosceles triangle PSS' the angle PSS' by the formula

$$\cos PSS' = \tan \tfrac{1}{2} SS' \cot \Delta.$$

Hence we have the angle $ZSP = ZSS' - PSS'$. We have also $PS = \Delta$ and $ZS = z$, and hence by Napier's analogies we find immediately angle $ZPS = h$, and afterwards we can find $ZP = \gamma$.

10. To find the errors of the deduced colatitude and hour-angle ($\delta\gamma$ and δh), corresponding to errors δz and $\delta z'$ of the observed zenith distances.

Let, in the accompanying figure, Z and S be the correct places of the zenith and the star when the correct zenith-distance of the star is $z - \delta z$; and Z' and S' the places deduced from erroneous values of the zenith-distance.

EFFECT OF Z. D. ERRORS ON THE TIME AND COLAT. 115

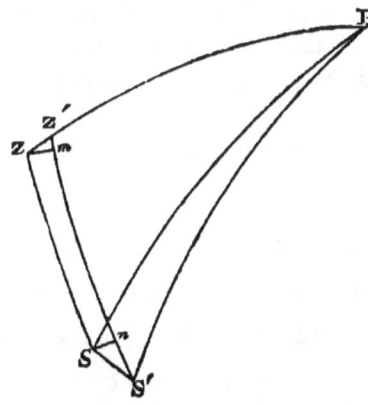

Then the error of the colatitude is $-\delta\gamma$; the correct colatitude γ being diminished by that quantity. Draw now Zm and Sn perpendicular to $Z'S'$.

Then $\delta z = Z'm + S'n$ very nearly,

$\quad = ZZ' \cos ZZ'm + SS' \cos SS'n,$

$\quad = -\delta\gamma \cos \text{south azimuth} + \delta h \sin \Delta \sin Z'S'P$

$\quad = -\delta\gamma \cos A + \delta h \sin A \sin \gamma.$

Similarly, at the second observation,

$$\delta z' = -\delta\gamma \cos A' + \delta h \sin A' \sin \gamma.$$

From which equations we can easily deduce

$$\delta\gamma = \frac{\delta z' \sin A - \delta z \sin A'}{\sin (A' - A)},$$

$$\delta h = \frac{\delta z' \cos A - \delta z \sin A'}{\sin \gamma \sin (A' - A)}.$$

Hence, for given error of zenith-distance, the effect on the colatitude and the time will be smaller in proportion as $\sin (A' - A)$ is larger; and therefore $A' - A$ should be as near $90°$ as possible, so that if one observation is made on the meridian, the other should be made near the prime vertical.

11. *To find the time by observing when two known stars have the same altitude or zenith-distance, the zenith-distance itself being unknown.*

116 *TIME BY OBSERVED EQUAL ALTI. OF TWO STARS.*

Let α and α', Δ and Δ' be the Right Ascensions and North Polar Distances of the stars; z their common zenith-distance; and h and h' their hour-angles, at the times t and t'.

Then
$$h - h' = 15\,(t' - t) - (\alpha' - \alpha) = d \text{ (suppose)}.$$

And we have
$$\cos z = \sin \gamma \cos h \sin \Delta + \cos \gamma \cos \Delta,$$
$$\text{and } \cos z = \sin \gamma \cos h' \sin \Delta' + \cos \gamma \cos \Delta',$$
$$= \sin \gamma \cos (h + d) \sin \Delta' + \cos \gamma \cos \Delta',$$
$$= \sin \gamma \cos h \cos d \sin \Delta'$$
$$\quad - \sin \gamma \sin h \sin d \sin \Delta' + \cos \gamma \cos \Delta',$$

therefore, by subtracting, we get
$$0 = \sin \gamma \cos h\,(\cos d \sin \Delta' - \sin \Delta) - \sin \gamma \sin h \sin d \sin \Delta'$$
$$\quad + \cos \gamma \cos \Delta' - \cos \gamma \cos \Delta,$$
or
$$(\cos d \sin \Delta' - \sin \Delta) \cos h - \sin d \sin \Delta' \sin h$$
$$= \cot \gamma\,(\cos \Delta - \cos \Delta')$$
$$= 2 \cot \gamma \sin \frac{\Delta' - \Delta}{2} \sin \frac{\Delta' + \Delta}{2}.$$

Let now ϕ be an arc such that
$$\cot \phi = \frac{\cos d \sin \Delta' - \sin \Delta}{\sin d \sin \Delta'}.$$

Then we have
$$\sin d \sin \Delta' \{\cot \phi \cos h - \sin h\}$$
$$= \frac{\sin d \sin \Delta' \cos (h + \phi)}{\sin \phi}$$
$$= 2 \cot \gamma \sin \frac{\Delta' - \Delta}{2} \sin \frac{\Delta' + \Delta}{2},$$
or
$$\cos (h + \phi) = \frac{2 \sin \phi \cot \gamma}{\sin d \sin \Delta'} \sin \frac{\Delta' - \Delta}{2} \sin \frac{\Delta' + \Delta}{2},$$

which equation determines $h + \phi$ and therefore h; and from this, knowing α the R.A. of the first star, the time of observation is immediately determined.

TIME BY TWO STARS IN THE SAME VERTICAL.

12. To find the time by observing when two known stars are in the same vertical.

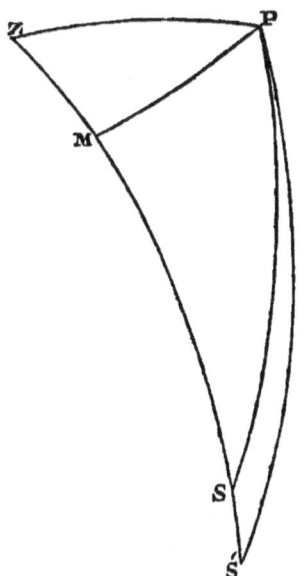

Let, in the accompanying diagram, S and S' be two stars (whose Right Ascensions and North Polar Distances are a, a', Δ, Δ' respectively) in the same vertical ZSS'. Let, as usual, h be the hour-angle for star S.

Draw PM perpendicular to ZS. Let angle $SPS' = a' - a = d$, and let angle $MPS = \phi$.

Then $\cos \phi = \tan PM \cot \Delta$,

and $\cos (\phi + d) = \tan PM \cot \Delta'$.

Hence
$$\frac{\cos (\phi + d)}{\cos \phi} = \frac{\cot \Delta'}{\cot \Delta},$$

or $\tan \dfrac{d}{2} \tan \left(\phi + \dfrac{d}{2}\right) = \dfrac{\sin (\Delta' - \Delta)}{\sin (\Delta' + \Delta)}$,

or $\tan \left(\phi + \dfrac{d}{2}\right) = \cot \dfrac{d}{2} \, \dfrac{\sin (\Delta' - \Delta)}{\sin (\Delta' + \Delta)}$,

which determines ϕ.

Again, in the triangle ZPM,

$\cos ZPM = \tan PM \cot \gamma$

or $\cos (h - \phi) = \cos \phi \tan \Delta \cot \gamma$,

from which h, and therefore the time of observation, is determined.

Some of the preceding problems for the determination of time must be considered, as they are here given, rather as exercises for the student, than as belonging to the direct theory or practice of Astronomy, though amongst them are found the methods in general use in the practice of Nautical Astronomy. If the student should wish for a more practical knowledge of these methods of determining time, he should consult Inman's or Raper's *Navigation*, and go through the actual computations of some of the examples.

13. Assuming so much of the theory of the Sun's motion in its orbit as to grant that it moves with a varying velocity, which has its maximum at perigee (the point nearest to the earth), and its minimum at apogee (the point farthest from the earth), and that perigee and apogee occur a little after the winter and summer solstices respectively, the following graphical illustration may be given of the variations of the equations of time.

Let t_1 and t_2 be the portions of the equation due respectively to the obliquity of the ecliptic and to the unequal motion in the ecliptic. Then the maximum value of t_1 is about 10 minutes of time, and that of t_2 is about $8^m.24^s$. Also, from an equinox to the following solstice, t_1 is negative, and, from a solstice to the following equinox, t_1 is positive; while, from perigee to apogee t_2 is positive, and, from apogee to perigee, it is negative.

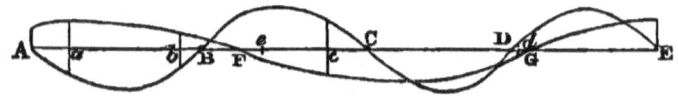

Let the tropical year be the line of abscissæ in the accompanying diagram, A and C being the times of the vernal and autumnal equinoxes, and B and D those of the summer and winter solstices. Let also F and G be the times of apogee and perigee. Then, the separate parts of the equation of time may be represented by the ordinates of two curves as drawn in the figure, the nodal points of the first being A, B, C, D, E (E corresponding to the next vernal equinox); and of the second, F and G; the maximum ordinates occurring half-way between the nodal points. Hence, it is plain that the equation of time will vanish at the four points a, b, c, d, where the positive and negative ordinates (marked in the figure) are equal to each other; and that the maximum value which occurs first after the summer solstice (as at e where the causes oppose each other), is much smaller than that next before the vernal equinox where the two causes act in the same direction.

CHAPTER VI.

ON THE CORRECTIONS TO BE APPLIED TO THE OB-SERVED PLACES OF THE HEAVENLY BODIES, ON ACCOUNT OF THE POSITION OF THE OBSERVER ON THE SURFACE OF THE EARTH, AND OF THE PROPERTIES OF LIGHT.

IN all that has preceded, though we have been obliged to make occasional reference to the corrections indicated in the title of this Chapter, yet it is generally assumed either that such corrections are not needed, or that they have been applied to the observed places. It is however now necessary, before proceeding farther, to develope the theory of them, as far as can be done in an elementary treatise like the present.

We will first consider the corrections which are required on account of the properties of light.

These are of two kinds, namely, 1st, those which arise from the refraction of the rays of light in passing from a heavenly body to the eye of the observer through the strata of the earth's atmosphere; and 2dly, those which arise from the progressive motion of light in coming from a heavenly body to the eye of the observer. The first class of corrections is comprehended under the term *Refraction;* the second under the term *Aberration*.

ON REFRACTION.

1. The earth is surrounded with an atmosphere of a variable density (the densest part being of course that nearest to the surface), and extending appreciably only a few miles beyond the

13. Assuming so much of the theory of the Sun's motion in its orbit as to grant that it moves with a varying velocity, which has its maximum at perigee (the point nearest to the earth), and its minimum at apogee (the point farthest from the earth), and that perigee and apogee occur a little after the winter and summer solstices respectively, the following graphical illustration may be given of the variations of the equations of time.

Let t_1 and t_2 be the portions of the equation due respectively to the obliquity of the ecliptic and to the unequal motion in the ecliptic. Then the maximum value of t_1 is about 10 minutes of time, and that of t_2 is about $8^m . 24^s$. Also, from an equinox to the following solstice, t_1 is negative, and, from a solstice to the following equinox, t_1 is positive; while, from perigee to apogee t_2 is positive, and, from apogee to perigee, it is negative.

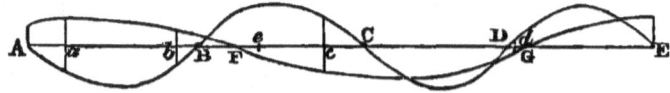

Let the tropical year be the line of abscissæ in the accompanying diagram, A and C being the times of the vernal and autumnal equinoxes, and B and D those of the summer and winter solstices. Let also F and G be the times of apogee and perigee. Then, the separate parts of the equation of time may be represented by the ordinates of two curves as drawn in the figure, the nodal points of the first being A, B, C, D, E (E corresponding to the next vernal equinox); and of the second, F and G; the maximum ordinates occurring half-way between the nodal points. Hence, it is plain that the equation of time will vanish at the four points $a, b, c, d,$ where the positive and negative ordinates (marked in the figure) are equal to each other; and that the maximum value which occurs first after the summer solstice (as at e where the causes oppose each other), is much smaller than that next before the vernal equinox where the two causes act in the same direction.

CHAPTER VI.

ON THE CORRECTIONS TO BE APPLIED TO THE OBSERVED PLACES OF THE HEAVENLY BODIES, ON ACCOUNT OF THE POSITION OF THE OBSERVER ON THE SURFACE OF THE EARTH, AND OF THE PROPERTIES OF LIGHT.

In all that has preceded, though we have been obliged to make occasional reference to the corrections indicated in the title of this Chapter, yet it is generally assumed either that such corrections are not needed, or that they have been applied to the observed places. It is however now necessary, before proceeding farther, to develope the theory of them, as far as can be done in an elementary treatise like the present.

We will first consider the corrections which are required on account of the properties of light.

These are of two kinds, namely, 1st, those which arise from the refraction of the rays of light in passing from a heavenly body to the eye of the observer through the strata of the earth's atmosphere; and 2dly, those which arise from the progressive motion of light in coming from a heavenly body to the eye of the observer. The first class of corrections is comprehended under the term *Refraction;* the second under the term *Aberration.*

On Refraction.

1. The earth is surrounded with an atmosphere of a variable density (the densest part being of course that nearest to the surface), and extending appreciably only a few miles beyond the

surface. With respect to this atmosphere we may assume that, supposing the temperatures to be the same at any two points at equal distances above the surface, and the densities at the surface to be the same, then the densities at these two points will be the same. Or, in other words, if the whole be in equilibrium, the atmosphere is arranged round the surface in concentric layers of equal density (or in *couches de niveau*).

Secondly, we may assume that the whole space through which a ray of light is refracted in arriving obliquely through the atmosphere at the eye of the observer, is exceedingly small, and that the refraction itself is also very small, so that when we have found the differential expression for the refraction, we may in the integration use very approximate values of the variables concerned.

Thirdly, since the density of the atmosphere varies continuously in going from the earth's surface, and since the amount of refraction depends upon the density, the ray of light will describe a continuous curve in passing through the atmosphere, and the object seen will appear in the direction of the tangent to the curve at the point where it enters the eye of the observer.

Fourthly, the angular difference between this tangential direction, and that in which the ray would have come in a straight line from the object to the eye, is the amount of the *Refraction*.

2. In proceeding to deduce the general expression for the path of a ray of light in passing through the earth's atmosphere, we may first remark that the amount of refraction depends not only upon the direction of the ray, but upon the densities of the strata of air through which it passes, and ultimately upon the density of the air at the surface as measured at a given temperature by the barometer; and, the direction being given, the refraction is assumed to *vary as the density*. In what follows we shall first assume that the refraction is calculated for some mean values of the pressure and temperature, and afterwards show how, from this *mean refraction*, the true refraction for any values of the pressure may be determined.

Since the time of Bradley, astronomers have generally calculated the *mean refraction* for the temperature 50° Fahrenheit, and for the pressure corresponding to the barometer-reading 29·6 inches.

It is assumed that the reader is tolerably familiar with the laws of the refraction of light, but for the sake of precision we may here state them briefly.

(1) When a ray of light travelling through any medium arrives at the surface of a medium of different density, it does not continue in a straight line, but is *refracted* or bent, but so as to remain in the same plane.

(2) If a normal be drawn to the common surface of the media at this point, then the sines of the angles formed with this normal by the two portions of the ray, before and after incidence, will be in a constant ratio, whatever be the value of the angle of incidence before refraction.

Thus if μ be the constant ratio, and Z and Z' the angles of incidence and refraction, we shall have $\sin Z = \mu \sin Z'$, where μ is called the *refractive index* for the two media.

$$\text{Let } Z = Z' + r;$$

$$\therefore \sin(Z' + r) = \mu \sin Z',$$

$$\text{or } \sin Z' + r \sin 1'' \cos Z' = \mu \sin Z' \text{ (nearly)},$$

$$\text{or } r = \frac{(\mu - 1) \tan Z'}{\sin 1''}.$$

And since, in the case of the atmosphere which we are considering, Z is approximately the zenith-distance of the object from which the rays of light come, we see that the refraction will *cæteris paribus* vary approximately as the tangent of the zenith-distance.

3. To form the general differential equation for the refraction of a heavenly body in zenith-distance.

Let AB be a section of the surface of the earth; C its centre; ZAC the vertical line to an observer at A.

Imagine now the atmosphere to be made up of a series of concentric layers of small thickness and uniform density, but that the density of each, and therefore the refractive index of each, increases from the outer boundary of the atmosphere to-

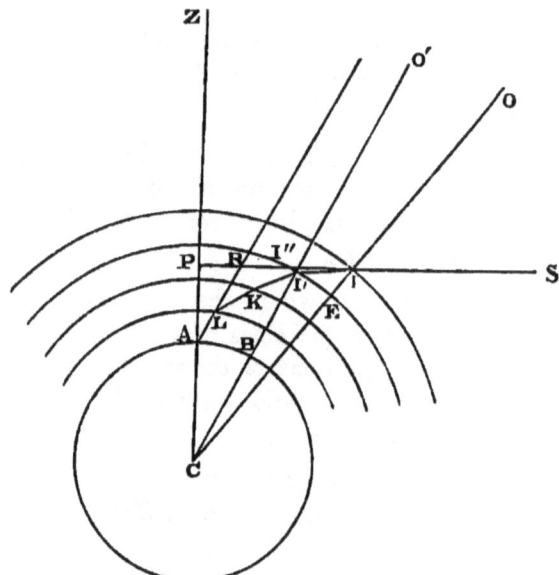

ward the surface of the earth; and let there be n such layers, the refractive indices being respectively

$$\mu_n, \mu_{n-1}, \mu_{n-2}, \ldots \mu_1, \mu_0.$$

Let also $SII'KLA$ be the path of a ray of light proceeding from the star S to the eye at A.

Join $CI (= r_n)$ and produce it to O, and let the first angle of incidence $OIS = \iota_n$, and let the others be denoted by ι_{n-1}, $\iota_{n-2}, \ldots \iota_0 (= z$ the apparent zenith-distance $ZAL)$, and let the other radii CI', &c., be denoted by

$$r_{n-1}, r_{n-2}, \ldots r_1, \text{ and } a \,(= CA).$$

Then $\dfrac{\sin \iota_n}{\sin I'IC} = \dfrac{\mu_{n-1}}{\mu_n}$,

and $\dfrac{\sin \iota_{n-1} \,(= \sin O'I'I)}{\sin I'IC} = \dfrac{r_n}{r_{n-1}}$;

$$\therefore \dfrac{\sin \iota_n}{\sin \iota_{n-1}} = \dfrac{r_{n-1} \mu_{n-1}}{r_n \mu_n}.$$

DIFFERENTIAL EQUATION OF REFRACTION.

Similarly, $\dfrac{\sin \iota_{n-1}}{\sin \iota_{n-2}} = \dfrac{r_{n-2}\mu_{n-2}}{r_{n-1}\mu_{n-1}},$

&c. = &c.

and $\dfrac{\sin \iota_1}{\sin \iota_0 (=\sin z)} = \dfrac{a\mu_n}{r_1\mu_1};$

therefore, by multiplication,

$$\dfrac{\sin \iota_n}{\sin z} = \dfrac{a\mu_0}{r_n\mu_n},$$

or $r_n\mu_n \sin \iota_n = a\mu_0 \sin z = $ a constant quantity.

Hence, generally,

$$r\mu \sin \iota = a\mu_0 \sin z \dots\dots\dots\dots(1).$$

Produce now SI to meet the vertical in P.

Then, since the star S is supposed to be at an infinite or very great distance, the lines PS and AS may be supposed parallel, and therefore ZPS is the true zenith-distance; also the refraction, that is the angle between the first direction, SRP and the last direction ALR, is the angle $PRA = \delta\theta$ (suppose).

Hence true zenith-distance ZPS

$$= z + \delta\theta.$$

Again, the angle $ZPI = $ angle $PIC + $ angle PCI

$$= \iota + v \text{ suppose};$$

$$\therefore z + \delta\theta = \iota + v,$$

and, differentiating, since z is constant (that is, is not concerned in the variations produced in passing from one medium to another),

$$d(\delta\theta) = d\iota + dv.$$

Farther, we have

$$\tan I''IE = \tan \iota = \dfrac{EI''}{IE}$$

$$= \dfrac{r dv}{dr} \text{ (at the limit)},$$

or $dv = \dfrac{dr}{r} \tan \iota.$

Hence, $d(\delta\theta) = d\iota + \dfrac{dr}{r} \tan \iota$.

But, by differentiating logarithmically equation (1), we have,

$$\frac{dr}{r} + \frac{d\mu}{\mu} + \cot \iota \, d\iota = 0,$$

or $\dfrac{dr}{r} \tan \iota + d\iota = -\dfrac{d\mu}{\mu} \tan \iota;$

$$\therefore d(\delta\theta) = -\frac{d\mu}{\mu} \tan \iota \dotfill (2).$$

But since, from (1),

$$\sin \iota = \frac{a\mu_0 \sin z}{\mu r},$$

and $\therefore \cos \iota = \sqrt{1 - \dfrac{a^2 \mu_0^2 \sin^2 z}{\mu^2 r^2}},$

$$\therefore \tan \iota = \frac{a\mu_0 \sin z}{\mu r \sqrt{1 - \dfrac{a^2 \mu_0^2 \sin^2 z}{\mu^2 r^2}}}$$

$$= \frac{\dfrac{a}{r} \mu_0 \sin z}{\sqrt{\mu^2 - \dfrac{a^2}{r^2} \mu_0^2 \sin^2 z}},$$

and therefore from (2),

$$d(\delta\theta) = -\frac{\dfrac{a}{r} \mu_0 \sin z \, d\mu}{\mu \sqrt{\mu^2 - \dfrac{a^2}{r^2} \mu_0^2 \sin^2 z}} \dotfill (A),$$

which is the general differential equation for the refraction, independently of any assumption as to the law of the variation of μ, that is, of the law of variation of density of the different strata of the atmosphere.

DIFFERENTIAL EQUATION OF REFRACTION.

4. La Place and others have assumed, following the steps of Newton, that if ρ be the density of the atmosphere, corresponding to the refractive index μ, and C a constant, then

$$\mu = \sqrt{1 + C\rho},$$

and $\therefore \mu_0 = \sqrt{1 + C\rho_0},$

ρ_0 being the density at the surface of the earth.

Hence
$$d\mu = \frac{\frac{C}{2} d\rho}{\sqrt{1 + C\rho}},$$

and the equation (A) becomes

$$d(\delta\theta) = \frac{-\frac{a}{r}\sin z \cdot \sqrt{1 + C\rho_0} \cdot \frac{\frac{C}{2} d\rho}{\sqrt{1 + C\rho}}}{\sqrt{1 + C\rho} \cdot \sqrt{1 + C\rho - \frac{a^2}{r^2}\sin^2 z (1 + C\rho_0)}}$$

$$= -\frac{\frac{a}{r}\sin z \cdot \frac{C}{2}\sqrt{1 + C\rho_0} \cdot d\rho}{(1 + C\rho)\sqrt{1 + C\rho - \frac{a^2}{r^2}\sin^2 z (1 + C\rho_0)}}.$$

Put now $\frac{a}{r} = 1 - s$, where s is a very small quantity, and

$$a = \frac{\frac{C}{2}\rho_0}{1 + C\rho_0}, \quad \text{or } C\rho_0 = \frac{2a}{1 - 2a},$$

and
$$1 + C\rho_0 = \frac{1}{1 - 2a},$$

and we shall then have

$$d(\delta\theta) = -\frac{(1-s)\sin z \frac{1}{\rho_0}\cdot\frac{\alpha}{1-2\alpha}\cdot\frac{d\rho}{\sqrt{1-2\alpha}}}{\left(1+\frac{2\alpha}{1-2\alpha}\cdot\frac{\rho}{\rho_0}\right)\sqrt{1+\frac{2\alpha}{1-2\alpha}\cdot\frac{\rho}{\rho_0}-(1-2s+s^2)\sin^2 z \frac{1}{1-2\alpha}}}$$

$$= -\frac{(1-s)\sin z \frac{\alpha}{\rho_0}\cdot d\rho}{\left(1-2\alpha+2\alpha\frac{\rho}{\rho_0}\right)\sqrt{1-2\alpha+2\alpha\frac{\rho}{\rho_0}-(1-2s+s^2)\sin^2 z}}$$

$$= -\frac{(1-s)\sin z \frac{\alpha}{\rho_0} d\rho}{\left\{\left(1-2\alpha\left(1-\frac{\rho}{\rho_0}\right)\right)\right\}\sqrt{\cos^2 z - 2\alpha\left(1-\frac{\rho}{\rho_0}\right)+(2s-s^2)\sin^2 z}} \quad \ldots \text{(B)},$$

which equation can only be integrated when the relation is known between ρ and s.

5. To integrate the equation given above according to the theories given by Newton, La Place, Bessel, Lubbock, &c. would scarcely fall within the limits of an elementary treatise. We shall therefore be contented with determining the amount of the refraction according to the theory of Thomas Simpson, which is not only simple and beautiful, but was made the basis of Bradley's Tables of Refraction, which were used for so long a time at Greenwich.

Simpson's assumption is that the refractive index diminishes, for all heights of the atmosphere above the surface of the earth, according to a law represented by the equation

$$\frac{a}{r}(=1-s) = \left(\frac{\mu}{\mu_0}\right)^m,$$

where m is a quantity to be determined by observations.

Substituting therefore in equation (A) we get

$$d(\delta\theta) = -\frac{\left(\frac{\mu}{\mu_0}\right)^m \mu_0 \sin z\, d\mu}{\mu\sqrt{\mu^2 - \left(\frac{\mu}{\mu_0}\right)^{2m}\mu_0^2 \sin^2 z}}$$

$$= -\frac{\frac{\mu^m}{\mu_0^{m-1}} \sin z \, d\mu}{\mu \sqrt{\mu^2 - \frac{\mu^{2m}}{\mu_0^{2m-2}} \cdot \sin^2 z}} = -\frac{\left(\frac{\mu}{\mu_0}\right)^{m-1} \sin z \, d\mu}{\mu \sqrt{1 - \left(\frac{\mu}{\mu_0}\right)^{2m-2} \cdot \sin^2 z}},$$

and, putting
$$\zeta = \frac{\mu^{m-1}}{\mu_0^{m-1}} \sin z,$$

and $\therefore d\zeta = \frac{(m-1)\mu^{m-2} \sin z}{\mu_0^{m-1}} \cdot d\mu,$

$$d(\delta\theta) = -\frac{1}{m-1} \cdot \frac{d\zeta}{\sqrt{1-\zeta^2}},$$

the integral of which is

$$\delta\theta = C - \frac{1}{m-1} \sin^{-1} \zeta$$

$$= C - \frac{1}{m-1} \sin^{-1} \left(\frac{\mu^{m-1}}{\mu_0^{m-1}} \sin z\right),$$

to be taken between the limits $\mu = \mu_0$, and $\mu = \mu$;

$$\therefore \delta\theta = \frac{1}{m-1} \left\{ z - \sin^{-1} \left(\frac{\mu^{m-1}}{\mu_0^{m-1}} \sin z\right) \right\}.$$

At the superior limit of the atmosphere, or, for a vacuum, $\mu = 1$.

Hence the whole refraction

$$r = \frac{1}{m-1} \left\{ z - \sin^{-1} \left(\frac{\sin z}{\mu_0^{m-1}}\right) \right\},$$

or, $\quad \sin\{z - (m-1)r\} = \frac{\sin z}{\mu_0^{m-1}},$

or, $\quad \dfrac{\sin z}{\sin\{z-(m-1)r\}} = \mu_0^{m-1},$

and hence

$$\tan\frac{m-1}{2}r = \frac{\mu_0^{m-1}-1}{\mu_0^{m-1}+1} \tan\left(z - \frac{m-1}{2}r\right) \quad \ldots\ldots\ldots\ldots \text{(C)}.$$

Or, since r is very small,

$$r = \frac{2}{(m-1)\sin 1''} \frac{\mu_0^{m-1}-1}{\mu_0^{m-1}+1} \tan\left(z - \frac{m-1}{2}r\right), \text{ very nearly.}$$

To determine the value of this constant (m), let $z = 90°$, and let R be the corresponding value of r, or the horizontal refraction.

Then
$$\tan\frac{m-1}{2}R = \frac{\mu_0^{m-1}-1}{\mu_0^{m-1}+1}\cot\frac{m-1}{2}R,$$

or,
$$\tan^2\frac{m-1}{2}R = \frac{\mu_0^{m-1}-1}{\mu_0^{m-1}+1},$$

where μ_0 is a quantity slightly greater than unity.

To expand this, we may proceed thus,

$$\frac{\mu_0^{m-1}-1}{\mu_0^{m-1}+1} = \frac{(1+\mu_0^2-1)^{\frac{m-1}{2}}-1}{(1+\mu_0^2-1)^{\frac{m-1}{2}}+1}$$

$$= \frac{\frac{m-1}{2}(\mu_0^2-1) + \frac{m-1}{2}\cdot\frac{m-3}{4}(\mu_0^2-1)^2 + \&c.}{2 + \frac{m-1}{2}(\mu_0^2-1) + \frac{m-1}{2}\cdot\frac{m-3}{4}(\mu_0^2-1)^2 + \&c.}$$

$$= \frac{m-1}{4}(\mu_0^2-1) - \frac{m-1}{8}(\mu_0^2-1)^2 + \&c.,$$

$$\therefore \tan^2\frac{m-1}{2}R = \frac{m-1}{4}(\mu_0^2-1) - \frac{m-1}{8}(\mu_0^2-1)^2 + \&c.,$$

or since, generally, $\theta = \tan\theta - \frac{1}{3}\tan^3\theta + \&c.,$

and
$$\therefore \theta^2 = \tan^2\theta - \frac{2}{3}\tan^4\theta + \&c.,$$

$$\left(\frac{m-1}{2}\right)^2 R^2 \sin^2 1'' = \frac{m-1}{4}(\mu_0^2-1) - \frac{m-1}{8}(\mu_0^2-1)^2 + \&c.$$

$$-\frac{2}{3}\cdot\frac{(m-1)^2}{16}(\mu_0^2-1)^2 + \&c.$$

$$= \frac{m-1}{4}(\mu_0^2-1) - \frac{2m^2+2m-4}{48}(\mu_0^2-1)^2 + \&c.$$

$$= \frac{m-1}{4}(\mu_0^2-1) - \frac{(m-1)(m+2)}{24}(\mu_0^2-1)^2 + \&c.$$

and $\therefore R^2 \sin^2 1'' = \dfrac{\mu_0^2-1}{m-1} - \dfrac{m+2}{6(m-1)}(\mu_0^2-1)^2 + \&c.$

and the values of μ_0 and R being known, we can, from this equation, determine the value of m.

6. To deduce Bradley's formula for the refraction, which is of the form
$$r = \frac{\beta}{\alpha} \tan(z - \alpha r).$$

Taking the equation
$$\frac{\sin z}{\mu_0^{m-1}} = \sin\{z - (m-1)r\},$$

we may write it thus,
$$a \sin z = \sin(z - br) \quad \ldots\ldots\ldots\ldots (a);$$

$$\therefore \frac{1-a}{1+a} = \frac{\tan\dfrac{br}{2}}{\tan\left(z - \dfrac{b}{2}r\right)},$$

or,
$$\tan \frac{br}{2} = \frac{1-a}{1+a} \tan\left(z - \frac{b}{2}r\right),$$

but, in equation (a), putting $z = 90°$, and $r = R$, we get
$$a = \cos bR,$$

and $\therefore \dfrac{1-a}{1+a} = \tan^2 \dfrac{b}{2} R.$

Hence $\tan\left(\dfrac{b}{2}r\right) = \tan^2\left(\dfrac{b}{2}R\right) \tan\left(z - \dfrac{b}{2}r\right),$

which, since r is very small, can be written
$$\frac{b}{2}r = \frac{b^2 R^2 \sin 1''}{4} \tan\left(z - \frac{b}{2}r\right);$$

or $r = \dfrac{bR^2 \sin 1''}{2} \tan\left(z - \dfrac{b}{2}r\right),$

which can easily be put into the form

$$r = \frac{\beta}{\alpha} \tan\left(z - \alpha r\right),$$

and hence the refraction varies very nearly as the tangent of the zenith-distance. The value of the constant $\frac{\beta}{\alpha}$ has been found by Bessel to be $57''\cdot538$, and Bradley assumed that α was equal to 3.

7. We have hitherto treated only of the *mean* refraction, that is, of the value of the refraction for mean values of the pressure and temperature of the air. As has been stated, the mean pressure is considered to be that corresponding to the barometric height 29·6 in., and the mean temperature to be 50° Fahrenheit. It is now necessary to show how to find the actual refraction corresponding to the barometric height b expressed in inches, and to any temperature t measured in degrees of Fahrenheit's scale.

Let the variations of pressure and temperature be considered separately and in order. Then since, by Mariotte's law, the pressure of the air varies within the atmospheric limits as the density, and that the refraction varies also as the density (Art. 2); therefore the refraction varies as the pressure, or as the height of the barometric column. Hence, if r_m be the mean refraction, then for barometer height b, and temperature 50° Fahrenheit, the true refraction is $\frac{b}{29\cdot6} r_m$.

Again, for the effect of change of temperature. It is found that between the boiling and the freezing points of the thermometric scale, that is, for 180° of Fahrenheit, a volume of air expands by very nearly three-eighths of its bulk. Hence, any quantity of air taken as the unit at the temperature 50°, would, at the temperature t, have expanded by about

$$\frac{3}{8} \cdot \frac{t - 50°}{180} = \cdot00208\,(t - 50°).$$

Or the volume would have expanded in the proportion of

$$1 : 1 + \cdot00208\,(t - 50°);$$

and therefore the density, and consequently the refraction, will have diminished in the same proportion.

Hence the preceding quantity $\frac{b}{29 \cdot 6} r_m$ must be multiplied by $\frac{1}{1 + \cdot 00208 (t - 50^\circ)}$, and the refraction for temperature t°, and barometric height b, becomes

$$\frac{b}{29 \cdot 6} \cdot \frac{r_m}{1 + \cdot 00208 (t - 50^\circ)}.$$

Hence generally the refraction, according to Bradley's formula,

$$= \frac{57'' \cdot 538}{1 + \cdot 00208 (t - 50^\circ)} \times \frac{b}{29 \cdot 6} \tan (z - 3r).$$

The expression given above will also require a correction for the expansion of the mercury between the temperatures 50° and t. This expansion has been found to be $\frac{1}{5500}$ part for every degree of rise of temperature as measured by the Centigrade Thermometer, or $\frac{1}{9900}$ part as measured by Fahrenheit's. Let this fraction be represented by c; then the preceding value of the refraction must be multiplied by

$$\frac{1}{1 + c (t - 50^\circ)} \text{ or by } 1 - c (t - 50^\circ) = 1 - \cdot 000101 (t - 50^\circ).$$

8. What has been given above will be sufficient to exhibit the principles on which the various theories of refraction are founded. For the complete integration of the general differential equation, and for the theory of Bessel, whose tables are generally preferred to any others, the English student may consult my translation of Brünnow's *Astronomy*.

There is also an excellent Prize Essay by Dr C. Bruhns[*], recently published, which gives the complete history of the subject, as well as the development of all the theories which have been proposed up to the present time.

---

[*] *Die Astronomische Strahlenbrechung in ihren historischen entwickelung dargestellt von Dr C. Bruhns.* Leipzig, 1861.

9. To determine the constant of refraction from observations of circumpolar stars*.

Let z and z' be the observed zenith-distances of the same circumpolar star at its upper and lower transit, and suppose that at its upper transit it passes very near the zenith. Let also $\alpha f(z)$ and $\alpha f(z')$ be the refractions. Then the true zenith-distances will be $z + \alpha f(z)$ and $z' + \alpha f(z')$, and the colatitude γ will be the half sum of these zenith-distances; that is,

$$2\gamma = z + z' + \alpha \{f(z) + f(z')\} \quad \ldots\ldots\ldots\ldots(1).$$

Similarly if z_1 and z_1' be the zenith-distances similarly observed, of another circumpolar star, we should have

$$2\gamma = z_1 + z_1' + \alpha \{f(z_1) + f(z_1')\} \quad \ldots\ldots\ldots\ldots(2),$$

and, eliminating γ between these equations, we should find

$$\alpha = \frac{z_1 + z_1' - (z + z')}{f(z) + f(z') - \{f(z_1) + f(z_1')\}}.$$

To use this method with effect it is plain that pairs of stars must be chosen differing considerably in zenith-distance, and therefore in N.P.D.

10. When an object is observed at its meridian passage, the whole effect of refraction in the direction of zenith-distance is also in the direction of N.P.D., the effect in Right Ascension being nothing. But if an object, such as a planet or comet, be observed at a distance from the meridian, expressions must be found for the parts of the refraction resolved in the directions of right ascension and North Polar Distance.

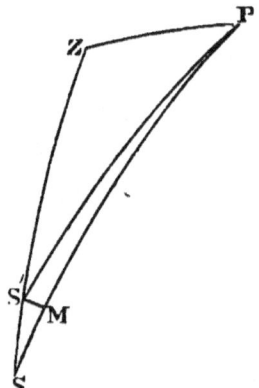

Let as usual Z and P be the zenith and pole of the heavens, and S the

---

* For the details of this method, as well as others, the reader may consult my Memoir on the Constant of Refraction, printed in Vol. XXVI. of the *Memoirs of the Royal Astronomical Society*.

true position of an object raised to S' by the amount of the refraction $S'S$.

Then is $S'S = \alpha \tan ZS'$, where $\alpha = 57''{\cdot}5$ nearly.

$\qquad = \alpha \tan ZS$ very nearly, in seconds of angle.

Draw $S'M$ perpendicular to SP;
therefore refraction in Right Ascension in seconds of time

$$= \frac{1}{15} \angle S'PS$$

$$= \frac{S'M}{15 \sin SP}$$

$$= \frac{S'S \sin S}{15 \sin SP}$$

$$= \frac{\alpha}{15} \cdot \frac{\tan z}{\sin \Delta} \sin S$$

$$= \frac{\alpha}{15} \cdot \tan z \sin P \frac{\sin \gamma}{\sin z}$$

$$= \frac{\alpha}{15} \cdot \frac{\sin P \sin \gamma}{\cos z \sin \Delta}$$

$$= \frac{\alpha}{15} \cdot \frac{\sin P \sin \gamma}{\sin \Delta (\cos P \sin \Delta \sin \gamma + \cos \Delta \cos \gamma)}$$

$$= \text{(if } \tan \phi = \cos P \tan \gamma \text{)}$$

$$\frac{\alpha}{15} \cdot \frac{\sin P \tan \gamma \cos \phi}{\cos (\Delta - \phi) \sin \Delta}.$$

Again, refraction in N.P.D.

$= SM = \alpha \tan z \cos S$

$$= \alpha \tan z \cdot \frac{\cos \gamma - \cos \Delta \cos z}{\sin \Delta \sin z}$$

$$= \alpha \frac{\cos \gamma - \cos \Delta (\cos P \sin \Delta \sin \gamma + \cos \Delta \cos \gamma)}{\sin \Delta (\cos P \sin \Delta \sin \gamma + \cos \Delta \cos \gamma)}$$

$$= \alpha \frac{\cos \gamma \sin \Delta - \cos P \sin \gamma \cos \Delta}{\cos \gamma \cos \Delta + \cos P \sin \gamma \sin \Delta}$$

$$= \alpha \tan \Delta \cdot \frac{1 - \cos P \tan \gamma \cot \Delta}{1 + \cos P \tan \gamma \tan \Delta}.$$

This may very easily be adapted to logarithmic computation in the following way.

Let ϕ be an angle such that $\cot\phi = \cos P \tan\gamma$; therefore refraction in N.P.D.

$$= \alpha \tan\Delta \cdot \frac{1 - \cot\phi \cot\Delta}{1 + \cot\phi \tan\Delta}$$

$$= \alpha \tan\Delta \cdot \frac{\sin\phi \sin\Delta - \cos\phi \cos\Delta}{\sin\phi \cos\Delta + \cos\phi \sin\Delta} \cdot \cot\Delta$$

$$= \alpha \cot\{180° - (\Delta + \phi)\}.$$

The method given above would be found laborious and troublesome when applied to every case in a series of observations made with the equatorial, and the following will be found preferable.

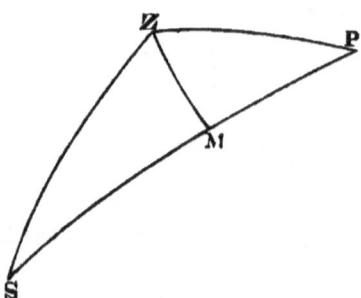

Draw ZM perpendicular to PS.

Then, as before, refraction in R.A. in seconds of time

$$= \frac{\alpha}{15} \cdot \frac{\tan z}{\sin\Delta} \sin S$$

$$= \frac{\alpha}{15} \cdot \frac{\tan z}{\sin\Delta} \cdot \frac{\sin ZM}{\sin z}$$

$$= \frac{\alpha}{15} \cdot \frac{\sin ZM}{\sin\Delta \cos z}$$

$$= \frac{\alpha}{15} \cdot \frac{\sin ZM}{\sin\Delta \cos ZM \cos SM}$$

$$= \frac{\alpha}{15} \cdot \frac{\tan ZM}{\sin\Delta \cos(\Delta - PM)}.$$

Again, refraction in N.P.D.
$$= a \tan z \cos S$$
$$= a \tan z \cot z \tan SM$$
$$= a \tan SM$$
$$= a \tan (\Delta - PM).$$

Now, for any given observatory, that is, for any given value of ZP, tables can be formed of the values of PM and log tan ZM for values of the hour-angle P at small intervals, and the computation then becomes very easy, and can be applied with great facility to a great number of observations. This is the method used at Greenwich.

It must be observed, however, that in strictness the apparent value of z should be used instead of the true value, as this method supposes, since the value of the vertical refraction is $a \times$ tan app. Z.D. But Bessel has given a table (Vol. x. No. 219 of the *Astronomische Nachrichten*), in which the argument for the refraction is the *true* zenith-distance, and, in general, since it is only the differential effect of refraction on the place of the planet or comet which comes into use, the difference of results is insignificant except in cases wherein the object observed is near the horizon.

11. The following problems are added rather as exercises for the student than as important in the theory of refraction.

(1) To find the refraction on Cassini's hypothesis, namely, that the atmosphere is of uniform density.

Let C be the centre of the earth; A the position of an observer whose zenith is Z, SDA the path of a ray coming from the star S, and refracted at the upper surface of the atmosphere.

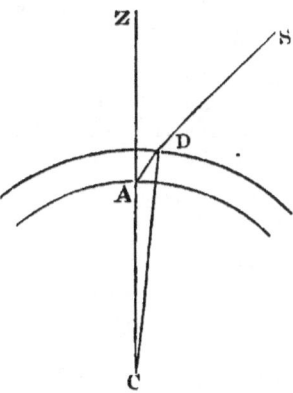

$ZAD = z$, the apparent zenith-distance; μ the index of refraction; $CA = a$.

Let also the height of the atmosphere be $n \times CA = na$.

Then we have seen (page 121) that, if r be the refraction,

$$r = \frac{\mu - 1}{\sin 1''} \tan CDA,$$

where μ is the refractive index out of air into vacuo, and does not differ greatly from unity.

Now $\dfrac{\sin ZAD}{\sin ADC} = \dfrac{CD}{AC} = 1 + n,$

or $\sin ADC = \dfrac{\sin z}{1 + n};$

$\therefore \cos ADC = \sqrt{1 - \dfrac{\sin^2 z}{(1+n)^2}}$

$\qquad = \dfrac{1}{1+n} \sqrt{\cos^2 z + 2n + n^2},$

and $\therefore \tan ADC = \dfrac{\sin z}{\sqrt{\cos^2 z + 2n + n^2}} = \dfrac{\sin z}{\sqrt{\cos^2 z + 2n}}$ (nearly)

$\qquad = \dfrac{\tan z}{\sqrt{1 + 2n \sec^2 z}} = \tan z (1 - n \sec^2 z)$

$\qquad = \tan z - n \tan z \sec^2 z.$

Hence refraction $= \dfrac{\mu - 1}{\sin 1''} (\tan z - n \tan z \sec^2 z).$

(2) To find the effect of refraction on the rising or setting of a star.

If, generally, h be the hour-angle; z and Δ the zenith-distance and N.P.D. of the star; and γ the colatitude; then

$$\cos h = \frac{\cos z - \cos \gamma \cos \Delta}{\sin \gamma \sin \Delta},$$

and $\sin h \, \delta h = \dfrac{\sin z \, \delta z}{\sin \gamma \sin \Delta}.$

At rising, $z = 90°$, and $\delta z = R$ the horizontal refraction.

EFF. OF REF. ON TIME OF RISING AND SETTING.

Hence $\cos h = -\dfrac{\cos \gamma \cos \Delta}{\sin \gamma \sin \Delta}$ and $\sin h = \sqrt{1 - \cot^2 \gamma \cot^2 \Delta}$;

$$\therefore \delta h = \dfrac{\delta z}{\sin h \sin \gamma \sin \Delta} = \dfrac{\delta z}{\sqrt{(1 - \cot^2 \gamma \cot^2 \Delta) \sin^2 \gamma \sin^2 \Delta}}$$

$$= \dfrac{R}{\sqrt{\sin^2 \gamma \sin^2 \Delta - \cos^2 \gamma \cos^2 \Delta}}$$

$$= \dfrac{R}{\sqrt{\cos(\Delta - \gamma) \cos(180^\circ - \Delta - \gamma)}}.$$

Hence the alteration of the hour-angle in time, or $\dfrac{\delta h}{15}$, is known.

COR. Let the star be in the equator, or $\Delta = 90^\circ$.

Then $\dfrac{\delta h}{15} = \dfrac{1}{15} \cdot \dfrac{R}{\sqrt{\sin^2 \gamma}} = \dfrac{R}{15 \sin \gamma}$.

If now we could observe the time t at which the star rose, and the time t' at which it set,

$$\text{then } t' - t - \dfrac{2R}{15 \sin \gamma} = 12^h,$$

from which R could be determined.

(3) To find the alteration produced by refraction on any diameter of the moon.

Assuming that for the extent of the lunar disk the differences of refraction are proportional to the differences of altitude, it is evident that the moon's disk will assume the form of an ellipse, the major-axis being horizontal. More properly it will consist of two semi-ellipses of different excentricities above and below the horizontal diameter.

Consider now the case of the semi-ellipse above the horizontal diameter or major-axis, which we take as the axis of x, the centre being the origin of co-ordinates.

Let a be the semi-axis major.

$a - r$ the semi-axis minor (r being the difference of refraction of the centre of the moon and the point of the limb immediately above it).

Then $y^2 = \dfrac{(a-r)^2}{a^2} (a^2 - x^2)$ (y being an ordinate at the distance x from the centre).

And, if R be any radius vector inclined at an angle α to the major axis,
$$y = R \sin \alpha,$$
$$x = R \cos \alpha,$$

or $\quad R^2 \sin^2 \alpha = (a-r)^2 - \dfrac{(a-r)^2}{a^2} R^2 \cos^2 \alpha,$

or $\quad R^2 = \dfrac{(a-r)^2}{\sin^2 \alpha + \dfrac{(a-r)^2}{a^2} \cos^2 \alpha}$

$\qquad = \dfrac{a^2 - 2ar}{1 - \dfrac{2r}{a} \cos^2 \alpha}$, very nearly,

$\qquad = a^2 \left(1 - \dfrac{2r}{a} \sin^2 \alpha\right)$, very nearly,

and $R = a \left(1 - \dfrac{r}{a} \sin^2 \alpha\right)$, very nearly.

Let now d be the true horizontal diameter of the moon, every point of which is apparently lifted up equally in a vertical circle by the refraction ρ.

Then $\quad \dfrac{\sin(z + \rho)}{\sin z} = \dfrac{d}{2a},$

or $\quad 1 + \rho \cot z = \dfrac{d}{2a},$

and $\therefore a = \dfrac{d}{2(1 + \rho \cot z)}$

$\qquad = \dfrac{d}{2}(1 - \rho \cot z);$

$\therefore R = \dfrac{d}{2}(1 - \rho \cot z)\left(1 - \dfrac{r}{a} \sin^2 \alpha\right).$

(4) To find the length of the twilight at any period of the year.

This is a problem which, though not immediately connected with atmospheric refraction, may properly be introduced here as analogous to that of the acceleration and retardation produced by the refraction in the rising and setting of a star.

If there were no atmosphere, none of the sun's rays could reach us after his actual setting or before his rising; but, by means of the atmosphere, a portion of the rays which before the rising and after the setting of the sun pass through the atmosphere near the surface of the earth are reflected by it and by the clouds and vesicles of moisture which it holds suspended, in an irregular manner, so as to illuminate objects on the surface, and thus is produced that subdued, and gradually increasing or diminishing light, called twilight.

It is generally considered that the twilight terminates, or absolute darkness takes place, when the sun is $18°$ below the horizon, though this determination is not susceptible of great accuracy.

Using the ordinary notation, if h be the hour-angle corresponding to the time of the termination of twilight, h' the hour-angle corresponding to sunset, and Δ the N.P.D. of the sun which determines the time of the year,

$$\cos h = \frac{\cos z - \cos \gamma \cos \Delta}{\sin \gamma \sin \Delta}$$

$$= -\frac{\sin 18° + \cos \gamma \cos \Delta}{\sin \gamma \sin \Delta},$$

and $\cos h' = -\dfrac{\cos \gamma \cos \Delta}{\sin \gamma \sin \Delta} = -\cot \gamma \cot \Delta.$

From which equations h and h' may be determined, and therefore $\dfrac{h - h'}{15}$, or the duration of twilight.

In summer the greatest depression of the sun below the horizon (at midnight) is equal to his N.P.D. (Δ) diminished by the latitude (λ) of the place of observation. Hence there will be twilight all night as long as $\Delta - \lambda$ is less than 18°.

(5) *To find the time of the year for a given latitude when the twilight is shortest.*

This problem is solved most conveniently by geometrical considerations.

Let Z be the zenith, P the pole, and S the sun at the commencement of twilight.

Then $ZS = 108°$.

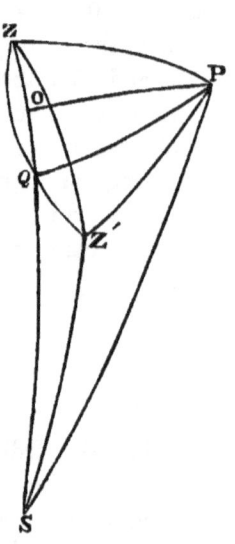

Draw the small circle ZQZ' round the pole P, and take $SZ' = 90°$.

Join ZZ' and PZ' by arcs of great circles.

Then PZ' = colatitude, $Z'S = 90°$, and PS = sun's N.P.D.

Hence $Z'PS$ is the hour-angle at sunrise, and ZPS at the commencement of twilight; and the angle ZPZ' corresponds to the duration of twilight; and is smallest when ZZ' is smallest.

This will manifestly be the case when Z' coincides with Q, the intersection of the great circle ZS with the small circle ZQZ', since ZZ' is never less than $ZS - Z'S$*. Hence we have this construction. Take $ZQ = 18°$, and let it intercept the small circle ZQZ' in Q; produce ZQ to S till $ZQS = 108°$. Then is S the position of the sun at the commencement of the shortest twilight, and PS is his corresponding N.P.D.

To find the value of PS, and of angle ZPQ.

Draw PO perpendicular to ZQ. Hence the triangle ZPQ is bisected, and $ZO = OQ = 9°$.

---

* Thus, $ZZ' + Z'S$ is always greater than ZS; ∴ ZZ' is greater than $ZS - Z'S$, till Z' lies in the same great circle with ZS, when $ZQ = ZS - QS$.

Hence $\sin ZO = \sin ZP \sin ZPO$,

or $\sin ZPO = \dfrac{\sin 9°}{\sin \gamma}$ ....(1).

Again, $\cos ZP = \cos PO \cos ZO$,

and $\cos SP = \cos PO \cos OS$;

$\therefore \dfrac{\cos SP}{\cos ZP} = \dfrac{\cos OS}{\cos ZO}$,

or $\cos \Delta = \cos \gamma \dfrac{\cos 99°}{\cos 9°}$

$\quad\quad\quad = -\cos \gamma \tan 9°$ ....(2).

Equation (1) gives the length of the shortest twilight, which is equal to $\dfrac{2}{15}$ angle ZPO; and (2) gives the value of the sun's N.P.D., which determines the time of the year when it occurs.

CHAPTER VI.

(PART SECOND.)

ON ABERRATION.

---

1. ABERRATION is the apparent displacement produced in the positions of the stars and other heavenly bodies by the progressive motion of light combined with the motion of the earth in its orbit.

2. The fact of the progressive motion of light was detected by the celebrated astronomer Roëmer by means of the observed times of the eclipses of Jupiter's satellites. By a great number of observations of the immersion and emersion of the satellites in the shadow of the body of Jupiter at various distances of that planet from the earth their motions were tolerably well known, and the time at which an eclipse of any one of them ought to happen could be predicted with tolerable accuracy. It was found however by Roëmer that when Jupiter was at a distance from the earth, considerably greater than his mean distance, the observed time of the eclipse was later than the predicted time, and that when he was nearer than the mean distance, the observed time was earlier than the predicted time. The inference from this fact is plainly that some time was expended during the passage of the reflected light from the satellite to the earth, or, that the motion of light is sensibly progressive, since, on that supposition, the time would be longer, the more distant the earth is from the planet.

From the best modern discussions it has been determined that the time taken by a ray of light to traverse a space equal to the mean distance of the earth from the sun is $8^m.18^s$.*

3. The illustrations which have been generally employed to explain the fact of the aberration of light are of the following nature:

1st. Supposing a traveller in a carriage with an open window in front, and that rain was falling vertically downwards. Then it is plain that the drops of rain falling immediately in front of the carriage would before reaching the ground be received into it; and the traveller, not attending to his own motion, would imagine that it was *beating* in or moving towards him with an inclined motion.

2ndly. Imagine a tube inclined to the vertical and moving forwards horizontally with a certain velocity, to be so placed as always to keep within it a ball falling vertically with a uniform velocity. Then it can be easily proved that the tube must be inclined from the vertical in the direction towards which it is moving, and at such an angle that the tangent of its elevation shall be equal to the velocity of the falling ball divided by its own velocity. Thus

Let AB be the tube at a given time, and let it move forwards to the position ab, in the horizontal direction Bb. Draw AC and ac in the vertical directions. Then if the ball be at this time in the tube, it must be at E the point of intersection of AC and ab.

Hence it has descended through the space AE or aD in the same time that the tube has described the space Bb or Cc or DE; and

$$\tan ABc = \tan aED = \frac{aD}{DE}$$

$$= \frac{\text{velocity of the ball}}{\text{velocity of the tube}};$$

* This is the value found by Professor W. Struve in his memoir entitled "*Sur le Coefficient Constant de l'Aberration des Etoiles Fixes.*" St Petersburg, 1843.

which determines the angle at which the tube must be held so that the ball may be always in it, and move along it.

3rdly. Imagine that a ship is passing a battery, and that a ball fired at her in the direction at right angles to her path, passes through her sides. It is evident then that it will pass through the side farthest from the battery farther astern than at the entering side, and the sailors not attending to their own motion will think that it was not fired correctly across their path but in a direction towards the stern of the vessel.

4thly. We now proceed, by considerations similar to the above, to explain the phenomena of the aberration of light.

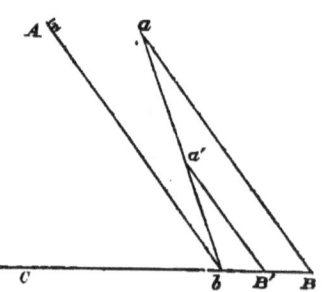

Let BC be the tangent to the earth's orbit at any point b: Bb an elemental arc of the orbit which ultimately coincides with the tangent at b, and is described uniformly with the velocity the earth has at b. Let also ab be the direction in which the light of a star (or other heavenly body) moves from the star to the earth at b. Also let a be the point at which the light has arrived when the earth is at B. Then, we can shew that as the line aB moves parallel to itself in consequence of the earth's motion, the light will pass over successive points of it, in its motion from a to b; and may therefore be said to *describe* the moving line aB.

For, if $B'a'$ be *any* intermediate position of Ba, cutting ba in a'; then,

$$\frac{BB'}{aa'} = \frac{bB}{ba} = \frac{\text{velocity of earth}}{\text{velocity of light}},$$

and therefore aa' is described by the light in the same time as BB' by the earth; and thus the light continually arrives at successive points of the fixed line ab, and the moving line aB, simultaneously; or, the light describes on its passage to the earth, the line aB, which moves with the observer.

This line aB is therefore the *apparent* direction in which the light comes from the star to the eye of the observer, or is the

VALUE OF COEFFICIENT OF ABERRATION. 145

apparent direction of the star: the angle between this and the real direction ab is called the aberration.

. Hence

$$\frac{\sin . \text{ aberration}}{\sin CBa} = \frac{bB}{ba}$$

$$= \frac{\text{velocity of Earth}}{\text{velocity of light}},$$

or, since this is a small fraction, and the aberration is therefore small,

$$\text{aberration} = \frac{\text{vel. of Earth}}{\text{vel. of light}} \cdot \frac{\sin CBa}{\sin 1''}$$

nearly, when expressed in arc.

It should be remarked that the angle CBa, formed by the line joining the Earth and star and that representing the direction of the Earth's motion, is called the *Earth's Way*.

4. To find the value of the *Constant Coefficient of Aberration*, or of $\dfrac{\text{vel. of Earth}}{\text{vel. of light} \times \sin 1''}$.

Let a represent the semi-axis major of the Earth's orbit, or the mean distance of the Earth from the Sun.

Then the velocity of light per second of time $= \dfrac{a}{498}$, since light takes $8^m . 18^s = 498^s$ in traversing a space equal to the radius of the Earth's orbit.

Also the mean motion of the Earth per day $= \dfrac{2\pi a}{365\frac{1}{4}}$, and therefore the mean motion per second

$$= \frac{2\pi a}{365\frac{1}{4} \times 24 \times 60 \times 60} = \frac{\pi a}{4383 \times 60 \times 60};$$

$$\therefore \frac{\text{vel. of Earth}}{\text{vel. of light}} = \frac{498\pi}{4383 \times 60 \times 60} = \frac{83\pi}{2629800},$$

also $\dfrac{1}{\sin 1''} = 206265.$

M. A.

Hence, coefficient of aberration

$$= \frac{83 \times 206265 \times \pi}{2629800}$$

$$= \frac{83 \times 206265\pi}{2629800} \text{ (where } \pi = 3\cdot 14159 \text{ &c.)}$$

$$= 20''\cdot 45.$$

The exact value which Struve has deduced for the constant of aberration is $20''\cdot 445$, corresponding to the time $8^m.17^s\cdot 78$ taken by a ray of light to traverse a space equal to the mean distance of the Earth from the Sun.

The value of the constant which I have myself deduced by a discussion of the observations made at Greenwich with the Reflex Zenith Tube, is $20''\cdot 335$*.

5. *To find the value of the aberration of a star with reference to any given plane.*

We have seen that the value of the aberration in general is $20''\cdot 45 \times$ sine Earth's way, and that it is estimated in the plane passing through the tangent to the Earth's path, or direction of the Earth's motion at the given time, and the line joining the Earth and star. Since however the distance of the star is infinite, this plane will be sensibly parallel to the plane passing through the line joining the Sun and star, and that drawn in the

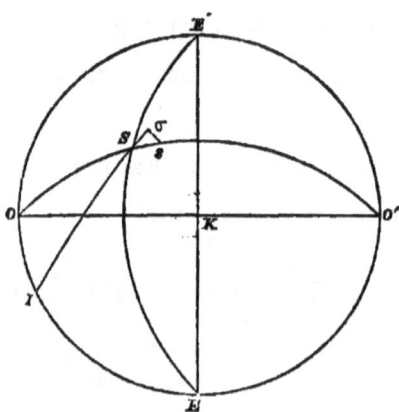

* See *Memoirs of the Royal Astronomical Society*, Vol. XXIX. p. 190.

ABERRATION IN LONGITUDE AND LATITUDE. 147

plane of the Earth's orbit through the Sun parallel to the tangent before mentioned.

Let E be the position of the Earth in its orbit $EOE'O'$ supposed circular.

Draw the diameter EKE', and OKO' at right angles to it. And, S being the place of the star, draw the great circles OSO' and ESE'. Then OS is evidently the Earth's way, and the aberration $Ss = 20''\cdot 45 \times \sin OS$. If then IS be the plane perpendicular to which the aberration is to be estimated, draw $s\sigma$ perpendicular to IS produced. Thus

$$s\sigma = Ss \sin S$$
$$= 20''\cdot 45 \sin OS \sin S$$
$$= 20''\cdot 45 \sin I \sin OI$$
$$= 20''\cdot 45 \sin I \cos IE.$$

6. To find the aberration of a given star in longitude and latitude.

Other things remaining as before, through K the pole of the ecliptic draw great circles KSA and KsA', and draw $S\sigma$ perpendicular to KA'.

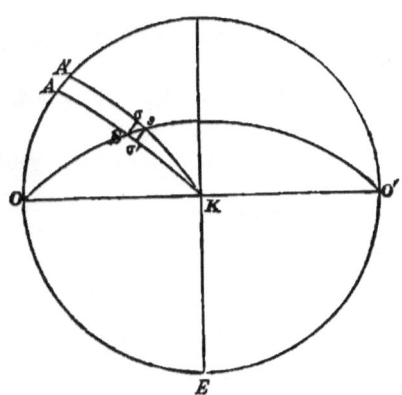

Then angle SKs is the aberration in longitude.

Now $SKs = -\dfrac{S\sigma}{\sin SK}$ (the aberration diminishing the longitude)

$= -\dfrac{Ss \cos \sigma Ss}{\sin SK}$

$= -\dfrac{20''\cdot 45 \sin SO \sin OSA}{\sin SK}$

$= -\dfrac{20''\cdot 45 \sin OA}{\cos AS} = +\dfrac{20''\cdot 45 \cos AE}{\cos AS}.$

Or, if λ be the latitude of the star, $\odot$ the longitude of the Sun ($=$ Earth's long. $-180°$), and l the longitude of the star,

Aberration in longitude $= +\dfrac{20''\cdot 45 \cos (180° + \odot - l)}{\cos \lambda}$

$= -\dfrac{20''\cdot 45 \cos (\odot - l)}{\cos \lambda}$ .... (1).

Again, aberration in latitude

$= s\sigma = 20''\cdot 45 \sin SO \cos OSA$

$= 20''\cdot 45 \cos OA \sin SO \sin O$

$= 20''\cdot 45 \cos OA \sin AS$

$= 20''\cdot 45 \sin \lambda \cos (AE - 90°)$

$= 20''\cdot 45 \sin \lambda \cos (180° + \odot - l - 90°)$

$= -20''\cdot 45 \sin \lambda \sin (\odot - l)$ .... (2).

Cor. If the Sun be in the vernal equinox, the circle OKO' passes through the pole of the equator, and therefore a star, whose longitude is $270°$, will also lie in this circle.

Thus $\odot - l = -270°,$

and aberration in latitude

$= -20''\cdot 45 \sin \lambda$

$= -20''\cdot 45 \cos (\Delta - \omega).$

And, since the star is displaced altogether in the solsticial colure EK, the aberration in latitude is equal to that in declination, and the aberration in right ascension vanishes.

Similarly, at the autumnal equinox, the aberration in declination

$$= + 20''{\cdot}45 \cos (\Delta - \omega).$$

7. To find the effect of aberration on the Right Ascension and N.P.D. of a star, in terms of α and Δ.

Let E be the Earth in the ecliptic, of which ΥE is a portion, Υ being the first point of Aries. ΥQ a portion of the equator, and P its pole. S the position of the star, and SS' the effect of aberration parallel to ΥQ, or perpendicular to the great circle PSs.

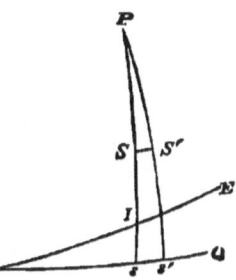

The obliquity of ecliptic $= \omega$ as usual.

Then, aberration in R.A. $= \dfrac{SS'}{\sin \Delta}$

$$= 20''{\cdot}45 \, \frac{\sin I \cos IE}{\sin \Delta}$$

$$= 20''{\cdot}45 \, \frac{\sin I \cos (\Upsilon E - \Upsilon I)}{\sin \Delta}$$

$$= \frac{20''{\cdot}45}{\sin \Delta} (\cos \Upsilon E \sin I \cos \Upsilon I + \sin \Upsilon E \sin I \sin \Upsilon I).$$

But $\sin I \sin \Upsilon I = \sin \alpha$,

$$\therefore \sin I \cos \Upsilon I = \sin \alpha \cot \Upsilon I$$
$$= \sin \alpha \cos \omega \cot \alpha$$
$$= \cos \omega \cos \alpha.$$

And $\Upsilon E =$ Earth's longitude

$$= 180° + \odot,$$

therefore aberration in R.A.

$$= \frac{20''{\cdot}45}{\sin \Delta} \{\cos (180° + \odot) \cos \omega \cos \alpha + \sin (180° + \odot) \sin \alpha\}$$

$$= - \frac{20''{\cdot}45}{\sin \Delta} (\cos \odot \cos \omega \cos \alpha + \sin \odot \sin \alpha).$$

Again, for aberration in N.P.D. (see accompanying figure), draw the great circle SMI perpendicular to PSs, meeting the equator produced in M, and the ecliptic produced in I, and let SS' be the aberration in N.P.D.

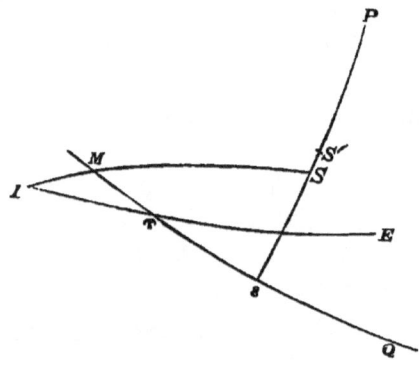

Then

$$SS' = +20''\!\cdot\!45 \sin I \cos EI$$
$$= +20''\!\cdot\!45 \sin I \cos (E\Upsilon + \Upsilon I)$$
$$= +20''\!\cdot\!45 (\cos E\Upsilon \sin I \cos \Upsilon I - \sin E\Upsilon \sin I \sin \Upsilon I).$$

But $\sin I \sin \Upsilon I = \sin M \sin \Upsilon M = \cos \Delta \cos a$, ($M$ being the pole of PSs),

and $\cos \Upsilon I = \dfrac{\cos M + \cos \Upsilon \cos I}{\sin \Upsilon \sin I}$

$$= \dfrac{\cos M + \cos \Upsilon (\cos M\Upsilon \sin M \sin \Upsilon - \cos M \cos \Upsilon)}{\sin \Upsilon \sin I}$$

$$= \dfrac{\cos M \sin \Upsilon + \sin M \cos \Upsilon \cos M\Upsilon}{\sin I};$$

$\therefore \sin I \cos \Upsilon I = \cos M \sin \Upsilon + \sin M \cos \Upsilon \cos M\Upsilon$

$$= \cos \omega \sin a \cos \Delta - \sin \omega \sin \Delta.$$

And aberration in N.P.D.
$$= +20''\!\cdot\!45 \{\cos (180° + \odot) \cdot (\cos \omega \sin a \cos \Delta - \sin \omega \sin \Delta)$$
$$- \sin (180° + \odot) \cos a \cos \Delta\}$$
$$= -20''\!\cdot\!45 \{\cos \Delta (\cos \odot \cos \omega \sin a - \sin \odot \cos a)$$
$$- \cos \odot \sin \omega \sin \Delta\}.$$

ABERRATION-CURVE. 151

8. To prove that the apparent place of a fixed star, as affected by aberration, describes in the course of a year an ellipse about the true place.

At the true place of the star let a tangent-plane be drawn to the sphere of the heavens, and take for the axes of x and y the lines of intersection of the circles of parallel and latitude with this plane. We may then assume that, for such small quantities as the aberration in longitude and latitude, this tangent-plane coincides with the spherical surface; and (referring to the figure on page 147) we shall have

$$x = s\sigma' = a \cos(\odot - l), \text{ (where } a = 20''\cdot 45),$$
and
$$y = s\sigma' = a \sin \lambda \sin(\odot - l).$$

Hence
$$\frac{x^2}{a^2} + \frac{y^2}{a^2 \sin^2 \lambda} = 1,$$

which is the equation to an ellipse, of which the semi-axis major is a and the semi-axis minor is $a \sin \lambda$.

If $\lambda = 90°$, or the star be in the pole of the ecliptic, $x^2 + y^2 = a^2$, which is the equation to a circle.

If $\lambda = 0$, then, since $x^2 \sin^2 \lambda + y^2 = a^2 \sin^2 \lambda$,

$$y = 0 \text{ for all values of } x,$$

or the whole effect of aberration is in a circle parallel to the ecliptic.

9. We have already deduced the values of the aberration in R.A. and N.P.D. in terms of α and Δ, it appears however to be desirable, for the benefit of the more advanced class of students, to give the investigation of Bessel, which is remarkable for its elegance and symmetry*.

Let a be the position of the eye of the observer, who sees a star in the apparent direction ba at the time t.

Let b be the position of a ray of light (coming from the star), at the time $t - \delta t$, and, in the interval δt, let the observer by the motion of the Earth be carried from a

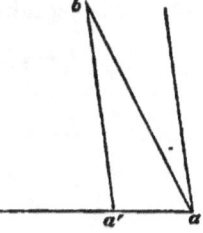

* See the *Tabulæ Regiomontanæ*, p. xvii; and also the Introduction to Carrington's *Red Hill Catalogue of Stars*.

to a' in a line sensibly straight. Then is ba' the *true* direction of the ray, and the angle $a'ba$ is the aberration.

Referring now the positions of the points a' and b to rectangular co-ordinates, let the plane of xz pass through the equinoctial points, and the plane of yz through the solsticial points, their intersection, or axis of z, being parallel to the Earth's axis. Suppose also x to be positive for right ascensions between $270°$ and $90°$, y positive for right ascensions between $0°$ and $180°$, and z positive for north declinations.

Let then, at time t, the co-ordinates of a' be x, y, z, and those of b, x', y', z'.

Then, at the time $t - \delta t$, the co-ordinates of a are

$$x - \frac{dx}{dt}\delta t, \quad y - \frac{dy}{dt}\delta t, \quad \text{and } z - \frac{dz}{dt}\delta t.$$

And, if $a'b = \lambda$, and the true and apparent R.A. and declination of the star be represented by α, δ; α', δ' respectively, we shall have

$$\left.\begin{array}{l}\lambda \cos \delta \cos \alpha = x' - x, \\ \lambda \cos \delta \sin \alpha = y' - y, \\ \lambda \sin \delta \phantom{{}={}} = z' - z,\end{array}\right\} \quad \ldots\ldots\ldots\ldots (\alpha).$$

Also, if $ab = \lambda'$,

$$\left.\begin{array}{l}\lambda' \cos \delta' \cos \alpha' = x' - x + \dfrac{dx}{dt}\delta t, \\[4pt] \lambda' \cos \delta' \sin \alpha' = y' - y + \dfrac{dy}{dt}\delta t, \\[4pt] \lambda' \sin \delta' \phantom{{}={}} = z' - z + \dfrac{dz}{dt}\delta t,\end{array}\right\} \quad \ldots\ldots (\beta).$$

And, if k be the time in which a ray of light describes the unit of distance, or the radius of the Earth's orbit, or $\lambda k = \delta t$, we get, by elimination between equations (α) and (β),

$$L \cos \delta' \cos \alpha' = \cos \delta \cos \alpha + \frac{dx}{dt}k, \quad \ldots\ldots\ldots (1),$$

$$L \cos \delta' \sin \alpha' = \cos \delta \sin \alpha + \frac{dy}{dt}k, \quad \ldots\ldots\ldots (2),$$

$$L \sin \delta' \phantom{{}={}} = \sin \delta + \frac{dz}{dt}k, \quad \ldots\ldots\ldots (3),$$

where $L = \dfrac{\lambda'}{\lambda}$.

BESSEL'S INVESTIGATION.

From these equations we readily find (by multiplying (1) by $\cos \alpha$ and (2) by $\sin \alpha$ and adding, and then multiplying (2) by $\cos \alpha$, and (1) by $\sin \alpha$, and subtracting)

$$L \cos \delta' \cos (\alpha' - \alpha) = \cos \delta + k \left(\frac{dy}{dt} \sin \alpha + \frac{dx}{dt} \cos \alpha \right),$$

$$L \cos \delta' \sin (\alpha' - \alpha) = k \left(\frac{dy}{dt} \cos \alpha - \frac{dx}{dt} \sin \alpha \right),$$

or

$$\tan (\alpha' - \alpha) = \frac{k \left(\frac{dy}{dt} \cos \alpha - \frac{dx}{dt} \sin \alpha \right)}{\cos \delta + k \left(\frac{dy}{dt} \sin \alpha + \frac{dx}{dt} \cos \alpha \right)}$$

$$= \frac{k \sec \delta \left(\frac{dy}{dt} \cos \alpha - \frac{dx}{dt} \sin \alpha \right)}{1 + k \sec \delta \left(\frac{dy}{dt} \sin \alpha + \frac{dx}{dt} \cos \alpha \right)}.$$

Let now $\frac{dy}{dt} \cos \alpha - \frac{dx}{dt} \sin \alpha = b \sin \theta$, where b is the Earth's velocity, then it is evident that $\frac{dy}{dt} \sin \alpha + \frac{dx}{dt} \cos \alpha = b \cos \theta$, since the sum of the squares is equal to $\frac{dx^2}{dt^2} + \frac{dy^2}{dt^2}$, which is equal to b^2.

Hence we have an equation of the form

$$\tan y = \frac{a \sin \theta}{1 + a \cos \theta}, \quad (\text{where } a = kb \sec \delta).$$

For $\sin y$ and $\sin \theta$ put the well-known values

$$\frac{e^{y\sqrt{-1}} - e^{-y\sqrt{-1}}}{2\sqrt{-1}} \text{ and } \frac{e^{\theta\sqrt{-1}} - e^{-\theta\sqrt{-1}}}{2\sqrt{-1}},$$

and for $\cos \theta$ put

$$\frac{e^{\theta\sqrt{-1}} + e^{-\theta\sqrt{-1}}}{2}.$$

Hence

$$\frac{e^{2y\sqrt{-1}} - 1}{e^{2y\sqrt{-1}} + 1} = \frac{\frac{a}{2} \left(e^{\theta\sqrt{-1}} - e^{-\theta\sqrt{-1}} \right)}{1 + \frac{a}{2} \left(e^{\theta\sqrt{-1}} + e^{-\theta\sqrt{-1}} \right)},$$

and
$$e^{2y\sqrt{-1}} = \frac{1 + ae^{\theta\sqrt{-1}}}{1 + ae^{-\theta\sqrt{-1}}},$$

or, taking the logs,
$$2y\sqrt{-1} = \log(1 + ae^{\theta\sqrt{-1}}) - \log_e(1 + ae^{-\theta\sqrt{-1}}),$$

whence, expanding the logarithms, we easily get
$$y = a\sin\theta - \frac{a^2}{2}\sin 2\theta + \frac{a^3}{3}\sin 3\theta - \&c.$$
$$= a\sin\theta - a^2\sin\theta\cos\theta, \text{ (to the second order)},$$

or $a' - a = k\sec\delta\left(\frac{dy}{dt}\cos\alpha - \frac{dx}{dt}\sin\alpha\right)$

$\quad - k^2\sec^2\delta\left(\frac{dy}{dt}\cos\alpha - \frac{dx}{dt}\sin\alpha\right) \times \left(\frac{dy}{dt}\sin\alpha + \frac{dx}{dt}\cos\alpha\right),$

or thus,
$$a' - a = -k\sec\delta\left(\frac{dx}{dt}\sin\alpha - \frac{dy}{dt}\cos\alpha\right)$$
$$+ k^2\sec^2\delta\left(\frac{dx}{dt}\sin\alpha - \frac{dy}{dt}\cos\alpha\right)\cdot\left(\frac{dx}{dt}\cos\alpha + \frac{dy}{dt}\sin\alpha\right) \quad \ldots\ldots (\gamma).$$

To obtain the value of $\delta' - \delta$, proceed thus:

Multiply (1) by $\sin\delta\cos\alpha$, and (2) by $\sin\delta\sin\alpha$, and add. We thus get
$$L\cos\delta'\sin\delta\cos(\alpha' - \alpha)$$
$$= \sin\delta\cos\delta + k\left(\frac{dx}{dt}\sin\delta\cos\alpha + \frac{dy}{dt}\sin\delta\sin\alpha\right),$$

also from (3),
$$L\sin\delta'\cos\delta = \sin\delta\cos\delta + k\frac{dz}{dt}\cos\delta.$$

Subtracting these equations (first dividing the first by $\cos(\alpha' - \alpha)$ and remembering that to the second order
$$\frac{1}{\cos(\alpha' - \alpha)} = 1 + \frac{1}{2}(\alpha' - \alpha)^2),$$

$$L \sin (\delta' - \delta) = -\frac{1}{2} \sin \delta \cos \delta \times (\alpha' - \alpha)^2$$
$$- k \left(\frac{dx}{dt} \sin \delta \cos \alpha + \frac{dy}{dt} \sin \delta \sin \alpha - \frac{dz}{dt} \cos \delta \right).$$

Again, multiply (1) by $\cos \delta \cos \alpha$, and (2) by $\cos \delta \sin \alpha$ and add; then

$$L \cos \delta' \cos \delta \cos (\alpha' - \alpha)$$
$$= \cos^2 \delta + k \left(\frac{dx}{dt} \cos \delta \cos \alpha + \frac{dy}{dt} \cos \delta \sin \alpha \right),$$

also $L \sin \delta' \sin \delta = \sin^2 \delta + k \dfrac{dz}{dt} \sin \delta.$

Therefore, in the same manner as before, we get

$$L \cos (\delta' - \delta) = 1 + \frac{1}{2} \cos^2 \delta \times (\alpha' - \alpha)^2$$
$$+ k \left(\frac{dx}{dt} \cos \delta \cos \alpha + \frac{dy}{dt} \cos \delta \sin \alpha + \frac{dz}{dt} \sin \delta \right);$$

$$\therefore \tan (\delta' - \delta)$$
$$= - \frac{\frac{1}{2} \sin \delta \cos \delta . (\alpha' - \alpha)^2 + k \left(\frac{dx}{dt} \sin \delta \cos \alpha + \frac{dy}{dt} \sin \delta \sin \alpha - \frac{dz}{dt} \cos \delta \right)}{1 + \frac{1}{2} \cos^2 \delta . (\alpha' - \alpha)^2 + k \left(\frac{dx}{dt} \cos \delta \cos \alpha + \frac{dy}{dt} \cos \delta \sin \alpha + \frac{dz}{dt} \sin \delta \right)},$$

and, expanding to the second power, and therefore for $\tan (\delta' - \delta)$ putting $\delta' - \delta$, and, for $(\alpha' - \alpha)^2$,

$$- k^2 \sec^2 \delta \left(\frac{dx}{dt} \sin \alpha - \frac{dy}{dt} \cos \alpha \right)^2,$$

we finally get

$$\delta' - \delta = - k \left(\frac{dx}{dt} \sin \delta \cos \alpha + \frac{dy}{dt} \sin \delta \sin \alpha - \frac{dz}{dt} \cos \delta \right)$$
$$- \frac{1}{2} k^2 \tan \delta \left(\frac{dx}{dt} \sin \alpha - \frac{dy}{dt} \cos \alpha \right)$$
$$+ k^2 \left(\frac{dx}{dt} \sin \delta \cos \alpha + \frac{dy}{dt} \sin \delta \sin \alpha - \frac{dz}{dt} \cos \delta \right)$$
$$\times \left(\frac{dx}{dt} \cos \delta \cos \alpha + \frac{dy}{dt} \cos \delta \sin \alpha + \frac{dz}{dt} \sin \delta \right) \ldots \ldots (\delta).$$

10. Take now the centre of the Sun as the origin of co-ordinates, and let $\odot$ denote the longitude (= Earth's longitude $-180°$) and ω the obliquity of the ecliptic. Then, remembering that the axis of x passes through the equinoxes, and that the plane of xy is the equator, we have

$$x = R \cos \text{Earth's longitude}$$
$$= -R \cos \odot,$$
$$y = -R \sin \odot \cos \omega,$$
$$z = -R \sin \odot \sin \omega,$$

when R is the Earth's distance from the Sun.

And
$$\frac{dx}{dt} = +R \sin \odot \frac{d\odot}{dt},$$
$$\frac{dy}{dt} = -R \cos \odot \cos \omega \frac{d\odot}{dt},$$
$$\frac{dz}{dt} = -R \cos \odot \sin \omega \frac{d\odot}{dt}.$$

Substituting these values in equations (γ) and (δ), and retaining only terms of the first order, we have

$$\alpha' - \alpha = -kR \frac{d\odot}{dt} (\sin \odot \sin \alpha + \cos \odot \cos \omega \cos \alpha) \sec \delta,$$

and
$$\delta' - \delta = +kR \frac{d\odot}{dt} \{\cos \odot (\sin \alpha \sin \delta \cos \omega - \cos \delta \sin \omega)$$
$$- \sin \odot \cos \alpha \sin \delta\},$$

where, if the Earth's orbit be supposed circular, we may put $R = 1$.

To obtain the value of the constant, $k \dfrac{d\odot}{dt}$, the mean arc described by the Sun in a day, or in 86400 seconds, is $59'.8''\cdot 33$.

Hence
$$\frac{d\odot}{dt} = 0''\cdot 04107,$$

and we have seen that $k = 498$.

Hence
$$k \frac{d\odot}{dt} = 20''\cdot 45.$$

And we have

$$\alpha' - \alpha = -20''{\cdot}45\,(\cos \odot \cos \omega \cos \alpha + \sin \odot \sin \alpha) \sec \delta,$$
$$\delta' - \delta = +20''{\cdot}45\,\{\cos \odot\,(\sin \alpha \sin \delta \cos \omega - \cos \delta \sin \omega)$$
$$- \sin \odot \cos \alpha \sin \delta\}.$$

11. The terms of the second order in the value of $\alpha' - \alpha$ will be

$$-\frac{k^2}{4}\left(\frac{d\odot}{dt}\right)^2 \sin 1''\sec^2\delta\,\{\cos 2\odot\,\sin 2\alpha\,(1+\cos^2\omega)$$
$$- 2\sin 2\odot \cos 2\alpha \cos \omega\},$$

of which the numerical value is

$$- 0''{\cdot}000933\,\sec^2\delta\,\sin 2\alpha \cos 2\odot$$
$$+ 0''{\cdot}000930\,\sec^2\delta\,\cos 2\alpha \sin 2\odot.$$

Similarly, the terms of the second order in the value of $\delta' - \delta$ will be

$$-\frac{k^2}{8}\left(\frac{d\odot}{dt}\right)^2 \sin 1''\tan \delta\,[\cos 2\odot\,\{\cos 2\alpha\,(1+\cos^2\omega)-\sin^2\omega\}$$
$$+ 2\sin 2\odot \sin 2\alpha \cos \omega],$$

of which the numerical value is

$$+\,(0''{\cdot}0000401 - 0''{\cdot}000468 \cos 2\alpha)\,\tan \delta \cos 2\odot$$
$$- 0''{\cdot}000466 \tan \delta \sin 2\alpha \sin 2\odot.$$

These terms may therefore in general be neglected for stars not nearer to the pole than $3°$.

12. The expressions for the aberration in longitude and latitude may be easily deduced from the preceding general formula.

Thus referring the co-ordinates to the plane of the ecliptic, and to a perpendicular to it,

$$x = -R \cos \odot,$$
$$y = -R \sin \odot,$$
$$z = 0,$$

and $\dfrac{dx}{dt} = + R \sin \odot \dfrac{d\odot}{dt}$,

$\dfrac{dy}{dt} = - R \cos \odot \dfrac{d\odot}{dt}$;

therefore if, in the general formulæ, we put l and λ in place of α and δ, we get

$$l' - l = - kR (\sin \odot \sin l + \cos \odot \cos l) \sec \lambda$$
$$= - kR \cos (\odot - l) \cos \lambda,$$

and $\lambda' - \lambda = - kR (\sin \odot \cos l - \cos \odot \sin l) \sin \lambda$
$$= - kR \sin (\odot - l) \sin \lambda,$$

in which, if the Earth's orbit be supposed circular, R may be put equal to unity.

13. Since the Earth revolves on its axis, the diurnal motion will of itself produce an aberration. This is called *Diurnal Aberration*, and its amount may be thus investigated.

Let λ be the latitude of the place of observation;

r the radius of the Earth supposed spherical.

Then the circumference of the circle of parallel at latitude λ will be $2\pi a \cos \lambda$, and the velocity per second of rotation of any point of it will be $\dfrac{2\pi r \cos \lambda}{86400}$.

Also velocity of light $= \dfrac{a}{498}$ (a being the mean distance of the Earth from the Sun).

Therefore the tangent of the angle of aberration (by which objects appear too far east, or come too late to the meridian) is

$$\dfrac{498 \times 2\pi r \cos \lambda}{86400 \times a} = \dfrac{\pi r \cos \lambda}{87 a} \text{ very nearly,}$$

$$= (\text{since } \dfrac{r}{a} = \dfrac{1}{23750} \text{ nearly}) \dfrac{\pi \cos \lambda}{2066250}$$

in parts of the radius.

Hence, in seconds of space,

$$\text{Diurnal Aberration} = \frac{\pi \cos \lambda \times 206265}{2066250}$$

$$= \frac{\pi \cos \lambda}{10\cdot0175} \text{ very nearly.}$$

EXAMPLE. For Oxford $\lambda = 51^\circ.45'$ nearly.

Hence $\log \pi = \log 3\cdot14159 = 0\cdot4971495$

$\log \cos \lambda = 9\cdot7917566$

Ar. co. $\log 10\cdot0175 = 8\cdot9992407$

$\log \text{ aberration } 9\cdot2881468$

aberration $= 0''\cdot194$

And the time of transit of a star whose declination is δ will be retarded by the quantity $\frac{0''\cdot194}{15} \sec \delta$.

And in the reduction of transit observations, the diurnal aberration, considered negative, must be incorporated with the error of collimation.

14. Hitherto we have treated only of the laws of the aberration of light for the fixed stars, that is, of the corrections to be made to the apparent directions of rays of light proceeding from bodies absolutely fixed, on account of the successive propagation of light combined with the motion of the Earth in its orbit. For the sun, moon, and planets, however, which have motions of their own, there is another effect quite distinct from the former, and having its origin in the circumstance that we see them in the directions which they had with respect to the Earth, when the rays by which they are rendered visible left them, and not in the direction which they really have when these rays enter the eye of the observer. That is, we always see them too late by the time required by light to traverse the space between them and us.

The mode of correcting for this error is very simple. Let t be the time when the rays by which a planet is rendered visible left its surface; t' the time of observation; D its distance from the Earth. Then (the Earth's mean distance from the Sun being the unit of distance) the planet is observed too late by the time $498^s \times D$, for 498^s is the time light takes to describe the distance from the Sun to the Earth, or

$$t' = t + 498 \times D,$$

the *apparent* place (as affected by aberration) at the time t' corresponding to the *true* place which it had at the time t. If then we wish to compare with observations the true places of a body interpolated from an Ephemeris of its daily motions, we need simply calculate the intervals of time corresponding to the quantity $498^s \times D$, and subtract them from the times of observation. The places interpolated for these times will thus correspond to the observed places without any further correction, the whole relative motion of the planet with respect to the Earth being taken into account by referring it to the Earth as the origin of co-ordinates.

If we wish however to obtain the *true* places of the object which has been observed, then the motion (whether of R.A. or N.P.D.) of the body for the time $498^s \times D$, computed from the tables of its daily motion, must be added to the observed or apparent places to obtain the true places at the times corresponding to t.

15. We must not leave the subject of Aberration without saying a few words respecting the history of its discovery by Bradley. For the purpose of observing the zenith distances of a few stars which pass the meridian near the zenith places not very far from Greenwich, he made use of a zenith sector which is still kept in good preservation at Greenwich. Fortunately one of these stars was γ Draconis, of the 2nd magnitude, and therefore likely to be observed very frequently. We have seen also (Cor. to No. 7 of this section) that stars which have the maximum amount of aberration in N.P.D. or in Z.D. must be situated at the pole of the ecliptic. Now the R.A. of γ Draconis is very nearly 18^h, and its N.P.D. equal to about $38°.29'$. Hence it is situated very near to the solsticial colure, and at a distance of only $15°$ from the pole of the ecliptic. It was therefore admi-

rably suited for investigation of the amount of the aberration, after the discovery of the phenomenon, and the inequalities which were produced in the places of the stars before its detection led Bradley to those sagacious speculations on the origin of the observed discrepancies which resulted in his grand discovery.

This will perhaps be seen most clearly by taking the expression for the aberration in declination previously investigated (10), namely,

$$\delta' - \delta = + 20''\cdot 45 \{\cos \odot (\sin \alpha \sin \delta \cos \omega - \cos \delta \sin \omega) - \sin \odot \cos \alpha \sin \delta\}.$$

At the vernal equinox, putting

$$\alpha = 18^h = 270°, \text{ and } \odot = 0,$$

we get
$$\delta' - \delta = - 20\cdot 45 (\sin \delta \cos \omega + \cos \delta \sin \omega)$$
$$= - 20\cdot 45 \sin (\delta + \omega)$$
$$= - 20\cdot 45 \cos (\Delta - \omega),$$

where $\quad \Delta = 90° - \delta = \text{N.P.D.},$

and, at the autumnal equinox, where $\odot = 180°$,

$$\delta' - \delta = + 20''\cdot 45 \sin (\delta + \omega)$$
$$= + 20''\cdot 45 \cos (\Delta - \omega),$$

or $\Delta - \Delta' = $ (at the vernal equinox) $- 20'''\cdot 45 \cos (\Delta - \omega)$
$\qquad\qquad = $ (at the autumnal equinox) $+ 20''\cdot 45 \cos (\Delta - \omega),$

as in Cor. Art. 7.

The star is therefore at the vernal equinox carried apparently farther from the pole of the equator by the quantity $20'''\cdot 45 \cos (\Delta - \omega)$, and, at the autumnal equinox, brought nearer to it by the same quantity.

The difference of the apparent values of N.P.D. or of Greenwich meridian N.Z.D. of γ Draconis, would be equal to

$$40''\cdot 9 \cos (\Delta - \omega)$$
$$= 40''\cdot 9 \cos (36°.29' - 23°.29')$$
$$= 40''\cdot 9 \cos 15°$$
$$= 40''\cdot 9 \times 0\cdot 966$$
$$= 39''\cdot 5.$$

Now the accuracy of Bradley's Zenith tube observations was pretty nearly equal to that attainable by instruments of modern times, and therefore even an error in the mean of several observations amounting to 1" or 2" was scarcely admissible. He therefore set seriously to work to determine the theoretical cause of these curious anomalies, and after several failures, and by the exercise of a patience and a sagacity beyond all praise, was rewarded by his famous discovery of the aberration of light.

CHAPTER VI.

(PART THIRD.)

ON PARALLAX.

---

1. IN all the preceding investigations we have supposed the places of the heavenly bodies to be such as would be determined by an observer situated at some point of the *surface* of the Earth; but ultimately it is necessary to reduce all such positions to those which would have been observed at the Earth's centre, both for the sake of comparison with places calculated from theory, and for the comparison of observations made at different stations.

The correction which it is necessary to apply to the observed place of a body on this account is called *Parallax*, and is evidently equal to the angle contained between the two lines drawn from the star to the centre of the Earth and to the place of observation.

For the fixed stars, which are generally at an infinite distance, this angle is inappreciable, but, in the case of all other bodies, including the Sun, the Moon, Planets, and Comets, the correction must be rigorously applied to the observed places before any theoretical use can be made of the observations.

2. Since the amount of the parallax of any object depends primarily on the distance between the observer's position on the surface of the Earth and its centre, it is plain that a knowledge of the size and figure of the Earth is necessary before we can proceed with the investigation of the laws of parallax, and the

present part of the treatise is therefore the most suitable for treating of this part of the subject.

3. *Determination of the Magnitude and Figure of the Earth.*

The Earth, though not accurately, is very approximately, a spheroid of revolution, with its axes very nearly in the proportion of 299 : 300, the shorter axis passing through the poles; and the quantity $\dfrac{300-299}{300} = \dfrac{1}{300}$ is called the *compression*. This we shall denote by e. That is, if a and b be the semi-axes major and minor of any elliptic section by a plane passing through the axis of revolution, $\dfrac{a-b}{a} = e$.

4. A tolerable approximation was made to the correct magnitude of the Earth by Eratosthenes of Samos, about 300 years before Christ, on the same principles as are now employed for the measurement. Imagine the Earth in the accompanying diagram to be a sphere; C its centre, A and B two points on the same meridian on its surface, and SA, $S'B$ rays (sensibly

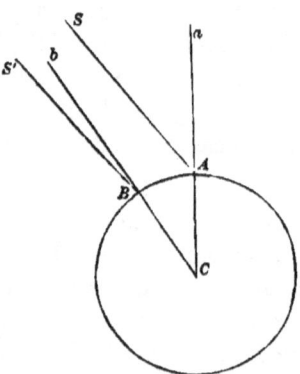

parallel), proceeding from a star or very distant body S in the plane BAC. Produce CA and CB to a and b. Then it is plain that the angle ACB is equal to the difference of the angles SAa and $S'Bb$, that is, to the difference of the meridian zenith distances of the object as observed at A and B.

Hence, if the length of the arc AB can be measured in terms of any known unit of length, and if the zenith distance of the object be observed simultaneously at A and B, we have the value of the radius AC in terms of known quantities by the equation

$$\pi \times AC = \frac{180°}{\angle BCA} \times AB.$$

Eratosthenes made use of two stations in Egypt, Alexandria and Syene, which he knew to be very nearly on the same meridian, and of which the distance was estimated at about 5000 stadia. He observed also that, on the day of the summer solstice, bodies at noon at Syene cast no shadow, that is, that the Sun was exactly vertical, while at Alexandria its distance from the zenith was about 7°.12'. Hence the arc of the meridian between Alexandria and Syene was 7°.12', or $\frac{1}{50}$th part of the whole circumference.

Hence therefore, the circumference of the earth expressed in stadia was $5000 \times 50 = 250{,}000$ stadia.

This investigation was very remarkable for the correctness of the principles on which it was based, though of course, the numbers are very erroneous.

5. The principle on which are based the methods used in modern times for measuring the magnitude and ellipticity of the earth is precisely the same, though the details are widely different. It would, for example, be totally impracticable to measure an arc of sufficient length along a meridian, and this is never attempted.

The first and most important part of the operation is the measure of a straight line called a *base line*, several miles in length, with very great accuracy, by means of compensation bars, which have been themselves carefully compared with some recognized standard of length, and which do not change their lengths under different temperatures. Each extremity of this base is very carefully marked by a dot or pin, and its azimuths at the extremities are carefully observed, that is, the angle which it makes with the meridian at each extremity. These points then form the commencement of a chain of triangles of which the angles are measured by means of a theodolite, the most conspicuous stations on each side of the arc of meridian which is to be measured, being selected. By the principles of spherical trigonometry, with some additional modifications introduced specially for geodetic operations, the sides of the triangles are successively computed, commencing with the measured base as the side of the first triangle.

When this has been done it is a mere matter of calculation to deduce from the measures the length of the arc of meridian included within their limits, another base for *verification* being measured before the close of the operations, and its measured value being compared with that deduced from calculation as a side of one of the triangles.

As a distinct part of the operation the zenith distances of the same star or of several stars are observed at the extremities of the arc to be measured, with a zenith-sector provided with every means for ensuring accuracy, and their difference gives accurately the angle formed, at the centre of the osculating circle to the elliptic meridian, by the verticals drawn through the extremities of the arc. Hence the length of a degree of arc can be determined at this point of the meridian, or the length of the radius of the osculating circle for the point corresponding to the middle of the arc can be determined.

6. If now two such arcs be measured, the one in a high northern or southern latitude and the other near the equator, we have the means of determining the value of the *compression* of the earth, or the ratio of the major and minor axes of the elliptic section in which the measures are made. We will now proceed to shew how this is effected.

Let x and y be co-ordinates of a point P of the elliptic meridian, connected by the equation

$$\frac{x^2}{a^2} + \frac{y^2}{b^2} = 1,$$

$\phi =$ the astronomical latitude of the point,

or inclination of the normal at P to the axis of x.

FORMULA FOR RADIUS OF CURVATURE.

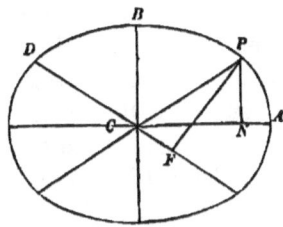

Then
$$x = \frac{a \cos \phi}{\sqrt{1 - \epsilon^2 \sin^2 \phi}},$$

$$y = \frac{a(1-\epsilon^2) \sin \phi}{\sqrt{1 - \epsilon^2 \sin^2 \phi}},$$

where $\epsilon =$ the ellipticity, or $1 - \epsilon^2 = \dfrac{b^2}{a^2}$.

Hence, employing the usual letters in the figure, the radius of curvature ρ, at the point x, y,

$$= \frac{CD^2}{PF} = \frac{CD^3}{PF \times CD} = \frac{CD^3}{ab}$$

$$= \frac{(a^2 - \epsilon^2 x^2)^{\frac{3}{2}}}{ab}$$

$$= \frac{\left(a^2 - \dfrac{a^2 \epsilon^2 \cos^2 \phi}{1 - \epsilon^2 \sin^2 \phi}\right)^{\frac{3}{2}}}{a^2 \sqrt{1 - \epsilon^2}}$$

$$= \frac{(a^2 - a^2 \epsilon^2)^{\frac{3}{2}}}{a^2 \sqrt{1 - \epsilon^2} (1 - \epsilon^2 \sin^2 \phi)^{\frac{3}{2}}}$$

$$= \frac{a(1 - \epsilon^2)}{(1 - \epsilon^2 \sin^2 \phi)^{\frac{3}{2}}}.$$

Now $\epsilon^2 = 1 - \dfrac{b^2}{a^2} = 1 - (1-e)^2 = 2e - e^2,$

$$\therefore \rho = \frac{a(1-e)^2}{\{1 - (2e - e^2) \sin^2 \phi\}^{\frac{3}{2}}}$$

$$= a(1-2e)(1 + 3e \sin^2 \phi) \text{ very nearly}$$

$$= a(1 - 2e + 3e \sin^2 \phi) \text{ very nearly.}$$

near the equator, the chief astronomers employed being Maupertuis, La Condamine, Bouguer, and Clairaut. In the time of the French republic, a large arc was measured, extending from Formentara, an island in the Mediterranean, to Dunkirk. In the great Indian survey also, conducted successively for the British Government by Colonel Lambton and Colonel Everest, a large arc of meridian was measured. Again, the triangulation of Russia has been admirably executed by Professor W. Struve, the director of the observatory of Poulkova, and that of Prussia by the celebrated Professor Bessel.

Finally, for complete discussions of all the measured arcs, we may refer to two admirable memoirs by Mr Airy and Professor Bessel, the first of which will be found in the Article on the "Figure of the Earth," in the *Encyclopædia Metropolitana*, and the other in Nos. 333 to 336, and No. 438 of the *Astronomische Nachrichten*.

Airy's results are:
    Equatorial diameter = 7925·648 miles,
    Polar diameter   = 7899·170 ...

Bessel's results are:
    Equatorial diameter = 7925·604 ...
    Polar diameter   = 7899·114 ...

From which we obtain very approximately $e = \dfrac{1}{300}$.

9. Let now C be the centre of the Earth; B the North Pole; and P a position on the surface in the meridian plane APB.

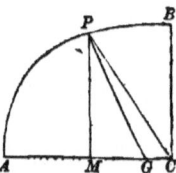

Join $PC = r$, and draw the normal PG.

Then is the angle $AGP (= \phi)$ the *astronomical latitude* of the point P, or that determined by observation; $ACP (= \phi')$

ANGLE OF THE VERTICAL.

is the *geocentric latitude*; and the angle $GPC (= AGP - ACP)$ is the *angle of the vertical*.

We will now proceed to obtain expressions for $\phi - \phi'$ and for r in terms of the latitude ϕ, and of the axes of terrestrial spheroid.

Draw PM perpendicular to AC.

Then $CM = x$.

and $GM =$ (subnormal $=$) $\dfrac{b^2}{a^2} x$,

Hence $\dfrac{\tan \phi'}{\tan \phi} = \dfrac{\frac{PM}{CM}}{\frac{PM}{GM}} = \dfrac{GM}{CM} = \dfrac{b^2}{a^2}$,

or $\tan \phi' = \dfrac{b^2}{a^2} \tan \phi$,

or $\dfrac{e^{\phi'\sqrt{-1}} - e^{-\phi'\sqrt{-1}}}{e^{\phi'\sqrt{-1}} + e^{-\phi'\sqrt{-1}}} = \dfrac{b^2}{a^2} \cdot \dfrac{e^{\phi\sqrt{-1}} - e^{-\phi\sqrt{-1}}}{e^{\phi\sqrt{-1}} + e^{-\phi\sqrt{-1}}}$,

or $\dfrac{e^{2\phi'\sqrt{-1}} - 1}{e^{2\phi'\sqrt{-1}} + 1} = \dfrac{b^2}{a^2} \cdot \dfrac{e^{2\phi\sqrt{-1}} - 1}{e^{2\phi\sqrt{-1}} + 1}$;

and $e^{2\phi'\sqrt{-1}} = \dfrac{(a^2 + b^2) e^{2\phi\sqrt{-1}} + a^2 - b^2}{(a^2 - b^2) e^{2\phi\sqrt{-1}} + a^2 + b^2}$

$= e^{2\phi\sqrt{-1}} \dfrac{1 + \dfrac{a^2 - b^2}{a^2 + b^2} e^{-2\phi\sqrt{-1}}}{1 + \dfrac{a^2 - b^2}{a^2 + b^2} e^{2\phi\sqrt{-1}}}$

$= e^{2\phi\sqrt{-1}} \dfrac{1 + m e^{-2\phi\sqrt{-1}}}{1 + m e^{2\phi\sqrt{-1}}}$,

where $m = \dfrac{a^2 - b^2}{a^2 + b^2}$.

And, taking the logarithms,

$$2\phi'\sqrt{-1} = 2\phi\sqrt{-1} + \log_e(1 + me^{-2\phi\sqrt{-1}}) - \log_e(1 + me^{2\phi\sqrt{-1}})$$
$$= 2\phi\sqrt{-1} - m(e^{2\phi\sqrt{-1}} - e^{-2\phi\sqrt{-1}})$$
$$+ \frac{m^2}{2}(e^{4\phi\sqrt{-1}} - e^{-4\phi\sqrt{-1}}),$$

or $\phi' = \phi - m\sin 2\phi + \frac{m^2}{2}\sin 4\phi - \&c.,$

or, in seconds of space,

$$\phi' = \phi - \frac{m}{\sin 1''}\sin 2\phi + \frac{m^2}{2\sin 1''}\sin 4\phi - \&c.$$

Now $m = \dfrac{a^2 - b^2}{a^2 + b^2} = \dfrac{1 - \dfrac{b^2}{a^2}}{1 + \dfrac{b^2}{a^2}} = \dfrac{1 - (1-e)^2}{1 + (1-e)^2} = \dfrac{2e - e^2}{2 - 2e + e^2}$

$$= \dfrac{e\left(1 - \dfrac{e}{2}\right)}{1 - e + \dfrac{e^2}{2}}$$

$$= e\left(1 - \frac{e}{2}\right)\left\{1 + \left(e - \frac{e^2}{2}\right) + \left(e - \frac{e^2}{2}\right)^2 + \&c.\right\}$$

$$= e\left(1 - \frac{e}{2}\right)\left(1 + e + \frac{e^2}{2}\right)$$

$$= e\left(1 + \frac{e}{2}\right) \text{ very nearly (the coefficient of } e^3 \text{ vanishing)}$$

$$= \frac{1}{300} \times \left(1 + \frac{1}{600}\right) = \frac{601}{180000}.$$

To calculate the coefficients, therefore, we have

Log 601 = 2·7788745
Ar. co. log 180000 = 4·7447275
Ar. co. log sin 1″ = 5·3144251
Sum = log 688″·70 = 2·8380271

VALUE FOR OXFORD.

Hence, the coefficient of sin 2ϕ, or the value of

$$\frac{m}{\sin 1''} = 688''\cdot 70 = 11'.28''\cdot 70.$$

To calculate the coefficient of

$$\sin 4\phi, \text{ or } \frac{1}{2}\left(\frac{m}{\sin 1''}\right)^2 \times \sin 1'',$$

$$\text{Log}\left(\frac{m}{\sin 1''}\right)^2 = 2\log\left(\frac{m}{\sin 1''}\right) = 5\cdot 6760542$$

$$\text{Log} \sin 1'' = 4\cdot 6855749$$

$$\text{Ar. co. log } 2 = 9\cdot 6989700$$

$$\text{Sum} = \log 1'''\cdot 150 = \overline{0\cdot 0605991}$$

Hence, generally,

$$\phi' = \phi - 11'.28'''\cdot 70 \times \sin 2\phi + 1'''\cdot 150 \times \sin 4\phi - \&c.$$

For the Radcliffe Observatory, Oxford,

$$\phi = \overset{\circ}{51}.\overset{'}{45}.\overset{''}{35};$$

$$\therefore 2\phi = 103.31.10 \quad \log \sin 2\phi = +9\cdot 9877961$$

$$4\phi = 207.\;\;2.20 \quad \log \sin 4\phi = -9\cdot 6576248.$$

Hence
$$\text{Log } 688''\cdot 70 = 2\cdot 8380271$$
$$\text{Log sin } 2\phi = 9\cdot 9877961$$
$$\text{Sum log } 669''\cdot 61 = \overline{2\cdot 8258232}$$

$$\text{And log } 1'''\cdot 150 = \;\;\;0\cdot 06060$$
$$\text{Log sin } 4\phi = -9\cdot 65762$$
$$\text{Sum} = -\log 0''\cdot 52 = \overline{-9\cdot 71822}$$

Hence $\phi' = \phi - 11'.9''\cdot 61 - 0''\cdot 52$
$$= \phi - 11'.10'''\cdot 13$$
or $\phi - \phi' = 11'.10'''\cdot 13$

which is the value of the angle of the vertical for the Radcliffe Observatory.

10. To find the value of $\log_e r$ in terms of cosines of multiples of ϕ.

The equation to the ellipse in polar co-ordinates is

$$\frac{\cos^2 \phi'}{a^2} + \frac{\sin^2 \phi'}{b^2} = \frac{1}{r^2};$$

whence
$$r^2 = \frac{b^2}{\sin^2 \phi' + \frac{b^2}{a^2} \cos^2 \phi'}.$$

Now $\tan \phi' = \frac{b^2}{a^2} \tan \phi$,

or $\tan^2 \phi' = \frac{b^4}{a^4} \tan^2 \phi$,

or $\frac{1 - \cos^2 \phi'}{\cos^2 \phi'} = \frac{b^4}{a^4} \tan^2 \phi$,

or $\cos^2 \phi' = \dfrac{1}{1 + \dfrac{b^4}{a^4} \tan^2 \phi}$;

$\therefore \sin^2 \phi' = \dfrac{\dfrac{b^4}{a^4} \tan^2 \phi}{1 + \dfrac{b^4}{a^4} \tan^2 \phi}$;

$\therefore r^2 = \dfrac{b^2 \left(1 + \dfrac{b^4}{a^4} \tan^2 \phi\right)}{\dfrac{b^2}{a^2} + \dfrac{b^4}{a^4} \tan^2 \phi}$

$= a^2 \dfrac{1 + \dfrac{b^4}{a^4} \tan^2 \phi}{1 + \dfrac{b^2}{a^2} \tan^2 \phi}$

$= a^2 \dfrac{1 + \dfrac{b^4}{a^4} \dfrac{1 - \cos 2\phi}{1 + \cos 2\phi}}{1 + \dfrac{b^2}{a^2} \dfrac{1 - \cos 2\phi}{1 + \cos 2\phi}}$

$= \dfrac{a^4 + b^4 + (a^4 - b^4) \cos 2\phi}{a^4 + b^2 + (a^2 - b^2) \cos 2\phi}.$

VALUE OF THE LOG. OF EARTH'S RADIUS.

Let now $a^2 + b^2 = \alpha$, and $a^2 - b^2 = \beta$; $a + b = \gamma$, and $a - b = \delta$;

$\therefore a^4 + b^4 = \dfrac{\alpha^2 + \beta^2}{2}$, $a^4 - b^4 = \alpha\beta$, $a^2 + b^2 = \dfrac{\gamma^2 + \delta^2}{2}$, $a^2 - b^2 = \gamma\delta$.

Let also $2 \cos 2\phi = x^2 + \dfrac{1}{x^2}$.

Hence
$$r^2 = \dfrac{\alpha^2 + \alpha\beta\left(x^2 + \dfrac{1}{x^2}\right) + \beta^2}{\gamma^2 + \gamma\delta\left(x^2 + \dfrac{1}{x^2}\right) + \delta^2}$$

$$= \dfrac{(\alpha + \beta x^2)\left(\alpha + \dfrac{\beta}{x^2}\right)}{(\gamma + \delta x^2)\left(\gamma + \dfrac{\delta}{x^2}\right)},$$

and, taking the logarithms,

$2 \log_e r = 2 \log_e \dfrac{\alpha}{\gamma} + \log_e \left(1 + \dfrac{\beta}{\alpha} x^2\right) + \log_e \left(1 + \dfrac{\beta}{\alpha x^2}\right)$

$\qquad - \log_e \left(1 + \dfrac{\delta}{\gamma} x^2\right) - \log_e \left(1 + \dfrac{\delta}{\gamma x^2}\right)$

$= 2 \log_e \dfrac{\alpha}{\gamma} + \dfrac{\beta}{\alpha} x^2 - \dfrac{1}{2} \dfrac{\beta^2}{\alpha^2} x^4 + \dfrac{1}{3} \dfrac{\beta^3}{\alpha^3} x^6 - \&c.$

$\qquad\qquad - \left(\dfrac{\delta}{\gamma} x^2 - \dfrac{1}{2} \dfrac{\delta^2}{\gamma^2} x^4 + \dfrac{1}{3} \dfrac{\delta^3}{\gamma^3} x^6 - \&c.\right)$

$\qquad + \dfrac{\beta}{\alpha} \dfrac{1}{x^2} - \dfrac{1}{2} \dfrac{\beta^2}{\alpha^2} \dfrac{1}{x^4} + \dfrac{1}{3} \dfrac{\beta^3}{\alpha^3} \dfrac{1}{x^6} - \&c.$

$\qquad\qquad - \left(\dfrac{\delta}{\gamma} \dfrac{1}{x^2} - \dfrac{1}{2} \dfrac{\delta^2}{\gamma^2} \dfrac{1}{x^4} + \dfrac{1}{3} \dfrac{\delta^3}{\gamma^3} \dfrac{1}{x^6} - \&c.\right)$

$= 2 \log_e \dfrac{\alpha}{\gamma} + 2 \dfrac{\beta}{\alpha} \cos 2\phi - \dfrac{2}{2} \dfrac{\beta^2}{\alpha^2} \cos 4\phi + \dfrac{2}{3} \dfrac{\beta^3}{\alpha^3} \cos 6\phi - \&c.$

$\qquad\qquad - \left(2 \dfrac{\delta}{\gamma} \cos 2\phi - \dfrac{2}{2} \dfrac{\delta^2}{\gamma^2} \cos 4\phi + \dfrac{2}{3} \dfrac{\delta^3}{\gamma^3} \cos 6\phi - \&c.\right),$

or $\log_e r = \log_e \frac{\alpha}{\gamma} + \left(\frac{\beta}{\alpha} - \frac{\delta}{\gamma}\right) \cos 2\phi - \frac{1}{2}\left(\frac{\beta^2}{\alpha^2} - \frac{\delta^2}{\gamma^2}\right) \cos 4\phi$

$$+ \frac{1}{3}\left(\frac{\beta^3}{\alpha^3} - \frac{\delta^3}{\gamma^3}\right) \cos 6\phi - \&c.$$

$$= \log_e \frac{a^2 + b^2}{a + b} + \left(\frac{a^2 - b^2}{a^2 + b^2} - \frac{a - b}{a + b}\right) \cos 2\phi$$

$$- \frac{1}{2}\left\{\left(\frac{a^2 - b^2}{a^2 + b^2}\right)^2 - \left(\frac{a - b}{a + b}\right)^2\right\} \cos 4\phi$$

$$+ \frac{1}{3}\left\{\left(\frac{a^2 - b^2}{a^2 + b^2}\right)^3 - \left(\frac{a - b}{a + b}\right)^3\right\} \cos 6\phi - \&c.$$

or, passing to the common system of logarithms,

$$\log r = \log \frac{a^2 + b^2}{a + b} + M\left[\left(\frac{a^2 - b^2}{a^2 + b^2} - \frac{a - b}{a + b}\right) \cos 2\phi\right.$$

$$- \frac{1}{2}\left\{\left(\frac{a^2 - b^2}{a^2 + b^2}\right)^2 - \left(\frac{a - b}{a + b}\right)^2\right\} \cos 4\phi$$

$$\left.+ \frac{1}{3}\left\{\left(\frac{a^2 - b^2}{a^2 + b^2}\right)^3 - \left(\frac{a - b}{a + b}\right)^3\right\} \cos 6\phi - \&c.\right]$$

where M is the modulus of the common system of logarithms, and $10 + \log M = 9\cdot6377843$.

11. We will now proceed to calculate the numerical values of the coefficients, as far as e^3.

First, we have $\dfrac{a^2 + b^2}{a + b} = a\,\dfrac{2 - 2e + e^2}{2 - e}$

$$= a\left(1 - \frac{e}{2} + \frac{e^2}{4} + \frac{e^3}{8}\right)$$

$$= a\left(1 - \frac{1}{600} + \frac{1}{360000} + \frac{1}{216000000}\right)$$

$$= a\,\frac{215640601}{216000000}.$$

VALUE OF THE LOG. OF EARTH'S RADIUS.

Next,
$$\frac{a^2-b^2}{a^2+b^2} = e\left(1+\frac{e}{2}\right),$$

and
$$\frac{a-b}{a+b} = \frac{e}{2-e} = \frac{e}{2}\left(1+\frac{e}{2}+\frac{e^2}{4}\right);$$

$$\therefore \frac{a^2-b^2}{a^2+b^2} - \frac{a-b}{a+b} = \frac{e}{2}\left(1+\frac{e}{2}-\frac{e^2}{4}\right)$$

$$= \frac{360599}{360000 \times 600} = \frac{1}{599 \cdot 003}.$$

Similarly,
$$\left(\frac{a^2-b^2}{a^2+b^2}\right)^2 = e^2(1+e),$$

and
$$\left(\frac{a-b}{a+b}\right)^2 = \frac{e^2}{4}(1+e);$$

$$\therefore \left(\frac{a^2-b^2}{a^2+b^2}\right)^2 - \left(\frac{a-b}{a+b}\right)^2 = \frac{3e^2}{4}(1+e)$$

$$= \frac{301}{36000000}.$$

And
$$\left(\frac{a^2-b^2}{a^2+b^2}\right)^3 = e^3,$$

$$\left(\frac{a-b}{a+b}\right)^3 = \frac{e^3}{8};$$

$$\therefore \left(\frac{a^2-b^2}{a^2+b^2}\right)^3 - \left(\frac{a-b}{a+b}\right)^3 = \frac{7}{8}e^3$$

$$= \frac{7}{216000000};$$

$$\therefore \log r = \log a + \log\left(1-\frac{e}{2}+\frac{e^2}{4}+\frac{e^3}{8}\right) + \frac{Me}{2}\left(1+\frac{e}{2}-\frac{e^2}{4}\right)\cos 2\phi$$

$$- \frac{3M}{8}e^2(1+e)\cos 4\phi + \frac{7M}{24}e^3\cos 6\phi$$

$$= \log a + \log 215640601 - \log 216000000 + \frac{M}{599}\cos 2\phi$$

$$- M\frac{301}{72000000}\cos 4\phi + \frac{7M}{24 \times 27000000}\cos 6\phi$$

$$= \text{(if } a=1 \text{, and therefore } \log a = 0\text{)}$$

$$9 \cdot 9992767 + 0 \cdot 0007250 \cos 2\phi - 0 \cdot 0000018 \cos 4\phi.$$

For the Radcliffe Observatory, Oxford, of which the latitude is 51°.45′.35″

$$\log r = 9 \cdot 9992767 - 0 \cdot 0001692 + 0 \cdot 0000016$$
$$= 9 \cdot 9991091.$$

12. To find the value of $\log r$ in terms of the geocentric latitude ϕ'.

Here we have

$$r^2 = \frac{a^2(1-\epsilon^2)}{1-\epsilon^2 \cos^2 \phi'}, \text{ (where } \epsilon \text{ is the } \textit{excentricity}\text{)}$$

$$= \frac{a^2(1-\epsilon^2)}{1-\frac{\epsilon^2}{2}\cos 2\phi' - \frac{\epsilon^2}{2}}$$

$$= \frac{a^2(1-\epsilon^2)}{a^2 - 2\alpha\beta \cos 2\phi' + \beta^2}$$

$$\left(\text{if } 1 - \frac{\epsilon^2}{2} = a^2 + \beta^2 \text{ and } \frac{\epsilon^2}{2} = 2\alpha\beta\right)$$

$$= (\text{as before}) \frac{a^2(1-\epsilon^2)}{(\alpha - \beta x^2)\left(\alpha - \frac{\beta}{x^2}\right)},$$

$$\therefore 2 \log_e r = 2 \log_e a + \log(1-\epsilon^2) - 2\log_e \alpha - \log_e \left(1 - \frac{\beta}{\alpha} x^2\right)$$
$$- \log_e \left(1 - \frac{\beta}{\alpha x^2}\right)$$

$$= (\text{by expanding the logarithms}),$$

$$2\log_e a + \log_e (1-\epsilon^2) - 2\log_e \alpha + 2\frac{\beta}{\alpha}\cos 2\phi' + \frac{2}{2}\frac{\beta^2}{\alpha^2}\cos 4\phi'$$
$$+ \frac{2}{3}\frac{\beta^3}{\alpha^3}\cos 6\phi' + \&c.$$

and $\log r = \log a + \frac{1}{2}\log(1-\epsilon^2) - \log \alpha$
$$+ M\left(\frac{\beta}{\alpha}\cos 2\phi' + \frac{1}{2}\frac{\beta^2}{\alpha^2}\cos 4\phi' + \frac{1}{3}\frac{\beta^3}{\alpha^3}\cos 6\phi' + \&c.\right)$$

in the common system of logarithms, where

$$10 + \log M = 9 \cdot 6377843.$$

13. By solving the equations

$$1 - \frac{e^2}{2} = \alpha^2 + \beta^2, \text{ and } \frac{e^2}{2} = 2\alpha\beta,$$

we find
$$\alpha = \frac{1 + \sqrt{1 - e^2}}{2} = 1 - \frac{e}{2},$$

and
$$\beta = \frac{1 - \sqrt{1 - e^2}}{2} = \frac{e}{2}.$$

Then, by substituting in the expression for $\log r$ we should find (correctly to e^3),

$$\log r = \log a + \log(1 - e) - \log\left(1 - \frac{e}{2}\right)$$
$$+ M\left\{\frac{e}{2-e}\cos 2\phi' + \frac{1}{2}\frac{e^2}{(2-e)^2}\cos 4\phi' + \frac{1}{3}\frac{e^3}{(2-e)^3}\cos 6\phi' + \&c.\right\}$$

$$= (\text{if } a = 1),$$

$$9\cdot 9992744 + M\left\{\frac{e}{2-e}\cos 2\phi' + \frac{1}{2}\frac{e^2}{(2-e)^2}\cos 4\phi'\right.$$
$$\left. + \frac{1}{3}\frac{e^3}{(2-e)^3}\cos 6\phi' + \&c.\right\}$$

$$= 9\cdot 9992744 + 0\cdot 0007250 \cos 2\phi' + 0\cdot 0000006 \cos 4\phi'.$$

To compute $\log r$ for Oxford by this formula,

we have
$$\phi' = 51°.45'.35'' - 11'.10''$$
$$= 51°.34'.25''$$
$$2\phi' = 103°.8'.50''; \log \cos = -9\cdot 35687$$
$$4\phi' = 206°.17'.40''; \log \cos = -9\cdot 64637.$$
$$\therefore \log r = 9\cdot 9992744 - 0\cdot 0001649 - 0\cdot 0000003$$
$$= 9\cdot 9991092$$

which agrees very exactly with the former value.

14. In some computations the values of the co-ordinates of the place of observation, x and y, are needed.

We have then $\quad x = r \cos \phi'$,

and $y = r \sin \phi'$,

or, for Oxford, $\quad \log x = \log r + \log \cos \phi'$
$$= 9{\cdot}7925563$$

and $\quad \log y = \log r + \log \sin \phi'$
$$= 9{\cdot}8930968$$

15. We may now proceed to the direct discussion of PARALLAX.

Let O be the position of the observer, and C the centre of the earth; S the position of a planet. Produce CO to meet

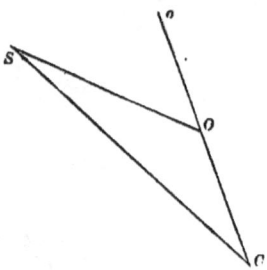

the sphere of the heavens in o; then is o the *geocentric zenith* of the observer.

Let the angle SCO, or the geocentric zenith-distance $= z$,

.... SOo, or true distance from geocentric zenith
$$= z + p.$$
Then is p the parallax of the body in zenith-distance.

Let $SC = D$ and $CO = r$;

then $\dfrac{CO}{SC} = \dfrac{\sin OSC}{\sin SOo}$;

or $\dfrac{r}{D} = \dfrac{\sin p}{\sin (p+z)}$;

$\therefore \sin p = \dfrac{r}{D} \sin (p+z) = \dfrac{r}{D} \sin z'$, where $z' = z + p$.

Let now P represent the horizontal parallax for a station on the earth's equator, or the *Horizontal Equatorial Parallax*.

FORMULÆ FOR PLANETS AND THE MOON.

Then $z' = 90°$ and $r = a$;

$$\therefore \sin P = \frac{a}{D};$$

and $\dfrac{\sin p}{\sin P} = \dfrac{r}{a} \sin z'$,

or $\sin p = \dfrac{r}{a} \sin P \sin z'$.

For the planets, p is always a very small quantity, never exceeding a few seconds of space, and we may with the utmost accuracy, put p for $\sin p$ and P for $\sin P$.

Hence $\quad p = \dfrac{r}{a} P \sin z'$;

where z', in every case of meridian observations, is given by the observation of zenith-distance, the observed zenith-distance, corrected for refraction, being diminished by the angle of the vertical.

For the moon this process is scarcely correct enough, but we can easily deduce a correction which will make the same formula applicable.

Let $\quad \sin p = \alpha \sin P \sin z'$,

and, as a first approximation, let

$$p = \alpha P \sin z'.$$

Then, since $\quad \sin p = p - \dfrac{p^3}{1 . 2 . 3} + \&c.$

and $\quad \sin P = P - \dfrac{P^3}{1 . 2 . 3} + \&c.$

$$p - \frac{p^3}{1 . 2 . 3} = \alpha \sin z' \left(P - \frac{P^3}{1 . 2 . 3} \right),$$

and, substituting for p in the small term $\dfrac{p^3}{1 . 2 . 3}$ its approximate value $\alpha \sin z' \times P$,

we have, $\quad p - \dfrac{\alpha^3 \sin^3 z' \times P^3}{6} = \alpha \sin z' \times P - \dfrac{\alpha \sin z' \times P^3}{6}$;

$$\therefore p = aP \sin z' - \frac{aP^3}{6} \sin z' (1 - a^2 \sin^2 z')$$

$$= \text{(since } a = 1 \text{ very nearly)}$$

$$aP \sin z' - \frac{aP^3}{6} \sin z' \cos^2 z',$$

or, since p and P must be expressed in seconds of space,

$$p'' \sin 1'' = aP'' \sin z' \sin 1'' - \frac{aP''^3}{6} \sin z' \cos^2 z' \times \sin^3 1'';$$

$$\therefore p'' = aP'' \sin z' - \frac{aP''^3}{6} \sin z' \cos^2 z' \sin^2 1'' ;$$

where, as we have seen (page 178) log $a =$ (for Oxford) 9·9991091.

As this more accurate formula is only needed for the moon, we may put, in the small term on the second side of the equation, for P, the mean value of the moon's Horizontal Equatorial Parallax, or $57' = 3420''$. We shall then find that the logarithm of the value of the factor $\dfrac{aP^2}{6} \sin^2 1''$ is 9·19418,

or $\dfrac{aP^2}{6} \sin^2 1'' = [9\cdot19418]$ according to the usual notation.

Hence $p'' = aP'' \sin z' - 0''\cdot156 \sin z' \cos^2 z'$.

The second term of the right-hand side of the equation may be computed for convenient intervals of zenith-distance. If we take values of z' for every 5° of zenith-distance from $z' = 10°$ to $z' = 90°$, the table will be as follows:

z'	Correction.	z'	Correction.
°	''	°	''
10	−0·026	50	−0·050
15	·038	55	·042
20	·047	60	·034
25	·054	65	·025
30	·059	70	·017
35	·060	75	·010
40	·059	80	·005
45	−0·055	85	−0·001

TABULATED RATIOS OF SIN TO ARC.

We might also proceed thus:

$$\sin p = a \sin P \sin z',$$

or $p\left(\dfrac{\sin p}{p}\right) = aP\left(\dfrac{\sin P}{P}\right)\sin z',$

$$\therefore p = aP\left(\dfrac{p}{\sin p}\right)\left(\dfrac{\sin P}{P}\right)\sin z';$$

(an approximate value of p being used on the right-hand side of the equation) and we might then tabulate the values of $\left(\dfrac{p}{\sin p}\right)$ and $\left(\dfrac{\sin P}{P}\right)$ or of their logarithms, between the limiting values in the case of the moon.

The following is the table which would be required.

Arc	Log$\left(\frac{\text{Arc}}{\text{Sin}}\right)$	Arc	Log$\left(\frac{\text{Arc}}{\text{Sin}}\right)$	Arc	Log$\left(\frac{\text{Arc}}{\text{Sin}}\right)$	Arc	Log$\left(\frac{\text{Arc}}{\text{Sin}}\right)$
16′	0·0000016	31′	0·0000058	46′	0·0000129	61′	0·0000228
17	18	32	62	47	135	62	235
18	20	33	66	48	141	63	243
19	22	34	70	49	147	64	251
20	24	35	74	50	153	65	259
21	26	36	78	51	159	66	267
22	29	37	83	52	165	67	276
23	32	38	88	53	171	68	284
24	35	39	93	54	178	69	292
25	38	40	98	55	185	70	0·0000301
26	41	41	103	56	192		
27	44	42	108	57	199		
28	47	43	113	58	206		
29	51	44	118	59	213		
30	0·0000055	45	0·0000124	60	0·0000221		

The values of $\log\left(\dfrac{\sin}{\text{arc}}\right)$ are the reciprocals of $\log\left(\dfrac{\text{arc}}{\sin}\right)$ or are equal to $10 - \log\left(\dfrac{\text{arc}}{\sin}\right)$, and it is therefore unnecessary to exhibit them in the table. It would be however convenient in practice, for the sake of taking out readily from the Table the values of $\left(\frac{p}{\sin p}\right)$, to add as another argument the approximate logarithm of the number of seconds of "Arc."

Or, we may proceed thus:

$$\text{generally, } \sin p = p - \frac{p^3}{6} + \&c.;$$

$$\therefore \frac{\sin p}{p} = 1 - \frac{p^2}{6}$$

$$= 1 - \frac{1}{3}\frac{p^2}{2}$$

$$= \left(1 - \frac{p^2}{2}\right)^{\frac{1}{3}}$$

$$= \sqrt[3]{\cos p} \text{ nearly,}$$

$$\text{and } p = aP\frac{\sqrt[3]{\cos P}}{\sqrt[3]{\cos p}}\sin z'.$$

Thus, if $P = 54'$, $\log \cos P = 9\cdot9999464$;

$$\therefore \log \sqrt[3]{\cos P} = 9\cdot9999821,$$

essentially the same value as the reciprocal of that taken from the Table for

$$\log \frac{\text{circ. measure of } 54'}{\sin 54'}.$$

16. In observing the moon's zenith-distance, it is of course necessary to observe that of the upper or lower limb, and the parallax must be calculated for the part of the limb observed. In this case, supposing a plane to be drawn through the Earth's radius for the place of observation, and through the centre of the moon, and in this plane tangents from the Earth's centre and from the plane of observation to be drawn to the section of the moon made by this plane, then the inclination of these two lines will represent the parallax which is to be applied to the observed zenith-distance of the limb. This involves a correction to the horizontal parallax amounting at the maximum to about

PARALLAX IN TERMS OF GEOC. ZEN. DIST. 185

a tenth of a second, but it is scarcely necessary to give the investigation in this place. The reader may consult the *Greenwich Observations* for 1847, or subsequent volumes, for the investigation of this minute correction, and for its tabulated amount.

17. Thus far the parallax has been considered as a function of the true zenith-distance. If we consider it as a function of the geocentric zenith-distance, we must take the equation

$$\sin p = \alpha \sin P \sin(z + p).$$

To expand p in terms of $\sin z$, $\sin^2 z$, &c.,

$$\text{put } \sin p = \frac{e^{p\sqrt{-1}} - e^{-p\sqrt{-1}}}{2\sqrt{-1}},$$

$$\sin(z + p) = \frac{e^{(z+p)\sqrt{-1}} - e^{-(z+p)\sqrt{-1}}}{2\sqrt{-1}};$$

$$\therefore e^{p\sqrt{-1}} - e^{-p\sqrt{-1}} = \alpha \sin P \left(e^{(z+p)\sqrt{-1}} - e^{-(z+p)\sqrt{-1}} \right),$$

or $e^{2p\sqrt{-1}} - 1 = \alpha \sin P \left(e^{(z+2p)\sqrt{-1}} - e^{-z\sqrt{-1}} \right),$

or $e^{2p\sqrt{-1}} \left(1 - \alpha \sin P e^{z\sqrt{-1}} \right) = 1 - \alpha \sin P e^{-z\sqrt{-1}},$

or $e^{2p\sqrt{-1}} = \dfrac{1 - \alpha \sin P e^{-z\sqrt{-1}}}{1 - \alpha \sin P e^{z\sqrt{-1}}}.$

Hence, taking the logarithms,

$$2p\sqrt{-1} = \alpha \sin P e^{z\sqrt{-1}} + \frac{1}{2}\alpha^2 \sin^2 P e^{2z\sqrt{-1}}$$

$$+ \frac{1}{3}\alpha^3 \sin^3 P e^{3z\sqrt{-1}} + \&c.$$

$$- \alpha \sin P e^{-z\sqrt{-1}} - \frac{1}{2}\alpha^2 \sin^2 P e^{-2z\sqrt{-1}}$$

$$- \frac{1}{3}\alpha^3 \sin^3 P e^{-3z\sqrt{-1}} - \&c.$$

and $p = \alpha \sin P \sin z + \dfrac{1}{2}\alpha^2 \sin^2 P \sin 2z$

$$+ \frac{1}{3}\alpha^3 \sin^3 P \sin 3z + \&c.,$$

or, expressed in seconds of space,

$$p'' \sin 1'' = \alpha \sin P \sin z + \frac{1}{2} \alpha^2 \sin^2 P \sin 2z$$

$$+ \frac{1}{3} \alpha^3 \sin^3 P \sin 3z + \&c.$$

To compute the coefficients of the second and third terms of this expansion, take the mean value of $P = 57' = 3420''$;

then, Ar. co. log 2 = 9·6989700
Log α = 9·9991091 (for Oxford).
Again = 9·9991091
Log sin P = 8·2195811
Again = 8·2195811
Ar. co. log sin 1″ = 5·3144251
———————
Log 2nd coef. = 1·4507755
———————
2nd coef. = 28″·23
———————

Again, Ar. co. log 3 = 9·5228787
3 log α = 9·9973273
3 log sin P = 4·6587433
Ar. co. log sin 1″ = 5·3144251
———————
Log 3rd coef. = 9·4933744
———————
3rd coef. =   0″·31
———————

$$\therefore p'' = \frac{\alpha}{\sin 1''} \sin P \sin z + 28''{\cdot}23 \sin 2z + 0''{\cdot}31 \sin 3z + \&c.$$

(for the latitude of Oxford)

$$= [5{\cdot}3135342] . \sin P \sin z + 28''{\cdot}23 \sin 2z$$
$$+ 0''{\cdot}31 \sin 3z + \&c.$$

$$= [9{\cdot}9991091] \times P'' \left(\frac{\sin P}{P}\right) \sin z + 28''{\cdot}23 \sin 2z$$
$$+ 0''{\cdot}31 \sin 3z + \&c.$$

18. The preceding investigation has given the expression for the parallax of the moon or a planet in zenith-distance, without any regard to its position with respect to the meridian of the place of observation. In fact, the whole effect of parallax takes place in the direction ·of zenith-distance, that is, of a great circle drawn through the geocentric zenith of the place of observation, and the object observed is depressed towards the horizon by the amount of the parallax, or its observed zenith-distance is too great by that amount. If now the object be on the meridian, the direction of zenith-distance coinciding with that of polar-distance, the whole effect of parallax is in this latter direction, and the right ascensions of objects observed on the meridian are not at all affected by it. If on the contrary the object be not on the meridian (as is generally the case with objects such as comets and small planets observed with an equatorial) it will be necessary to shew how to calculate the effect of the parallax in right ascension (or hour-angle) and in N.P.D. This we shall proceed to do.

19. *To determine the effect of parallax on the Right Ascension and North Polar Distance of an object observed at a distance from the meridian.*

Let Z' be the geocentric zenith of the place of observation (so that $Z'P =$ colat. $+$ angle of the vertical).

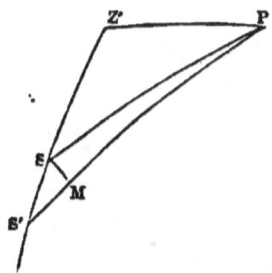

P the pole of the heavens,

S the geocentric place of a body depressed by parallax to S' in the vertical circle $Z'S$.

Then $SS' = P' \sin Z'S$

(where $P' = \dfrac{r}{a} \times$ Horizontal Equatorial Parallax).

Draw $S'P$, and SM perpendicular to $S'P$.
Then parallax in hour-angle
$= -$ parallax in R.A.

$= $ angle $SPS' = \dfrac{SM}{\sin \text{N.P.D.}}$

$= \dfrac{SS' \sin SS'M}{\sin \text{N.P.D.}}$.

$= \dfrac{P' \sin Z'S \times \sin Z'SP}{\sin \text{N.P.D.}}$ (very approximately)

$= \dfrac{P' \sin Z'P \times \sin Z'PS}{\sin \text{N.P.D.}}$

$= \dfrac{P' \sin Z'P \times \sin \text{hour-angle}}{\sin \text{N.P.D.}}$.

Again, parallax in N.P.D. $= S'M$
$= P' \sin Z'S \cos Z'S'P$
$= P' \sin Z'S \cos Z'SP$ very approximately.

But, since in any spherical triangle whose angles are A, B, C, and opposite sides a, b, c, by a well-known formula,

$\sin c \cos A = \cos a \sin b - \cos C \sin a \cos b$,

we shall have

$P' \sin Z'S \cos Z'SP = P' (\cos Z'P \sin SP$
$\qquad\qquad\qquad\qquad - \cos Z'PS \sin Z'P \cos SP)$
$\qquad = P' (\cos Z'P \sin \text{N.P.D.}$
$\qquad\qquad - \cos \text{hour-angle} \sin Z'P \cos \text{N.P.D.})$.

If as usual, we put Δ for the N.P.D.; γ' for the colatitude $+$ angle of the vertical; h for the hour-angle ($=$ sidereal time $-$ R.A.), we shall have

parallax in R.A. $= - P' \dfrac{\sin \gamma' \sin h}{\sin \Delta}$,

.... in N.P.D. $= P'(\cos \gamma' \sin \Delta - \cos h \sin \gamma' \cos \Delta)$.

The latter formula may easily be put in a shape fit for logarithmic calculation.

Thus, if we compute the angle ϕ from the equation,

$$\tan \phi = \cos h \cot \Delta,$$

the parallax in N.P.D. will be

$$= P' \frac{\sin \Delta \, \cos (\gamma' + \phi)}{\cos \phi}.$$

20. But, practically, the parallaxes in R. A. and N. P. D. can be found much more easily by means of appropriate tables in the following manner.

Every thing else remaining as before, draw $Z'M$ perpendicular to SP.

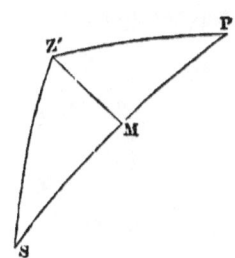

Then parallax in R. A.

$$= \frac{P' \sin Z'S \times \sin Z'SP}{\sin SP}$$

$$= \frac{P' \sin Z'M}{\sin \Delta} \quad (1)$$

and, parallax in N. P. D.

$$= P' \sin Z'S \cdot \cos Z'SP$$
$$= P' \sin Z'S \cdot \tan SM \cot Z'S$$
$$= P' \cos Z'S \cdot \tan SM$$
$$= P' \cos SM \cdot \cos Z'M \tan SM$$
$$= P' \sin SM \cdot \cos Z'M$$
$$= P' \sin (\Delta - PM) \cos Z'M. \quad (2)$$

If then, for a given latitude, that is, for a given value of $Z'P$ or γ' there be constructed a table of the value of PM from the formula, $\cos h = \tan PM \cot \gamma'$ and also of log sin $Z'M$ and log cos $Z'M$ from the formula, $\sin Z'M = \sin h \sin \gamma'$, for all values of the hour-angle at small intervals (for instance for every two minutes of the hour-angle expressed in time) the calculation of formulæ (1) and (2) will become very simple and easy.

This is the method pursued at Greenwich.

21. To find the value of P', or of the horizontal parallax, in terms of the sun's horizontal equatorial parallax at his mean distance from the earth.

Let the sun's mean distance from the earth be taken for the unit of distance, and let the planet's distance (D) be expressed in multiples or parts of this unit. Let also $a(= 8''\cdot 90)$ be the sun's horizontal equatorial parallax. Then, since the horizontal parallax will vary inversely as the distance, (see page 181), the planet's horizontal equatorial parallax will be $\dfrac{a}{D}$, or $P = \dfrac{a}{D}$;

And therefore $P' (=$ horizontal parallax for radius r of the terrestrial spheroid$) = \dfrac{a}{D} \cdot \dfrac{r}{a}$

$\qquad = \dfrac{a}{D} \cdot r$, if r is referred to a as the unit of distance.

22. To find the equatorial horizontal parallax of the moon.

The mean distance of the earth from the moon is about 60 radii of the earth, or 240,000 miles, and therefore the tangent of horizontal parallax is about $\dfrac{1}{60}$, or the parallax itself is about 57'. It is obvious then from purely geometrical considerations, that the parallax being of such a magnitude can be very accurately determined by means of observations of declination made in two places lying nearly on the same meridian, the one in a high northern, and the other in a low southern latitude. Two observatories both belonging to the British Government exist which are admirably adapted for such a determination, namely the Greenwich Observatory and that of the Cape of Good Hope, the former in North latitude 51°. 28' and the latter in South latitude 33°. 56', the longitude of the latter being only 1^h.13^m.55^s. East of Greenwich.

In fact the parallax of the moon was thus determined, as well as that of the planet Mars (the latter however imperfectly) about the middle of the last century by comparison of observations

INVESTIGATION OF THE PARALLAX OF THE MOON. 191

made by La Caille at the Cape, with those made at several European observatories, including Greenwich. The late Professor Henderson made also a new determination of the parallax by observations made in the years 1832 and 1833, for which the reader may consult the 10th volume of the Memoirs of the Royal Astronomical Society.

We will now explain the principle of this method of determining the parallax by observations of meridian zenith-distances made at two observatories thus situated.

In the first place we may remark, that the change of meridian zenith-distance or of polar-distance of the moon, in passing from the meridian of the Cape to that of Greenwich, can be accurately calculated by means of the table of her motions, and therefore we may determine the meridian zenith-distance at which the moon would be observed by an observer on the meridian of Greenwich at a place which has the same latitude as the observatory at the Cape; and we may thus practically consider the observatories to be on the same meridian.

Let OAO' be an elliptic section of the earth's spheroid by this meridian; O and O' the positions of the two observatories;

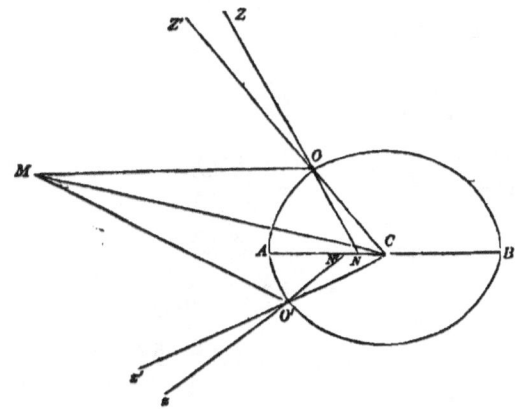

NOZ, and $N'O'z$ the true verticals, and COZ' and $CO'z'$ lines drawn from the centre of the earth through O and O' towards the geocentric zeniths.

Then if M be the position of the moon on the meridian, we shall have $MOZ = z$ and $MO'z = z'$, the observed zenith-distances. Join CM, and let the actual parallaxes at the time of observation, namely the angles OMC and $O'MC$, be respectively p and p'.

Then, denoting the angles of the vertical at O and O' by v and v', and the horizontal equatorial parallax by P, we have (taking as the unit of length the earth's equatorial radius)

$$\sin p = r \sin P \sin (z - v)$$
$$\text{and } \sin p' = r' \sin P \sin (z' - v');$$

again, since $z - v = \angle OCM + \angle OMC$,

$$\text{and } z' - v' = \angle O'CM + \angle O'MC;$$
$$\therefore z + z' - v - v' = \angle OMO' + \angle OCO'$$
$$= p + p' + \phi - v + \phi_1 - v',$$

(where ϕ and ϕ_1 are the astronomical latitudes)

or $\qquad z + z' = p + p' + \phi + \phi_1,$

and $\qquad p + p' = z + z' - (\phi + \phi_1)$, a known quantity,

$$= a \text{ suppose.}$$

Hence we have $\sin p = r \sin P \sin (z - v)$,

$$\text{and } \sin (a - p) = r' \sin P \sin (z' - v'),$$

or $\qquad \dfrac{\sin (a - p)}{\sin p} = \dfrac{r'}{r} \cdot \dfrac{\sin (z' - v')}{\sin (z - v)};$

or $\qquad \dfrac{\sin a}{\tan p} - \cos a = \dfrac{r'}{r} \cdot \dfrac{\sin (z' - v')}{\sin (z - v)};$

or $\tan p = \dfrac{\sin a}{\cos a + \dfrac{r'}{r} \cdot \dfrac{\sin (z' - v')}{\sin (z - v)}}$

$$= \dfrac{r \sin a \sin (z - v)}{r' \sin (z' - v') + r \cos a \sin (z - v)};$$

whence p is known,

and finally $\qquad \sin P = \dfrac{\sin p}{r \sin (z - v)}$, from which equation P is determined.

23. In this investigation we have assumed that the *centre* of the moon has been observed at the two observatories. This however is not the case, and the observation is always that of the upper or the lower limb (one limb only being in general fully illuminated when the moon is on the meridian). To deduce from the observed zenith-distance of the limb affected by parallax the zenith-distance of the centre similarly affected, it is necessary to apply the semidiameter *corrected for parallax*, and this introduces some rather complicated considerations into the problem. As there is however no real difficulty in the solution, it will be sufficient to refer the student to the complete investigation given in Brunnow's *Sphärischen Astronomie*, page 373, as our limits will not allow many details.

24. The method which has been applied to determine the moon's parallax is not generally applicable to the planets, because of their much greater distance, and the consequent smallness of the parallaxes. In the case of Mars however, it has been attempted to determine the parallax by observations of zenith-distance at different observations, by taking advantage of the fact that, owing to the excentricity of his orbit, he comes much nearer to us at some oppositions than at others, so near indeed that in some cases the horizontal parallax has amounted to as much as $22''$.

For the purpose of giving greater efficiency to the use of this method, there is published in the Nautical Almanac, for each opposition of the planet, a list of stars situated so near his path as to be conveniently compared with him either by the use of meridian instruments or of an equatorial.

The way in which the amount of parallax is deduced is sufficiently obvious. Thus, let z and z' be as before the true meridian zenith-distances of the planet as affected with the parallaxes $Pr \sin z$, and $Pr' \sin z'$ (and let the observation made at one station be reduced to the meridian of the other station, by the motion in N.P.D. of the planet in its passage from the more easterly to the more westerly meridian); let also z_1 and z_1' be the true meridian zenith-distances of the star observed at the two stations, and γ and γ' the co-latitudes of the stations (the one referred to the North Pole and the other to the South Pole).

Then the true geocentric N.P.D's of the planet will be $\gamma + z - Pr \sin z$, and $180° - (\gamma' + z' - Pr' \sin z')$ and the N.P.D's of the stars will be

$$\gamma + z_1 \text{ and } 180° - (\gamma' + z_1'),$$

and therefore the difference of N.P.D. of the planet and star, will be at the first station (the Cape for example) $z - z_1 - Pr \sin z$, and at the second

$$z_1' - z' + Pr' \sin z';$$

and these must manifestly be equal.

Hence $$P = \frac{z - z_1 + z' - z_1'}{r \sin z + r' \sin z'}.$$

The advantage of this method is that it requires only the difference of meridian zenith-distances or polar-distances of the star and planet, and therefore there will in all cases be got rid of the greater part of the uncertainty of ill-determined refraction, since only the *difference* of refraction for the star and planet comes into play. We may also apply the same method and avail ourselves of extra-meridional observations, since an equatorial (which is in general not to be trusted for giving accurate values of absolute right ascension and declination), will give the differences of those quantities for neighbouring objects very accurately.

If however the equatorial be used, and therefore the observation be not made at the meridian passage, the formulæ just given will require a little modification.

Thus, let, at the two stations, Δ and Δ' be the observed N.P.D's of the planet corrected for refraction (page 134), at the Greenwich mean solar times t and t'; m the hourly motion in seconds of space of the planet in N.P.D., $Prf(\Delta)$ and $Pr'f(\Delta')$ the parallaxes applicable to observed N.P.D's.

Then, reducing all to the time t, the geocentric N.P.D's will be

$$\Delta - Pr f(\Delta), \text{ and } \Delta' + Pr' f(\Delta') - \frac{t' - t}{3600} \times m,$$

$t' - t$ being expressed in seconds of time.

OBSERVATIONS OF R.A. OF MARS FOR PARALLAX.

Again, let the observed N.P.D's of the star be Δ_1 and Δ_1',

∴ difference of geocentric N.P.D's of planet and star at Greenwich

$$= \Delta_1 - \Delta + Pr f(\Delta),$$

and, at the Cape of Good Hope,

$$= \Delta_1' - \Delta' - Pr' f(\Delta') + \frac{t'-t}{3600} \times m,$$

and these must be equal,

or
$$P = \frac{\Delta_1' - \Delta' - (\Delta_1 - \Delta) + \frac{t'-t}{3600} \times m}{r f(\Delta) + r' f(\Delta')},$$

where $f(\Delta)$ and $f(\Delta')$ can be calculated by the formulæ on page 189.

25. Observations of right ascension of Mars when nearest to us, made with a good equatorial at only one station, at considerable distances East and West of the meridian, may also be made available for determining the parallax.

Thus, referring to the figure on page 187, it will be seen that, as the planet is depressed by parallax in the vertical circle from S to S', the hour-angle (whether East or West) is *increased* by the angle SPS', or by its equivalent $\frac{Pr \sin \gamma' \sin h}{\sin \Delta}$, where h is the hour-angle.

Let then h be the eastern and h' the western hour-angle expressed in time, corresponding to the true values α and α', Δ and Δ' of R.A. and N.P.D., and to sidereal times t and t'; and let α_1 and α_1' be in time the observed values of R.A., or values resulting from observation, corrected for refraction only.

Then is
$$\alpha_1 = t + h, \text{ and } \alpha_1' = t' - h',$$

and
$$\alpha = t + h - \frac{Pr \sin \gamma' \sin h}{15 \sin \Delta};$$

$$\alpha' = t' - h' + \frac{Pr \sin \gamma' \sin h'}{15 \sin \Delta'};$$

13—2

if therefore $m =$ motion in R.A. (in time) of the planet in the interval $t'-t$,

$$\alpha' - \alpha = m = t' - t - (h' + h) + \frac{Pr \sin \gamma'}{15} \left(\frac{\sin h'}{\sin \Delta'} + \frac{\sin h}{\sin \Delta} \right),$$

and therefore $P = \dfrac{15 \{h' + h - (t' - t) + m\}}{r \sin \gamma \left(\dfrac{\sin h'}{\sin \Delta'} + \dfrac{\sin h}{\sin \Delta} \right)}.$

If we neglect the planet's motion in N.P.D. in the time $t'-t$, which will generally be small, $\Delta' = \Delta$;

$$\therefore P = \frac{15 \{h' + h - (t' - t) + m\} \sin \Delta}{r \sin \gamma' (\sin h' + \sin h)}$$

$$= \frac{15}{2} \cdot \frac{\{h' + h - (t' - t) + m\} \sin \Delta}{r \sin \gamma \sin \dfrac{h'+h}{2} \cos \dfrac{h'-h}{2}}.$$

26. At the last opposition of Mars in 1862, great pains were taken to secure good co-operation of different observatories for the deduction of the parallax of the planet and therefore of the Sun's parallax, and pamphlets were circulated containing specific recommendations for conducting the observations, and maps in which were laid down the positions of all the stars lying very near the track of Mars.

The observations which were made at various northern and southern observatories, in compliance with the recommendations, have not all been given to the public, but comparisons have been made between the results of observations of two northern and two southern observatories, which agree in shewing that the received value of the solar parallax, as deduced from the Transit of Venus in 1769, namely 8"·57, must be considerably increased. In the *Astronomische Nachrichten*, No. 1409, for example, M. Winnecke, one of the astronomers of the Russian observatory at Pulkowa, gives the results of thirteen observations of declination of Mars made at that observatory, compared with those made at the observatory of Santiago de Chili, by M. Moesta, and finds that the resulting solar parallax is 8"·964. Also in the *Monthly Notices* of the Royal Astronomical Society, is a paper by Mr Stone, first assistant of the Royal Observatory at Greenwich, in which he gives the results of comparison between twenty-two observations of declination of Mars and comparison-stars made at Greenwich and at Williamstown, Victoria, in Australia; and the resulting solar parallax is in this case $8''\cdot 932$.

The mean of these two results, which are so nearly identical, would therefore deserve considerable weight, even if it was not supported by other considerations which render the essential correctness of it indisputable, and a brief account of these other considerations becomes absolutely necessary.

M. Le Verrier, the celebrated French astronomer, has recently made a redetermination of the orbits of Mercury, Venus, and Mars, and found that it was impossible to represent the motions of the perihelia of Mercury and Mars, and of the nodes of Venus, so as to make them agree with observation (assuming the received value of the solar parallax), without an inadmissible increase of the values of the planetary masses. In his discussion of his results given in a paper in the *Comptes Rendus* of Jan. 6. 1862, he states that an increase of the mass of the earth by about one-tenth part would get rid of nearly all the discrepancies between theory and observation, but he observes that there is a difficulty in the way of this alteration, because this would disturb the relation which exists between the force of gravity at the surface of the earth, the mass of the earth, and the solar parallax, unless the solar parallax were itself increased by about one-thirtieth part. In the face of this difficulty he was inclined rather to believe that the disturbing influence arises from a ring of small planets as yet undiscovered.

In the meanwhile M. Foucault was engaged in endeavouring to determine by experiment the actual velocity of light by means of an apparatus consisting of a series of reflecting mirrors, one of which was made to revolve uniformly with a very great velocity, and the conclusion at which he arrived was that the velocity of light was considerably less than its received value as deduced originally from the eclipses of Jupiter's satellites. His experiments were repeated again and again with so much care that no reasonable doubt could be entertained about its correctness.

Now the constant of aberration has been determined (as has been seen) by considerations quite independent of the velocity of light, that is, by the observed apparent displacement of the stars, and, assuming Struve's value, or 20″·445, this gives us immediately the following equation,

$$\frac{\text{velocity of the earth}}{\text{velocity of light}} = 20\cdot 445 \times \sin 1''.$$

Hence if it be found necessary to diminish the velocity of light, that of the earth must be diminished in the same proportion, but, in any case, if the velocity of light be known, the velocity of the earth is given by the preceding equation.

Now the velocity of the earth depends on the dimensions of the solar orbit, or on the solar parallax, and may be expressed by the following equation,

$$v = \frac{2\pi a}{T},$$

where a = radius of earth's orbit supposed circular,

v = its velocity, or space described in a second of time,

and T = the time of revolution, or length of a sidereal year, which is accurately known from observation.

Hence if v be diminished, a or the mean distance of the earth from the Sun will be diminished in the same proportion, and therefore the solar parallax, which is equal to $\dfrac{\text{earth's radius}}{a}$, will be increased.

M. Foucault thus found that it would be necessary to increase the Sun's parallax by about one-thirtieth part, and his deduced value was actually 8″·86.

Now M. Le Verrier, in his planetary researches had been led to assume 8″·93, as giving the best agreement between theory and observation, and we have seen that two independent results derived from observations of Mars give 8″·95.

There can therefore be little doubt of the essential correctness of this value, or of the incorrectness of that which has been assumed up to the present time as deduced from the Transit of Venus across the Sun's disk, namely, 8″·57. It will be desirable in this place to explain the principle of finding the parallax by this latter method.

27. Both the inferior planets, Mercury and Venus, in arriving at inferior *conjunction* (that is, in passing in their orbits between the Sun and the earth), occasionally appear to *transit* the disk of the Sun. When this phenomenon occurs for Venus it affords very good means for determining the solar parallax, and, at the last two *transits*, which occurred in 1761 and 1769, expeditions to several northern and southern stations were fitted out by the British and other Governments for ensuring observations best adapted for the determination of the parallax.

The problem taken in all its generality is a complicated one, and may be referred to the Chapter which treats of the motions of the planets, but the general explanation presents no difficulty.

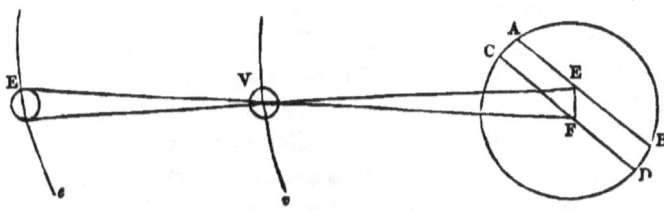

It is presumed that the student has sufficient elementary knowledge of the motions of the planets to be aware that they move all in the same direction, in nearly circular orbits round the Sun, in planes inclined at different small angles to the plane of the earth's motion, and with greater velocities in proportion as they are nearer to the Sun. If then it should happen that, when Venus is passing between the earth and the Sun, she should be *very near* the ecliptic, or very nearly in a direct line with the Sun as seen from the earth, she would appear projected upon the disk of the Sun. Let then E and V be simultaneous positions of the Earth and Venus, moving in their orbits in the directions Ee and Vv (which are in different planes), and imagine two observers, one stationed near the north pole of the earth and the other near the south pole. Then, if lines be drawn from those stations through V, they will meet the Sun's disk at points EF, and therefore for this instant the observers will see Venus projected on the Sun at those points. Thus the planet will appear to describe upon the Sun's disk the very nearly straight lines or chords AB, CD, and, if we could by any means measure the angular lengths of these chords, we should plainly (knowing the value of the angular diameter of the Sun) be able to calculate the angular value of EF, that is, the distance between the chords.

Now the simplest observation by which this can be effected is that of the times of apparent ingress and egress of the planet on the Sun's disk, since by this means, we shall know the time occupied by the planet in traversing the chords, and the angular velocities being known from the tables of the motion of Venus, the angular spaces described, namely, AB and CD, will be known.

Again, by the laws of planetary motion, the *ratio* of the distances of Venus and the Earth from the Sun is known by their periods of revolution, that is, $EF : VF :: 95 : 68$ nearly, and therefore, $VF : EV :: 68 : 27$, or as $2\frac{1}{2} : 1$ nearly, and therefore EF as measured on the Sun's disk will be $2\frac{1}{2}$ times the distance between the stations on the earth's surface; and, if we assume that the distance between the stations is equal to the earth's diameter or to twice the earth's radius, then is the angular measure of EF equal to five times the Sun's parallax, and the latter quantity may therefore be determined.

The sketch given above is exceedingly imperfect, and particularly in this respect that it does not take into account the rotation of the earth during the progress of the transit of the planet across the disk, but it is perhaps sufficient to shew the principle of the method, which will be given in detail in a following Chapter.

CHAPTER VII.

ON PRECESSION AND NUTATION.

On the corrections to be applied to a star's place, on account of the motions of the Equator and Ecliptic.

1. HITHERTO, the planes of the equator and ecliptic, and consequently the position of the first point of Aries, have been regarded as fixed, and this is approximately true. But, since the Earth is not a sphere, the attractions of the Sun and Moon do not in general act through its centre, and the axis of the Earth does not retain a fixed direction in space. Since the ellipticity of the Earth is small, the motion of the axis, being due to the ellipticity, is also small. When this motion is investigated, it is found that the *mean* motion of the pole of the equator is in a small circle about the pole of the ecliptic, whose angular radius is about $23°.28'$; that is, the distance between the poles will be sometimes greater and sometimes less, than that quantity,—according to the positions of the Sun and Moon, and of the node of the Moon's orbit: also the motion in this circle is not quite uniform, the pole being sometimes before, sometimes behind its mean place, but the distance of the pole, from its mean place, is always small.

The *mean* motion of the pole is called 'Precession,' and the deviation from the mean place is considered as a correction to be applied to the Precession, and is called 'Nutation.'

The effect of the Precessional motion of the Earth's pole will be, that the First Point of Aries will move uniformly in the ecliptic (in the contrary direction to the Sun's motion), while the obliquity of the ecliptic will remain unchanged.

The formulæ which express this motion of the pole have been investigated by Rigid Dynamics, and its amount has been computed numerically.

2. It is evident from the explanation given above that the latitudes of the stars are unaltered by the motion of the equator, while the longitudes, as measured from the First Point of Aries, are all changed by the same amount; and that the motion of the equator is completely determined when we know for a given time the true value of the obliquity of the ecliptic, and the quantity by which the longitudes of the stars are altered.

Now, from the investigations of Physical Astronomy, it is found that, if $\odot$, $\mathcal{D}$, and Ω be the longitudes of the Sun, Moon, and ascending node of the Moon's orbit at the time (in years) $1750 + t$, then the increase of true longitude of a star for the latter epoch, over its mean longitude for 1750, will be represented by the following expression,

$$50''\cdot 37572 t - 0''\cdot 000121795 t^2$$

$$- 16''\cdot 78332 \sin \Omega + 0''\cdot 20209 \sin 2\Omega$$

$$- 1''\cdot 33589 \sin 2\odot - 0''\cdot 20128 \sin 2\mathcal{D},$$

while the true value of the obliquity of the ecliptic, for $1750 + t$, is

$$23°.28'.18''\cdot 0 + 8''\cdot 97707 \cos \Omega - 0''\cdot 08773 \cos 2\Omega$$

$$+ 0''\cdot 57990 \cos 2\odot + 0''\cdot 08738 \cos 2\mathcal{D},$$

using Bessel's constants.

The terms which are non-periodical functions of the time are considered under the head Precession; and the periodical under Nutation: thus, there is no precession in obliquity, and the precession in longitude varies (nearly) as the time.

3. As yet, we have considered the motion of the *equator* only; but, on account of the mutual actions of the planets, the ecliptic or plane of the earth's orbit is not fixed, although its motion is very small.

PRECESSIONAL MOTION OF THE ECLIPTIC. 203

By a motion of the ecliptic on the equator, it is evident that the R.A's of all stars will be altered by the same amount, while their N.P.D's are unchanged.

The formulæ which express this effect of the motion of the ecliptic in the interval from 1750 to $1750 + t$ are,

1st, a diminution a of R.A. of all stars, whose value is

$$a = 0''{\cdot}17926 t - 0''{\cdot}0002660394 t^2.$$

And 2ndly, a change in the obliquity of the ecliptic,

$$= - 0''{\cdot}48368 t - 0''{\cdot}0000027230 t^2.$$

The motions in these formulæ arise from the *secular variation of the inclination, and longitude of the node* of the Earth's orbit, considered with reference to a plane absolutely fixed, due to the action of the planets; they are in reality periodic quantities, but their periods are immense, so that for the ordinary purposes of Astronomy, for even moderately large intervals of time, we may consider the R.A's to be *continually increasing*, and the obliquity *continually diminishing* according to the formulæ given above.

This motion of the ecliptic is called 'Planetary Precession;' that due to the action of the Sun and Moon on the spheroidal Earth being distinguished as 'Lunisolar Precession.'

4. The Lunisolar Precession, as given in Art. (2), was calculated on the supposition of the ecliptic being fixed; if the motion of the ecliptic be taken into account, there will be found to be a small precessional change of the inclination of the equator to the fixed ecliptic of 1750, so that at time $1750 + t$—correcting for precession only—the equator will be inclined to this *fixed* ecliptic at the angle

$$\omega_0 = 23°. 28'. 18''{\cdot}0 + 0''{\cdot}00000984233 t^2.$$

We will now proceed to apply the above results of theory to determine the corrections to be applied to the place of a star due to the motion of its planes of reference. And we will first consider

Precession.

5. On inspection of the above formulæ, it is seen, that by far the most considerable part of precession consists in a uniform motion of the Earth's pole about the pole of the ecliptic in a circle: and that we may very approximately consider the ecliptic as *fixed*.

Thus the latitudes of stars are unaltered, but the longitudes have a yearly increase of about $50''\cdot 2$ by the combined effect of the Lunisolar and Planetary Precession (called the General Precession); and we may hence deduce expressions for the precession in R.A. and N.P.D.

6. Let π, P be the pole of the ecliptic and equator, at a given epoch: S any given star of which the R.A. $= a$, decli-

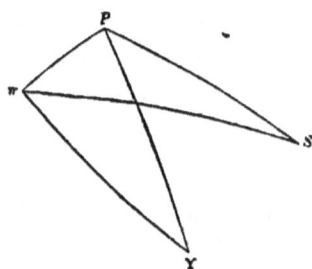

nation $= \delta$, longitude $= l$, and latitude $= \lambda$: also let obliquity of ecliptic $= \omega$: then, in triangle πPS,

$$\pi P = \omega; \quad PS = 90^\circ - \delta; \quad \angle \pi PS = 90^\circ + a,$$
$$\pi S = 90^\circ - \lambda; \quad \angle P\pi S = 90^\circ - l.$$

Since P moves in a circle about π, πP is unaltered; and from triangle πPS

$$\sin \delta = \sin \lambda \cos \omega + \cos \lambda \sin \omega \sin l;$$

therefore differentiating,—since λ and ω are unchanged,

$$d\delta \cos \delta = \cos \lambda \sin \omega \cos l \,.\, dl.$$

And, $\quad \dfrac{\cos l}{\cos \delta} = \dfrac{\sin P}{\cos \lambda} = \dfrac{\cos a}{\cos \lambda};$

$$\therefore d\delta = \cos \alpha \sin \omega \cdot dl,$$

or, since $\dfrac{dl}{dt} = 50''\cdot 2$ nearly,

$$\frac{d\delta}{dt} = \frac{d\delta}{dl} \cdot \frac{dl}{dt} = 50''\cdot 2 \cos \alpha \sin \omega,$$

which give the rate of change of declination of the star.

Again,
$$\sin \lambda = \cos ES$$
$$= \sin \delta \cos \omega - \cos \delta \sin \omega \sin \alpha,$$

therefore differentiating, and remembering that λ and ω are unaltered, we have

$$\cos \delta \sin \omega \cos \alpha \frac{d\alpha}{d\delta} = \cos \delta \cos \omega + \sin \delta \sin \omega \sin \alpha;$$

or, since
$$\frac{d\delta}{dt} = 50''\cdot 2 \cos \alpha \sin \omega,$$

$$\cos \delta \frac{d\alpha}{dt} = 50''\cdot 2 (\cos \delta \cos \omega + \sin \delta \sin \omega \sin \alpha);$$

or
$$\frac{d\alpha}{dt} = 50''\cdot 2 (\cos \omega + \sin \omega \sin \alpha \tan \delta).$$

7. The preceding article considers only the *principal* terms in precession. We proceed to the more accurate investigation.

Let AA_0, EE_0 be the equator and ecliptic for the year 1750: and $A'A''$, EE' their positions for the year $1750 + t$ (of course

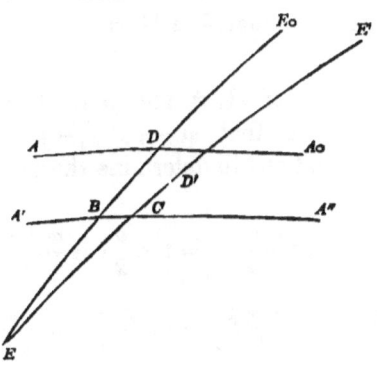

neglecting nutation): then, BD, on the *fixed ecliptic* EE_0, is the lunisolar precession in t years; let it $= p_1$.

Then, from Art. (2),

$$p_1 = + 50''\cdot 37572 t - 0''\cdot 000121795 t^2.$$

And BC, being the motion of the ecliptic on the equator $A'A''$ considered fixed, $= a$, where a is the planetary precession in t years; and is equal to $0''\cdot 17926 t - 0''\cdot 0002660394 t^2$.

Also $BCE =$ inclination of the *true* ecliptic to the equator,

$$= 23^\circ.28'.18''\cdot 0 - 0''\cdot 48368 t - 0''\cdot 0000027230 t^2 = \omega, \text{ say.}$$

And, $A'BE\ (= \omega_0) =$ inclination of the *fixed* ecliptic

$$= 23^\circ.28'.18''\cdot 0 + 0'''\cdot 00000984233 t^2,$$

thus $\omega - \omega_0$ is small.

On EE', take $ED' = ED$; and let $CD' = p$; p is called the 'General Precession:' also $p_1 - p = BD - CD'$, and is evidently very small.

Let $\pi = \angle E_0 EE'$: and $\Pi =$ longitude of the *ascending* node of the true on the fixed ecliptic, $= 180^\circ - DE$, E being the *descending* node;

$$\therefore EB = 180^\circ - \Pi - p_1;$$

and, $\qquad EC = ED' - CD' = ED - CD'$

$$= 180^\circ - \Pi - p.$$

Now in the triangle EBC, $BC = a$; $\angle C = \omega$; and $\angle B = 180^\circ - \omega_0$; which are all known: and hence the remaining parts of the triangle, and therefore Π, π, p, are known.

8. The calculation of Π, π, and p is effected by Napier's Analogies, remembering that $\omega - \omega_0$, $p_1 - p$ and π are very small. Thus, the equations to determine the required quantities are

$$\tan \frac{p_1 - p}{2} \cos \frac{\omega - \omega_0}{2} = \tan \frac{a}{2} \cos \frac{\omega + \omega_0}{2},$$

$$\tan \frac{\pi}{2} \sin \left(\Pi + \frac{p_1 + p}{2} \right) = \sin \frac{p_1 - p}{2} \tan \frac{\omega + \omega_0}{2},$$

$$\tan\frac{\pi}{2}\cos\left(\Pi+\frac{p_1+p}{2}\right)=\cos\frac{p_1-p}{2}\tan\frac{\omega-\omega_0}{2}.$$

Hence, since $\frac{\omega+\omega_0}{2}=\omega_0+\frac{\omega-\omega_0}{2}$, the first equation gives, neglecting $(\omega-\omega_0)^2$,

$$p_1-p=a\cos\omega_0-\frac{1}{2}a(\omega-\omega_0)\sin\omega_0\sin 1''\quad\ldots\ldots\quad(a).$$

Again, dividing the second equation by the third, and using the first,

$$\tan\left(\Pi+\frac{p_1+p}{2}\right)=\tan\frac{a}{2}\frac{\sin\frac{\omega+\omega_0}{2}}{\sin\frac{\omega-\omega_0}{2}};$$

whence, $\tan\left(\Pi+\frac{p_1+p}{2}\right)=\frac{a\sin\omega_0}{\omega-\omega_0}+\frac{1}{2}a\cos\omega_0\sin 1''\quad\ldots\ldots\quad(b).$

Lastly, adding the squares of the second and third,

$$\tan^2\frac{\pi}{2}=\left(\tan^2\frac{p_1-p}{2}\tan^2\frac{\omega+\omega_0}{2}+\tan^2\frac{\omega-\omega_0}{2}\right)\cos^2\frac{p_1-p}{2},$$

whence, very approximately,

$$\pi^2=(p_1-p)^2\tan^2\left(\omega_0+\frac{\omega-\omega_0}{2}\right)+(\omega-\omega_0)^2$$

$$=(p_1-p)^2\tan^2\omega_0\left(1+\frac{\omega-\omega_0}{\sin\omega_0\cos\omega_0}\sin 1''\right)+(\omega-\omega_0)^2$$

$$=(p_1-p)^2\tan^2\omega_0+a^2\tan\omega_0(\omega-\omega_0)\sin 1''+(\omega-\omega_0)^2,\text{ by }(a)$$

$$=a^2\sin^2\omega_0-a^2(\omega-\omega_0)\sin\omega_0\cos\omega_0\tan^2\omega_0\sin 1''$$
$$\qquad+a^2\tan\omega_0(\omega-\omega_0)\sin 1''+(\omega-\omega_0)^2$$

$$=a^2\sin^2\omega_0+a^2\sin\omega_0\cos\omega_0(\omega-\omega_0)\sin 1''+(\omega-\omega_0)^2\quad\ldots\ldots\quad(c).$$

If we put in (a), (b), (c), the known values of a, ω_0, $\omega-\omega_0$, p_1, they give for p, Π, and π the following values,

$$p=50''\cdot 21129t+0''\cdot 0001221483t^2,$$

$$\Pi=171°.36'.10''-5''\cdot 21t,$$

$$\pi=0''\cdot 48892t-0''\cdot 0000030719t^2,$$

where it is to be remembered that

$$DE = 180° - \Pi, \text{ and } EC = 180° - \Pi - p.$$

9. Let F be the ascending node: S a star; SL, SL' per-

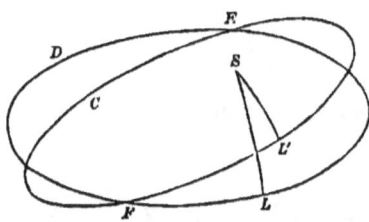

pendicular to the fixed, and true ecliptic; and the points C, D, &c. as in the last figure.

Then,
$$DF = \Pi; \quad CF = \Pi + p.$$

We can now easily find for any given interval of time t, the precession of S in *latitude and longitude*.

Let, at the beginning of the interval, L, Λ be the longitude and latitude referred to the fixed ecliptic: and l, λ to the true; then, since D and C are the positions of the fixed and true First Point of Aries,

$$FL' = CL' - CF = l - \Pi - p,$$
and $$FL = DL - DF = L - \Pi,$$
also $SL = \Lambda$; $SL' = \lambda$.

Hence, if we take two systems of rectangular axes, one set being in and perpendicular to the plane EDF, and the other in and perpendicular to plane ECF, and if one of the axes of each system be at F; the co-ordinates of S referred to them are

$$\left.\begin{array}{l}\cos \Lambda \cos (L - \Pi) \\ \cos \Lambda \sin (L - \Pi) \\ \sin \Lambda\end{array}\right\} \text{ and } \left\{\begin{array}{l}\cos \lambda \cos (l - \Pi - p) \\ \cos \lambda \sin (l - \Pi - p) \\ \sin \lambda.\end{array}\right.$$

Thus, transforming from the second system to the first, we have, as in Chap. III., page 89, putting, for convenience, x for $L - \Pi$, and y for $l - \Pi - p$,

$$\begin{aligned}\cos \lambda \cos y &= \cos \Lambda \cos x, \\ \cos \lambda \sin y &= \cos \Lambda \sin x \cos \pi + \sin \Lambda \sin \pi \\ \sin \lambda &= -\cos \Lambda \sin x \sin \pi + \sin \Lambda \cos \pi \end{aligned} \right\} \quad \ldots\ldots\ldots \text{(A)}.$$

Now, in an interval of t years, if t be not very large, the precession in latitude and longitude will be $\frac{d\lambda}{dt}t$, $\frac{dl}{dt}t$; and differentiating the first two equations above, we have, since L and Λ are constants,

$$\sin \lambda \cos y \, d\lambda + \cos \lambda \sin y \, dy = \cos \Lambda \sin x \, dx,$$

and $\sin \lambda \sin y \, d\lambda - \cos \lambda \cos y \, dy = -\cos \Lambda \cos x \cos \pi \, dx - \sin \lambda \, d\pi.$

Eliminate $d\lambda$, and for dx write $-d\Pi$;

$\therefore \cos \lambda \, dy = \sin \lambda \cos y \, d\pi - \cos \Lambda \, (\sin x \sin y + \cos x \cos y \cos \pi) \, d\Pi.$

And, from the last two equations of (A),

$$\cos \Lambda \sin x = \cos \lambda \sin y \cos \pi - \sin \lambda \sin \pi;$$

also $\quad \cos \Lambda \cos x = \cos \lambda \cos y;$

$\therefore (\sin x \sin y + \cos x \cos y \cos \pi) \cos \Lambda$

$\qquad = \cos \lambda \cos \pi - \sin \lambda \sin \pi \sin y,$

whence, eliminating Λ from the expression for dy,

$$dy = \tan \lambda \cos y \, d\pi - (\cos \pi - \sin \pi \tan \lambda \sin y) \, d\Pi \quad \ldots\ldots \text{(}\alpha\text{)},$$

or, since π is very small,

$$dy = \tan \lambda \cos y \, . \, d\pi - (1 - \pi \tan \lambda \, . \, \sin y) \, d\Pi,$$

that is, $\quad d(l - p) = \tan \lambda \cos y \, . \, d\pi + \pi \tan \lambda \sin y \, d\Pi,$

or, since $\pi = \frac{d\pi}{dt} \, . \, t$, nearly,

$$\frac{d(l - p)}{dt} = \tan \lambda \, . \, \frac{d\pi}{dt} \, . \, \cos\left(y - t \frac{d\Pi}{dt}\right) \quad \ldots\ldots\ldots\ldots \text{(1)}.$$

Again, from the last equation in (A), we have,—using the 2nd to get rid of Λ,

$$\cos \lambda . d\lambda = -\cos \Lambda \cos x \sin \pi . dx - \cos \lambda \sin y . d\pi;$$

$$\therefore d\lambda = -\cos y \sin \pi . dx - \sin y . d\pi \dots\dots\dots\dots (\beta)$$

$$= -\pi \cos y . dx - \sin y . d\pi, \text{ nearly};$$

$$\therefore \frac{d\lambda}{dt} = \pi \cos y . \frac{d\Pi}{dt} - \sin y . \frac{d\pi}{dt}$$

$$= -\frac{d\pi}{dt} \sin\left(y - t\frac{d\Pi}{dt}\right) \dots\dots\dots\dots\dots (2).$$

From (1) and (2), since $y (= l - \Pi - p)$ is known in terms of t, and $\frac{d\pi}{dt}$, $\frac{d\Pi}{dt}$ are known, we get the rate of change of longitude and latitude, through precession, in time t.

10. To find the precession in right ascension and declination, we use two sets of axes, one in and at right angles to the ecliptic for 1750, EE_0, and the other in and at right angles to the equator for $1750 + t$, $A'A''$, the point B corresponding to an axis in both systems.

Since $BD = p_1$, and D is the true equinox for 1750, the longitude of a star, *reckoned from B* on $EE_0 = L + p_1$, L being the *true* longitude for 1750; so C being the true equinox for $1750 + t$, the R.A. *reckoned from* $B = a + a$.

Thus the co-ordinates of the star referred to EBE_0 and $A'BA''$ are,

$$\left.\begin{array}{c}\cos \Lambda \cos (L + p_1) \\ \cos \Lambda \sin (L + p_1) \\ \sin \Lambda\end{array}\right\} \text{ and } \left\{\begin{array}{c}\cos \delta . \cos (\alpha + a) \\ \cos \delta . \sin (\alpha + a) \\ \sin \delta,\end{array}\right.$$

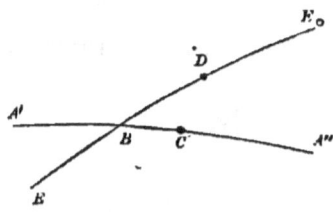

also, angle at $B = \omega_0$: whence, putting x for $L + p_1$, and y for $\alpha + a$, we get,

$$\left.\begin{array}{l}\cos \delta \cos y = \cos \Lambda \cos x \\ \cos \delta \sin y = \cos \Lambda \sin x \cos \omega_0 - \sin \Lambda \sin \omega_0 \\ \sin \delta = \cos \Lambda \sin x \sin \omega_0 + \sin \Lambda \cos \omega_0\end{array}\right\} \ldots \ldots (B),$$

which are identical in form with (A), if we put in (A) δ for λ, and $-\omega_0$ for π; we thus get, by repeating the process of article (9), i.e. by differentiating, and eliminating Λ, instead of equations (α) and (β), the equations

$$d(\alpha + a) = -\tan \delta \cos (\alpha + a) \, d\omega_0$$
$$+ \{\cos \omega_0 + \sin \omega_0 \tan \delta \sin (\alpha + a)\} \, dp_1,$$

and $d\delta = \cos (\alpha + a) \sin \omega_0 \, dp_1 + \sin (\alpha + a) \, d\omega_0$;

thus $\dfrac{d\alpha}{dt} = -\dfrac{da}{dt} + (\cos \omega_0 + \sin \omega_0 \tan \delta \sin \alpha) \dfrac{dp_1}{dt}$

$$+ \left(a \sin \omega_0 \dfrac{dp_1}{dt} - \dfrac{d\omega_0}{dt}\right) \tan \delta \cos \alpha, \text{ approximately,}$$

and $\dfrac{d\delta}{dt} = \cos \alpha \sin \omega_0 \dfrac{dp_1}{dt} - \left(a \sin \omega_0 \dfrac{dp_1}{dt} - \dfrac{d\omega_0}{dt}\right) \sin \alpha.$

Here a is the *circular measure* of a very small angle which is expressed in seconds in Art. (7); hence a will be a very small fraction; and $\dfrac{dp_1}{dt}$, p_1, ω_1, are given in the same article, from which it is seen that $\dfrac{d\omega_0}{dt}$ is very small, and $\dfrac{dp_1}{dt}$ not large. Thus the coefficient $a \sin \omega_0 \dfrac{dp_1}{dt} - \dfrac{d\omega_0}{dt}$ is very small, and its numerical value is easily found to be $-0''\cdot0000022472t$: we may therefore safely reject it.

Thus $\quad \dfrac{d\alpha}{dt} = m + n \tan \delta \sin \alpha,$

$\quad\quad\quad \dfrac{d\delta}{dt} = n \cos \alpha,$

where
$$m = -\frac{da}{dt} + \cos\omega_0 \frac{dp_1}{dt},$$

and
$$n = \sin\omega_0 \frac{dp_1}{dt},$$

and, putting for ω_0, $\frac{da}{dt}$, $\frac{dp_1}{dt}$ their values, we find

$$m = 46''\cdot 02824 + 0''\cdot 0003086450\, t,$$

$$n = 20''\cdot 06442 - 0''\cdot 0000970204\, t.$$

11. We will now shew how these formulæ are applied to calculate the precession of a star in any interval.

It is easily seen that we shall get a very accurate result by supposing $\frac{d\alpha}{dt}$, $\frac{d\delta}{dt}$ constant during the interval and equal to their value corresponding to the middle of the interval. For putting the interval $= 2\tau$; and $f(t)$ for the change in α or δ during time t from the middle of the interval: we have, by Stirling's theorem,

$$f(\tau) = f(0) + \tau f'(0) + \frac{\tau^2}{1.2} f''(0) + \ldots\ldots$$

$$f(-\tau) = f(0) - \tau f'(0) + \frac{\tau^2}{1.2} f''(0) - \ldots\ldots$$

$$\therefore f(\tau) - f(-\tau) = 2\tau f'(0),$$

to the 2nd order in τ: and $f'(0)$ is the rate of precession at the middle of the interval. Of course the same applies to the precession in l or λ.

The following method is also very useful in certain cases where greater accuracy is required.

Let p_1, p_2, p_3 be the annual precessions for a star not very near the pole, in R.A. or N.P.D. for equidistant epochs, t_1, t_2, t_3; and let the whole interval of time from t_1 to t_3 be equal to T or to 2τ. Then, if P be the whole precessional motion for the interval $t_3 - t_1$ or T,

$$\frac{dP}{dT} = p_1 + \left(\frac{dp_1}{dT}\right)_0 \cdot T + \frac{1}{2}\left(\frac{d^2p_1}{dT^2}\right)_0 T^2 + \&c.$$

integrating from $T = 0$ to $T = 2\tau$, we get

$$P = 2p_1\tau + 2\left(\frac{dp_1}{dT}\right)_0 \cdot \tau^2 + \frac{4}{3}\cdot\left(\frac{d^2p_1}{dT^2}\right)_0 \tau^3 \quad \dots\dots\dots\dots (1),$$

also $\quad p_2 = p_1 + \left(\frac{dp_1}{dT}\right)_0 \tau + \frac{1}{2}\left(\frac{d^2p_1}{dT^2}\right)_0 \tau^2,$

and $\quad p_2\tau = p_1\tau + \left(\frac{dp_1}{dT}\right)_0 \tau^2 + \frac{1}{2}\left(\frac{d^2p_1}{dT^2}\right)_0 \tau^3 \quad \dots\dots\dots\dots (2),$

and similarly, $p_3\tau = p_1\tau + 2\left(\frac{dp_1}{dT}\right)_0 \tau^2 + 2\left(\frac{d^2p_1}{dT^2}\right)_0 \tau^3 \quad \dots\dots (3);$

therefore by eliminating, between the equations (1), (2), and (3) the differential coefficients $\left(\frac{dp_1}{dT}\right)_0$ and $\left(\frac{d^2p_1}{dT^2}\right)_0$, we get

$$P = \frac{1}{6}(p_1 + 4p_2 + p_3) \times 2\tau$$

$$= \frac{T}{6}(p_1 + 4p_2 + p_3).$$

EXAMPLE. In Bessel's *Fundamenta*, we find for α Aquilæ at the epoch 1755, R.A. $= 294°.42'.24''\cdot 0$

$$= 19^h.38^m.49^s\cdot 60,$$

also p_1 for $1755 = 43\cdot 410 = 2\cdot 894$ ⎫
$\quad p_2 \ \dots \ 1800 = 43\cdot 399 = 2\cdot 893$ ⎬ reducing to Peters' value of the precession;
$\quad p_3 \ \dots \ 1845 = 43\cdot 385 = 2\cdot 892$ ⎭

$$\therefore P = T \times 2\cdot 893, \text{ where, } T = 90,$$

and R.A. for $1845 = 19^h.38^m.49^s\cdot 60 + 4^m.20^s\cdot 37$

$$= 19^h.43^m.9^s\cdot 97.$$

Now from the *Greenwich Observations* for 1845, we find that the observed R.A. was $19^h.43^m.13^s\cdot 10$.

Hence the proper motion of the star in R.A. for 90 years is $+3''\cdot 13$; and the annual proper motion is $+0''\cdot 035$.

We now proceed to

Nutation.

12. It is clear from what has been said of Nutation that, if we refer a star to the *mean* ecliptic and equator at time t, (i. e. to the positions of those planes as determined by precession), the *nutation* in the position of the star will be the error which the deviation of the true plane of the equator from its mean position causes in the calculated place of the star.

The ecliptic has no nutation, the periodic terms in the expressions for its motion as disturbed by the planets being inconsiderable: so that the motion may be considered entirely secular or non-periodic: and thus, nutation does not affect a star's *latitude*.

The nutational motion of the equator is given by the *periodic* terms in Art. (2); i. e. by a change Δl in the longitude of all stars, and a change $\Delta \omega$ in the obliquity of the ecliptic, where Δl, $\Delta \omega$ contain only periodic terms.

13. To find the nutation in right ascension and declination, i. e. to find the change of place of a star in R.A. and N.P.D., due to the deviation of the true equator from its *mean* place $A'A''$—fig. Art. (7),—we may pursue the same method as that by which we obtained the precession. The only difference is that in the case of precession we referred the star to the *fixed* ecliptic EE_0: and in nutation, we refer it to the *mean* ecliptic EE'. From the figure it is easily seen that this is the same as putting in the formulæ of Art. (10), α for $\alpha + a$, l for $L + p_1$, λ for Λ, and ω for ω_0: δ being unchanged.

The formulæ so modified are

$$\cos \delta \cos \alpha = \cos \lambda \cos l,$$
$$\cos \delta \sin \alpha = \cos \lambda \sin l \cos \omega - \sin \lambda \sin \omega,$$
$$\sin \delta = \cos \lambda \sin l \sin \omega + \sin \lambda \cos \omega,$$

and are of course easily obtained independently by repeating the process of Art. (10), the planes of reference being EE', $A'A''$.

FORMULÆ FOR NUTATION. 215

Thus, if $\Delta\alpha$, $\Delta\delta$ be the nutations in α and δ:

$$\Delta\alpha = (\cos\omega + \sin\omega \tan\delta \sin\alpha)\, \Delta l - \cos\alpha \tan\delta\, \Delta\omega,$$

$$\Delta\delta = \cos\alpha \sin\omega\, \Delta l + \sin\alpha\, \Delta\omega.$$

And $\cos\omega$, $\sin\omega$ being multiplied by the small quantities Δl, $\Delta\omega$, there will be no appreciable error, if we put for ω its value for the beginning of the year 1800, or $23°.27'.54''$: substituting then for Δl, $\Delta\omega$ their values, $\Delta\alpha$ and $\Delta\delta$ can be found.

14. If we wish to retain second or higher powers of Δl, $\Delta\omega$, we must use Taylor's Theorem. Thus

$$\Delta\alpha = \frac{d\alpha}{dl}\Delta l + \frac{d\alpha}{d\omega}\Delta\omega + \frac{1}{2}\frac{d^2\alpha}{dl^2}\Delta l^2 + \frac{d^2\alpha}{dl.d\omega}\Delta l.\Delta\omega$$
$$+ \frac{1}{2}\frac{d^2\alpha}{d\omega^2}\Delta\omega^2 + \ldots\ldots$$

where, by the formulæ of Art. (13),

$$\frac{d\alpha}{dl} = \cos\omega + \sin\omega \tan\delta \sin\alpha,$$

$$\frac{d\alpha}{d\omega} = -\cos\alpha \tan\delta,$$

whence $\frac{d^2\alpha}{dl^2}$, &c. may be found, and thence $\Delta\alpha$; similarly, we can find $\Delta\delta$.

15. If the principal terms only in Δl, $\Delta\omega$ be retained, viz. the terms in $\sin\Omega$, $\cos\Omega$, the motion of the true pole is in an ellipse described about the mean place.

For, let P, p be the *mean* and true pole at time t, i.e. P the place of the pole as determined by applying precession, and p its place after again correcting for nutation: pq perpendicular to EP produced; let $Pq = x$, $pq = y$;

$$\begin{aligned} \text{then} \quad x &= Eq - EP \\ &= Ep - EP \text{ nearly,} \\ &= \Delta\omega; \\ \text{also} \quad y &= \sin Ep \times \angle pEq, \\ &= \sin \omega \,.\, \Delta l, \text{ nearly.} \\ \text{And} \quad \therefore \quad x &= a \cos \Omega, \\ y &= b \sin \Omega, \end{aligned}$$

where a and b are known constants;

$$\text{hence} \quad \frac{x^2}{a^2} + \frac{y^2}{b^2} = 1,$$

and thus the motion of p is in an ellipse about P, whose major-axis points to E.

16. We have now shewn how, supposing the motion of the equator on the ecliptic, or Lunisolar Precession and Nutation, and the motion of the ecliptic on the equator or Planetary Precession, to be known, we can, from the latitude and longitude, or right-ascension and declination, at any assumed time, deduce the same for any future time. Conversely, if we obtain by observation the right-ascension and declination of a star at two epochs, separated by a considerable interval, we can, from the difference between these observed values, obtain equations to determine m and n. It is found that all stars do not give the same values: this shews that the changes of place of some stars are not wholly due to the motions of the planes of reference, but that part of the change must be due to some *proper motion* (as it is called), either of the solar system, or of the stars themselves, or of both.

If, however, we determine m and n by a large number of stars, it is probable that in the *mean* of the values thus found, the proper motion will be eliminated or nearly so; those which increase m or n being on the whole counterbalanced by those which diminish them. And, the positions of stars being calculated by these *mean* values, the errors in their positions (if too large to be considered as errors of observation) may be assumed as due to proper motion. It is in this way that the proper motions of stars are determined. (See page 213.)

17. The corrections for refraction, aberration, precession, and nutation, enable us to deduce from the observed place of a star at any given epoch, the place in which it would be observed at any subsequent time.

The observed place of a star cleared of refraction gives the R.A. and N.P.D. referred to the equator and First Point of Aries at the time of observation, affected with the error of aberration.

Correcting for aberration we get the place of the star referred to the true equinox and equator corresponding to the time of observation. Next, correcting for nutation, we get the *mean* place, i.e. the place referred to the mean equator and mean equinox of the time of observation.

If then the place be wanted at an interval t from the time of observation, we apply the precession for the time t to the mean place of the star found as above: we thus have the mean place at the time t; whence the apparent place is found by correcting for nutation; then, applying aberration, we have the place in which the star would be observed, allowance being made for refraction.

18. We proceed to shew how, by means of tables, the labour of calculating the corrections is abbreviated, and the corrections applied to any number of stars with great facility: and we will first consider precession and nutation.

Let α_0, δ_0 be the *mean* R.A. and declination of a star at the year 1750; α, δ the *apparent* R.A. and declination at the epoch $1750 + t$ (neglecting aberration),

then $\alpha - \alpha_0 =$ precession for interval t
$\qquad\qquad +$ nutation at time $1750 + t$.

Now in the formulæ for precession α and δ stand for the *mean* R.A. and declination at time t: but the error introduced by considering them to be the *apparent* R.A. and declination is inconsiderable; thus from Arts. (10) and (13),

$$\alpha - \alpha_0 = (m + n \tan \delta \sin \alpha)\, t + (\cos \omega + \sin \omega \tan \delta \sin \alpha)\, \Delta l$$
$$- \cos \alpha \tan \delta\, \Delta \omega,$$

where

$$m + n \tan \delta \sin \alpha = -\frac{da}{dt} + (\cos \omega_0 + \sin \omega_0 \tan \delta \sin \alpha) \frac{dp_1}{dt},$$

in which for ω_0 we may put ω without sensible error; thus

$$\alpha - \alpha_0 = (m + n \tan \delta \sin \alpha) t + \left(m + n \tan \delta \sin \alpha + \frac{da}{dt} \right) \frac{\Delta l}{\frac{dp_1}{dt}} - \cos \alpha \tan \delta\, \Delta \omega,$$

$$= (m + n \tan \delta \sin \alpha) \left(t + \frac{\Delta l}{\frac{dp_1}{dt}} \right) - \cos \alpha \tan \delta\, \Delta \omega + \frac{\Delta l}{\frac{dp_1}{dt}} \cdot \frac{da}{dt},$$

whence, putting for Δl, $\Delta \omega$, $\frac{dp_1}{dt}$, $\frac{da}{dt}$ and m and n their values, $\alpha - \alpha_0$ is known in terms of α, δ, $\odot$, $\mathrm{)}$, and Ω.

Now $\odot$, $\mathrm{)}$, and Ω are functions of the *time only*, i.e., are determined when the time is given; hence, neglecting the last term, which is very small, we have, putting c for $m + n \tan \delta \sin \alpha$, d for $\cos \alpha \tan \delta$, C for $t + \dfrac{\Delta l}{\frac{dp_1}{dt}}$; and D for $\Delta \omega$,

$$\alpha - \alpha_0 = Cc + Dd,$$

where C, D are functions of the *time*, and c, d of the star's place.

19. Again, taking into account the correction for aberration, there will be found (on inspecting the form of the aberration in R.A.) to be two terms, which we may write $Aa + Bb$;

where
$A = -20{\cdot}445'' \cos \omega \cos \odot,$

$B = -20{\cdot}445'' \sin \odot,$

$a = \cos \alpha \sec \delta,$

$b = \sin \alpha \sec \delta,$

A and B being functions of the *time*, and a, b of the star's place.

If we denote by Δc the annual proper motion of the star in R.A. we have, then,

apparent R.A. $= a_0 + Aa + Bb + Cc + Dd + t \Delta c$.

Now, in the *Nautical Almanac*, at page xx. of every month, are given the logarithms of A, B, C, D for mean midnight throughout the month: also the *British Association Catalogue* contains the mean R.A. and N.P.D. for January 1, 1850, of more than 8000 stars, with their annual precessions and proper motions, as well as the logarithms of a, b, c, d for all of them.

If then the star in question be one of those in this catalogue, the apparent R.A. at any time can be found by a very simple calculation.

The apparent Declination is found in a precisely similar manner.

20. When the star is not in the catalogue, the logarithms of a, b, c, d are not known and must be computed from the formulæ previously given.

CHAPTER VIII.

ON THE PLANETS.

Section I. The Laws of Planetary Motion.

1. In the preceding portion of this treatise has been given, it is hoped, adequate information respecting the methods pursued in modern observatories both in the making and reducing of observations. The whole of these operations have for their object the determination of the positions of the heavenly bodies with respect to the equator, that is, to the determination of their right-ascensions and declinations measured from the moveable equinox and the moveable equator. With regard to the fixed stars, which are generally at immeasurable distances from us, the processes of reduction to a fixed epoch have necessitated the discussion of the theories of refraction, aberration, precession, and nutation, and the mode of application of these corrections, so that, from the raw observations, the student has been able to trace the successive steps by which the mean *place of a star for a given epoch* can be found. By this means, catalogues of the mean places of all the stars which have been observed at any observatory can be made, and these are the representations of all the star-work which has been performed at that observatory, and the *apparent places* of all the stars contained in them can be found for any time whatever, by the converse application of the precession, nutation, and aberration to the mean places. For the planets, which are not at an infinite distance, the dis-

cussion of parallax was needed, but this did not require any detailed statement of the planetary movements, the only element involved in those movements being the distance from the earth, at a given instant, which could be assumed to be known.

It is now however proper to explain the elementary principles of the motions of the planets in their orbits.

2. The planets all describe orbits round the sun in the same direction, that is, in the order of the signs of the zodiac, each orbit lying in a separate plane having a determinate inclination to the ecliptic or the plane of the earth's motion.

3. The laws of elliptic motion were first discovered and enumerated by Kepler without the help of any physical theory, and by means of the study of the motions of the planet Mars. They are as follows:

I. The planets, including the earth, describe ellipses round the sun having the sun in one of their foci.

II. They describe round the sun equal areas in equal times.

III. The squares of their periodic times are as the cubes of the semi-major axes of their orbits, or of their mean distances from the sun.

4. We will now proceed to develop the mathematical theory of the motions of the planets from the laws enunciated above.

Let AB be the major axis of the ellipse described by any one of the planets, round the sun in the focus at S; and let AMB be a semicircle on the same diameter.

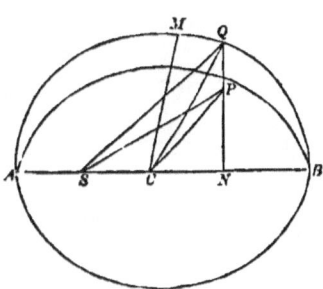

Then is A, the point nearest to the sun, called the *Perihelion* of the orbit, and the opposite point B is called the *Aphelion*.

At any time t (reckoned from the passage of the Perihelion) let P be the position of the planet; and draw QPN perpendicular to AB; and join SP and CQ, (C being the center). Imagine also another body moving uniformly with the planet's mean motion in the circle AMB, and, setting out from A at the same time, to be at M when the planet is at P so that the ellipse and circle are described in the same periodic time.

If therefore P be the *periodic time*, or time of describing the whole orbit measured in some unit of time (for instance the mean solar day), and n the *mean motion* of the planet, or the motion of the fictitious planet in its circular orbit, in this unit of time; then angle $ACM = nt = \dfrac{2\pi t}{P}$.

But by the equable description of areas,

$$\frac{t}{P} = \frac{\text{area } ASP}{\text{area of ellipse}} = \frac{\text{area } ASQ \times \frac{b}{a}}{\pi ab}$$

$$= \frac{\text{area } ACQ - \text{area } SCQ}{\pi a^2}.$$

Let now angle $ASQ = v$, called the *true anomaly*,

and angle $ACQ = u$, called the *excentric anomaly*.

Then area $ACQ = \dfrac{1}{2} a^2 u$ (a being as usual the semi-major axis);

and area $SCQ = \dfrac{1}{2} a^2 e \sin u$ (ae being equal to SC);

$\therefore$ area $ACQ - $ area $SCQ = \dfrac{a^2}{2}(u - e \sin u)$;

$\therefore nt = m = u - e \sin u$ .... (1).

Again, let $SP = \rho$.

RELATION OF EXCENTRIC AND TRUE ANOMALY.

Then
$$SP^2 = SN^2 + PN^2$$
$$= (SC + CN)^2 + QN^2 \times \frac{b^2}{a^2};$$
$$= (ae - a\cos u)^2 + (1 - e^2)\, a^2 \sin^2 u;$$
$$= a^2 - 2a^2 e \cos u + a^2 e^2 \cos^2 u;$$
$$= a^2(1 - e\cos u)^2;$$

or $\rho = a(1 - e\cos u)$.

Lastly,
$$\frac{SN}{SP} = -\cos v = \frac{ae - a\cos u}{a(1 - e\cos u)};$$

or $\cos v = \dfrac{\cos u - e}{1 - e\cos u};$

$$\therefore \frac{1 - \cos v}{1 + \cos v} = \frac{1 - \cos u + e(1 - \cos u)}{1 + \cos u - e(1 + \cos u)}$$
$$= \frac{1 + e}{1 - e} \cdot \frac{1 - \cos u}{1 + \cos u},$$

or
$$\tan^2 \tfrac{1}{2} v = \frac{1 + e}{1 - e} \tan^2 \tfrac{1}{2} u;$$

$$\therefore \tan \tfrac{1}{2} v = \sqrt{\frac{1 + e}{1 - e}} \tan \tfrac{1}{2} u \dots\dots\dots (2).$$

5. We have therefore two equations, of which (1) gives the relation between the mean and excentric anomaly, and (2) that between the true and the excentric anomaly; and, as the object of the problem is to determine the true anomaly in terms of the mean, we must in the next place eliminate u between the two equations.

This must be done by Lagrange's Theorem.

Thus, since $\tan \dfrac{v}{2} = \sqrt{\dfrac{1 + e}{1 - e}} \tan \dfrac{u}{2}$

$$= \alpha \tan \frac{u}{2} \text{ (suppose)},$$

224 TRUE ANOMALY IN TERMS OF MEAN ANOMALY.

we shall easily find, (see page 171),

$$v = u + 2\frac{\alpha-1}{\alpha+1}\sin u + \left(\frac{\alpha-1}{\alpha+1}\right)^2 \sin 2u + \&c.$$

or $\quad v = u + e\left(1 + \frac{e^2}{4}\right)\sin u + \frac{e^2}{4}\left(1 + \frac{e^2}{2}\right)\sin 2u + \frac{e^3}{12}\sin 3u + \&c.,$

(where it must be remembered that, for the sake of present convenience, v and u are still expressed in circular measure, or $v = v'' \times \sin 1''$, and $u = u'' \times \sin 1''$).

Also $m = u - e \sin u$.

Hence, by Lagrange's Theorem, since $v = fu$, and

$$u = m + e \sin u,$$

$$\therefore v = fm + \sin m \cdot f'm \cdot e + \frac{d}{dm}\{(\sin m)^2 \cdot f'm\}\frac{e^2}{1 \cdot 2}$$

$$+ \frac{d^2}{dm^2}\{(\sin m)^3 \cdot f'm\}\frac{e^3}{1 \cdot 2 \cdot 3} + \&c.$$

where

$$fm = m + \left(e + \frac{e^3}{4}\right)\sin m + \left(\frac{e^2}{4} + \frac{e^4}{8}\right)\sin 2m + \frac{e^3}{12}\sin 3m + \&c.,$$

and therefore

$$f'm = 1 + \left(e + \frac{e^3}{4}\right)\cos m + \left(\frac{e^2}{2} + \frac{e^4}{4}\right)\cos 2m + \frac{e^3}{4}\cos 3m + \&c.,$$

$$\sin m \cdot f'm = \sin m + \left(\frac{e}{2} + \frac{e^3}{8}\right)\sin 2m$$

$$+ \left(\frac{e^2}{4} + \frac{e^4}{8}\right)(\sin 3m - \sin m) + \&c.,$$

$$\sin^2 m \cdot f'm = \sin^2 m + \left(\frac{e}{4} + \frac{e^3}{16}\right)(\cos m - \cos 3m) + \&c.,$$

$$\frac{d(\sin^2 m \cdot f'm)}{dm} = \sin 2m + \left(\frac{e}{4} + \frac{e^3}{16}\right)(3 \sin 3m - \sin m) + \&c.$$

Similarly, $\dfrac{d^2(\sin^3 m \cdot f'm)}{d^2 m} = \dfrac{9}{4}\sin 3m - \dfrac{3}{4}\sin m,$

$$\therefore v = m + \left(e + \frac{e^3}{4}\right)\sin m + \frac{e^2}{4}\sin 2m + \frac{e^3}{12}\sin 3m + \&c.$$

$$+ e\sin m + \frac{e^2}{2}\sin 2m + \frac{e^3}{4}(\sin 3m - \sin m) + \&c.$$

$$+ \frac{e^2}{2}\sin 2m + \frac{e^3}{8}(3\sin 3m - \sin m) + \&c.$$

$$+ \frac{e^3}{8}(3\sin 3m - \sin m) + \&c.$$

$$= m + \left(2e - \frac{e^3}{4}\right)\sin m + \frac{5e^2}{4}\sin 2m + \frac{13e^3}{12}\sin 3m + \&c.$$

6. We must now expand the radius-vector ρ in terms of nt or m; that is, we must eliminate u between the two equations

$$\rho = a(1 - e\cos u),$$

and $\qquad m = u - e\sin u,$

or, $\qquad u = m + e\sin u.$

Hence, by Lagrange's Theorem, we have as before,

$$\rho = fm + \{\sin m \cdot f'm\}e + \frac{d}{dm}\{(\sin m)^2 \cdot f'm\}\frac{e^2}{1.2}$$

$$+ \frac{d^2}{dm^2}\{(\sin m)^3 \cdot f'm\}\frac{e^3}{1.2.3} + \&c.$$

where $\qquad fm = a(1 - e\cos m),$

and therefore $\qquad f'm = ae\sin m,$

$$\sin m \cdot f'm = ae\sin^2 m = \frac{1}{2}ae(1 - \cos 2m),$$

$$(\sin m)^2 \cdot f'm = ae\sin^3 m,$$

and $\qquad \dfrac{d}{dm}\{(\sin m)^2 \cdot f'm\} = 3ae\sin^2 m \cos m$

$$= \frac{3ae}{2}\sin 2m \sin m$$

$$= \frac{3ae}{4}(\cos m - \cos 3m),$$

$$\sin^3 m \cdot f'm = ae \sin^4 m,$$

$$\frac{d}{dm}(\sin^3 m \cdot f'm) = 4ae \sin^3 m \cos m,$$

$$\frac{d^2}{dm^2}(\sin^3 m \cdot f'm) = 12ae \sin^2 m \cos^2 m - 4ae \sin^4 m$$

$$= 4ae(3\cos^2 m - \sin^2 m)\sin^2 m$$
$$= ae\{3(1+\cos 2m) - (1-\cos 2m)\} \times (1-\cos 2m)$$
$$= ae(2 + 4\cos 2m)(1 - \cos 2m)$$
$$= 2ae(1 + \cos 2m - 2\cos^2 2m)$$
$$= 2ae\{1 + \cos 2m - (1 + \cos 4m)\}$$
$$= 2ae(\cos 2m - \cos 4m);$$

$$\therefore \rho = a\left\{1 - e\cos m + \frac{e^2}{2}(1 - \cos 2m) + \frac{3e^3}{8}(\cos m - \cos 3m)\right.$$
$$\left. + \frac{e^4}{3}(\cos 2m - \cos 4m) + \&c.\right\}$$

or $\rho = a\left\{1 + \frac{e^2}{2} - e\left(1 - \frac{3e^2}{8}\right)\cos m - \frac{e^2}{2}\left(1 - \frac{2e^2}{3}\right)\cos 2m\right.$
$$\left. - \frac{3e^3}{8}\cos 3m - \&c.\right\}$$

7. We may here remark that the difference between the *true* and the *mean* anomaly is called the *Equation of the Centre*, this being the first equation or correction to be applied to the mean motion in the calculation of the place of a planet.

8. To find the greatest equation of the centre in a given elliptic orbit.

Since $v - m$ is a maximum,

$$\frac{dv}{du} = \frac{dm}{du}.$$

Now $m = u - e \sin u,$

$$\therefore \frac{dm}{du} = 1 - e \cos u,$$

and
$$\tan \frac{v}{2} = \sqrt{\frac{1+e}{1-e}} \tan \frac{u}{2};$$

$$\therefore \frac{dv}{du} = \sqrt{\frac{1+e}{1-e}} \frac{\sec^2 \frac{u}{2}}{\sec^2 \frac{v}{2}}$$

$$= \sqrt{\frac{1+e}{1-e}} \frac{\sec^2 \frac{u}{2}}{1 + \tan^2 \frac{v}{2}}$$

$$= \sqrt{\frac{1+e}{1-e}} \frac{1}{\cos^2 \frac{u}{2} \left(1 + \frac{1+e}{1-e} \tan^2 \frac{u}{2}\right)}$$

$$= \frac{\sqrt{1-e^2}}{(1-e)\cos^2 \frac{u}{2} + (1+e)\sin^2 \frac{u}{2}}$$

$$= \frac{\sqrt{1-e^2}}{1 - e \cos u};$$

$$\therefore 1 - e \cos u = \frac{\sqrt{1-e^2}}{1 - e \cos u},$$

or $1 - e \cos u = \sqrt[4]{1-e^2}$

$$= 1 - \frac{1}{4}e^2 - \frac{3}{32}e^4 - \&c.,$$

or $\cos u = \dfrac{e}{4} + \dfrac{3e^3}{32} + \&c.$

Let now $u = 90° - u'$;

$$\therefore \sin u' = \frac{e}{4} + \frac{3e^3}{32} + \&c.$$

$$= u' - \frac{u'^3}{6} + \&c.,$$

whence we should easily find, by assuming
$$u' = Ae + Be^3 + \&c.,$$

and equating coefficients of the two expansions, that

$$u' = \frac{e}{4} + \frac{37e^3}{384} + \&c.$$

$$\text{or } u = \frac{\pi}{2} - \frac{e}{4} - \frac{37e^3}{384} - \&c.$$

Again, since $\rho = \dfrac{a(1-e^2)}{1+e\cos v} = a(1-e\cos u)$

$$= a\sqrt[4]{1-e^2};$$

$\therefore 1 + e \cos v = (1-e^2)^{\frac{3}{4}}$

$$= 1 - \frac{3}{4}e^2 - \frac{3}{32}e^4 - \&c.,$$

$$\text{or } \cos v = -\frac{3}{4}e - \frac{3}{32}e^3 - \&c.,$$

or, if $v = v' + \dfrac{\pi}{2}$,

$$\sin v' = \frac{3}{4}e + \frac{3}{32}e^3 + \&c.;$$

whence, by the same process as before,

$$v' = \frac{3e}{4} + \frac{21e^3}{128} + \&c.,$$

$$\text{or } v = \frac{\pi}{2} + \frac{3e}{4} + \frac{21e^3}{128} + \&c.$$

Finally, $\sin u = \sqrt{1 - \cos^2 u}$

$$= \sqrt{1 - \frac{e^2}{16} - \&c.}$$

$$= 1 - \frac{e^2}{32} - \&c.;$$

$\therefore e \sin u = e - \dfrac{e^3}{32} - \&c.$

Hence if E be the greatest equation of the centre,

$$E = v - nt$$
$$= v - u + e \sin u$$
$$= \frac{\pi}{2} + \frac{3e}{4} + \frac{21e^3}{128} + \&c.$$
$$- \frac{\pi}{2} + \frac{e}{4} + \frac{37e^3}{384} + \&c.$$
$$+ e - \frac{e^3}{32} + \&c.$$
$$= 2e + \frac{88e^3}{384} + \&c.$$
$$= 2e + \frac{11e^3}{48} + \&c.$$

It needs scarcely be mentioned that E is here expressed in circular measure. To express it in seconds of angle we must multiply by $\frac{1}{\sin 1''}$.

EXAMPLE. For the Earth's orbit, or the apparent solar orbit,
$$e = 0 \cdot 01685,$$
$$\text{or } 2e = 0 \cdot 02370.$$

Hence, Log $0 \cdot 02370 = 8 \cdot 3747483$
Ar. co. log sin $1'' = 5 \cdot 3144251$

Sum $= \log 4888''\cdot 49 = 3 \cdot 6891734$

Again, Log $e^3 = 4 \cdot 6797997$
Log $11 = 1 \cdot 0413927$
Ar. co. log $48 = 8 \cdot 3187588$
Ar. co. log sin $1'' = 5 \cdot 3144251$

Sum $= \log 0''\cdot 23 = 9 \cdot 3543763$

Hence $E = 4888''\cdot 72$
$= 1°. 21'. 28'''\cdot 72,$

and the mean sun can never separate from the true sun farther than by this quantity*.

9. In the preceding investigations the expansions have been made according to powers of the excentricity of the orbit, and the series will converge rapidly only when the excentricity is small, or for planets moving in nearly circular orbits. For comets, which generally move either in parabolic orbits or orbits of very great excentricity, a different method must be employed. We will at present confine ourselves to two problems of great elegance and simplicity.

10. *To find the radius-vector and the time corresponding to a given value of the true anomaly, in orbits of very great excentricity.*

Generally we have

$$\rho = \frac{a(1-e^2)}{1+e \cos v}$$

$$= \frac{a(1-e^2)}{\cos^2 \frac{v}{2} + \sin^2 \frac{v}{2} + e\left(\cos^2 \frac{v}{2} - \sin^2 \frac{v}{2}\right)}$$

$$= \frac{a(1-e^2)}{(1+e)\cos^2 \frac{v}{2} + (1-e)\sin^2 \frac{v}{2}}$$

$$= \frac{1}{\cos^2 \frac{v}{2}} \cdot \frac{a(1-e^2)}{1+e+(1-e)\tan^2 \frac{v}{2}}$$

$$= \frac{1}{\cos^2 \frac{v}{2}} \cdot \frac{a(1-e^2)}{1+e+(1+e)\tan^2 \frac{u}{2}}$$

$$= a(1-e) \frac{\cos^2 \frac{u}{2}}{\cos^2 \frac{v}{2}}$$

$$= p \frac{\cos^2 \frac{u}{2}}{\cos^2 \frac{v}{2}},$$

if p be the perihelion distance.

* See Price's *Infinitesimal Calculus*, Vol. III. p. 515.

ORBITS OF GREAT EXCENTRICITY.

Again, to find the time from perihelion, if P be the periodic time, and μ the force of the sun at the unit of distance,

$$P = \frac{2\pi a^{\frac{3}{2}}}{\mu^{\frac{1}{2}}},$$

hence, if the year be the *unit* of time, and the sun's mean distance the unit of distance,

$$\frac{P}{1} = \frac{a^{\frac{3}{2}}}{1}, \text{ or } P = a^{\frac{3}{2}}.$$

But, since the area described round the focus in the time dt is $\frac{1}{2}\rho^2 dv$, and the areas are proportional to the times,

$$\frac{dt}{P} = \frac{dt}{a^{\frac{3}{2}}} = \frac{\frac{1}{2}\rho^2 dv}{\text{area of ellipse}}$$

$$= \frac{a^2(1-e^2)^2 dv}{2\pi ab(1+e\cos v)^2}$$

$$= \frac{a^2(1-e^2)^2 dv}{2\pi a^2 \sqrt{1-e^2}\cdot(1+e\cos v)^2},$$

or $\dfrac{dt}{dv} = \dfrac{a^{\frac{3}{2}}}{2\pi}\cdot\dfrac{(1-e^2)^{\frac{3}{2}}}{(1+e\cos v)^2}$

$$= \frac{p^{\frac{3}{2}}}{2\pi}\cdot\frac{(1+e)^{\frac{3}{2}}}{(1+e\cos v)^2}$$

$$= (\text{if } c = 1-e)\;\frac{p^{\frac{3}{2}}}{2\pi}\cdot\frac{(2-c)^{\frac{3}{2}}}{(1+e\cos v)^2}.$$

Let now $x = \tan\dfrac{v}{2}$; $\therefore \dfrac{dv}{dx} = \dfrac{2}{1+x^2}$,

and $1 + e\cos v = \cos^2\dfrac{v}{2} + \sin^2\dfrac{v}{2} + e\left(\cos^2\dfrac{v}{2} - \sin^2\dfrac{v}{2}\right)$

$$= (1+e)\cos^2\frac{v}{2} + (1-e)\sin^2\frac{v}{2}$$

$$= \frac{1 + e + (1-e)\tan^2\dfrac{v}{2}}{1 + \tan^2\dfrac{v}{2}}$$

$$= \frac{2 - c + cx^2}{1 + x^2}$$

$$= \frac{2 - c(1 - x^2)}{1 + x^2};$$

$$\therefore \frac{dt}{dx} = \frac{dt}{dv} \cdot \frac{dv}{dx}$$

$$= \frac{2}{1+x^2} \cdot \frac{p^{\frac{3}{2}}(2-c)^{\frac{3}{2}}}{2\pi} \cdot \frac{(1+x^2)^2}{\{2-c(1-x^2)\}^2}$$

$$= \frac{p^{\frac{3}{2}}(2-c)^{\frac{3}{2}}}{\pi} \cdot \frac{1+x^2}{\{2-c(1-x^2)\}^2}$$

$$= \frac{p^{\frac{3}{2}}\left(1-\frac{c}{2}\right)^{\frac{3}{2}}}{\pi\sqrt{2}} \cdot \frac{1+x^2}{\{1-\frac{c}{2}(1-x^2)\}^2}$$

$$= \frac{p^{\frac{3}{2}}}{\pi\sqrt{2}} \left(1 - \frac{3c}{4} + \frac{3c^2}{32}\right) \cdot (1+x^2) \cdot \{1 + c(1-x^2)$$

$$+ \frac{3c^2}{4}(1-x^2)^2 + \&\text{c.}\}$$

$$= \frac{p^{\frac{3}{2}}}{\pi\sqrt{2}} \left(1 - \frac{3c}{4} + \frac{3c^2}{32}\right) \{1 + x^2 + c(1-x^4)$$

$$+ \frac{3c^2}{4} \cdot (1-x^2)^2 (1+x^2) + \&\text{c.}\};$$

$$\therefore t = C + \frac{p^{\frac{3}{2}}}{\pi\sqrt{2}} \left(1 - \frac{3c}{4} + \frac{3c^2}{32}\right) \left\{ x + \frac{x^3}{3} + c\left(x - \frac{x^5}{5}\right) \right.$$

$$\left. + \frac{3c^2}{4}\left(x - \frac{x^3}{3} - \frac{x^5}{5} + \frac{x^7}{7}\right) + \&\text{c.} \right\};$$

and, if the time be measured from perihelion, then $t = 0$ when $v = 0$, and therefore when $x = 0$.

Hence $C = 0$;

$$\therefore t = \frac{p^{\frac{3}{2}}}{\pi\sqrt{2}} \left\{ x + \frac{x^3}{3} + c\left(\frac{x}{4} - \frac{x^3}{4} - \frac{x^5}{5}\right) + \frac{3c^2}{32}\left(x - \frac{7x^3}{3} + \frac{8x^7}{7}\right) + \&\text{c.} \right\}$$

$$= \frac{p^{\frac{3}{2}}}{\pi\sqrt{2}} \left\{ \tan\frac{v}{2} + \frac{1}{3}\tan^3\frac{v}{2} + c\left(\frac{\tan\frac{v}{2}}{4} - \frac{\tan^3\frac{v}{2}}{4} - \frac{\tan^5\frac{v}{2}}{5}\right) \right.$$

$$\left. + \frac{3c^2}{32}\left(\tan\frac{v}{2} - \frac{7}{3}\tan^3\frac{v}{2} + \frac{8}{7}\tan^7\frac{v}{2}\right) + \&\text{c.} \right\}.$$

LAMBERT'S THEOREM. 233

If $c = 0$ or $e = 1$, the orbit becomes a parabola, and

$$t = \frac{p^{\frac{3}{2}}}{\pi \sqrt{2}} \left(\tan \frac{v}{2} + \frac{1}{3} \tan^3 \frac{v}{2} \right),$$

also

$$\rho = \frac{p}{\cos^2 \frac{v}{2}}.$$

NOTE. In the actual use of the preceding formula for the determination of the true anomaly in cometary orbits, it is usual to construct a table of the values of t corresponding to the values of v for orbits in which $p = 1$.

Let now t and t' represent the times from perihelion for which the true anomaly is v, in two orbits whose least distances from the centre of force are p and 1.

Then
$$t = \frac{p^{\frac{3}{2}}}{\pi \sqrt{2}} \left\{ \tan \frac{v}{2} + \frac{1}{3} \tan^3 \frac{v}{2} \right\},$$

and
$$t' = \frac{1}{\pi \sqrt{2}} \left\{ \tan \frac{v}{2} + \frac{1}{3} \tan^3 \frac{v}{2} \right\};$$

$$\therefore t' = \frac{t}{p^{\frac{3}{2}}}.$$

We must therefore first divide the time from perihelion by $p^{\frac{3}{2}}$, and then entering the table with the time thus resulting, we shall find the required true anomaly v.

11. *To find the time of describing any arc of a parabola in terms of its chord and the focal distances of its extremities.*

Let ρ and ρ' be the two focal distances; v and v' the corresponding true anomalies; c the chord.

Then, the preceding notation being retained,

$$\rho = \frac{p}{\cos^2 \frac{v}{2}} = p(1 + x^2), \text{ and } \rho' = p(1 + x'^2),$$

and the included sectorial area

$$= \frac{1}{2}\int \rho^2 dv = \frac{p^2}{2}\int \left(1 + \tan^2 \frac{v}{2}\right)^2 dv$$

$$= p^2 \int \left(1 + \tan^2 \frac{v}{2}\right) d\left(\tan \frac{v}{2}\right)$$

$$= p^2 \left(\tan \frac{v}{2} + \frac{1}{3}\tan^3 \frac{v}{2}\right),$$

$$= \text{(between the limits } v \text{ and } v')$$

$$p^2 \left\{x' - x + \frac{1}{3}(x'^3 - x^3)\right\}$$

$$= p^2(x' - x) \cdot \left\{1 + \frac{1}{3}(x'^2 + x'x + x^2)\right\}$$

$$= \frac{p^2}{3}(x' - x) \cdot (1 + x'^2 + 1 + x'x + 1 + x^2).$$

Again, in the triangle of which the sides are ρ, ρ', and c, and the angle included by ρ and ρ' is $v' - v$,

we have $\cos \frac{1}{2}(v' - v) = \sqrt{\dfrac{s(s-c)}{\rho \rho'}}$ where $s = \dfrac{\rho + \rho' + c}{2}$;

$$\therefore 1 + xx' = 1 + \tan \frac{v}{2} \tan \frac{v'}{2} = \cos \frac{v' - v}{2} \sec \frac{v}{2} \sec \frac{v'}{2}$$

$$= \sqrt{\frac{s(s-c)}{\rho \rho'}} \cdot \frac{\sqrt{\rho \rho'}}{p} = \frac{1}{p}\sqrt{s(s-c)},$$

also
$$1 + x^2 = \frac{\rho}{p},$$

$$1 + x'^2 = \frac{\rho'}{p};$$

and
$$(x' - x)^2 = x'^2 - 2xx' + x^2$$

$$= 1 + x'^2 + 1 + x^2 - 2(1 + xx')$$

$$= \frac{1}{p}(\rho + \rho' - 2\sqrt{s(s-c)})$$

$$= \frac{1}{p}\{s - 2\sqrt{s(s-c)} + s - c\};$$

$$\therefore x' - x = \frac{1}{\sqrt{p}} (\sqrt{s} - \sqrt{s-c});$$

and sectorial area

$$= \frac{\sqrt{p}}{3} \{(\sqrt{s} - \sqrt{s-c}) \cdot \{\rho + \rho' + \sqrt{s(s-c)}\}$$

$$= \frac{\sqrt{p}}{3} \{(\sqrt{s} - \sqrt{s-c}) \cdot \{s + \sqrt{s(s-c)} + s - c\}$$

$$= \frac{\sqrt{p}}{3} \{s^{\frac{3}{2}} - (s-c)^{\frac{3}{2}}\}$$

$$= \frac{\sqrt{p}}{6\sqrt{2}} \{(\rho + \rho' + c)^{\frac{3}{2}} - (\rho + \rho' - c)^{\frac{3}{2}}\},$$

but the area described in the unit of time is $\sqrt{\frac{\mu p}{2}}$, where μ is the value of the central force at the unit of distance, therefore the time of describing the sectorial area represented above, is

$$\frac{1}{6\sqrt{\mu}} \{(\rho + \rho' + c)^{\frac{3}{2}} - (\rho + \rho' - c)^{\frac{3}{2}}\}.$$

NOTE. A slight knowledge of physical astronomy has been here assumed in the expression, area in unit of time $= \sqrt{\frac{\mu p}{2}}$, but this expression is easily arrived at by the consideration that area in unit of time $= \frac{1}{2} p \times$ velocity at vertex of parabola, and that the velocity $= \sqrt{\frac{2\mu}{p}}$.

12. *Elements of the orbit of a Planet.*

We have thus far only treated of the laws regulating the motion of a planet or comet in its elliptic orbit. We must now shew how by means of these, we are able to represent the position of a body in the heavens; or, in other words, to find its latitude or longitude when referred either to the sun or the earth in the plane of the ecliptic, and its right ascension or declination when referred to the centre of the earth and the plane of the earth's equator.

Now the orbit of a planet (neglecting perturbations) lies in one plane, which has a definite position with respect to the ecliptic. .For example, it has a definite angle of *Inclination* to the ecliptic, and cuts it in two points at the opposite extremities of a line passing through the sun's centre. These points are called the *Ascending and Descending Nodes* of the orbit; ascending when the planet is passing from the south to the north side of the ecliptic, and descending when passing from north to south.

Hence the two elements which determine the position of the planet's orbit with respect to the ecliptic are the *Inclination* and the *Longitude of the Node*.

Next with regard to the orbit itself, the position of the body at any time will depend upon the following quantities:

(1) Upon the position of the major axis of the orbit, defined by the *longitude of the perihelion or aphelion*.

(2) On the magnitude of the orbit, or the value of *the semi-major axis*, or of the periodic time.

(3) On the excentricity of the orbit.

(4) On the mean longitude of the body in its orbit at a given time, or upon the *Epoch of Mean Longitude*.

These six quantities, then, namely: 1. The Inclination; 2. The Longitude of the Node; 3. The Longitude of the Perihelion; 4. The Semi-major Axis; 5. The Excentricity; and 6. The Epoch of Mean Longitude, will fully determine the position of the planet at a given time. It remains to shew how these quantities are introduced into the calculation.

Let S be the centre of the sun taken as the centre of the sphere of the heavens, and the origin of co-ordinates. $\Upsilon E'$ and ΥE traces of the ecliptic and equator on the sphere, intersecting in the first point of Aries (Υ) from which longitudes are measured; N_1Nm the similar trace of the orbit of a planet; m the position of the planet at time t.

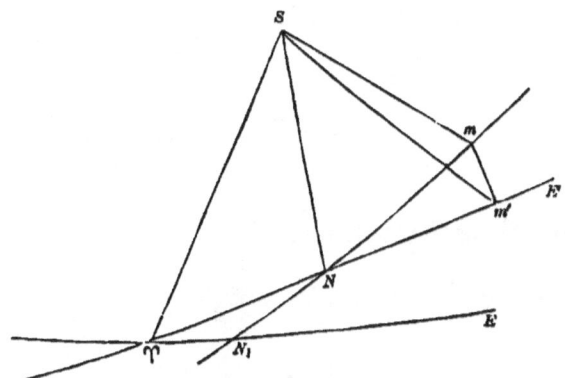

Then is N the ascending node of the orbit, and its longitude is angle $\Upsilon SN = \Omega$; also angle mNE' is the inclination $= i$.

The longitude of the planet in its orbit (l) is the sum of the arcs, ΥN (measured along the ecliptic to the node) and Nm (measured on the orbit). And, if we draw an arc of great circle mm' perpendicular to $\Upsilon NE'$, $\Upsilon m'$ is called the reduced longitude (l'). Finally, $mm' (= \beta)$ is the latitude of the planet.

All the above-mentioned quantities are of course *heliocentric*.

Sm is the radius-vector of the orbit $= \rho$; and we will call Sm', its projection on the ecliptic, ρ'.

We have therefore plainly $\rho' = \rho \cos \beta$.

13. *To find the reduced longitude.*

In the triangle Nmm', we have

$$\tan Nm' = \cos N \tan Nm,$$

or
$$\tan (l' - \Omega) = \cos i \tan (l - \Omega).$$

Let
$$l' - \Omega = x,$$

and
$$l - \Omega = y;$$

$$\therefore \frac{e^{2x\sqrt{-1}}-1}{e^{2x\sqrt{-1}}+1} = \cos i \cdot \frac{e^{2y\sqrt{-1}}-1}{e^{2y\sqrt{-1}}+1},$$

or
$$e^{2x\sqrt{-1}} = \frac{1-\cos i + (1+\cos i)\, e^{2y\sqrt{-1}}}{1+\cos i + (1-\cos i)\, e^{2y\sqrt{-1}}}$$

$$= e^{2y\sqrt{-1}} \frac{1+\tan^2 \frac{i}{2} e^{-2y\sqrt{-1}}}{1+\tan^2 \frac{i}{2} e^{2y\sqrt{-1}}};$$

therefore, taking the logarithms,

$$2x\sqrt{-1} = 2y\sqrt{-1} + \log_e\left(1+\tan^2\frac{i}{2} e^{-2y\sqrt{-1}}\right)$$

$$- \log_e\left(1+\tan^2\frac{i}{2} e^{2y\sqrt{-1}}\right)$$

$$= 2y\sqrt{-1} + \tan^2\frac{i}{2} e^{-2y\sqrt{-1}} - \frac{1}{2}\tan^4\frac{i}{2} e^{-4y\sqrt{-1}}$$

$$+ \frac{1}{3}\tan^6\frac{i}{2} e^{-6y\sqrt{-1}} - \&c.$$

$$- \tan^2\frac{i}{2} e^{2y\sqrt{-1}} + \frac{1}{2}\tan^4\frac{i}{2} e^{4y\sqrt{-1}} - \frac{1}{3}\tan^6\frac{i}{2} e^{6y\sqrt{-1}} + \&c.$$

\or $x = y - \tan^2\frac{i}{2}\sin 2y + \frac{1}{2}\tan^4\frac{i}{2}\sin 4y - \frac{1}{3}\tan^6\frac{i}{2}\sin 6y + \&c.$

or $l' = l - \tan^2\frac{i}{2}\sin 2(l-\Omega) + \frac{1}{2}\tan^4\frac{i}{2}\sin 4(l-\Omega)$

$$- \frac{1}{3}\tan^6\frac{i}{2}\sin 6(l-\Omega) + \&c.$$

or, when expressed in seconds of arc,

$$l' - l \,(= \textit{reduction to the ecliptic})$$

$$= -\tan^2\frac{i}{2} \cdot \frac{\sin 2(l-\Omega)}{\sin 1''} + \frac{\tan^4\frac{i}{2}\sin 4(l-\Omega)}{\sin 2''}$$

$$- \frac{\tan^6\frac{i}{2}\sin 6(l-\Omega)}{\sin 3''} + \&c.$$

TRUE LONGITUDE IN TERMS OF MEAN LONGITUDE. 239

14. Let now the mean longitude of a planet at the commencement of the time t be ϵ; n the mean daily motion in the orbit; ϖ the longitude of the perihelion.

Then is $nt + \epsilon - \varpi$ the mean anomaly at the time t. And, substituting this for m in the expression for the true anomaly (page 225), we have

$$\text{True anomaly} = nt + \epsilon - \varpi + \left(2e - \frac{e^3}{4}\right) \sin(nt + \epsilon - \varpi)$$

$$+ \frac{5e^2}{4} \sin 2(nt + \epsilon - \varpi) + \frac{13}{12} e^3 \sin 3(nt + \epsilon - \varpi) + \&c.,$$

and true longitude (in orbit)$_{\bullet} = l$

$$= nt + \epsilon + \left(2e - \frac{e^3}{4}\right) \sin(nt + \epsilon - \varpi) + \frac{5e^2}{4} \sin 2(nt + \epsilon - \varpi)$$

$$+ \frac{13}{12} e^3 \sin 3(nt + \epsilon - \varpi) + \&c.$$

We shall have occasion to return to this equation again, for the purpose of explaining the method of determining from observation the errors of the assumed elements of a planet's orbit. At present it is necessary to determine the relations which exist between the geocentric and heliocentric quantities which define the position of the planet.

15. Let S be the centre of the Sun (supposed to be in the ecliptic, the sun's latitude being neglected) at a given time.

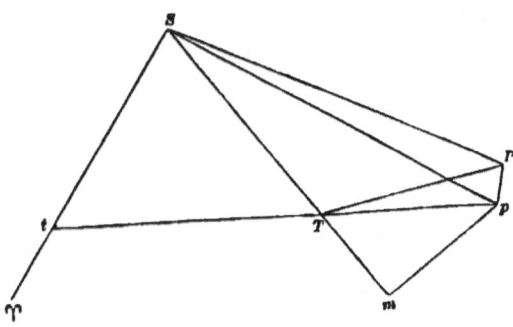

240 GEOCENTRIC AND HELIOCENTRIC RELATIONS.

T the earth, and P a planet, projected on the ecliptic by the perpendicular Pp. $S\Upsilon$ the direction of the first point of Aries from which the longitudes are measured.

Join SP, Sp, pT (produced to t), and draw pm perpendicular to ST produced.

Let angle $\Upsilon Sp = l' =$ heliocentric reduced longitude,

... $\Upsilon tT = L =$ geocentric longitude.

$SP = \rho$ and $Sp = \rho'$,

$ST = R$, $TP = \Delta$ and $Tp = \Delta'$.

Angle $PSp = \beta =$ heliocentric latitude,

... $PTp = \lambda =$ geocentric latitude,

... $\Upsilon ST =$ earth's longitude $= \odot + 180°$.

Then we have immediately the following relations and equalities:

Angle $\quad tTS = pTm = \Upsilon tT - \Upsilon ST$

$\qquad\qquad = L - \odot - 180°$.

Angle $\quad tpS = \Upsilon tp - \Upsilon Sp$

$\qquad\qquad = L - l'$.

Angle $\quad TSp = \Upsilon Sp - \Upsilon ST$

$\qquad\qquad = l' - \odot - 180°$.

$Sp = SP \cos \beta$,

or $\quad \rho' = \rho \cos \beta$;

and $\quad Tp = TP \cos \lambda$,

or $\quad \Delta' = \Delta \cos \lambda$.

Again, $\quad \dfrac{ST}{Tp} = \dfrac{\sin TpS}{\sin TSp} = \dfrac{\sin (L - l')}{\sin (l' - \odot - 180°)}$,

or $\quad \dfrac{R}{\Delta'} = - \dfrac{\sin (L - l')}{\sin (l' - \odot)}$,

or $\quad R \sin (l' - \odot) + \Delta' \sin (L - l') = 0$ ....(1).

Also, $Sp = ST \cos TSp + Tp \cos TpS$,

or $\rho' = R \cos (l' - \odot - 180°) + \Delta' \cos (L - l')$

$ = - R \cos (l' - \odot) + \Delta' \cos (L - l')$ ....(2).

Finally, $Pp = SP \sin PSp = TP \sin PTp$,

$$\left. \begin{array}{c} \text{or} \quad \rho \sin \beta = \Delta \sin \lambda \\ \text{or thus,} \quad \rho' \tan \beta = \Delta' \tan \lambda \end{array} \right\} \quad \text{............(3).}$$

Other equations between geocentric and heliocentric positions may be thus deduced:

$pm = Tp \sin pTm = Sp \sin pSm$,

or $\Delta' \sin (L - \odot - 180°) = \rho' \sin (l' - \odot - 180°)$,

or $\Delta' \sin (L - \odot) = \rho' \sin (l' - \odot)$ ....(4),

$Sm = ST + Tm = ST + Tp \cos pTm$,

or $\rho' \cos (l' - \odot - 180°) = R + \Delta' \cos (L - \odot - 180°)$,

or $\Delta' \cos (L - \odot) = R + \rho' \cos (l' - \odot)$ ....(5).

The equations (4) and (5) serve immediately for determining the geocentric quantities Δ' and L from the heliocentric ρ' and l', or *vice versâ*, while equations (3) will determine the geocentric from the heliocentric latitude, or the contrary.

If we project Sp, ST, and Tp upon the line of the equinoxes $S\Upsilon$, and in the direction perpendicular to it, we shall plainly have

$\rho' \cos l' = R \cos (180° + \odot) + \Delta' \cos L$,

$\rho' \sin l' = R \sin (180° + \odot) + \Delta' \sin L$;

or $\rho' \cos l' = \Delta' \cos L - R \cos \odot$ ....(6),

$\rho' \sin l' = \Delta' \sin L - R \sin \odot$ ....(7),

which equations are sometimes useful.

16. *To find the relation between the geocentric and the heliocentric errors of longitude, latitude, &c.*

To do this conveniently it will be better to investigate first the variations of the parts of the plane triangle whose sides are a, b, c, and opposite angles A, B, C.

Taking the well-known equations,
$$c \sin A = a \sin C,$$
and $c \cos A = b - a \cos C,$

let $c \sin A = P,$

and $c \cos A = Q;$

then $\delta P = \sin A \, \delta c + c \cos A \, \delta A,$

and $\delta Q = \cos A \, \delta c - c \sin A \, \delta A,$

from which we get easily
$$\delta c = \sin A \, \delta P + \cos A \, \delta Q,$$
$$c \cdot \delta A = \cos A \, \delta P - \sin A \, \delta Q;$$

but $P = a \sin C,$

and $Q = b - a \cos C;$

$\therefore \delta P = \sin C \, \delta a + a \cos C \, \delta C,$

and $\delta Q = \delta b - \cos C \, \delta a + a \sin C \, \delta C;$

whence by substitution we shall easily find
$$\delta c = \cos A \, \delta b + \cos B \, \delta a + a \sin B \, \delta C,$$
$$\delta A = \frac{1}{c} \left\{ - \sin A \, \delta b + \sin B \, \delta a - a \cos B \, \delta C \right\},$$

or, since $\delta C = \delta C'' \times \sin 1''$; and $\delta A = \delta A'' \sin 1'',$
$$\delta c = \cos A \, \delta b + \cos B \, \delta a + a \sin B \sin 1'' \, \delta C'',$$
$$\delta A'' = - \frac{\sin A}{c \sin 1''} \delta b + \frac{\sin B}{c \sin 1''} \delta a - \frac{a \cos B}{c} \delta C''.$$

Taking now our triangle SpT, and comparing it side by side with the triangle ABC,

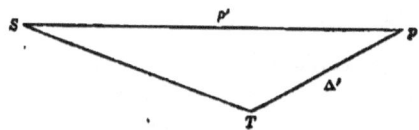

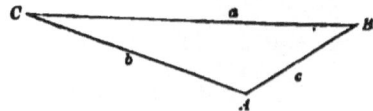

that is, putting $c = \Delta'$, and $a = \rho'$, we shall have

$$A = \angle T$$
$$= -(L - \odot),$$
$$B = \angle p$$
$$= (L - l'),$$
$$C = \angle S$$
$$= l' - \odot - 180°.$$

Now generally

$$\delta L = \frac{dL}{dl'} \delta l' + \frac{dL}{d\rho'} \delta \rho',$$

$$\delta \Delta' = \frac{d\Delta'}{dl'} \delta l' + \frac{d\Delta'}{d\rho'} \delta \rho',$$

$$\delta \lambda = \frac{d\lambda}{d\beta} \delta \beta + \frac{d\lambda}{dl'} \delta l' + \frac{d\lambda}{d\rho'} \delta \rho'.$$

Comparing the first and second of these equations with the expression for δA and δc, (remarking that $\delta b = 0$, if we assume that the Earth's place is correct), we have

$$\frac{dL}{dl'} = -\frac{a \cos B}{c} = -\frac{\rho'}{\Delta'} \cos(L - l'),$$

$$\frac{dL}{d\rho'} = \frac{\sin B}{c \sin 1''} = +\frac{\sin(L - l')}{\Delta' \sin 1''},$$

$$\frac{d\Delta'}{dl'} = a \sin B \sin 1'' = \rho' \sin 1'' \sin(L - l'),$$

$$\frac{d\Delta'}{d\rho'} = \cos B = \cos(L - l'),$$

also $\delta A = -\delta L;$

$$\therefore \delta L = +\frac{\rho'}{\Delta'}\cos(L-l')\,\delta l' - \frac{\sin(L-l')}{\Delta'\sin 1''}\,\delta\rho'\ldots\ldots(\alpha).$$

$$\delta\Delta' = \rho'\sin 1''\sin(L-l')\,\delta l' + \cos(L-l')\,\delta\rho'\ldots\ldots(\beta).$$

To find the error of heliocentric latitude, we have

$$\rho'\tan\beta = \Delta'\tan\lambda;$$

$$\therefore \frac{\rho'\sin 1''}{\cos^2\beta}\delta\beta + \tan\beta\,\delta\rho' = \frac{\Delta'\sin 1''}{\cos^2\lambda}\delta\lambda + \tan\lambda\,\delta\Delta';$$

$$\therefore \delta\beta = \frac{\Delta'\cos^2\beta}{\rho'\cos^2\lambda}\delta\lambda + \frac{\tan\lambda\cos^2\beta}{\rho'\sin 1''}\delta\Delta' - \frac{\sin\beta\cos\beta}{\rho'\sin 1''}\delta\rho'$$

$$= \frac{\Delta\cos\beta}{\rho\cos\lambda}\delta\lambda + \frac{\tan\lambda\cos^2\beta}{\rho'\sin 1''}\left\{\rho'\sin 1''\sin(L-l')\,\delta l' + \cos(L-l')\,\delta\rho'\right\} - \frac{\sin\beta\cos\beta}{\rho'\sin 1''}\delta\rho'$$

$$= \frac{\Delta\cos\beta}{\rho\cos\lambda}\delta\lambda + \tan\lambda\cos^2\beta\sin(L-l')\,\delta l'$$

$$+ \frac{\cos\beta}{\rho'\sin 1''}\left\{\tan\lambda\cos\beta\cos(L-l') - \sin\beta\right\}\delta\rho'$$

$$= \frac{\Delta\cos\beta}{\rho\cos\lambda}\delta\lambda + \tan\lambda\cos^2\beta\sin(L-l')\,\delta l'$$

$$+ \frac{\cos\beta}{\rho'\sin 1''}\left\{\frac{\rho'}{\Delta'}\sin\beta\cos(L-l') - \sin\beta\right\}\delta\rho'$$

$$= \frac{\Delta\cos\beta}{\rho\cos\lambda}\delta\lambda + \tan\lambda\cos^2\beta\sin(L-l')\,\delta l'$$

$$- \frac{R\sin\beta\cos\beta}{\rho'\Delta'\sin 1''}\cos(L-\odot)\,\delta\rho'\ldots\ldots\ldots(\gamma).$$

It is however more convenient to have $\delta\beta$ expressed in terms of error of geocentric longitude (δL), instead of heliocentric longitude ($\delta l'$), because this is the quantity deduced from observation.

Since then

$$\delta L = +\frac{\rho'}{\Delta'}\cos(L-l')\,\delta l' - \frac{\sin(L-l')}{\Delta'\sin 1''}\delta\rho',$$

we have

$$\delta l' = \frac{\Delta'}{\rho'\cos(L-l')}\delta L + \frac{\tan(L-l')}{\rho'\sin 1''}\delta\rho';$$

HELIOCENTRIC AND GEOCENTRIC ERRORS. 245

therefore, substituting in the last stage but one above,

$$\delta\beta = \frac{\Delta \cos\beta}{\rho \cos\lambda}\delta\lambda + \frac{\Delta'}{\rho'}\tan\lambda \cos^2\beta \tan(L-l')\delta L$$

$$+ \frac{\tan\lambda \cos^2\beta}{\rho' \sin 1''} \cdot \frac{\sin^2(L-l')}{\cos(L-l')}\delta\rho'$$

$$+ \frac{\sin\beta \cos\beta}{\Delta' \sin 1''}\cos(L-l')\delta\rho'$$

$$- \frac{\sin\beta \cos\beta}{\rho' \sin 1''}\delta\rho'$$

$$= \frac{\Delta \cos\beta}{\rho \cos\lambda}\delta\lambda + \sin\beta \cos\beta \tan(L-l')\delta L$$

$$+ \frac{\sin\beta \cos\beta}{\Delta' \sin 1''} \cdot \frac{\sin^2(L-l')}{\cos(L-l')}\delta\rho'$$

$$- \frac{\sin\beta \cos\beta}{\Delta' \sin 1''}\cos(L-l')\delta\rho'$$

$$- \frac{\sin\beta \cos\beta}{\rho' \sin 1''}\delta\rho'$$

$$= \frac{\Delta \cos\beta}{\rho \cos\lambda}\delta\lambda + \sin\beta \cos\beta \tan(L-l')\delta L$$

$$+ \left(\frac{\sin\beta \cos\beta}{\Delta' \sin 1'' \cos(L-l')} - \frac{\sin\beta \cos\beta}{\rho' \sin 1''}\right)\delta\rho'$$

$$= \frac{\Delta \cos\beta}{\rho \cos\lambda}\delta\lambda + \sin\beta \cos\beta \tan(L-l')\delta L$$

$$+ \frac{\sin\beta \cos\beta}{\rho'\Delta' \sin 1'' \cos(L-l')}\{\rho' - \Delta' \cos(L-l')\}\delta\rho'$$

$$= \frac{\Delta \cos\beta}{\rho \cos\lambda}\delta\lambda + \sin\beta \cos\beta \tan(L-l')\delta L$$

$$- \frac{\sin\beta \cos\beta}{\rho'\Delta' \cos(L-l') \sin 1''} \times R\cos(l'-\odot)\delta\rho'$$

$$= \frac{\Delta \cos\beta}{\rho \cos\lambda}\delta\lambda + \sin\beta \cos\beta \tan(L-l')\delta L$$

$$- \frac{R \tan\lambda \cos^2\beta}{\rho'^2 \cos(L-l') \sin 1''}\cos(l'-\odot)\delta\rho'$$

$$= \frac{\Delta \cos\beta}{\rho \cos\lambda}\delta\lambda + \sin\beta \cos\beta \tan(L-l')\delta L$$

$$- \frac{R \tan\lambda \cos(l'-\odot)}{\rho'^2 \cos(l-l') \sin 1''}\delta\rho'\ldots\ldots(\delta).$$

This is the form used at Greenwich.

17. We have hitherto neglected the errors of the Earth's place.

They may easily be taken into account in the following way.

$$\text{Generally} \quad \delta L = \frac{dL}{d\odot}\delta\odot + \frac{dL}{dR}\delta R,$$

$$\delta\Delta' = \frac{d\Delta'}{d\odot}\delta\odot + \frac{d\Delta'}{dR}\delta R.$$

Comparing the same triangles as before, only interchanging a and b, A and B, and considering the planet's place to be correct, that is, making $\delta\rho' = 0$, or $\delta a = 0$,

we have

$$\delta B = \frac{\sin A}{c \sin 1''}\delta b - \frac{b \cos A}{c}\delta C;$$

and $\delta B = \delta L$, $\delta C = -\delta\odot$, $\delta b = \delta R$;

$$\frac{dL}{d\odot} = -\frac{b \cos A}{c} = -\frac{R}{\Delta'}\cos(L - \odot),$$

$$\frac{dL}{dR} = -\frac{\sin A}{c \sin 1''} = -\frac{\sin(L - \odot)}{\Delta' \sin 1''};$$

$$\therefore \delta L = \frac{R}{\Delta'}\cos(L - \odot)\delta\odot - \frac{\sin(L - \odot)}{\Delta' \sin 1''}\delta R.$$

Again, $\delta c = \cos A \, \delta b + b \sin A \sin 1'' \delta C$

or $\delta\Delta' = R \sin 1'' \sin(L - \odot)\delta\odot + \cos(L - \odot)\delta R.$

With respect to the larger planets, Mercury, Venus, Mars, Jupiter, Saturn, Uranus, and Neptune, the inclinations of whose orbits to the ecliptic are small, and of which the errors of the elements of the orbits are small also, we may in the formulæ above neglect the latitudes, that is, we may assume $\cos\beta$ and $\cos\lambda$ to be each equal to unity, and $\sin\beta$ or $\tan\beta$, $\sin\lambda$ or $\tan\lambda$, each equal to 0; but we cannot neglect the errors of the solar elements as compared with those of the planet's orbit.

We shall have, therefore,

$$\delta L = \frac{\rho}{\Delta} \cos (L - l') \, \delta l' - \frac{\sin (L - l')}{\Delta \sin 1''} \delta \rho'$$
$$+ \frac{R}{\Delta} \cos (L - \odot) \, \delta \odot - \frac{\sin (L - \odot)}{\Delta \sin 1''} \delta R,$$

$$\delta \Delta' = \rho' \sin 1'' \sin (L - l') \, \delta l' + \cos (L - l') \, \delta \rho'$$
$$+ R \sin 1'' \sin (L - \odot) \, \delta \odot + \cos (L - \odot) \, \delta R,$$

$$\delta \beta = \frac{\Delta}{\rho} \delta \lambda.$$

For the small recently discovered planets between Mars and Jupiter, the inclinations of whose orbits are not generally small, and of which the errors of the ephemerides are generally very much greater than those of the Sun's calculated places, we may assume the Sun's places as taken from the *Nautical Almanac* to be correct; but we must use the formulæ (*a*), (*β*) and (*δ*) rigorously.

18. We are now in a condition to explain the whole treatment of planetary observations, and to shew how they are made available for the correction of the elements of the orbits.

(1) By the observations of the limbs of the planets (both limbs being observed whenever it is practicable), the R.A.s. and N.P.D.s of the centres are obtained, and these can be cleared first of refraction, and secondly of parallax, according to the principles explained in Chapter VI. We thus obtain the geocentric R.A. and N.P.D. of the planet for a given mean time of observation.

(2) From the Nautical Almanac, or other similar work, can be taken immediately for the meridian of Greenwich, or can be deduced by an easy interpolation for other meridians, the R.A. and N.P.D. at the same instant, as calculated from assumed elements of the orbit; and these calculated places can be compared with the observed places. Thus are obtained the Tabular Errors of R.A. and N.P.D., the Error being equal to Tabular Place − Observed Place.

248   CORRECTION OF THE ELEMENTS OF THE ORBIT.

(3) The Tabular Errors of R.A. and N.P.D. can be converted into errors of geocentric longitude and latitude by the formulæ in No. 7 of Chapter III.; but since this would be exceedingly laborious if done for each separate observed position, it is usual to group the observations as far as is consistent with perfect accuracy, that is, so that for each group the mean of the errors of R.A. and N.P.D. may correspond accurately to the error for the mean of the days of observation. These *mean errors* are called *normal errors*, and the corresponding errors of geocentric longitude and latitude are computed from them.

(4) From the errors of *geocentric* longitude and latitude can be derived the errors of *heliocentric* longitude and latitude by means of the formulæ just now given. For the well-known planets every group of observations of R.A. and N.P.D. will give two equations of the following form, (neglecting the errors of the Sun's place or applying corrections derived from observations):

$$\delta L = a\delta l' + b\delta \rho',$$
$$\delta \beta = a'\delta \lambda.$$

Taking the first of these equations we must now proceed to express $\delta l'$ and $\delta \rho'$ in terms of the elements of the orbit. This is done by means of the formulæ at pages 239 and 226.

We have, for instance,

$$l' = l + \text{reduction to ecliptic}$$
$$= l + r'$$
$$= r' + nt + \epsilon + \left(2e - \frac{e^3}{4}\right)\sin(nt + \epsilon - \varpi) + \frac{5e^2}{4}\sin 2(nt + \epsilon - \varpi)$$
$$+ \frac{13}{12}e^3 \sin 3(nt + \epsilon - \varpi) + \&c.$$

∴ neglecting the error of r' and assuming n to be correct,

$$\delta l' = \delta \epsilon + \left(2 - \frac{3e^2}{4}\right)\sin(nt + \epsilon - \varpi)\delta e$$
$$+ \left(2e - \frac{e^3}{4}\right)\cos(nt + \epsilon - \varpi)\delta \epsilon$$
$$- \left(2e - \frac{e^3}{4}\right)\cos(nt + \epsilon - \varpi)\delta \varpi$$

CORRECTION OF THE ELEMENTS OF THE ORBIT. 249

$$+ \frac{5e}{2} \sin 2(nt + \epsilon - \varpi) \delta e$$

$$+ \frac{5e^2}{2} \cos 2(nt + \epsilon - \varpi) \delta \epsilon$$

$$- \frac{5e^2}{2} \cos 2(nt + \epsilon - \varpi) \delta \varpi$$

$$+ \&c.$$

$$= \left\{ \left(2 - \frac{3e^2}{4}\right) \sin m + \frac{5e}{2} \sin 2m + \frac{13e^2}{4} \sin 3m \right\} \delta e$$

$$+ \left(1 + 2e \cos m + \frac{5e^2}{4} \cos 2m + \&c.\right) \delta \epsilon$$

$$- \left(2e \cos m + \frac{5e^2}{4} \cos 2m + \&c.\right) \delta \varpi$$

(m being the mean anomaly),

$$= A \delta e + B \delta \epsilon + C \delta \varpi, \text{ suppose,}$$

since the values of the coefficients can be calculated immediately by the tables of the motions of the planet.

Similarly, since, from the formula in page 226,

$$\rho = a \left\{ 1 + \frac{e^2}{2} - e \left(1 - \frac{3e^2}{8}\right) \cos(nt + \epsilon - \varpi) - \frac{e^2}{2} \cos 2(nt + \epsilon - \varpi) \right.$$

$$\left. - \frac{3e^3}{8} \cos 3(nt + \epsilon - \varpi) - \&c. \right\}$$

$$\delta \rho = \left(1 + \frac{e^2}{2} - e \cos m - \frac{e^2}{2} \cos 2m - \&c.\right) \delta a$$

$$+ ae - a\left(1 - \frac{9e^2}{8}\right) \cos m\, \delta e$$

$$- ae \sin m\, \delta \epsilon$$

$$+ ae \sin m\, \delta \varpi$$

$$- ae \cos 2m\, \delta e$$

$$+ ae^2 \sin 2m\, \delta \epsilon$$

$$- ae^2 \sin 2m\, \delta \varpi$$

$$+ \&c.$$

$$= \left(1 + \frac{e^2}{2} - e\cos m - \frac{e^2}{2}\cos 2m - \&c.\right)\delta a$$

$$+ a\left\{e - \left(1 - \frac{9e^2}{8}\right)\cos m - e\cos 2m - \&c.\right\}\delta e$$

$$- a\,(e\sin m - e^2\sin 2m - \&c.)\,\delta\epsilon$$

$$+ a\,(e\sin m - e^2\sin 2m - \&c.)\,\delta\varpi$$

$$+ \&c.$$

$$= A'\delta a + B'\delta e + C'\delta\epsilon + D'\delta\varpi, \text{ suppose,}$$

and $\delta\rho' = \cos\beta\,\delta\rho$, will be of the same form, if we neglect error of latitude.

Hence, by substituting in the equation,

$$\delta L = a\delta l' + b\delta\rho',$$

we shall have an equation of the form

$$\delta L = A_{,}\delta a + B_{,}\delta e + C_{,}\delta\epsilon + D_{,}\delta\varpi;$$

and every group of observations will give a similar equation; and finally the values of δa, δe, $\delta\epsilon$, and $\delta\pi$ will be found by the method of least squares, or by some similar method.

19. The preceding investigation will shew how the errors of four of the elements of the orbit are to be determined (the value of δa being determined not as serving to correct the mean motion n, which is connected with it by the equation $a^{\frac{3}{2}} \times n = $ a constant quantity, but as shewing whether the magnitude of the *instantaneous* ellipse has been properly determined).

The remaining elements are the inclination to the ecliptic i, and the longitude of the node Ω.

These are connected by the equation

$$\tan\beta = \tan i\,\sin(l' - \Omega),$$

whence $\dfrac{\delta\beta}{\cos^2\beta} = \dfrac{\sin(l' - \Omega)}{\cos^2 i}\,\delta i + \tan i\,\cos(l' - \Omega)\,\delta(l' - \Omega),$

or $\dfrac{2\delta\beta}{\sin 2\beta} = \dfrac{2}{\sin 2i}\,\delta i + \cot(l' - \Omega)\,\delta(l' - \Omega).$

In general, for the orbits of the well-known planets, the error of the node may be tolerably large without producing any sensible effect on the calculated latitude of the planet, because the inclinations are generally small. Thus in the equation above

$$\delta\beta = \frac{\cos^2\beta}{\cos^2 i} \sin(l' - \Omega)\,\delta i + \cos^2\beta \tan i \cos(l' - \Omega)\,\delta(l' - \Omega);$$

therefore the maximum value of the error of latitude arising from an error of the node $\delta\Omega$, will be

$$-\cos^2\beta \tan i\,\delta\Omega.$$

If then $i =$ the inclination of the orbit of Mercury $= 7°$, this error cannot amount to

$$\frac{12}{100}\delta\Omega,$$

and for the greater number of the large planets it will be much smaller; and, as the error of longitude, in general, as computed from the best modern elements, amounts only to a few seconds, we may in the expression above neglect $\delta l'$, and we shall then have

$$\delta\beta = \frac{\cos^2\beta}{\cos^2 i} \sin(l' - \Omega)\,\delta i - \cos^2\beta \tan i \cos(l' - \Omega)\,\delta\Omega.$$

Every observation of R.A. and N.P.D. will furnish one such equation, and the whole of the observations made in several years may be combined and solved by the method of least squares for the determination of the most correct values of δi and $\delta\Omega$.

If finally the value of $\delta\Omega$ has been found within limits of accuracy comparable to that of $\delta l'$, we may substitute the value of $\delta l'$, which will have been found in the determination of the other elements, and thus obtain a better approximation to the values of δi and $\delta\Omega$.

20. In the preceding discussion we have assumed that, in the value of $\delta l'$, the error of the reduction to the ecliptic may be neglected, or that we may, in expressing the errors of the elements δa, δe, $\delta \epsilon$, and $\delta\varpi$ in terms of $\delta l'$, assume that $\delta l' = \delta l$. This is

practically the case in orbits of small inclination; but it is desirable to shew how $\delta l'$ is affected for orbits of any inclination whatever.

Let N be the position of the ascending node; m that of the planet in its orbit; and m' its place as referred to the ecliptic.

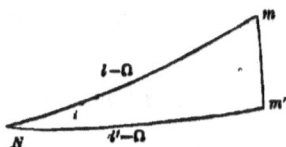

Then, using the same nomenclature as before, we shall have the following equations:

$$\tan(l' - \Omega) = \cos i \tan(l - \Omega) \quad\quad\quad (8),$$

$$\cos(l - \Omega) = \cos \beta \cos(l' - \Omega) \quad\quad\quad (9),$$

$$\left\{ \begin{array}{l} \sin \beta = \sin i \sin(l - \Omega) \\ \tan \beta = \tan i \sin(l' - \Omega) \end{array} \right\} \quad\quad\quad (10);$$

from which we shall easily deduce

$$\frac{dl'}{dl} = \frac{\cos i}{\cos^2 \beta}*,$$

$$\frac{dl'}{di} = -\tan \beta \cos(l' - \Omega),$$

$$\frac{dl'}{d\Omega} = 1 - \frac{\cos i}{\cos^2 \beta}.$$

---

* Thus, from equation (8),

$$\frac{dl'}{\cos^2(l' - \Omega)} = \cos i \cdot \frac{dl}{\cos^2(l - \Omega)},$$

or $\dfrac{dl'}{dl} = \cos i \cdot \dfrac{\cos^2(l' - \Omega)}{\cos^2(l - \Omega)} = \dfrac{\cos i}{\cos^2 \beta}$, from equation (9).

Also, $\dfrac{dl'}{di} \dfrac{1}{\cos^2(l' - \Omega)} = -\sin i \tan(l - \Omega) = -\tan i \tan(l' - \Omega);$

$\therefore \dfrac{dl'}{di} = -\tan i \sin(l' - \Omega) \cos(l' - \Omega) = -\tan \beta \cos(l' - \Omega).$

Hence, considering l' to be a function of l, i, and Ω, we shall have

$$\delta l' = \frac{dl'}{dl}\delta l + \frac{dl'}{di}\delta i + \frac{dl'}{d\Omega}\delta\Omega$$

$$= \frac{\cos i}{\cos^2 \beta}\delta l - \tan\beta\cos(l'-\Omega)\delta i + \left(1 - \frac{\cos i}{\cos^2\beta}\right)\delta\Omega,$$

and since $\delta l = \frac{dl}{da}\delta a + \frac{dl}{de}\delta e + \frac{dl}{d\epsilon}\delta\epsilon + \frac{dl}{d\pi}\delta\varpi$;

$$\therefore \delta l' = \frac{\cos i}{\cos^2\beta}\left\{\frac{dl}{da}\delta a + \frac{dl}{de}\delta e + \frac{dl}{d\epsilon}\delta\epsilon + \frac{dl}{d\pi}\delta\varpi\right\}$$

$$- \tan\beta\cos(l'-\Omega)\delta i + \left(1 - \frac{\cos i}{\cos^2\beta}\right)\delta\Omega.$$

By means of this formula we can easily evaluate the errors produced by making $\delta l' = \delta l$ in any particular case; that is, by the assumptions that $\frac{\cos i}{\cos^2\beta} = 1$, and $\tan\beta\cos(l'-\Omega) = 0$.

Again, for the node and inclination, we should easily find

$$\frac{d\beta}{d\Omega} = -\frac{d\beta}{dl} = -\sin i\cos(l'-\Omega)^*,$$

and $\dfrac{d\beta}{di} = \sin(l'-\Omega)$.

Hence, taking the equation

$$\sin\beta = \sin i\sin(l'-\Omega),$$

---

* Thus, by differentiating the first of equations (10) with respect to i, we get

$$\frac{d\beta}{di} = \frac{\cos i}{\cos\beta}\sin(l-\Omega)$$

$$= \sin(l'-\Omega),$$

and, differentiating the same equation with respect to Ω,

$$\frac{d\beta}{d\Omega} = -\frac{\sin i}{\cos\beta}\cos(l-\Omega)$$

$$= -\sin i\cos(l'-\Omega).$$

and considering β to be a function of i, Ω, and l, we have

$$\delta\beta = \frac{d\beta}{di}\,di + \frac{d\beta}{d\Omega}\,\delta\Omega + \frac{d\beta}{dl}\,\delta l$$
$$= \sin(l' - \Omega)\,\delta i + \sin i \cos(l' - \Omega)(\delta l - \delta\Omega);$$

which is simpler than the formula given at page 250.

21. *On the Geocentric Motion of the Planets.*

The planets, as has been explained, move all in the same direction round the Sun, that is, in the order of the signs of the zodiac, or from west to east; but, to an observer on the Earth's surface, the direction of the apparent motion is, on account of the Earth's motion, frequently changed, and sometimes they appear to be actually stationary. These phenomena of their motions may be investigated approximately by a mathematical process.

Referring to page 241 for the equations

$$\Delta' \cos L = \rho' \cos l' + R \cos \odot,$$
$$\Delta' \sin L = \rho' \sin l' + R \sin \odot,$$

and considering the orbit of the planet under consideration to be circular, and to coincide with the ecliptic, we may put

$$l' = l, \quad \rho' = a, \quad R = 1.$$

Hence $\Delta' \sin L = a \sin l + \sin \odot,$

$$\Delta' \cos L = a \cos l + \cos \odot;$$

$$\therefore \tan L = \frac{a \sin l + \sin \odot}{a \cos l + \cos \odot},$$

and, differentiating,

$$\frac{1}{\cos^2 L} \cdot \frac{dL}{dt}$$

$$= \frac{(a\cos l + \cos\odot)\cdot\left(a\cos l\frac{dl}{dt} + \cos\odot\frac{d\odot}{dt}\right) + (a\sin l + \sin\odot)\left(a\sin l\frac{dl}{dt} + \sin\odot\frac{d\odot}{dt}\right)}{(a\cos l + \cos\odot)^2}$$

$$= \frac{a^2 \frac{dl}{dt} + \frac{d\odot}{dt} + a \cos(l-\odot)\left(\frac{dl}{dt} + \frac{d\odot}{dt}\right)}{(a \cos l + \cos \odot)^2}$$

$$= \frac{\{a^2 + a \cos(l-\odot)\}\frac{dl}{dt} + \{1 + a \cos(l-\odot)\}\frac{d\odot}{dt}}{(a \cos l + \cos \odot)^2};$$

but, by Kepler's 3rd law,

$$\frac{d\odot}{dt} = a^{\frac{3}{2}} \frac{dl}{dt}.$$

Hence, putting $\left(\frac{\cos^2 L}{a \cos l + \cos \odot}\right)^2$, which is always positive, $=\beta^2$, we have

$$\frac{dL}{dt} = \beta^2 \{a^2 + a^{\frac{3}{2}} + (a + a^{\frac{1}{2}})\cos(l-\odot)\}\frac{dl}{dt};$$

and, from this expression, we can deduce the circumstances of the apparent geocentric motion.

Thus, if $l = \odot$, that is, if a superior planet be in conjunction, or an inferior planet be at conjunction farthest from the Earth, $\frac{dL}{dt}$ is essentially positive, or the apparent motion is direct.

If, on the contrary, $l - \odot = 180°$, that is, if a superior planet be in opposition, or an inferior planet be at inferior conjunction, that is, at conjunction nearest to the Earth,

$$\frac{dL}{dt} = \beta^2 \{a^2 + a^{\frac{3}{2}} - a - a^{\frac{1}{2}}\}\frac{dl}{dt}$$

$$= \beta^2 \{a(a-1) - a^{\frac{1}{2}}(a-1)\}\frac{dl}{dt}$$

$$= \beta^2 a(a-1)(1 - \sqrt{a}),$$

which is a negative quantity, whether a be greater or less than 1, or the apparent motion is retrograde.

STATIONARY POINT OF THE ORBIT.

If the planet be stationary, $\dfrac{dL}{dt} = 0$;

$$\therefore a^2 + a^{\frac{3}{2}} + (a + a^{\frac{1}{2}}) \cos (l - \odot) = 0,$$

$$\text{or } \cos (l - \odot) = - \frac{a^2 + a^{\frac{3}{2}}}{a + a^{\frac{1}{2}}}$$

$$= - \frac{a + a^{\frac{1}{2}}}{a^{\frac{1}{2}} + 1}$$

$$= - \frac{a^{\frac{1}{2}}}{a - a^{\frac{1}{2}} + 1}$$

$$= - \frac{1}{a^{\frac{1}{2}} + a^{-\frac{1}{2}} - 1};$$

and this equation will always be possible if $a^{\frac{1}{2}} + a^{-\frac{1}{2}} - 1$ be always greater than 1.

$$\text{Now } a^{\frac{1}{2}} + a^{-\frac{1}{2}} - 1 \text{ is} > 1,$$

$$\text{if } a^{\frac{1}{2}} + a^{-\frac{1}{2}} \text{ is} > 2,$$

$$\text{or } a - 2\sqrt{a} + 1 > 0,$$

$$\text{or } (\sqrt{a} - 1)^2 > 0;$$

which is manifestly the case, since it is a square number; therefore both for inferior or superior planets there is always a value of $l - \odot$, or a point in the orbit, where the planet will appear stationary.

Let α_i and α be the values of $l - \odot$ for the stationary point and for any other point;

then $\dfrac{dL}{dt} = \beta^2 \{a^2 + a^{\frac{3}{2}} + (a + a^{\frac{1}{2}}) \cos \alpha\} \dfrac{dl}{dt}$,

and $0 = \beta^2 \{a^2 + a^{\frac{3}{2}} + (a + a^{\frac{1}{2}}) \cos \alpha_i\} \dfrac{dl}{dt}$,

or $\dfrac{dL}{dt} = \beta^2 (a + a^{\frac{1}{2}}) (\cos \alpha - \cos \alpha_i) \dfrac{dl}{dt}$.

Hence in a synodic revolution, or from $\alpha = 0$ to $\alpha = 360°$, the geocentric apparent motion is retrograde as long as α is greater than α_i, and direct as long as α is less than α_i.

Section II. On the actually known Planetary Bodies.

1. Before the commencement of the present century, the planets actually known, reckoned in the order of their semi-major axes or mean distances from the Sun, were Mercury, Venus, the Earth, Mars, Jupiter, Saturn, and Uranus, of which Uranus alone was discovered with the help of the telescope by the elder Herschel in the year 1780.

At the commencement of the present century however began that series of discoveries, which has resulted in the addition, at the present time (July, 1863), of 78 additional bodies to the planetary system, and which is still proceeding without interruption. The bodies here referred to are small planets, for the most part requiring powerful telescopes to render them visible, revolving at nearly the same mean distance, in orbits lying between Mars and Jupiter. Of these, four were discovered very near the commencement of this century, namely Ceres, by Piazzi on Jan. 1, 1801; Pallas, by Olbers on March 28, 1802; Juno, by Harding on September 1, 1804; and Vesta, by Olbers on March 29, 1807. There was then a long intermission of discovery, till, in 1845, on December 8, Hencke discovered Astræa; and, since that time, the discovery of additional small planets has gone on with tolerable uniformity, till their number, as has been said, amounts to nearly eighty.

The motions of these small bodies differ in no respect from those of the larger planets, excepting that the excentricities and inclinations of their orbits to the ecliptic are generally larger. By means of the immense amount of labour (both of observation and calculation) which has been bestowed upon them since their discovery, the elements of the orbits of the greater number of them are known pretty exactly.

But the greatest and most remarkable planetary discovery of the present century is that of Neptune, almost simultaneously by M. Le Verrier and Professor Adams, by analytical investigations of Physical Astronomy based upon the unexplained disturbances which had been observed in the motions of Uranus.

2. In all that follows, we shall confine ourselves to the larger planets first mentioned, restricting ourselves to a few peculiarities of each which admit of mathematical development*.

It will be desirable in the first place to give a Synoptical Table of the Elements of the orbits, and relative magnitudes of the large planets.

The elements which follow have been mainly taken from Chambers' *Handbook of Astronomy*, and are abundantly accurate for our present purpose. They are subject to *secular variation*. Those given are for 1800, Jan. 1, 0^h. The apparent angular diameters at the unit of distance for Mercury, Venus, Mars, Jupiter, and Saturn, are deduced from the measures made by the author at Greenwich and Oxford; and, in deducing the distances of the planets from the sun, and their diameters in miles, the solar parallax $8''\cdot 90$ has been assumed, as there appears to be no reasonable doubt of the accuracy of this value.

* It would be both needless, and out of place in the present treatise, to dwell upon the physical peculiarities of the separate planets, as there are so many books of easy reference. Such are Hind's *Solar System;* the author's *Rudimentary Astronomy;* Webb's *Celestial Objects for Common Telescopes;* Chambers' *Handbook of Descriptive and Practical Astronomy.*

TABLE OF THE ELEMENTS OF THE ORBITS.

Planet.	Mean Distance from Sun.		Excentricity.	Mean Long. 1800, Jan. 1.	Longitude of Perihelion.	Inclination of Orbit.	Longitude of Ascending Node.	Apparent Diameter at Unit of Distance.	Equatorial Diameter in Miles.
		Miles.							
Mercury......	0·38710	35,551,710	0·20549	112.16. 4	74.20.42	7. 0. 5	45.57.38	6.89	3,067
Venus.........	0·72333	66,431,450	0·00687	146.44.56	128.43. 6	3.23.29	74.51.41	17.55	7,814
Earth	1·00000	91,841,100	0·01679	100.53.30	99.30.29	....	....		7,925
Mars	1·52369	139,937,400	0·09311	233.57.34	332.22.51	1.51. 6	47.59.38	9.38	4,178
Jupiter.........	5·20290	477,831,000	0·04816	81.54.49	11. 7.38	1.18.52	98.25.45	197.39	87,890
Saturn.........	9·53885	876,058,600	0·05615	123. 6.29	89. 8.20	2.29.36	111.56. 7	166.93	74,327
Uranus.........	19·18273	1,761,763,900	0·04667	173.30.37	167.30.24	0.46.28	72.59.21		33,200
Neptune	30·03628	2,758,566,000	0·00872	335. 8.58	47.14.37	1.46.59	130. 6.52		36,100

3. On the Phases of the Planets.

The planets are opaque bodies, and are made visible to us only by the solar light reflected from their surface.

The amount of *phase*, or the proportion of the illuminated surface to the whole disk of the inferior planets, including the Moon, our own satellite, will therefore depend on two circumstances, namely, 1st, on the position of the body with respect to the Sun, which determines the illuminated hemisphere, and, 2ndly, on the position with respect to the earth, which determines the hemisphere visible to us.

As the planets are all very approximately spherical bodies, and the inclinations of their orbits to the ecliptic, including the Moon, are all small, we will assume, in all which follows, that they are perfectly spherical and that they move in the ecliptic.

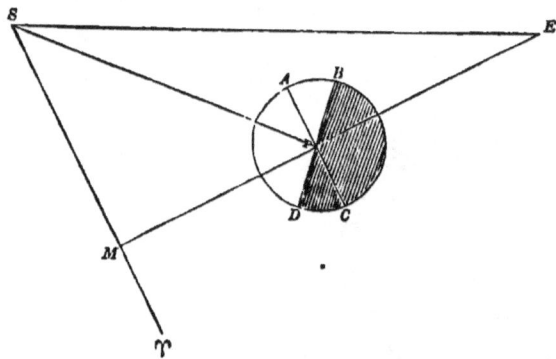

Let then S, E, and P represent the relative positions of centres of the Sun, the Earth, and a planet at any time, all lying in the ecliptic, and let ABC be a section of the planet by the ecliptic.

Draw $S\Upsilon$ towards the First Point of Aries; and produce EP to meet it in M.

Draw also AC and BD through the centre P at right angles to EP and SP respectively.

Then is the hemisphere of which ABC is a section that which is visible from the Earth, and that of which BAD is a section is the illuminated hemisphere.

Hence the arc AB is the section of that part of the surface of the planet which is illuminated as seen from the Earth; and this is measured by the angle APB or the angle SPM, which is equal to the difference of the Geocentric and Heliocentric Longitudes of the planet diminished by 180°.

In the case of the moon this angle, which we will denote by d, is called the Exterior Angle of Elongation.

Also the arc AB of the section of the planet which represents its greatest phase will be seen orthogonally projected on the diameter AC, and will therefore be represented by the versed-sine of the arc.

Hence the measure of the phase, or of the illuminated part of the diameter of the planet transverse to the line joining the cusps, will be semi-diameter × versin d.

It is plain that the whole of the illuminated portion of the disk of the planet, of which the expression above is the measure, will be a *lune* formed by planes passing through AP and BP perpendicular to the ecliptic, and that every part of this lune will be projected on the plane of which AP is the section, and therefore that the projections of all the points corresponding to B on this plane will be an ellipse whose major axis is to the minor axis as $1 : \cos d$.

4. PROBLEM. *To find when Venus, on approaching her inferior conjunction, is at her greatest brightness, neglecting the excentricity of the orbit.*

It is plain that the brightness of Venus will vary directly as the breadth of the phase of illumination, and inversely as the square of her distance from the earth, or as $\dfrac{1-\cos SPM}{EP^2}$.

Let then $SE =$ (unit of distance =) 1,

$SP = a$,

$EP = x$.

Then $SE^2 = SP^2 + PE^2 + 2SP \times PE \times \cos SPM,$

or $1 = a^2 + x^2 + 2ax \cos SPM;$

$\therefore \cos SPM = -\dfrac{a^2 + x^2 - 1}{2ax};$

and $\dfrac{1 - \cos SPM}{EP^2} = \dfrac{1}{x^2}\left(1 + \dfrac{a^2 + x^2 - 1}{2ax}\right)$

$= \dfrac{(a + x)^2 - 1}{2ax^3}.$

Hence $\dfrac{(a + x)^2 - 1}{x^3} = $ maximum,

$2x^3(a + x) - 3x^2\{(a + x)^2 - 1\} = 0,$

$2ax + 2x^2 - 3a^2 - 6ax - 3x^2 + 3 = 0,$

or $x^2 + 4ax + 3(a^2 - 1) = 0,$

whence $x = \sqrt{a^2 + 3} - 2a.$

5. To find the angle which the line joining the cusps of the Moon makes with the great circle passing through the poles of the earth, or with the declination circle.

Let O be the centre of the planet or of the moon (supposed to be horned, or not half illuminated) on a circle of declination

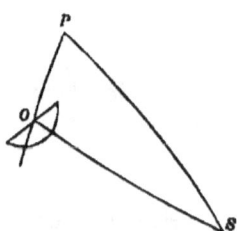

PO, P being the pole; S the position of the Sun. Draw the arcs of a great circle SO and SP; then will SO be manifestly perpendicular to the line of cusps.

Let $PS = \Delta_s,\ PO = \Delta_p,$

and angle $POS = 90° \pm \theta.$

CORRECTION FOR DEFECTIVE ILLUMINATION. 263

Then $\cot(90° \pm \theta) = \operatorname{cosec} P \sin \Delta_p \cot \Delta_s - \cot P \cos \Delta_p$,
where θ is plainly the inclination of the line of cusps to the declination circle, and P is the difference of R.A. of the Sun and Planet.

Imagine now that PO is the meridian of the place of observation, and that the zenith-distance of the moon is observed, when the line of cusps is nearly but not quite coincident with the meridian, that is, is nearly vertical. In this case, one limb (in the figure the south limb) will be full, but the other will be not fully illuminated; and, by what has preceded, the correction required to the observed zenith distance of the *north* limb will be   — (angular semi-diameter) × vers θ.

The same correction will apply to an observation of Venus or Mercury, but in this case θ may have any value whatever without affecting the accuracy of the observation.

If the Moon be *gibbous* we must proceed as follows:

Draw a great circle through the Moon at right angles to the meridian passing through the Moon, and let it meet the meridian passing through the Sun. The point where it meets this latter meridian will determine the position of a fictitious sun, which would fully illuminate both the north and south limbs of the Moon; and the elevation or depression of the true Sun above or below the great circle joining the moon and the fictitious sun, measured in the plane of that circle, will represent the angle by which the lowest or highest part of the illuminated hemisphere is distant from the limb, and therefore the angle whose versed sine multiplied into the semi-diameter is the correction required to observed zenith distance of defective limb.

Thus (Fig. on page 264), let P be the north pole of the heavens; M the centre of the Moon on the meridian; S the true Sun. Draw MS_1 perpendicular to PM, meeting PS produced in S_1; then is S_1 the place of the fictitious sun. Draw also SO perpendicular to MS_1.

Let $PS = \Delta$, $PM = \Delta_m$, $PS_1 = \Delta_1$, $SO = \theta$, $SS_1 = \theta_1$, $SO = \theta$.

Then $\qquad \cos P = \tan PM \cot PS_1$
$\qquad\qquad\qquad = \tan \Delta_m \cot \Delta_1,$

or $\tan \Delta_i = \tan \Delta_m \sec P$,

and $SS_i = \theta_i = \Delta_i - \Delta$,

$\therefore \sin SO = \sin \theta = \sin \theta_i \sin PS_i M$

$= \sin \theta_i \dfrac{\sin \Delta_m}{\sin \Delta_i}$,

whence θ is known, and the correction as before is semi-diameter × vers θ.

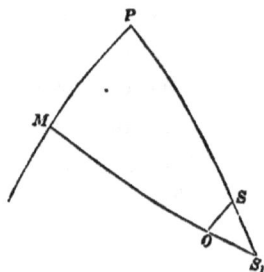

For an inferior *planet* the investigation is the same as for the Moon, excepting that a correction must be introduced depending upon the distance of the planet from the Earth and Sun.

Thus, SO or θ representing the angular distance of the Sun from the plane of the great circle MOS, as seen from the Earth, the sine of the angular distance as seen from the planet will be evidently $\dfrac{\text{distance of Earth from Sun}}{\text{distance of planet from Sun}} \times \sin \theta = \sin \phi$ (suppose); and ϕ represents in this case the angle by which the lowest or highest point of the illuminated hemisphere is distant from the limb as viewed by an observer anywhere in the plane of this great circle. The correction will therefore be

planet's semi-diameter × versin ϕ.

6. On the Transits of Mercury and Venus across the Disk of the Sun.

The inclinations of the orbits of these planets being very small, namely, for Mercury 7°.0′, and for Venus 3°.23′, it is plain that if the inferior conjunction of either of them with the

Earth happens when the planet is near the node of its orbit, it will be very nearly in a direct line between the Earth and the centre of the Sun, and will appear to cross or to transit the disk of the Sun.

If, for example, the latitude of the planet at inferior conjunction be less than the Sun's semi-diameter, that is, than 16', a transit will take place, and since generally

$$\tan \beta = \sin (l' - \Omega) \tan i,$$

we shall have (putting $\beta = 16'$) for Mercury,

$$l' - \Omega = 2°.10';$$

and for Venus,

$$l' - \Omega = 4°.31';$$

as the limiting values for which a transit is possible, supposing the observer to be stationed at the centre of the Earth.

To find the intervals of recurrence of the transits of Mercury or Venus, it must be observed, that since a transit can take place only when the planet is very near its node at the time of conjunction, each must make a complete number of sidereal revolutions after one such conjunction, before another will take place. Let then between two transits the planet make m complete revolutions, and the Earth n revolutions, the periods being respectively P_1 and P_2. We shall have then the indeterminate equation

$$mP_1 = nP_2,$$

and therefore

$$\frac{m}{n} = \frac{P_2}{P_1};$$

and we must find what *integral* numbers when substituted for P_1 and P_2 will give pretty correctly the value of the fraction $\frac{m}{n}$ or $\frac{P_2}{P_1}$.

Now, for Mercury, $P_1 = 87\cdot969$ days,

and $P_2 = 365\cdot 256,$

$$\therefore \frac{P_1}{P_2} = \frac{87 \cdot 969}{365 \cdot 256}$$

$$= \frac{1}{4+} \frac{1}{6+} \frac{1}{1+} \frac{1}{1+} \frac{1}{2+} \frac{1}{1+} \frac{1}{5+\&c.}$$

Hence the series of fractions which approximately represent the value of $\frac{P_1}{P_2}$ is

$$\frac{7}{29}, \frac{13}{54}, \frac{33}{137}, \frac{46}{191}, \frac{263}{1092};$$

or transits of Mercury may take place at the same node after intervals of 7, 13, 33, or 46 years.

Transits in fact have been observed at the descending node in the month of May of the years 1661, 1707, 1740, 1753, 1786, 1799, 1832, and 1845; and at the ascending node in the month of November of the years 1677, 1697, 1723, 1736, 1743, 1756, 1769, 1782, 1789, 1802, 1848, and 1861.

All these transits (excepting that for 1861) have been discussed by M. Le Verrier in his determination of the orbit of the planet contained in Vol. II. of the *Annales de l'Observatoire Impérial de Paris*.

Again, for Venus,

$$\frac{P_1}{P_2} = \frac{224 \cdot 700}{365 \cdot 256}$$

$$= \frac{1}{1+} \frac{1}{1+} \frac{1}{1+} \frac{1}{1+} \frac{1}{2+} \frac{1}{29+} \frac{1}{3+} \frac{1}{1+} \frac{1}{19+\&c.}$$

Hence the converging fractions are

$$\frac{8}{13}, \frac{235}{382}, \frac{713}{1159},$$

and transits may be expected to occur *at the same node* after intervals of 8, 235, or 713 years.

The transits of Venus at the ascending node to the end of the present millenary period, commencing with 1631, are those which occurred in the month of December in the years 1631, 1639, and which will occur in 1874 and 1882; and those at the descending node are the celebrated ones of 1761 and 1769, which occurred in the month of June, and that which will occur in the same month of 2004.

7. *To find the Sun's horizontal equatorial parallax from the difference of the durations of the same transit of Venus observed at different places on the Earth's surface.*

The principle on which is founded this method of finding the Sun's parallax has been explained in a preceding chapter (page 199). We now propose to exhibit the mathematical details of the calculations.

The first thing to be done is to find the times of the first and last contact as viewed from the centre of the Earth.

Let c be the sum or the difference of the angular semi-diameters of the Sun and the planet (the sum corresponding to the external contact of the limbs and the difference to the internal contact);

L and $\odot$ the geocentric longitudes of the centres of the planet and the Sun at the time of first or last contact;

λ and Λ the geocentric latitudes at the same time.

Then we have the following equations:

$$\cos c = \sin \lambda \sin \Lambda + \cos \lambda \cos \Lambda \cos (L - \odot),$$

or $\sin^2 \dfrac{c}{2} = \sin^2 \dfrac{\lambda - \Lambda}{2} + \cos \lambda \cos \Lambda \sin^2 \dfrac{L - \odot}{2}$.

Also, since, at the time of the transit, c, λ, and $L - \odot$ are very small arcs, we may in general put the arcs for the sines, when we shall have

$$c^2 = (\lambda - \Lambda)^2 + (L - \odot)^2 *.$$

In the *Nautical Almanac* the values of the Geocentric Longitudes and Latitudes of the planets are not given, but they can

---

* M. Le Verrier at first retains the terms of the fourth order in the expansions of $\sin^2 \dfrac{c}{2}$, $\sin^2 \dfrac{\lambda - \Lambda}{2}$, &c., but he finally neglects them as producing no sensible effect. (*Annales de l'Observatoire de Paris*, Tome v. page 63.)

be calculated from the Heliocentric Longitudes and Latitudes by the formulæ at page 241, or they can be taken immediately from the Spanish *Nautical Almanac* (*Almanique Nautico calculado en el Observatorio de San Fernando*). Let these then be computed for three times at equal intervals of four hours, this being, with respect to the duration of the transit, a convenient interval, and let the middle time (T) correspond pretty nearly to the time of conjunction in longitude. We shall then have, for the times $T-4^h$, T, and $T+4^h$, the *true* longitudes and latitudes of the Sun and Venus. These must then be converted into *apparent* longitudes and latitudes by the application of the aberration, unless the *apparent* places are given in the Ephemeris.

Then for any time $T+t$ (t being less than four hours, and the hour being taken as the unit of time,) we shall be able to express the latitudes and longitudes in the form $a + bt + ct^2$, and consequently we shall have, for $\lambda - \Lambda$ and $L - \odot$, expressions of the form

$$\lambda - \Lambda = n + n't + n''t^2,$$

and $\quad L - \odot = m + m't + m''t^2,$

and, substituting these values in the equation

$$c^2 = (\lambda - \Lambda)^2 + (L - \odot)^2,$$

we shall have an equation of the form

$$c^2 = e + ft + gt^2 + ht^3,$$

or, putting $\dfrac{c^2}{g} - \dfrac{e}{g} - \dfrac{h}{g}t^3 = k,$

$$t^2 + \frac{f}{g}t - k = 0,$$

from which

$$t = -\frac{f}{2g} \pm \sqrt{\left(\frac{f}{2g}\right)^2 + k},$$

which will give the two epochs for which the distance of the centres of the Sun and planet is equal to c.

The term of k involving t^3 will, of course, be neglected in the first approximation, but, when an approximate value of t has been found, it can be easily taken into account, though it has an exceedingly small influence on the result.

Let now τ and τ' be the times calculated in the manner explained above, when the first and last contact would be seen at the centre of the Earth;

$\tau + \delta\tau$ and $\tau' + \delta\tau'$ the times at one of the observing stations, $\delta\tau$ and $\delta\tau'$ being the effects of parallax;

π the Sun's horizontal equatorial parallax,

π' the horizontal equatorial parallax of Venus,

n' and m' the relative horary motions of the Sun and Venus in latitude and longitude respectively.

Then, knowing the hour-angle and declination of the point of contact at the time $t + \delta t$, we can calculate the coefficients of parallax in R.A. and declination by the formulæ on page 188, and, by the formulæ on page 76, these can be transformed into the coefficients of parallax in longitude and latitude. For the first contact let these coefficients be a and b; so that the whole variation of $L - \odot$ will be $a(\pi' - \pi) + m'\delta\tau$, and the whole variation of $\lambda - \Lambda$ will be $b(\pi' - \pi) + n'\delta\tau$.

But, differentiating the equation

$$c^2 = (\lambda - \Lambda)^2 + (L - \odot)^2,$$

considering c as constant,

$$(\lambda - \Lambda)(\delta\lambda - \delta\Lambda) + (L - \odot)(\delta L - \delta\odot) = 0;$$

$$\therefore \{a(\pi' - \pi) + m'\delta\tau\}(L - \odot) + \{b(\pi' - \pi) + n'\delta\tau\}(\lambda - \Lambda) = 0,$$

or $$\delta\tau = -\frac{a(L - \odot) + b(\lambda - \Lambda)}{m'(L - \odot) + n'(\lambda - \Lambda)}(\pi' - \pi)$$

$$= \alpha(\pi' - \pi), \text{ suppose.}$$

Similarly for $\delta\tau'$ we shall obtain an expression of the form

$$\delta\tau' = \beta(\pi' - \pi).$$

Hence, at the station where this observation is made, we shall have:

time of first contact $= \tau + \alpha(\pi' - \pi)$,

.... last contact $= \tau' + \beta(\pi' - \pi)$;

therefore duration of transit

$$= D = \tau' - \tau + (\beta - \alpha)(\pi' - \pi).$$

If now D' be the duration of transit at another station, and β' and α' similarly related quantities,

$$D' = \tau' - \tau + (\beta' - \alpha')(\pi' - \pi);$$

$$\therefore D' - D = (\beta' - \beta - \alpha' + \alpha)(\pi' - \pi),$$

$$\text{or } \pi' - \pi = \frac{D' - D}{\beta' - \beta - \alpha' + \alpha}.$$

Now $\dfrac{\pi'}{\pi} = \dfrac{\text{distance of Sun from the Earth}}{\text{distance of Venus from Earth}}$,

and, as this ratio is known by the theory of elliptic motion, let it be equal to k;

$$\therefore \frac{\pi' - \pi}{\pi} = k - 1,$$

and $\therefore \pi = \dfrac{\pi' - \pi}{k - 1}$

$$= \frac{D' - D}{(k - 1)(\beta' - \beta - \alpha' + \alpha)}.$$

This gives the value of the Sun's horizontal equatorial parallax for the day of observation. If then the radius-vector of the Earth's orbit for this day be r, we shall have at the unit of distance, for the constant of solar parallax, πr.

By Encke's most careful and laborious discussion of all the observations of the Transit of Venus in 1769, the constant of parallax was found to be $8''\cdot 5776$, which value however has been proved by modern discussions (page 198) to be considerably too small.

CHAPTER IX.

ON THE ORBIT OF THE MOON; AND ON THE SATELLITES OF JUPITER.

---

1. IN the Chapter on Parallax, the method has been explained by which the horizontal parallax of the moon has been determined by means of observations of zenith-distance made at two observatories having very different latitudes, but differing little in longitude. The mean value of the parallax thus found is about 57′, and the earth's equatorial semi-diameter being 7926 miles, the mean distance of the moon from the earth is about 240,000 miles, or about 60 semi-diameters of the earth. Also, the distance of the sun being about 92,000,000 miles from the earth, the ratio of the distances of the moon and sun from the earth is about $\frac{1}{400}$. These numbers it is desirable for the student to retain in the memory.

2. By observations of the moon's vertical diameter made on the meridian with the mural circle or transit circle, it appears that the moon's orbit must be nearly circular and described round the earth, since these diameters, when properly corrected for the difference of refraction and parallax of the upper and lower limbs, do not vary greatly during the period of a whole lunation. Thus, if we take the numbers in the Nautical Almanac to represent the results of observation (which they do very accurately), and confine ourselves to the August lunation of 1863, we find that the semi-diameter was least on August 11, at about 12^h, being 14′.44″·0, and greatest on August 26, at 12^h, being at that time 16′.36″·1.

These numbers then being reduced to seconds will represent the ratio of the greatest and least distances of the moon, and, if we assume that the orbit is an ellipse of which the excentricity is e, we shall have

$$\frac{1+e}{1-e} = \frac{996 \cdot 1}{884 \cdot 0},$$

or $e = \dfrac{112 \cdot 1}{1880 \cdot 1} = 0 \cdot 059625.$

This then may be considered as an approximate value of the excentricity of the orbit, and, if the elements of the orbit were unknown, observations of the diameter continued through several lunations would determine the mean value with some considerable accuracy. The mean value assumed by M. Hansen is $0 \cdot 05490807$.

3. On looking however at the longitudes of the Moon which correspond to her greatest and least distances, we shall find that when reduced to the longitudes in the orbit, these points do not lie at the extremities of a diameter.

Thus, on August 11, 12^h, moon's ecliptic longitude $= 110°.26'$; and on August 26, 12^h, ... $= 306°.54'$.

The increase of longitude is therefore $196°.28'$, or, neglecting the reduction from the ecliptic to the orbit, which does not amount to above $6'$, the *apse* or perigee appears in half a revolution to have progressed by about $16\frac{1}{2}°$.

If again we compare the moon's longitude at the next return to her perigee on Sept. 7, 23^h, with the apogee next preceding, we shall find that the increase of longitude is only $165°$, and therefore that in the latter half of the orbit the apse has *regressed* almost as much as it progressed in the preceding half, so that, in the whole lunation, the progress is about $2°$. Another month would shew in the same manner how large and irregular is the motion of the line of apsides, and therefore that it is only as a matter of convenience that the orbit is considered as an ellipse at all, the points of apogee and perigee never lying at the extremities of a diameter of the orbit, but deviating from it sometimes by $20°$.

4. But though the motion of the apse is so irregular during a single lunation, yet, as its motion is due to the disturbing influence of the Sun, and as the Sun in the course of a year is in every possible position with respect to the line of apsides, a mean or average annual *progression* is produced amounting to about 38°; so that it makes a complete revolution in about $9\frac{1}{2}$ years.

5. Every other element of the lunar orbit is subject to disturbances as great as those which affect the line of apsides.

For example, the nodes or points of intersection of the orbit with the ecliptic are not fixed, but, on account of the disturbing action of the Sun, sometimes progress and sometimes regress in a very irregular way, so that on the whole they retrograde with a mean yearly motion of about $19°.20'$, performing a tropical revolution in $6793\cdot39$ days, or in about $18\frac{1}{2}$ years.

The inclination of the orbit to the ecliptic is also variable on account of the Sun's disturbing action, and the mean value assumed by Professor Hansen is $5°.8'.39''\cdot96$.

To find the actual longitude of the Moon's node at any time, we must use observations made a little before and a little after the crossing of the node. For instance, by the tabulated latitudes, we can find the day when she crosses from north to south, or from south to north latitude, and find or make observations of R.A. and N.P.D. for a day or two before and after the passage of the node. These can be converted into longitudes and latitudes by the processes of Chapter III.

Let then l and l' be the resulting longitudes,

β and β' the latitudes (the first north, the second south),

and Ω the longitude of the descending node,

i the inclination of the orbit.

Hence we have

$$\tan i = \frac{\tan \beta}{\sin (\Omega - l)}$$

$$= \frac{\tan \beta'}{\sin (l' - \Omega)};$$

$$\therefore \frac{\sin(\Omega - l)}{\sin(l' - \Omega)} = \frac{\tan \beta}{\tan \beta'},$$

or
$$\frac{\tan \frac{l'-l}{2}}{\tan\left(\frac{l'+l}{2} - \Omega\right)} = \frac{\sin(\beta' + \beta)}{\sin(\beta' - \beta)},$$

or $\tan\left(\dfrac{l'+l}{2} - \Omega\right) = \dfrac{\sin(\beta' - \beta)}{\sin(\beta' + \beta)} \tan \dfrac{l'-l}{2},$

which gives $\dfrac{l'+l}{2} - \Omega$, and therefore Ω; and the inclination will be determined by the equation

$$\tan i = \frac{\tan \lambda}{\sin(\Omega - l)}.$$

This value of i would however be subject to great uncertainty, and the inclination should be found by latitudes determined from observations made when the moon is distant nearly 90° from the node, in a way analogous to that for finding the obliquity of the ecliptic in Chapter III.

EXAMPLE. In the *Nautical Almanac* for 1863, we find the following longitudes and latitudes of the moon computed from Hansen's Tables, and therefore representing observations very accurately.

	Longitude.	Latitude.
1863, June 14, 0ʰ,	62°.48′.54″·3	0°.22′.58″·2 N.
... . 12,	68°.51′. 5″·9	0°.10′.25″·4 S.

Here $l' - l = 6°.2'.11''·6,$ $\beta' + \beta = 33'.23''·6,$

and $\dfrac{l'-l}{2} = 3°.1'. 5''·8,$ $\beta' - \beta = -12'.32''·8;$

$$\log \sin(\beta' - \beta) = 7\cdot5622535$$
$$\text{Ar. Co. } \log \sin(\beta' + \beta) = -2\cdot0126209$$
$$\log \tan \frac{l'-l}{2} = 8\cdot7220386$$
$$\log \tan\left(\frac{l'+l}{2} - \Omega\right) = -8\cdot2969130$$

INEQUALITIES OF THE NODE AND INCLINATION.

$$\frac{l'+l}{2} - \Omega = -1°.8'.6''$$

and $\frac{l'+l}{2} = 65°.50'.0''$;

therefore Ω, or the longitude of the *descending* node, is equal to $66°.58'.6''$, and the longitude of the ascending node is $246°.58'.6''$.

6. The principal inequality of the longitude of the node is

$$+1°.30'.26'' \sin 2(\odot - \Omega),$$

(the value of the coefficient being only approximate), so that if Ω represent the mean longitude of the ascending node for a given epoch, the true longitude is

$$\Omega + 1°.30'.26'' \sin 2(\odot - \Omega).$$

For 1863, June 14, $8^h \odot = 83°.12'$

and $\Omega = 246.58$

therefore $\odot - \Omega = 196.14$

and $2(\odot - \Omega) = 32.28$

And $\log \sin 2(\odot - \Omega) = 9\cdot72982$

$\text{Log } 90'\cdot 43 = 1\cdot 95631$

$\text{Sum} = 1\cdot 68613$

$\text{Number} = 48'\cdot 54$

Now, in the *Nautical Almanac* for 1863, page 242, we have for Ω, $246°.2'\cdot 0$; therefore the true longitude (referred however to the mean equinox for 1863, Jan. 1), is $246°.50'\cdot 54$, agreeing nearly with that found by calculation.

7. The principal inequality of the inclination is

$$+8'.47'' \cos 2(\odot - \Omega),$$

so that if i be the mean inclination, the true inclination for any time is

$$i + 8'.47'' \cos 2(\odot - \Omega).$$

8. *The Moon's Mean Motion.*

If the moon were without disturbance, and the times of conjunction with the Sun could be accurately observed, then the time of a synodic period could be very easily and correctly determined. This, however, is not the case, as the gravitation of the moon towards the Earth is variously affected (and consequently the time of a revolution in her orbit is different) in different months of the year, and therefore the intervals of time between consecutive conjunctions will be different.

Thus, taking the *Nautical Almanac* for 1863, we find the following times of new moon:

	h. m.	Intervals. d. h. m.
January 19,	4 . 1·8	
		29 . 11 . 4·5
February 17,	15 . 6·3	
		29 . 11 . 30·9
March 19,	2 . 37·2	
		29 . 12 . 28·0
April 17,	15 . 5·2	
		29 . 13 . 43·3
May 17,	4 . 48·5	
		29 . 14 . 47·8
June 15,	19 . 36·3	
		29 . 15 . 17·3
July 15,	10 . 53·6	
		29 . 15 . 9·3
August 14,	2 . 2·9	
		29 . 14 . 38·9
September 12,	16 . 41·8	
		29 . 14 . 0·4
October 12,	6 . 42·2	
		29 . 13 . 17·2
November 10,	19 . 59·4	
		29 . 12 . 24·1
December 10,	8 . 23·5	

The intervals above increase with tolerable uniformity till the middle of the year, shewing a decrease of gravitation towards the Earth, or an increase of the radial disturbing force of the sun directed from the Earth, and then diminish with the same uniformity, shewing a decrease of radial disturbing force directed from the Earth.

The mean of the intervals, or the mean synodic period for the year, is however

$$29^d . 13^h . 29^{m} \cdot 2.$$

If now we were to take the conjunctions in the year 1862, we should find

for January, $29^d. 14^h. 49^m \cdot 5$,

and for December, $20^d. 17^h. 4^m \cdot 3$,

giving for eleven lunations a period of

$325^d. 2^h. 14^m \cdot 8$,

or for one synodic revolution,

$29^d. 13^h. 17. \cdot 7$.

A result agreeing pretty well with that for 1862; so that, as might be expected, we should get a moderately accurate result if we could observe the times of conjunction at intervals of a few years with moderate accuracy. Eclipses of the sun or moon of course offer the best method of doing this, and it fortunately happens that the records of the observations of several ancient eclipses of the moon have come down to us, which, when compared with observations of recent eclipses, have led to a very accurate determination of the synodic period of the moon or of the mean motion.

The most ancient of these eclipses was observed at Babylon, B.C. 721, March 19, as related by Ptolemy; and the others were, first, that said by Hipparchus to have been observed at Babylon in the 366th year of Nabonassar; and, secondly, that observed at Alexandria, B.C. 201, Sept. 22.

According to Laplace, the mean length of a synodic period of the moon, determined in this way, is

$29^d. 12^h. 44^m. 2^s \cdot 8032$, or $29^d \cdot 530588$.

9. To deduce from this the *tropical period*, or the time of a revolution of the moon with regard to the equinoxes, let this be represented by t; the length of a tropical year or $365^d \cdot 24224$ by T; and the synodic period of the moon by s.

Then the sun's mean daily motion being $\dfrac{360°}{T}$, and that of the moon $\dfrac{360°}{t}$, their relative daily motion is

$$\frac{360°}{t} - \frac{360°}{T} = 360° \left(\frac{1}{t} - \frac{1}{T} \right),$$

and therefore $360°. s. \left(\dfrac{1}{t} - \dfrac{1}{T}\right) = 360°.$

Hence $s = \dfrac{1}{\dfrac{1}{t} - \dfrac{1}{T}}$

$= \dfrac{tT}{t - T},$

or $t = \dfrac{sT}{s + T}.$

If we now substitute for s and T the values given above, we shall find

$t = 27^{d}\cdot 32158$

$= 27^{d}.\ 7^{h}.\ 43^{m}.\ 4^{s}\cdot 5.$

10. To find the length of a *sidereal revolution*.

Let $p \,(= 50'''\cdot 224)$ be the annual precession, and x the value of a sidereal revolution. Then, $\dfrac{px}{T}$ will be the precessional arc corresponding to the period x, and the time of the moon's describing it will be

$$\dfrac{t}{360 \times 60 \times 60} \cdot \dfrac{px}{T};$$

$\therefore x = t + \dfrac{tpx}{360 \times 60 \times 60\, T},$

or $x = \dfrac{t}{1 - \dfrac{tp}{1296000\, T}}$

$= t\left\{1 + \dfrac{tp}{1296000\, T} + \left(\dfrac{tp}{1296000\, T}\right)^{2} + \&\text{c.}\right\}$

$= t\,\{1 + \cdot 00000289887 + \cdot 000000000008\}$

$= t \times 1\cdot 00000289895$

$= 27^{d}\cdot 32158 + \cdot 000079$

$= 27^{d}\cdot 32166$

$= 27^{d}.\ 7^{h}.\ 43^{m}.\ 11^{s}\cdot 4.$

11. When the moon's synodic period of revolution is determined by comparison of ancient and modern eclipses, it is found that the most ancient eclipses give for the time of revolution a longer period than the more recent ones, or that the moon's mean motion is accelerated. This was known to Dr Halley, and the amount was approximately calculated by the Rev. Richard Dunthorne (*Phil. Trans.* for 1749), and was found to be about $10''$ in a century. Laplace first assigned the true physical cause of this *secular* acceleration, which arises from the diminution of the mean value of the sun's ablatitious disturbing force, on account of the secular diminution of the excentricity of the earth's orbit, and the consequent greater distance of the sun from the earth and moon on the average. He did not carry the approximation far, but he found that, as an approximate value of the correction to the moon's place required on this account, there should be added to the mean longitude, for the year $1800 + t$, calculated on the supposition of a uniform motion,

$$10''{\cdot}207 t^2 + 0''{\cdot}00185 t^3.$$

A very elaborate investigation of several ancient eclipses by Mr Airy and Professor Hansen has shewn that a still larger value of the coefficient of the acceleration is necessary to represent them properly, amounting at least to $12''$. On the other hand it was proved by Mr Adams, originally in a paper printed in the *Phil. Trans.* for 1853, and has been established since beyond controversy by several eminent mathematicians, including M. Delaunay, Professors Plana, Donkin, Cayley, and Sir John Lubbock, that the coefficient of the *acceleration* as derived from the theory of gravitation does not amount to more than $5''{\cdot}7$. For information on the interesting controversy which arose respecting the disputed value, the reader may consult the *Monthly Notices of the Royal Astronomical Society*. Here we content ourselves with stating, that a difficulty has arisen on account of the necessity of accepting Adams's value of the coefficient, because it is not large enough to satisfy the ancient eclipses; and we are driven either to the hypothesis of a resisting medium, or (according to Professor Hansen's views) to that of a minute change in the length of the sidereal day, which would produce apparent acceleration of the same kind, to make up the deficiency.

The node and the perigee of the lunar orbit are also affected with secular inequalities, connected with that of the mean motion; that of the node is negative, and its coefficient is about three times that of the mean motion; that of the perigee is also negative, and amounts to about three-fourths of that of the mean motion.

12. *On the equations of the moon's motion.*

It has been stated that the orbit of the moon is only approximately an ellipse, on account of the action of the sun's disturbing force, and that it is only for convenience of calculation that the orbit is assumed to be elliptical.

The chief disturbances of the orbit, or deviations from the longitude calculated on the elliptic theory, are three, namely, the *evection*, the *variation*, and the *annual equation*. The first and largest of these inequalities was discovered by Ptolemy in the first century after Christ, and the second by Tycho Brahe in the sixteenth century.

The *evection* has for its argument

$$\sin \{2 (\mathrm{D} - \odot) - m\},$$

where D and $\odot$ represent the mean longitudes of the moon and sun, and m the mean anomaly of the moon. And the value of its coefficient is, according to the most recent researches of Mr Airy, $4587''\cdot 01$.

The correction to be added to the elliptic longitude is

$$+ 4587''\cdot 01 \sin \{2 (\mathrm{D} - \odot) - m\}.$$

The evection includes the effect of the disturbances producing the irregular motion of the lunar perigee before referred to, and the change of excentricity of the orbit. The approximate position of the perigee at any time may be found by subtracting from the longitude, calculated on the supposition of its uniform progression, $\dfrac{15}{104} \sin 2$ (long. of perigee − long. of sun), and the longitude of the moon may then be calculated in an elliptic orbit, with this position of the perigee, and with an excentricity = mean excentricity $\times \{1 + \frac{15}{104} \cos 2$ (long. of perigee − long. of sun)$\}$. See Airy's *Tracts, Lunar Theory*, Art. 66.

The *variation* has for its argument $\sin 2 (\mathbb{D} - \odot)$, and the correct value of its coefficient is $2370''\cdot 7$.

The correction to moon's longitude on this account is

$$+ 2370''\cdot 7 \times \sin 2 (\mathbb{D} - \odot).$$

The *annual equation* depends of course on the position of the sun, and has for its argument sin sun's mean anomaly. The value of its coefficient is $669''\cdot 0$; and the correction to the longitude is

$$- 669''\cdot 0 \times \sin \text{ sun's mean anomaly}.$$

Taking account then of these inequalities only, the moon's longitude at any time = mean longitude + equation of the centre in assumed elliptic orbit ($+ 22639''\cdot 06 \sin m$)

$$+ 4587''\cdot 01 \sin \{2 (\mathbb{D} - \odot) - m\}$$
$$+ 2370''\cdot 7 \sin 2 (\mathbb{D} - \odot)$$
$$- 669''\cdot 0 \sin \text{ sun's mean anomaly}.$$

13. The researches of astronomers have been recently attended with complete success in developing the theory of the lunar inequalities, so that the places of the moon calculated by the tables of Professor Hansen, recently published, may at the present epoch be considered to represent the true places actually better than single observations, and, for the first time, we are able to say that, in the application of the method of Lunar Distances for finding the longitude at sea, the error of the result will not depend at all upon the inaccuracy of the assumed places of the moon. The places of the moon given in the *Nautical Almanac*, commencing with the year 1863, are computed from Hansen's tables; while, for all preceding years, commencing with 1834, they were computed from the tables of Burckhardt.

These latter gave places frequently in error to the amount of 30″, and sometimes to the amount of 45″*.

14. Since the same face of the moon is, with very trifling exceptions, always turned towards the earth (as proved by the fact that a map made at one epoch is found to represent with great accuracy the details of the surface presented to the earth at any other epoch), it is plain that she must rotate on an axis very nearly perpendicular to the plane of her orbit in the exact time of a mean revolution in her orbit round the earth.

Since, however, it is almost certain from the analogy of all other planets, that the velocity of rotation on her axis is uniform, while the velocity in the orbit is subject to considerable variations, it follows that occasionally a little more of the eastern limb and of the western limb will be visible than would be the case if the velocity in the orbit were uniform. This is called the *Libration in Longitude*.

It is observed also, that occasionally rather more is seen of the northern limb and of the southern limb than at other times. This is called the *Libration in Latitude*, and is assumed to arise from the circumstance of the axis of rotation not being exactly perpendicular to the plane of the orbit.

A third libration, called the *Diurnal Libration*, is due to parallax, or to the observer's position on the surface of the earth, the effect being that at rising and setting, parts near the upper limb are seen which would not be seen from the earth's centre, and which vary according to the altitude of the moon above the horizon.

On the Satellites of Jupiter.

15. Of the planets exterior to Mars, Jupiter has four satellites, Saturn has eight, Uranus several, and Neptune at least one. Saturn has also a system of luminous rings all lying in one plane. All these objects, excepting the satellites of Jupiter, concern speculative rather than practical astronomy, and the

---

* For a history of the successive improvements in the Lunar Tables, see the address on the presentation of the Gold Medal of the Royal Astronomical Society to Professor Hansen, in Vol. xx. of the *Monthly Notices*.

reader may consult more popular books for information respecting them.

The satellites of Jupiter, however, are of practical importance to astronomers, as the observation of their eclipses, at different distances from the earth, furnished a good approximation to the velocity of light (see page 142), and also affords a ready means of obtaining the difference of longitude of distant stations on the earth's surface. We may therefore devote a few words to them.

16. The satellites of Jupiter were discovered in 1610, by Galileo; their brightness, when the planet is near opposition, being generally equivalent to stars of about the 7th magnitude, and therefore rendering them visible by the use of small telescopes. They are, to their primary planet, what the moon is with respect to the earth, revolving round Jupiter in nearly circular orbits, casting a shadow on his disk, and disappearing on entering his shadow.

That their disappearances are owing to their eclipse in the shadow of Jupiter is proved by the fact of their taking place at different distances from his body according to the relative positions of Jupiter, the sun, and the earth, but always towards those parts, and on that side of the disk, where the shadow ought to be by computation.

That the satellites move *directly*, or according to the order of the signs of the zodiac, is proved from the fact that a satellite is never eclipsed or occulted except when it appears to move in this direction, that is, towards the east, while, on the other hand, transits over the disk always occur when the satellite is apparently moving from east to west.

The synodical period of each satellite is found by comparing the intervals between the times of successive eclipses, and especially those which occur near the time of opposition of the planet. Thus, the mean of the times of disappearance and reappearance of a satellite is the time when it is very nearly in the direction of the line joining the centres of the sun and Jupiter, and therefore, the difference of the times of two successive eclipses will be very nearly the synodic period, and from this, when it has been well determined, the sidereal period can be determined by the formula on page 278. If, instead of two *successive* eclipses, two separated by a long interval be chosen, which happen, when the earth, Jupiter, and the satellite, are nearly in the same relative positions, the difference of observed times divided by the number of revolutions of the satellite will give the time of a revolution with much greater accuracy.

17. That the satellites move in nearly circular orbits is proved from the fact, that their mean motions do not differ considerably from their true motions. The excentricities of the orbits of the first and second are insensible, those of the third and fourth small (that of the fourth being the larger) and variable, on account of their mutual perturbations.

The inclinations of the orbits to the plane of Jupiter's equator are very small, all being included within half a degree.

Their mean distances from the centre of Jupiter have been determined by micrometrical measures, or times of comparative transit, near the time of greatest elongation. They are approximately, measured in parts of Jupiter's semi-diameter, 6·05, 9·62, 15·35, and 27·00. Of course, when the periodic times are accurately known and the distance of one satellite, the distances of the others can be determined by Kepler's third law.

18. The following very curious relation has been found between the Jovicentric longitudes of the first three satellites at any time. If these be denoted by l_1, l_2, l_3, then

$$l_1 - 3l_2 + 2l_3 = 180°,$$

from which it follows that they cannot all be eclipsed at the same time, as this would require that $l_1 = l_2 = l_3$.

CHAPTER X.

ON THE DETERMINATION OF GEOGRAPHICAL LATITUDE AND LONGITUDE.

1. GEOGRAPHICAL *Latitude* has already been defined (p. 6), and it is there stated that it is equal to angular elevation of the celestial pole above the horizon of the place of observation, or that the *colatitude* is equal to the arc included between the observer's zenith and the pole. This suggests, for a fixed observatory furnished with a mural or a transit-circle, a very obvious method of finding the value of the colatitude, namely, by observing meridian distances of Polaris or some other circumpolar star, both above and below the pole, and taking the half sum of the results.

If, for instance, z_u be the zenith-distance (corrected for refraction) observed at the transit above the pole, and z_l, at the transit below, and γ the colatitude;

then $\qquad \gamma = \dfrac{1}{2}(z_u + z_l).$

Let, generally, the value of z_u be the mean result of m observations, and that of z_l the result of n observations; then (see Airy's *Theory of Errors of Observations*) the *probable error* of z_u will be the probable error of a single observation (e_u) divided by $\sqrt{m}$, and the probable error of z will be the probable error of a single observation (e_l) divided by $\sqrt{n}$; and therefore the (probable error)^2 of γ will be

$$\frac{(e_u)^2}{4m} + \frac{(e_l)^2}{4n},$$

and, if we assume that the observations above and below the pole are equally trustworthy, or that $e_u = e_l = e$,

$$\text{(Probable error)}^2 \text{ of } \gamma = \frac{e^2}{4}\left(\frac{1}{m} + \frac{1}{n}\right),$$

or, probable error of $\gamma = \dfrac{e}{2}\sqrt{\dfrac{m+n}{mn}}$,

and, since the weight of a result is inversely proportional to the square of its probable error, the weight of this value of γ, when brought into combination with values derived from other determinations, will be $\dfrac{mn}{m+n}$.

2. In the reduction of a long series of observations of meridian zenith-distances, it is usual, when the colatitude is approximately known, to deduce the North Polar Distances of all stars and other objects observed, from the observed zenith-distances, by application of an assumed colatitude; and, at the end of the year, to collect all the results of observations of circumpolar stars, for the correction of the colatitude.

Thus, using the same notation as before, let γ be the assumed colatitude, and $\gamma + \delta\gamma$ the correct colatitude; then, from a series of m observations of a star above the pole, giving z_u for the resulting north zenith-distance, corrected for all astronomical inequalities (such as refraction, aberration, precession, and nutation), we obtain for the correct mean N.P.D. $\gamma + \delta\gamma - z_u$; and, similarly, for the result of n observations below the pole, we get for the mean N.P.D. of the same star,

$$z_l - \gamma - \delta\gamma;$$

thus $\quad\gamma + \delta\gamma - z_u = z_l - \gamma - \delta\gamma,$

or $\quad\delta\gamma = \dfrac{1}{2}(z_l + z_u) - \gamma$

$\quad\quad = \dfrac{1}{2}(z_l - \gamma) - \dfrac{1}{2}(\gamma - z_u).$

Now, the quantities $z_u - \gamma$ and $\gamma - z_l$ are plainly the values of the N.P.D. of the star, deduced with the erroneous value (γ) of the colatitude, and therefore the error of the colatitude is half the difference or half the algebraical sum of the seconds of N.P.D., as deduced from observations of the same stars above and below the pole.

If several (p) circumpolar stars have been observed for the determination of the colatitude, and if, as before, m and n represent for one of them the number of observations above and below the pole; then, assuming them to be arranged in the order of their distance from the pole, and that the intervals of N.P.D. are tolerably equal, weights are given proportional to the numbers

$$2p \frac{mn}{m+n}, \quad 2(p-1)\frac{m'n'}{m'+n'}, \quad 2(p-2)\frac{m''n''}{m''+n''}, \quad \&c.,$$

to make allowance for the additional uncertainty of the observations made at successively greater distances from the zenith.

EXAMPLE. At Oxford, after reducing all the observations of the year 1861, on the assumed colatitude $38°. 14'. 24''\cdot8$, the stars in the following table, of which the headings of the respective columns give all necessary information, were used for the determination of the error of the assumption.

ERROR OF ASSUMED COLATITUDE.

Stars.	Number of Observations.	N.P.D. on assumed Colatitude.	Number of Observations.	Algebraic sum of Determination.	Weight.	Product.
		° ′ ″		″		″
λ Ursæ Minoris...	4	1. 6.26·3	7	+2·4	11	+26·4
... S.P.	3	− 1. 6.23·9				
Polaris	7	1.25.55·4	10	+3·6	13	+46·8
... S.P.	3	− 1.25.51·8				
R. H. C. 897*......	2	2.26.57·6	3	+2·2	4	+ 8·8
... S.P.	1	− 2.26.55·4				
Cephei 51. (Hev.)	2	2.45. 9·7	6	+0·9	8	+ 7·2
... S.P.	4	− 2.45. 8·8				
24 Ursæ Minoris.	4	3. 1.13·3	6	+0·4	7	+ 2·8
... S.P.	2	− 3. 1.12·9				
δ Ursæ Minoris...	4	3.23.53·1	7	+3·2	9	+28·8
... S.P.	3	− 3.23.49·9				
Radcliffe 2738 ...	1	3.41.47·2	2	+3·0	3	+ 9·0
... S.P.	1	− 3.41.44·2				
Radcliffe 2320 ...	2	5.32.54·5	4	+1·1	5	+ 5·5
... S.P.	2	− 5.32.53·4				
22 Ursæ Majoris.	1	17.10.52·3	2	−0·5	2	− 1·0
... S.P.	1	−17.10.52·8				
B. A. C. 3245......	1	17.18. 3·4	2	+0·4	2	+ 0·8
... S.P.	1	−17.18. 3·0				
β² Cephei	11	20. 2.57·8	14	−0·8	10	− 8·0
... S.P.	3	−20. 2.58·6				
β¹ Cephei	3	20. 3. 1·5	6	−1·3	6	− 7·8
... S.P.	3	−20. 3. 2·8				
6 Ursæ Majoris...	2	24.52. 6·0	5	−1·0	5	− 5·0
... S.P.	3	−24.52. 7·0				
α Ursæ Majoris...	2	27.29.58·3	4	+1·3	4	+ 5·2
... S.P.	2	−27.29.57·0				
α Cephei	9	28. 0.10·8	12	+1·4	8	+11·2
... S.P.	3	−28. 0. 9·4				
β Ursæ Majoris ..	1	32.52.24·6	4	+1·9	3	+ 5·7
... S.P.	3	−32.52.22·7				

* R.H.C. 897 denotes that the star is No. 897 in Mr Carrington's *Red Hill Catalogue of Circumpolar Stars*: in like manner, Radcliffe 2738, denotes that the star is No. 2738 in the *Radcliffe* or *Oxford Catalogue of Stars*, published in 1861.

For explanation of the weights attributed to the separate results it will be sufficient to compute that for λ Ursæ Minoris. Here $p = 16$, $m = 4$, $n = 3$. Hence the weight

$$= \frac{4 \times 3 \times 32}{4+3} = \frac{384}{7} = 55,$$

and to prevent the use of numbers too large, this, as well as all the other weights, has been divided by 5, from which we get the number 11 in the table.

Dividing then the sum of all the products by the sum of all the weights, we get the quantity $+ 1'''\!\cdot 36$, and, it will be readily seen from the formula previously given, that

$$2\delta\gamma + 1''\!\cdot 36 = 0,$$

or
$$\delta\gamma = -0''\!\cdot 68.$$

Hence, the true value of the colatitude, as deduced from the results of 1861, is

$$\gamma + \delta\gamma = 38^\circ.\, 14'.\, 24''\!\cdot 8 - 0''\!\cdot 68$$
$$= 38^\circ.\, 14'.\, 24'''\!\cdot 1.$$

Still, it would not be prudent to accept this result as unquestionable, since the assumed colatitude (undoubtedly subject to a small error from some cause) is that which was deduced by Mr Johnson by an elaborate discussion of the results of the observations of several years.

3. The method given above is quite independent of any assumed positions of the objects observed, and therefore serves for the independent determination of the N.P.Ds. of all objects observed; but an astronomer, on fitting up a new observatory, might obtain by means of a single evening's observations a tolerably accurate value of the latitude by comparison of the observed zenith-distances of a series of standard stars with their declinations or North Polar Distances, given in the *Nautical Almanac*.

Thus, if as usual z be the observed south zenith-distance of a star, corrected only for refraction; Δ its N.P.D.; and γ the required colatitude, we have

$$z + \gamma = \Delta,$$

or
$$\gamma = \Delta - z.$$

EXAMPLE. From the *Catalogue of the Places of Stars* observed at Oxford in 1858, the following results of observed zenith-distances are obtained by subtracting the assumed colatitude 38°. 14′. 24″·8 from the mean North Polar Distances.

Star.	Mean South Zenith Distance, 1858, Jan. 1.	Mean N.P.D. from N. A.	Resulting Colatitude.
	° ′ ″	° ′ ″	° ′ ″
α Andromedæ...	23.27.11·1	61.41.37·2	38.14.26·1
ε Piscium.........	44.38. 5·6	82.52.31·1	25·5
α Ceti	48.13.47·0	86.28.12·4	25·4
Capella............	5.54.41·3	44. 9. 5·8	24·5
β Tauri............	23.16.35·6	61.31. 1·4	25·8
δ Orionis	52.10. 4·8	90.24.28·7	23·9
δ Geminorum ...	29.31.12·6	67.45.36·8	24·2
Castor	19.33.51·4	57.48.16·0	24·6
Pollux	23.23.39·9	61.38. 4·9	25·0
6 Cancri	23.34.14·2	61.48.40·0	25·8
83 Cancri........	33.27.17·8	71.41.42·5	24·7
Regulus	39. 6. 0·6	77.20.25·8	25·2
γ Leonis	31.12. 4·8	69.26.30·6	25·8
ρ Leonis	41.43.24·7	79.57.50·5	25·8
l Leonis	40.27.50·3	78.42.16·0	25·7

The mean of the values of the colatitude in the table above is 38°. 14′. 25″·2, which agrees moderately well with the assumed colatitude 38°. 14′. 24″·8, and shews that for south stars the assumption is correct within very trifling limits of error. The consistency of the separate results also shews the goodness of the observations.

4. The method of finding the latitude given above is that practised in a fixed observatory, furnished with a mural or transit-circle, and depends on the observation of meridian zenith-distances of stars. The latitude may also be found by the use of the transit-instrument placed in the prime vertical (as has been explained in Chapter II., pages 33 to 39), and this method is available for finding the latitudes of stations by travellers or surveyors, furnished with a small transit-instrument, and with independent means of local time. But in general, both at such

stations and at sea, the sextant is employed for the determination, by measuring (by the help of a surface of mercury) the angular distance between the sun or a star, and their reflected images, that is, their double altitudes; and we will proceed to shew how, by a repetition and combination of such observations, the determination of latitude is effected.

5. *First Method.*

By observing the zenith-distance or altitude of the sun or a known star at any hour-angle h.

Using the usual notation

$$\cos z = \cos h \sin \Delta \sin \gamma + \cos \Delta \cos \gamma$$

$$= \cot \phi \cos \Delta \sin \gamma + \cos \Delta \cos \gamma,$$

(by making $\cot \phi = \cos h \tan \Delta$)

$$= \frac{\cos \Delta}{\sin \phi} \cdot \sin (\phi + \gamma);$$

whence $$\sin (\phi + \gamma) = \frac{\cos z \sin \phi}{\cos \Delta},$$

which determines $\phi + \gamma$ and therefore γ, since ϕ is determined by the equation

$$\cot \phi = \cos h \tan \Delta.$$

6. *Second Method.*

By observed altitudes or zenith-distances of any star observed near the meridian.

Let z be the zenith-distance corresponding to hour-angle h, and z_0 the meridian zenith-distance.

Then $$\cos h = \frac{\cos z - \cos \Delta \cos \gamma}{\sin \Delta \sin \gamma},$$

and $$1 = \frac{\cos z_0 - \cos \Delta \cos \gamma}{\sin \Delta \sin \gamma};$$

$$\therefore 1 - \cos h = \frac{\cos z_0 - \cos z}{\sin \Delta \sin \gamma},$$

or
$$\sin^2 \frac{h}{2} = \frac{\sin \frac{z-z_0}{2} \sin \frac{z+z_0}{2}}{\sin \Delta \sin \gamma}.$$

Let now $z - z_0 = x$ (a small arc),

then
$$\frac{z+z_0}{2} = z_0 + \frac{x}{2};$$

$$\therefore \sin \frac{x}{2} = \sin \Delta \sin \gamma \frac{\sin^2 \frac{h}{2}}{\sin \left(z_0 + \frac{x}{2}\right)}.$$

For a first approximation,

$$\sin \frac{x}{2} = \sin \Delta \sin \gamma \frac{\sin^2 \frac{h}{2}}{\sin z_0},$$

or
$$\frac{x}{2} \sin 1'' = \frac{1}{4} \frac{\sin \Delta \sin \gamma}{\sin z_0} h^2 \sin^2 1'',$$

or
$$x = \frac{1}{2} \frac{\sin \Delta \sin \gamma}{\sin z_0} h^2 \sin 1''.$$

Recurring now to the equation

$$\sin \frac{x}{2} = \sin \Delta \sin \gamma \frac{\sin^2 \frac{h}{2}}{\sin \left(z_0 + \frac{x}{2}\right)},$$

it will become by expansion

$$\sin \frac{x}{2} = \frac{\sin \Delta \sin \gamma \sin^2 \frac{h}{2}}{\sin z_0 \cos \frac{x}{2} + \cos z_0 \sin \frac{x}{2}}$$

$$= \frac{\sin \Delta \sin \gamma \sin^2 \frac{h}{2}}{\sin z_0 + \frac{1}{2} \cos z_0 \times x \sin 1''} \text{ (very nearly)}$$

$$= \frac{\sin \Delta \sin \gamma \sin^2 \frac{h}{2}}{\sin z_0} \left\{1 - \frac{1}{2} \cot z_0 \times x \sin 1''\right\},$$

or, substituting for x on the right-hand side of the equation, its approximate value,

$$\frac{x}{2}\sin 1'' = \frac{1}{4}\cdot\frac{\sin\Delta\sin\gamma.h^2}{\sin z_0}\sin^2 1''\times\{1-\frac{1}{4}\cdot\frac{\sin\Delta\sin\gamma\cos z_0}{\sin^2 z_0}h^2\sin^2 1''\},$$

or $\quad x = \frac{1}{2}\cdot\frac{\sin\Delta\sin\gamma}{\sin z_0}h^2\sin 1'' - \frac{1}{8}\cdot\frac{\sin^2\gamma\sin^2\Delta\cos z_0}{\sin^3 z_0}h^4\sin^3 1'',$

in which expression approximate values of γ and z_0 must be used.

$\therefore z_0 = z - x$ is determined,

and $\gamma = \Delta - z_0$ (z_0 being the meridian south zenith-distance) is known.

If greater accuracy be required, we can easily deduce the more correct expression

$$x = \frac{2\sin^2\frac{1}{2}h\sin\Delta\sin\gamma}{\sin z_0\sin 1''} - \left(\frac{\sin^2\frac{1}{2}h\sin\Delta\sin\gamma}{\sin z_0}\right)^2\cdot\frac{2\cot z_0}{\sin 1''}.$$

With a sextant or an altitude and azimuth-instrument, a series of zenith-distances, corresponding to different values of h, may be observed, and each of the observations will give a value of z_0, and therefore of γ.

In Schumacher's *Hülfstafeln* (Warnstorff's Edition) will be found tables of the values of the logs. of $\dfrac{2\sin^2\frac{h}{2}}{\sin 1''}$ and $\dfrac{2\sin^4\frac{h}{2}}{\sin 1''}$, to facilitate the use of the formula given above.

7. *Third method.*

By observations of zenith-distance of Polaris made at any hour-angle.

In this method the peculiarity is that, the N.P.D. of the star being small (about $1^\circ.25'$ at the present time), advantage may be taken of this circumstance to expand the difference between the colatitude and the zenith-distance, which is always small, in terms of the N.P.D.

LATITUDE BY POLARIS.

Let this difference be x, that is, let $\gamma = z + x$;

$\therefore \cos z = \cos h \sin(z+x) \sin \Delta + \cos(z+x) \cos \Delta$
$\quad = \cos h \sin \Delta \{\sin z \cos x + \cos z \sin x\}$
$\quad\quad + \cos \Delta \{\cos z \cos x - \sin z \sin x\}$,

and $\quad 1 = \cos h \sin \Delta \{\tan z \cos x + \sin x\}$
$\quad\quad + \cos \Delta \{\cos x - \tan z \sin x\}$
$\quad = \cos x \{\cos \Delta + \cos h \tan z \sin \Delta\}$
$\quad\quad + \sin x \{\cos h \sin \Delta - \tan z \cos \Delta\}$
$\quad = a \cos x - b \sin x \dots\dots\dots\dots\dots\dots(1),$

if $\quad a = \cos \Delta + \cos h \tan z \sin \Delta,$
and $\quad b = \tan z \cos \Delta - \cos h \sin \Delta.$

Then, developing a and b by powers of Δ to the third order, we have

$$a = 1 + \cos h \tan z \cdot \Delta - \frac{\Delta^2}{2} - \cos h \tan z \frac{\Delta^3}{6},$$

and $\quad b = \tan z - \cos h \cdot \Delta - \dfrac{\tan z}{2}\Delta^2 + \cos h \dfrac{\Delta^3}{6}.$

Recurring now to equation (1), or

$$1 = a \cos x - b \sin x,$$

we must proceed to find the value of x in terms of Δ by the method of indeterminate coefficients.

Let then $\quad x = A\Delta + B\Delta^2 + C\Delta^3 \dots\dots\dots\dots(2)$

(since, for a star at the pole, or for $\Delta = 0$, x would also be equal to 0, and therefore there is no term independent of Δ).

Then $\quad \cos x = 1 - \dfrac{x^2}{2}$

$$= 1 - \frac{1}{2}A^2\Delta^2 - AB\Delta^3,$$

and $\quad \sin x = x - \dfrac{x^3}{6}$

$$= A\Delta + B\Delta^2 + \left(C - \frac{A^3}{6}\right)\Delta^3.$$

LATITUDE BY POLARIS.

Substituting then in equation (1) the values given above, of a, b, $\sin x$, and $\cos x$, we have

$$1 = 1 + \cos h \tan z \cdot \Delta$$

$$- \left(\frac{1}{2}A^2 + \frac{1}{2} + B \tan z - A \cos h\right) \Delta^2$$

$$- \begin{cases} AB + \frac{1}{2}A^2 \cos h \tan z + \frac{1}{6} \cos h \tan z \\ + \left(C - \frac{A^3}{6}\right) \tan z - \frac{A}{2} \tan z - B \cos h \end{cases} \Delta^3;$$

and this equation must be identically true.

Hence $\quad A = \cos h$,

$$B \tan z = -\frac{1}{2}(1 + A^2) + A \cos h$$

$$= -\frac{1}{2}(1 - \cos^2 h)$$

$$= -\frac{1}{2}\sin^2 h,$$

and $\quad B = -\frac{1}{2}\sin^2 h \cot z.$

Also, since the terms in B of the coefficient of Δ^3 destroy each other,

$$\left(C - \frac{A^3}{6}\right)\tan z = -\frac{1}{6}\cos h \tan z (1 + 3A^2) + \frac{A}{2}\tan z,$$

whence $\quad C \tan z = \frac{1}{3}\cos h \tan z - \frac{1}{3}\cos^3 h \tan z;$

and $\quad C = \frac{1}{3}\sin^2 h \cos h;$

thus $\quad x = \cos h \cdot \Delta - \frac{1}{2}\sin^2 h \cot z \cdot \Delta^2 + \frac{1}{3}\sin^2 h \cos h \cdot \Delta^3.$

And $\gamma = z + x$

$$= z + \cos h \cdot \Delta - \frac{1}{2}\sin^2 h \cot z \cdot \Delta^2 + \frac{1}{3}\sin^2 h \cos h \cdot \Delta^3,$$

or, since x and Δ must be expressed in angle,

$$\gamma = z + \cos h \cdot \Delta - \frac{1}{2}\sin 1'' \sin^2 h \cot z \cdot \Delta^2$$

$$+ \frac{1}{3}\sin^2 1'' \sin^2 h \cos h \cdot \Delta^3.$$

The coefficient of Δ^2 is a function of h only, and may therefore be tabulated, as also the factor $\frac{1}{2}\sin 1'' \sin^2 h$ of the coefficient of Δ^2, but the last term is generally exceedingly small.

In the *Nautical Almanac* are given tables containing for Polaris the values of the second and third terms of the right-hand side of the equation above, calculated, with the sidereal time of observation as the argument, for the mean values of the R.A. and N.P.D., and there is an additional table giving the correction required for the true values of R.A. and N.P.D. on any given day. (See *Some Critical Remarks on the Tables in the Nautical Almanac, by the late John Riddle, Esq.* in Vol. xx. of the *Monthly Notices*, page 339.)

8. The development might also have been effected by Maclaurin's Theorem in the following way.

Let $\quad x = x_0 + \left(\dfrac{dx}{d\Delta}\right)_0 \Delta + \dfrac{1}{2}\left(\dfrac{d^2x}{d\Delta^2}\right)_0 \Delta^2 + \&c.$

Then we have seen that $x_0 = 0$.

And, taking the equation,

$$\cos z = \cos h \sin(z+x)\sin\Delta + \cos(z+x)\cos\Delta,$$

and differentiating it, x and Δ being the variables, we get

$$0 = \cos h \cos(z+x)\sin\Delta \frac{dx}{d\Delta} + \cos h \sin(z+x)\cos\Delta$$

$$- \sin(z+x)\cos\Delta \frac{dx}{d\Delta} - \cos(z+x)\sin\Delta,$$

and, making $x = 0$, and therefore

$$\frac{dx}{d\Delta} = \left(\frac{dx}{d\Delta}\right)_0,$$

and remembering that $\sin \Delta = 0$, we get,

$$\cos h \sin z - \sin z \left(\frac{dx}{d\Delta}\right)_0 = 0,$$

or
$$\left(\frac{dx}{d\Delta}\right)_0 = \cos h.$$

Differentiating again,

$$0 = \begin{cases} -\cos h \sin(z+x) \sin \Delta \left(\frac{dx}{d\Delta}\right)^2 + \cos h \cos(z+x) \cos \Delta \frac{dx}{d\Delta} \\ \qquad + \cos h \cos(z+x) \sin \Delta \frac{d^2x}{d\Delta^2} \\ -\cos(z+x) \cos \Delta \left(\frac{dx}{d\Delta}\right)^2 + \sin(z+x) \sin \Delta \frac{dx}{d\Delta} \\ \qquad - \sin(z+x) \cos \Delta \frac{d^2x}{d\Delta^2} \\ +\cos h \cos(z+x) \cos \Delta \frac{dx}{d\Delta} - \cos h \sin(z+x) \sin \Delta \\ +\sin(z+x) \sin \Delta \frac{dx}{d\Delta} - \cos(z+x) \cos \Delta; \end{cases}$$

and $\therefore \left. \begin{array}{c} \cos^2 h \cos z - \cos^2 h \cos z - \sin z \left(\frac{d^2x}{d\Delta^2}\right)_0 \\ + \cos^2 h \cos z - \cos z \end{array} \right\} = 0,$

or
$$\left(\frac{d^2x}{d\Delta^2}\right)_0 = -\sin^2 h \cot z,$$

and therefore
$$x = \cos h \cdot \Delta - \frac{1}{2} \sin^2 h \cot z \cdot \Delta^2,$$

as before.

The student will probably not be inclined to pursue the investigation to another differentiation, though it is not difficult, if the terms which vanish (or which contain $\sin \Delta$) are omitted in the writing down.

298   APPLICATION OF MACLAURIN'S THEOREM.

Thus, retaining only the terms which will not vanish when $x = 0$ and $\Delta = 0$, we shall find

$$0 = \begin{cases} -3\cos h \sin(z+x)\cos\Delta \left(\dfrac{dx}{d\Delta}\right)^2 + 2\cos h \cos(z+x)\cos\Delta \dfrac{d^2x}{d\Delta^2} \\[4pt] + \sin(z+x)\cos\Delta \left(\dfrac{dx}{d\Delta}\right)^3 - \cos(z+x)\cos\Delta \left(\dfrac{d^2x}{d\Delta^2}\right)\left(\dfrac{dx}{d\Delta}\right) \\[4pt] \qquad\qquad + 3\sin(z+x)\cos\Delta \dfrac{dx}{d\Delta} \\[4pt] - \cos(z+x)\cos\Delta \left(\dfrac{d^2x}{d\Delta^2}\right)\left(\dfrac{dx}{d\Delta}\right) \\[4pt] - \sin(z+x)\cos\Delta \left(\dfrac{d^3x}{d\Delta^3}\right) - \cos h \sin(z+x)\cos\Delta. \end{cases}$$

and, putting $x = 0$, and $\Delta = 0$, and substituting for

$$\left(\frac{dx}{d\Delta}\right)_0 \text{ and } \left(\frac{d^2x}{d\Delta^2}\right)_0 \text{ their values, we get}$$

$$0 = \begin{cases} -3\cos^3 h \sin z - 2\sin^2 h \cos h \cos z \cot z + \cos^3 h \sin z \\ + \sin^2 h \cos h \cos z \cot z + 3\cos h \sin z \\ + \sin^2 h \cos h \cos z \cot z - \sin z \left(\dfrac{d^3x}{d\Delta^3}\right)_0 \\ - \cos h \sin z, \end{cases}$$

or $\qquad 2\cos h \sin z - 2\cos^3 h \sin z - \sin z \left(\dfrac{d^3x}{d\Delta^3}\right)_0 = 0,$

and $\qquad\qquad \left(\dfrac{d^3x}{d\Delta^3}\right)_0 = 2\sin^2 h \cos h ;$

$$\therefore \frac{1}{1.2.3}\left(\frac{d^3x}{d\Delta^3}\right)_0 = \frac{1}{3}\sin^2 h \cos h,$$

which is the coefficient of Δ^3 as before.

9. *Fourth method.*

By two observed altitudes or zenith-distances of the same star at different hour-angles, to find both the local time and the colatitude.

LATITUDE BY TWO OBSERVED ALTITUDES. 299

Let α and Δ be the R.A. and N.P.D. of the star; S and S'' the positions of the star at the sidereal times t and t'; z and z' the zenith-distances ZS and ZS''; $PS = PS'' = \Delta$.

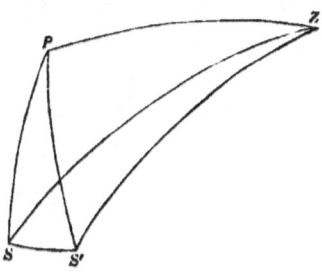

Draw SS' an arc of a great circle.

Then the angle $SPS' = 15 (t' - t) = \theta$ suppose.

And $\quad \sin \dfrac{SS'}{2} = \sin PS \sin \dfrac{\theta}{2} = \sin \Delta \sin \dfrac{\theta}{2}$,

which gives SS'.

Also $\cot PSS' = \cos \Delta \tan \dfrac{\theta}{2}$, which determines the angle PSS' or $PS'S$.

Next, in the triangle ZSS' we know the values of the three sides ZS, ZS', and SS', from which we can determine the values of the three angles ZSS', $ZS'S$, and SZS'.

Then the angle $PSZ = PSS' - ZSS'$ is known,

and $\quad \therefore \cos PZ = \cos S \sin PS \sin SZ + \cos PS \cos SZ$,

is determined, or the value of the colatitude is found.

Finally, the hour-angle (h) corresponding to the first observation can be computed in the triangle PSZ, and the sidereal time t of the observation $= \alpha - \dfrac{h}{15}$ is therefore determined.

The problem is but little altered if two known stars be observed, or the sun. In the latter case the N.P.D. or PS will not be constant, and the variation of R.A. during the interval $t' - t$, must be allowed for, in determining the angle SPS'.

10. It has been thought better not to complicate the preceding problems by considerations relating to the mode of observing the time, and the correction necessary to be applied for the losing or gaining rate of the chronometer. In the preceding instance the observed interval of time between the two observations must be reduced to the sidereal intervals by application of the rate. Let the daily losing rate be r seconds of time, and T the observed interval expressed in hours. Then in this time the chronometer will have lost (if it is going uniformly) $\dfrac{T}{24} r$; and therefore the true sidereal interval will be

$$T + \frac{T}{24} r = T \left(1 + \frac{r}{24}\right).$$

At sea there will be also a correction to be applied for the change of position of the ship on the earth's surface between the two observations. (See Francœur, *Astronomie Pratique*, page 230, edition of 1830. This book is well worthy of the attention of the student of Nautical Astronomy.)

11. *Fifth method, or that of Douwes.*

By two observed altitudes of the sun without a knowledge of the time of the observation.

Let z and z' be the observed zenith-distances, corrected for refraction and parallax.

Δ the N.P.D. of the sun's centre at the middle epoch between the observations, which is supposed to apply to both observations.

h and h' the hour-angles as usual.

Then $\quad \cos z = \cos \gamma \cos \Delta + \sin \gamma \sin \Delta \cos h \ldots \ldots (3),$

and $\quad \cos z' = \cos \gamma \cos \Delta + \sin \gamma \sin \Delta \cos h' \ldots \ldots (4);$

$\therefore \cos z - \cos z' = \sin \gamma \sin \Delta (\cos h - \cos h')$

$$= 2 \sin \gamma \sin \Delta \sin \frac{h' - h}{2} \sin \frac{h' + h}{2}$$

$$= 2 \sin \gamma \sin \Delta \sin y \sin \theta,$$

if we put $y = \frac{1}{2}(h' + h)$ = the mean of the hour-angles,

and $\theta = \frac{1}{2}(h' - h) = \frac{15}{2} \times$ known interval of time between the observations;

$$\therefore \sin y = \frac{\cos z - \cos z'}{2 \sin \gamma \sin \Delta \sin \theta},$$

which gives y or $\frac{h' + h}{2}$;

$\therefore h = y + \theta$ is known, or the hour-angle at the first observation, that is, the time before or after apparent noon.

Finally, from equation (1) we get

$$\cos z = \cos \gamma \cos \Delta + \sin \gamma \sin \Delta \{1 - (1 - \cos h)\}$$

$$= \cos(\Delta - \gamma) - 2 \sin^2 \frac{h}{2} \sin \gamma \sin \Delta,$$

or $\cos(\Delta - \gamma) = \cos z + 2 \sin^2 \frac{h}{2} \sin \gamma \sin \Delta;$

and, if the first hour-angle, or h, be small, we may substitute for γ on the right-hand side of the equation an approximate value deduced from the latitude by account, and we thus obtain the value of $\Delta - \gamma$, and a corrected value of γ.

12. *Determination of Geographical Longitude.*

If, through the axis of the earth, we suppose a series of planes to be drawn intersecting the surface; the great circles thus traced on the surface are called *Meridians;* and the angular distance between any two of these great circles is the difference of geographical longitude of any places whatever situated upon them. Different zeros of longitude are assumed by different nations, each taking for the zero the meridian which passes through the chief Observatory of its capital city.

The general principle for the investigation of differences of longitude will be readily understood from our notions of sidereal and mean solar time, as explained in the fifth Chapter.

302 DIFFERENT METHODS FOR FINDING LONGITUDE.

Sidereal time, for example, at any place is the hour-angle of the First Point of Aries for that place, and mean solar time is the hour-angle for the mean sun for that place. The difference of the hour-angles—whether sidereal or mean solar—for two places at the same instant of absolute time, that is, the difference of local times at the same instant, will therefore be the difference of the longitudes of the places. If therefore we could observe at two stations whose difference of longitude is required, the same phenomenon at the same instant, then it is plain that the difference of the observed local times at the two stations would be the difference required.

A great many different methods have been employed for the purpose of finding the longitude, and every one is aware that the finding of the longitude at sea is the most difficult, and, at the same time vitally important of the problems which the mariner has to solve; but all the methods are different applications of the principle mentioned above.

We will consider first, the methods which have been in use for determining the difference of longitudes of fixed observatories, and afterwards those employed for finding longitudes at sea.

13. The principal methods employed are the following:

(i) By signals previously agreed upon.

(ii) By transmission of chronometers backwards and forwards between the stations.

(iii) By eclipses of Jupiter's satellites.

(iv) By meridional transits of the moon and neighbouring stars—called the *Method of the Culmination of the Moon and Stars*.

(v) By sextant observations of the moon's greatest altitude.

(vi) By lunar distances.

(vii) By eclipses of the moon.

(viii) By eclipses of the sun.

(ix) By occultations of the fixed stars and the planets by the moon.

I. The Method of Signals.

14. This method was formerly employed only for stations within a short distance from each other, and the signals generally employed were either rockets or masses of gunpowder fired from the more elevated station. If the stations were too far apart, a chain of intermediate stations was selected, and the difference of longitude of each successive two was determined by the difference of the local times at which the explosion was observed.

The determination of local time with great accuracy at each station was however a very troublesome and expensive part of the operation, involving, where great accuracy was required, the establishment of a transit-instrument.

15. Of late years, however, the extension of telegraphic communication has, in the case of fixed Observatories, brought into use a new method of signals capable of application to any two Observatories or stations which are on or near a line of railway or a line of telegraphic wires; and of this some account must be given.

The idea is due entirely to some American astronomers, who about fifteen years ago invented a method of registration of transits of stars by the aid of galvanism. Several persons appear to have arrived almost simultaneously at the same leading principle, amongst whom were Dr Lock, Professor O. M. Mitchel, Professor Bond, and Mr Walker, though the methods of application were rather different. The method which has continued in ordinary use in the United States is that of Professor Bond, who applied it, so as to supersede the ordinary method of observing transits by the eye and ear, at the Observatory of Harvard College, Cambridge, Massachusetts. And our Astronomer Royal soon after its introduction in America, devised a similar apparatus, with some specific differences, for observing transits at the Royal Observatory, Greenwich.

16. The following account of the apparatus used at Greenwich is extracted mainly from the Introduction to the *Greenwich Observations* for 1860.

"In the ground-floor of the North dome there is mounted a clock of a peculiar construction, whose motion is governed by the conical rotation of a pendulum. One spindle of the clock gives motion to a revolving brass cylinder; and, as the clock with conical pendulum moves without jerks, the cylinder revolves without jerks, and with a motion sensibly uniform. The cylinder revolves in two minutes of time; and its cylindrical surface moves through about one-third of an inch in one second of time. The barrel is covered with woollen cloth, and upon this a sheet of paper is folded, the ends of the sheet being cemented together; and, when the sheet is filled by the register about to be described, the cement is softened, the paper is removed, and another sheet of paper is substituted in its place.

"Another spindle of the clock turns two long screws, both parallel to the axis of the cylinder, which cause a travelling-frame to traverse the whole length of the cylinder. In one revolution of the cylinder, the frame moves through 0·1 inch. This travelling-frame carries two levers, each lever being armed at one end with a pricking point; the mounting of each lever being such that, when the opposite end is pulled away from the cylinder the pricking end is impressed upon the cylinder, and makes a permanent puncture on the paper. The prickers are mounted in such a way that when their points have entered the paper, they yield laterally to the motion of the revolving cylinder, and do not scratch the paper. Two galvanic magnets are fixed on the travelling-frame, so as to attract the lever-ends opposite to the pricking points. All that is required therefore to cause these points to make punctures upon the paper, is, to send galvanic currents through the galvanic magnets.

"One of the prickers is devoted to the register of seconds of time through the transit-clock. For this purpose, the wires of its galvanic magnet (after passing through a galvanic battery) are led to the transit-clock, and the circuit is there completed at every second of time by the following mechanism. Upon the escape-wheel axle, a wheel of 60 teeth is mounted; and, at every second, the start of a tooth of this wheel presses together two springs, included in the galvanic circuit, during a very small fraction of a second. Thus a series of punctures is made upon the revolving cylinder, one at every second of the transit-clock.

Proper means are provided for breaking the circuit at pleasure, and at the same time stopping the movement of the travelling frame, so as to avoid unnecessary consumption of paper upon the revolving cylinder. The other pricker is used for the register of the times of the transits over the nine wires in the transit telescope. The wires of its galvanic magnet, after passing through a battery, are led to the pier of the transit-circle, and terminate in two large springs, which touch two large insulated brass rings upon the conical axis of the transit-circle. From these brass rings wires are led within the telescope, to a contact-piece near the eye-end, where the observer, by a touch of the finger, can complete circuit, and then make a puncture on the revolving cylinder."

17. At Greenwich, the transits of all objects observed are recorded by the apparatus described above, and it is easy to see how the difference of longitude of two Observatories (Greenwich and Paris for example), each furnished with similar means of self-registration by means of galvanism, may be determined.

As the extent of circuit of the galvanic wires used for recording the times of transit of stars observed with the transit-telescope is of no consequence, presuming that the current has strength enough to drive the pricker, we may conceive that one of them, instead of returning back to the battery, is put in connexion with one of the telegraph wires proceeding to Paris by means of branch wires proceeding from each Observatory to the nearest points of approach of the telegraph wire; then the wires proceeding from the other ends of the batteries being put in connexion with the earth, if the circuit is only broken arbitrarily at one point at each Observatory, the observer, by completing it at this point, will, by suitable arrangements made beforehand, put in action the galvanic magnets driving the prickers at both Observatories, so that the stars observed at each Observatory will in fact be recorded on the apparatuses for self-registration at both. And, supposing this to be done, the times of transit of stars observed at Paris will be recorded in terms of the Greenwich transit-clock, and the transits of the same stars, as they pass the meridian of Greenwich, will be recorded in terms of the Greenwich transit-clock. Similarly the transits of stars observed at both Observatories will be recorded in terms of Paris transit-clock. And thus every star observed at both Observatories gives a difference of longitude which is subject only to the errors arising from the velocity of transmission of the current, and the personal equations of the observers with the transit-instruments. The former is eliminated by taking the mean of the results as recorded at Greenwich and at Paris, and the latter by interchanging the observers during the operations.

18. The best determination of longitude by direct comparison with Greenwich was that made by the Astronomer-Royal and M. Le Verrier in the year 1854, for obtaining the difference of longitude of the Observatories of Greenwich and Paris, but the longitudes of the Observatories of Edinburgh and Brussels have been determined in a similar way. Many of the Observatories on the continents of Europe and America have also been connected by similar means, and the method has been extensively used for the large surveys of the United States.

For further information on this important subject, see *Monthly Notices of the R. A. S.*, Vols. X, XI, XV, and XVIII, and for a detailed account of the apparatus at Greenwich, see the *Gr. Ob. for* 1856, *Appendix*.

II. *Method by Transmission of Chronometers.*

19. The availability of this method depends upon the steadiness of the rates of the chronometers employed, and, on account of the excellence to which this class of instruments has arrived in the present century, it has been employed with advantage on several occasions.

One of the most remarkable applications of the method is that by which the Astronomer-Royal determined, in the year 1844, the longitude of a station in the island of Valentia, on the south-west coast of Ireland. This island is the most westerly point of Europe, and is in very nearly the same latitude as Greenwich; and it offers therefore peculiar advantages for the measure of an extensive arc of parallel by time-comparisons with the National Observatory.

For the greater convenience of carrying out the plan of operations, intermediate observing stations were established at Liverpool and at Kingstown near Dublin, transit-instruments being established at Kingstown and Valentia; and, omitting all details respecting the transmission of the chronometers (30 in number) by railway to Liverpool and by mail steamer to Kingstown, and of passing them on after comparison with the transit-clocks at those places to Valentia, the general plan of operations was as follows.

Immediately before leaving Greenwich the chronometers were compared with the Greenwich transit-clock, and were then taken in a carriage to London for transmission to Liverpool by railway, where the director of the Liverpool Observatory was in waiting to carry them to the mail steamer for conveyance to Kingstown. The person in charge of the observing-station at Kingstown was in waiting to receive them, and to compare them with his transit-clock, and they were then passed back again to Greenwich, and compared with the Greenwich transit-clock immediately on their arrival at the Observatory.

The chronometers were thus transmitted backwards and forwards as rapidly as possible, for about a month, making nine journeys from Greenwich to Kingstown, and eight journeys from Kingstown to Greenwich.

They then made four journeys each way (occupying about eight days) between Liverpool and Kingstown, and afterwards made ten journeys each way (occupying considerably more than a month) between Kingstown and Valentia, going to Limerick and Tralee by mail coach, and then by private carriage and boat to Valentia. Finally, they made about four journeys each way, between Liverpool and Greenwich, occupying about seven days.

20. The operation therefore consisted of three distinct portions, namely, of the determination of the independent differences of longitude between Greenwich and Liverpool, Liverpool and Kingstown, and Kingstown and Valentia, local time (or the error of the transit-clock on sidereal time) being determined with the transit instruments at Greenwich, Liverpool, Kingstown, and Valentia.

21. If the rates of the chronometers were equally steady, and, if they were the same while they were at rest as while travelling, the whole process of reduction for deduction of the differences of longitude would be much more simple than it actually is. But it is found that there is a well-marked difference between the rate of a chronometer while travelling and while at rest, and, to determine this, it was usual to compare the chronometers twice at some of the stations, that is immediately after arrival and before sending them away again, and this furnished materials for determining immediately the travelling as well as the stationary rate. Take, for example, the case of transmission between Greenwich and Liverpool. The comparisons taken at Greenwich before departure and after return, give the whole loss or gain of the chronomoter for that period, while the two comparisons at Liverpool give its loss or gain during the stationary period; the difference is therefore the loss or gain during the time it was travelling.

22. The application of the most probable rates to the chronometers so as to determine for each chronometer employed, with the greatest possible accuracy, the Greenwich sidereal time corresponding to the local sidereal time at the station where longitude is to be determined, at the time of the comparison of the chronometers, is a very difficult problem, and has been treated by Mr Airy with his accustomed clearness and fulness in his account of the results of the expedition in the Greenwich Observations for 1845. The general problem of the determination of longitude by means of chronometers presents however no other difficulty, and we need not dwell on it any longer, except by saying that the operations were repeated during the present summer.

23. By a rigorous and instructive comparison of the longitude obtained, with that given by the great Trigonometrical Survey, Mr Airy arrived at the satisfactory conclusion, " that no improvements can be made in the earth's figure, so far as they apply to the circumference of a parallel, or to the measure of 1" on the arc perpendicular to the meridian......." And he con-

cludes that, in latitude 51°.40', the length of 1" in an arc perpendicular to the meridian is 101·6499 feet.

24. I have gone into some detail with regard to this celebrated expedition, because it was impossible otherwise to give the student any notion of the difficulties or the large amount of work which have to be encountered in such a series of operations, though the general aspect of the problem mathematically considered is so simple. Another very important expedition of a similar kind was that undertaken by Professor W. Struve in 1844, for the determination of the difference of longitudes between Pulkowa and Greenwich. All the details of the operations are given in a work published by him, and entitled *Expédition Chronométrique*.

III. *Method by Eclipses of Jupiter's Satellites.*

25. Since the eclipses of Jupiter's satellites happen at the same instant of absolute time for all places on the earth's surface, they afford occasionally excellent means for determining longitude, by comparison with the predicted times in the *Nautical Almanac*, which are computed by the theory of the motions of the satellites. In all cases however the method is rendered less certain by the circumstance, that the times of observed diasappearance and reappearance depend upon the telescope employed, larger telescopes giving later times of disappearance and earlier times of reappearance than smaller ones. The method has been also up to the present time practically useless at sea, on account of the impossibility of keeping a telescope steady enough for observation on the deck of the vessel in motion. A few years ago, however, Professor Piazzi Smyth devised an apparatus called by him *A Free Revolver Stand*, which afforded a perfectly steady surface for observation, and by means of which he actually saw the satellites of Jupiter with perfect ease and comfort, while going to Teneriffe on board the yacht Titania. (See *Notices of the R.A.S.* Vol. XVII. page 36, and Vol. XVIII. page 65; also Smyth's *Teneriffe, an Astronomer's Experiment*).

IV. *Method by Meridional Transits of the Moon and neighbouring Fixed Stars; or the Method of the Culmination of the Moon and Stars.*

26. The use of the moon's motion in R.A. for the determination of longitude has been long known, and lunar transits observed over different meridians have been for a long period very generally employed for the purpose. In the year 1824, however, Mr Baily brought into general use a considerable improvement in the method by proposing that there should be observed, in addition to the moon's transit, the transits of certain stars preceding and following her, and lying as nearly as possible in the same parallel of declination. In accordance with the suggestion of Mr Baily, the Royal Astronomical Society undertook for some time the preparation and circulation of lists containing the places of the moon and the selected moon-culminating stars, till, at the reformation of the *Nautical Almanac* in 1834, the lists were incorporated in that work.

By consulting the *Nautical Almanac* for any year commencing with 1834, it will be seen that there are given the exact R.A. of the moon's bright limb (1 L before opposition and 2 L after opposition) and of the selected stars; the variation of R.A. in one hour of terrestrial longitude; and the sidereal time occupied by the transit of the moon's semi-diameter over the meridian; all computed for the Greenwich transit.

27. The object of observing stars in the same parallel (or nearly so) with the moon is that the difference of time between the transits of the star and the moon, on which the determination of the difference of longitude of two stations depends, will be essentially free from the errors of adjustment of the transit-instrument employed, these errors being simple functions of the zenith distances or the polar distances of the objects observed. Still it is desirable that the observations, in cases where great accuracy is necessary, should be rigorously corrected for instrumental errors, because an azimuthal deviation of any considerable amount would entail upon the resulting longitude an error depending upon the motion of the moon in R.A. while describing by the diurnal motion an arc equivalent to that deviation.

METHOD OF CULMINATION OF MOON AND STARS.

28. The process for finding the longitude of any station relatively to Greenwich, is as follows.

Suppose the moon's limb and one culminator to be observed at both Observatories, the station whose longitude is sought being l degrees east or west of Greenwich.

Let t_m' and t_s' be the Greenwich sidereal times of observed transit of the moon's limb and of the star at Greenwich,

t_m'' and t_s'' similar times for the other station,

s_1 the sidereal time of transit of moon's semi-diameter at Greenwich,

s_2 the sidereal time of transit at the other station),

(s_2 must be interpolated from the *Nautical Almanac* with an approximate value of the longitude,)

a the apparent R.A. of the star,

a_m' and a_m'' the R.A. of the centre of the moon at transit of centre over the two meridians.

Then $a - a_m' = t_s' - (t_m' \pm s_1) = \beta_1$, suppose (a known quantity),

and $\quad a - a_m'' = t_s'' - (t_m'' \pm s_2) = \beta_2$, suppose;

$$\therefore a_m'' - a_m' = \beta_1 - \beta_2 \dots\dots\dots\dots\dots(a).$$

This quantity $\beta_1 - \beta_2$ is the increase of moon's R.A. in its passage over an arc of terrestrial longitude l, and is positive, when the second station is west of Greenwich, and negative when it is east.

Let now I be the increase of moon's R.A. in one hour of longitude (given in the *Nautical Almanac* for Greenwich transit of the moon). Then, if the longitude l be expressed in seconds of time, we have the equation

$$\frac{l}{3600} = \frac{\beta_1 - \beta_2}{I},$$

or
$$l = 3600^s \times \frac{\beta_1 - \beta_2}{I}.$$

If the difference of longitude be small, it will be sufficient to take for the value of I that given in the *Nautical Almanac* for Greenwich transit; but, if it be large, (amounting to several hours for example,) it must be interpolated for the middle epoch, by the values given for successive lunar transits in the *Nautical Almanac*.

29. It will readily be seen from the process above that it is not absolutely necessary that the same star should be observed at the two stations; but in the case of different stars it would be necessary that their R.A.'s should be accurately known; and there is therefore liability to another source of inaccuracy.

Thus, let the R.A.'s of the two stars be α' and α''.

The equation (α) will take the shape

$$\alpha' - \alpha'' + \alpha_m'' - \alpha_m' = \beta_1 - \beta_2,$$

or
$$\alpha_m'' - \alpha_m' = \beta_1 - \beta_2 - (\alpha' - \alpha''),$$

and the result will be affected by the difference of the errors of α' and α'', but will still be independent of the assumed equinox used in obtaining those Right Ascensions.

In Vol. XIX. of the *Memoirs of the Royal Astronomical Society* will be found a paper by Mr Airy on the *Weights to be given to the separate Results for Terrestrial Longitudes*, which is well worthy of the attention of the student. One important conclusion arrived at by Mr Airy is that for observations on the same evening or for the same transit of the moon, the increase in the number of comparison-stars adds very little to the accuracy of the result; but that observations of the moon and stars on different evenings add to it very greatly.

That the increase of the number of stars on the same evening does not add much to the accuracy of the result is easily proved as follows:

Let p_m represent the error of observation of a transit of the moon,

p_s represent the error of observation of a transit of a star,

and suppose that n moon-culminating stars have been observed.

PROBABLE ERRORS OF RESULTS. 313

Then the probable error of (moon-transit − mean of star-transits)

$$= \sqrt{\frac{p_s^2}{n} + p_m^2},$$

and, if $p_s = p_m = p$, which may be generally assumed, the probable error of result

$$= p \sqrt{1 + \frac{1}{n}};$$

and therefore very little additional accuracy is gained by increasing the number of stars beyond three or four.

Thus, if we make successively $n = 1, 2, 3, 4, 5, 10, 20$, we get for the probable error of the result,

for $n = 1$, probable error $= p \times 1\cdot414$
... 2, ... $p \times 1\cdot225$
... 3, ... $p \times 1\cdot155$
... 4, ... $p \times 1\cdot118$
... 5, ... $p \times 1\cdot095$
... 10, ... $p \times 1\cdot049$
... 20, ... $p \times 1\cdot025$

30. As an example we will deduce the longitude of the Observatory of Sydney, New South Wales, by comparison of the transits of η Cancri and the moon's second limb, observed at Greenwich and Sydney on Jan. 9, 1860.

From the volumes of the Greenwich and Sydney observations we get the following data:

	Greenwich.	Sydney.
	h. m. s.	h. m. s.
Corrected transit of η Cancri	8 . 24 . 29·76	8 . 23 . 44·47
.... ☽ 2 L	8 . 46 . 23·91	8 . 19 . 25·74
$s_1 = -$	73^s·01	$s_2 = -$ 74^s·03
and (from N. A.) $I_1 =$	153^s·91	
$\therefore \beta_1 = -$ 20^m. 41^s·14		$\beta_2 = +$ 5^m. 32^s·76

$$\beta_1 - \beta_2 = -26^m . 13^s\cdot 90$$

$$= -1573^s\cdot 90.$$

Again, to determine the value of I at the Sidney transit of the moon, we must interpolate the value given in the *N. A.* for the upper and lower Greenwich transits of the moon, referring all the computations to Greenwich Mean Solar Time. Thus:

Greenwich Mean Solar Time.	I.	1st Difference.	2nd Difference.
h. m.	s.	s.	s.
Jan 8 . 12 . 30	163·55		
		−4·59	
9 . 1 . 0	158·96		−0·46
		−5·05	
9 . 13 . 30	153·91		−0·23
		−4·82	

Again, R.A. of moon on passing the meridian of Sydney (or *Sidney* Sidereal Time of Transit) $= 8^{h}. 19^{m}. 6^{s}$ on Jan. 9, and, if we assume the longitude of Sydney to be $10^{h}. 5^{m}$ east, the *Greenwich* Sidereal Time of Sydney Transit is Jan. 8, $22^{h}. 14^{m}. 6^{s}$, and the Greenwich Mean Solar Time is easily found by computation to be Jan. 9, $3^{h}. 0^{m}. 35^{s}$.

Hence, by interpolation, the value of I for Sydney transit of the moon is

$$158^{s}\!\cdot\!96 - \left(\frac{2}{12\cdot5}\right) \times 4^{s}\!\cdot\!82 - \left(\frac{2}{12\cdot5}\right)^{2} \times 0^{s}\!\cdot\!23$$

$$= 158^{s}\!\cdot\!96 - 0^{s}\!\cdot\!771 - 0^{s}\!\cdot\!006,$$

or $I_{2} = 158^{s}\!\cdot\!183,$

and $\qquad I = \dfrac{I_{1}+I_{2}}{2} = 156^{s}\!\cdot\!05.$

Hence $\quad l = - 3600 \times \dfrac{1573^{s}\!\cdot\!90}{156\cdot05} = - 36309^{s}\!\cdot\!1$

$$= 10^{h}. 5^{m}. 9^{s}\!\cdot\!1 \text{ east.}$$

Note. As the method of interpolation by second differences, which is applied without explanation in the text, may not be familiar to the student, I subjoin the following explanation of it.

Let x be a function capable of being expressed in the form
$$x = a + bt + ct^{2}.$$

And let x_{-1}, x_0 and x_{+1} be its values corresponding to values of t, -1, 0, and $+1$.

Then we have
$$x_{-1} = a - b + c,$$
$$x_0 = a,$$
$$x_{+1} = a + b + c,$$
and, differencing, we get,

1st diff.	2nd diff.
$b - c$	$2c$
$b + c$	

$\therefore 2b = $ sum of 1st differences of x for values x_{-1}, x_0 and x_{+1}, and $2c = $ second difference of x.

Hence the method in the text is obvious.

As a second example we will deduce the longitude of the Observatory at Washington, U. S., by comparison of the observed R. A. of moon's first limb, and ψ^2 Cancri, on Feb. 14, 1859, with the corresponding Greenwich observations. The Washington observations are given in the *Monthly Notices*, Vol. xx. p. 287.

	Greenwich.	Washington.
	h. m. s.	h. m. s.
R.A. of ☽ 1 L	7 . 28 . 55·67	7 . 43 . 14·47
.... ψ^2 Cancri	8 . 1 . 59·83	8 . 1 . 59·90
	$s_1 = + 76^{s}\!\cdot\!79$	$s_2 = + 76^{s}\!\cdot\!36$
	$\beta_1 = + 31^m . 47^{s}\!\cdot\!37$	$\beta_2 = + 17^m . 29^{s}\!\cdot\!07$
	$I_1 = 168^{s}\!\cdot\!02$	$I_2 = 166^{s}\!\cdot\!29$

$$\beta_1 - \beta_2 = + 14^m . 18^{s}\!\cdot\!30$$
$$= + 858^{s}\!\cdot\!30.$$

For computation of s_2 and I_2 we must proceed as before, assuming the longitude of Washington $5^h . 8^m$ west.

Thus, Washington sidereal time of transit of ☽'s centre............... $7^h . 44^m . 31^s$

Add west longitude..................... $5 . 8 . 0$

Greenwich sidereal time............... $12 . 52 . 31$
And, Greenwich mean time........... $15 . 14 . 6$

And, for interpolation, we have from the *N. A.*

	s.	1st Diff.	2nd Diff.	*I.*	1st Diff.	2nd Diff.
h. m.				s.		
Feb. 13, 21 . 21	77·56			171·11		
		−0·77			−3·09	
14, 9 . 53	76·79		−0·33	168·02		−1·32
		−1·10			−4·42	
14, 22 . 23	75·69			163·60		
		−0·94	−0·17		−3·76	−0·66

Hence $s_2 = 76^s\!\cdot\!79 - \dfrac{5\cdot 35}{12\cdot 5} \times 0^s\!\cdot\!94 - \left(\dfrac{5\cdot 35}{12\cdot 5}\right)^2 \times 0^s\!\cdot\!17$

$\qquad\quad = 76^s\!\cdot\!79 - 0^s\!\cdot\!40 - 0^s\!\cdot\!03$

$\qquad\quad = 76^s\!\cdot\!36,$

and $I_2 = 168^s\!\cdot\!02 - \dfrac{5\cdot 35}{12\cdot 5} \times 3^s\!\cdot\!76 - \left(\dfrac{5\cdot 35}{12\cdot 5}\right)^2 \times 0^s\!\cdot\!66$

$\qquad\quad = 168^s\!\cdot\!02 - 1^s\!\cdot\!61 - 0^s\!\cdot\!12$

$\qquad\quad = 166^s\!\cdot\!29,$

and $I = \dfrac{I_1 + I_2}{2} = 167^s\!\cdot\!16;$

$\qquad \therefore\ l = +3600 \times \dfrac{858^s\!\cdot\!30}{167\cdot 16}$

$\qquad\qquad = +18484^s\!\cdot\!6$

$\qquad\qquad = 5^h.\ 8^m.\ 4^s\!\cdot\!6\ \text{west}.$

The longitude given in the *N. A.* is

$\qquad\qquad 5^h.\ 8^m.\ 12^s\!\cdot\!0\ \text{west}.$

V. *Method by Sextant Observations of the Moon's Greatest Altitude.*

31. This method was recently proposed by Mr W. Spottiswoode as applicable to cases wherein the moon's motion in declination is rapid, and there is not time or opportunity to apply the more correct method of Lunar Distances. Mr Spottiswoode's paper is printed in Vol. XXIX. of the *Memoirs of the R. A. S.*

The method consists in determining the moon's declination at the time of her greatest altitude. This being ascertained, if the local time be known, we have merely to compare the Greenwich time, deduced from the *Nautical Almanac*, at which she has that declination, and the difference of times is of course the longitude expressed in time. If however the local time be not known, the hour-angle at the time of the greatest altitude must be computed from one of the formulæ derived from the investigation. The process is as follows.

With the usual notation, we have

$$\cos z = \cos \gamma \cos \Delta + \sin \gamma \sin \Delta \cos h \ \ldots\ldots\ldots (1),$$

and, if z be a minimum (the altitude being a maximum) we have $\dfrac{dz}{dh} = 0$;

$$\therefore\ 0 = \sin z \frac{dz}{dh}$$

$$= \cos \gamma \sin \Delta \frac{d\Delta}{dh} + \sin \gamma \sin \Delta \sin h - \sin \gamma \cos \Delta \cos h \frac{d\Delta}{dh};$$

or $(\cot \gamma - \cot \Delta \cos h) \dfrac{d\Delta}{dh} + \sin h = 0$,

or, putting $\dfrac{d\Delta}{dh} = m$,

$$m (\cot \gamma - \cot \Delta \cos h) + \sin h = 0 \ \ldots\ldots\ldots (2).$$

Now, since the time of greatest altitude takes place when the moon is very near the meridian, h will be very small, and $z + \gamma$ will differ from Δ by a small quantity.

Let therefore $z + \gamma = \Delta + x$, x being a small quantity.

Then from equation (1) we have

$$\cos h = 1 - \frac{h^2}{2} = \frac{\cos z - \cos \gamma \cos (z + \gamma - x)}{\sin \gamma \sin (z + \gamma - x)}$$

$$= \frac{\cos z - \cos \gamma \{\cos (z + \gamma) + x \sin (z + \gamma)\}}{\sin \gamma \{\sin (z + \gamma) - x \cos (z + \gamma)\}},\ \text{nearly};$$

$$= \text{(by reduction)}\ \frac{1 - x \cot \gamma}{1 - x \cot (z + \gamma)}$$

$$= 1 - x \frac{\sin z}{\sin \gamma \sin (z + \gamma)},\ \text{nearly};$$

and $\therefore\ h^2 = 2x \dfrac{\sin z}{\sin \gamma \sin (z + \gamma)}$.

Again, in equation (2), since h is small, we may put $\sin h = h$, and $\cos h = 1$,

$$\therefore h = -m(\cot \gamma - \cot \Delta)$$

$$= -m\frac{\sin(\Delta - \gamma)}{\sin \gamma \sin \Delta}$$

$$= -m\frac{\sin(z - x)}{\sin \gamma \sin \Delta}$$

$$= -m\frac{\sin z}{\sin \gamma \sin(z + \gamma)} \text{ (to the first order),}$$

and $\therefore h^2 = m^2 \cdot \dfrac{\sin^2 z}{\sin^2 \gamma \sin^2(z+\gamma)} = 2x \dfrac{\sin z}{\sin \gamma \sin(z+\gamma)}$,

or $x = \dfrac{m^2}{2} \cdot \dfrac{\sin z}{\sin \gamma \sin(z+\gamma)}$;

or, in seconds of space,

$$x = \frac{m^2}{2 \sin 1''} \cdot \frac{\sin z}{\sin \gamma \sin(z+\gamma)};$$

and $\Delta = z + \gamma - x$

$$= z + \gamma - \frac{m^2}{2 \sin 1''} \cdot \frac{\sin z}{\sin \gamma \sin(z+\gamma)}.$$

For the computation of m or of $\dfrac{d\Delta}{dh}$, we must remember that this expression reckoned in seconds of space is the value of the moon's change of declination in one second of hour-angle.

Now $\qquad \dfrac{d\Delta}{dh} = \dfrac{1}{15} \cdot \dfrac{d\Delta}{dt} \cdot \dfrac{15 dt}{dh};$

and, on account of the moon's motion in R.A. which has a tendency to diminish the hour-angle, the average value of $\dfrac{15 dt}{dh}$ is nearly 1·04.

But, if we take for $d\Delta$ the moon's motion in N.P.D. in one hour of longitude (given in the *Nautical Almanac* in the Section of *Moon-Culminating Stars*), dt will be 3600 seconds of longitude expressed in time, and $\dfrac{15 dt}{dh}$ will be equal to unity; and therefore $\dfrac{m^2}{2\sin 1''}$ in the expression above, will be (if we denote by m' the moon's motion in one hour of longitude)

$$\dfrac{m'^2}{2.15^2.(3600)^2 \sin 1''} = m'^2 \times [5\cdot54862].$$

COR. If m'' be the motion of the moon in N.P.D. in one minute of longitude, the value of $\dfrac{m^2}{2\sin 1''}$ will be

$$\dfrac{m''^2}{2.15^2.(60)^2 \sin 1''} = m''^2 \times [9\cdot10492],$$

and this may be easily tabulated for different values of m''.

VI. Method of Lunar Distances.

32. Of all the methods for obtaining the longitude by means of sextant observations, this is the most important and useful, especially at sea; and astronomers, from the infancy of nautical science to the present time, have used their utmost efforts, by tables and other means, to simplify for the use of sailors the rather intricate computations which are required.

The principle of the method is easily explained.

In the *Nautical Almanac* are given for every three hours of Greenwich mean solar time, the correct *Geocentric* angular distance of the moon from the large planets and certain bright stars easily observable with the sextant. These distances are computed from the places of the moon given by the best lunar tables, and from the most correct places of the stars. At the present time, or since the use of Hansen's lunar tables, the places of the moon are sensibly accurate, that is, the errors are within the limits of the errors incidental to observations made at Greenwich or other great Observatories; and the places of the stars are also sensibly without error. Therefore the lunar distances are sensibly accurate, and represent those which would be observed from the centre of the earth; and these are to be compared with the distances from the bright limb of the moon of some of the planets or fixed stars which have been observed with the sextant at the place of which the longitude is to be determined.

320   METHOD OF LUNAR DISTANCES.

These latter, or observed, distances, after the application of the augmented semi-diameter of the moon must be *cleared* from the effects of refraction and parallax before they are comparable with the *geocentric* distances, and, since these corrections are functions of the altitudes of the objects observed, it is necessary to observe with the sextant their altitudes above the horizon of the place of observation, in addition to the lunar distance. The observation of a lunar distance which can be depended on, involving as it does a series of altitudes of the moon and stars, so as to get by interpolation the altitudes at the time of the observation of the distance, is therefore a laborious operation. But, supposing this to be done, and the observed distance for a known instant of local mean solar time to have been cleared from the effects of refraction and parallax; then it is easy to find by interpolation in the *Nautical Almanac* the exact instant of Greenwich mean solar time at which the moon has this geocentric distance from the other object which has been observed; and the difference between the Greenwich time and the local time will be the required longitude.

33.   We will now proceed to shew how the *Clearing of the Lunar Distance* is effected, by the method proposed by Lieutenant Raper (*Monthly Notices of R. A. S.* Vol. XVIII. p. 303), though, for the deduction of the formula equivalent to Mr Raper's, we shall prefer to use simply the methods of Spherical Trigonometry, as recommended by Mr J. Riddle (*Monthly Notices*, Vol. XIX. No. 3).

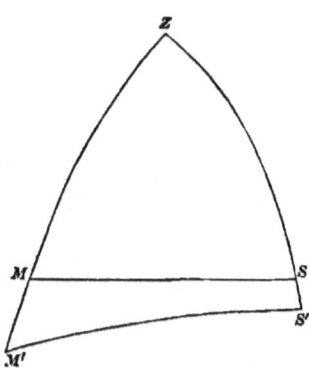

RAPER'S METHOD.

Let Z be the observer's zenith; M and M' the geocentric and apparent positions of the moon depressed by parallax in the vertical circle ZMM'; S and S' the geocentric and apparent positions of the planet, refraction not being taken into consideration, or being supposed to be allowed for independently.

Let MS, the true distance, $= \delta$,

$M'S'$, the apparent distance, $= \delta'$,

$ZS = 90° - \alpha$ and $ZS' = 90° - \alpha'$,

$ZM = 90° - \beta$ and $ZM' = 90° - \beta'$.

Then $\cos MZS = \dfrac{\cos \delta - \sin \alpha \sin \beta}{\cos \alpha \cos \beta} = \dfrac{\cos \delta' - \sin \alpha' \sin \beta'}{\cos \alpha' \cos \beta'}$;

$\therefore \cos \alpha' \cos \beta' \cos \delta - \cos \alpha \cos \beta \cos \delta' = \sin \alpha \cos \alpha' \sin \beta \cos \beta'$
$\qquad\qquad\qquad\qquad\qquad\qquad - \sin \alpha' \cos \alpha \sin \beta' \cos \beta$

$=$ (by adding and subtracting $\sin \alpha \cos \alpha' \cos \beta \sin \beta'$ on the right-hand side of the equation)

$\qquad \sin \alpha \cos \alpha' \sin(\beta - \beta') + \cos \beta \sin \beta' \sin(\alpha - \alpha')$.

Let now π and π' be the horizontal parallaxes of the moon and planet for the place and time of observation; then, $\alpha - \alpha'$ and $\beta - \beta'$ being the parallactic effects on the planet and the moon in altitude,

$\sin(\beta - \beta') = \cos \beta' \sin \pi$, and $\sin(\alpha - \alpha') = \cos \alpha' \sin \pi'$;

$\cos \alpha' \cos \beta' \cos \delta = \cos \alpha \cos \beta \cos \delta' + \sin \alpha \cos \alpha' \cos \beta' \sin \pi$
$\qquad\qquad\qquad\qquad\qquad\qquad + \cos \beta \sin \beta' \cos \alpha' \sin \pi'$;

or, $\cos \delta = \dfrac{\cos \alpha \cos \beta}{\cos \alpha' \cos \beta'} \cos \delta' + \sin \alpha \sin \pi + \cos \beta \tan \beta' \sin \pi'$

$\qquad = \dfrac{\cos \alpha \cos \beta}{\cos \alpha' \cos \beta'} \cos \delta' + \sin \alpha \sin \pi + \sin \beta \sin \pi'$ very nearly.

Cor. 1. If the object observed with the moon should be a fixed star, the last term of the preceding expression of course vanishes.

M. A.

COR. 2. Again, if m and s, m' and s' represent the distances of the moon and planet from the centre of the earth and from the observer's position, then it is plain that

$$\frac{m}{m'} = \frac{\cos \beta'}{\cos \beta}, \quad \text{and} \quad \frac{s}{s'} = \frac{\cos \alpha'}{\cos \alpha};$$

and the preceding expression becomes

$$\cos \delta = \frac{s'm'}{sm} \cos \delta' + \sin \alpha \sin \pi + \sin \beta \sin \pi'.$$

COR. 3. The correction of the distance for refraction which is supposed to have been previously applied, is approximately the sum of the resolved parts of the two vertical refractions; that is of the vertical refractions multiplied respectively by the cosines of the angles $ZM'S'$ and $ZS'M'$, which must therefore be calculated.

34. When the observed lunar distance has been cleared of refraction and parallax, or the true value of δ has been obtained, we must find, by interpolating between the values of δ given in the *Nautical Almanac* for intervals of 3^h, the exact Greenwich mean solar time at which the moon was at this distance from the star or planet observed.

In proceeding to take the first and second differences of the distances, we shall, as in the examples of longitude deduced from observations of the moon and culminators, have an equation of the form

$$\delta = a + bt + ct^2 \dots\dots\dots\dots\dots\dots(1),$$

where $\quad a =$ value of δ for middle epoch,

$b =$ half sum of first differences,

$c =$ half second difference,

and $t =$ required number of hours from middle epoch divided by 3.

This equation may be solved immediately, and t expanded

EXPANSION OF THE TIME IN A SERIES. 323

in powers of the small quantity $\delta - a (= x,$ suppose) by the Binomial Theorem.

Thus, we have
$$2ct + b = \pm \sqrt{b^2 + 4cx},$$
in which we take the upper sign, so that $t = 0$ when $x = 0$:

hence $\quad bt = x - \dfrac{cx^2}{b^2} + \dfrac{2c^2x^3}{b^4} - \dfrac{5c^3x^4}{b^6} + \dfrac{14c^4x^5}{b^8} - \ldots\ldots$ (2).

Or we may, without solving the equation, proceed at once by successive approximation, as follows. The equation may be written in the form
$$t = \frac{x}{b} - \frac{ct^2}{b} \ldots\ldots\ldots\ldots\ldots\ldots\ldots\ldots\ldots\ldots\ldots\ldots (3),$$

whence $\quad t = \dfrac{x}{b},$ to 1st power of $x,$

$\quad\quad\quad t = \dfrac{x}{b} - \dfrac{c}{b}\left(\dfrac{x}{b}\right)^2,$ to 2nd power of $x,$

so $\quad\quad t = \dfrac{x}{b} - \dfrac{c}{b}\left(\dfrac{x}{b} - \dfrac{cx^2}{b^3}\right)^2$

$\quad\quad\quad = \dfrac{x}{b} - \dfrac{cx^2}{b^3} + \dfrac{2c^2x^3}{b^5},$ to 3rd power of $x,$

and the process may be continued *ad libitum*.

This method may be applied with advantage in cases where 3rd or higher differences must be used; thus, in the case of 3rd differences we have an equation of the form
$$\delta = a + bt + ct^2 + dt^3;$$
whence $\quad t = \dfrac{x}{b} - \dfrac{ct^2}{b} - \dfrac{dt^3}{b},$

and, proceeding as above, we shall find
$$t = \frac{x}{b} - \frac{cx^2}{b^3} + \left(\frac{2c^2}{b^2} - \frac{d}{b}\right)\frac{x^3}{b^3} - 5\left(\frac{c^3}{b^3} - \frac{cd}{b^2}\right)\frac{x^4}{b^4} + \ldots\ldots$$

EXAMPLE. We will take the distances of α Aquilæ from the moon on June 1, 1863, and require the Greenwich mean solar time at which the distance was $52°. 30'. 33''.$ (*Nautical Almanac* for 1863, page 115.)

EXAMPLE.

The distances and differences will be thus arranged;

	Distance.	1st. Difference.	2nd. Differ.
June 1, 12^h	54°.34'.34''	−95'.27''	+38''
...... 15^h	52.59. 7	−94.49	$c = +19''$
...... 18^h	51.24.18	−95'.8''	
		$b = -5708''$	

Let now $x' = \dfrac{cx}{b^2}$.

Then $a = 52°.59'. 7''$ $\quad \dfrac{c}{b} = -\dfrac{19}{5708}$ $\quad \dfrac{x}{b} = +\dfrac{1714}{5708}$

$\delta = 52.30.33$

$x = -28'.34''$ $\quad x' = -\dfrac{19 \times 1714}{(5708)^2}$ $\quad = +0\cdot30028$

$\quad = -1714''$

$\text{Log } x' = -6\cdot9997964, \quad \text{number} = -0\cdot0009995,$

$\log (2x'^2) \doteq 4\cdot3006228, \quad \text{number} = 0\cdot0000020.$

Hence $3\,t = +0^h\cdot90084 \times 1\cdot0010015$

$\qquad\qquad = 0^h\cdot90174$

$\qquad\qquad = +54^m.6^s\cdot26,$

and the Greenwich mean solar time will be

$$\text{June 1, } 15^h.54^m.6^s\cdot26.$$

35. We will in addition give the method of clearing the lunar distance which has been in ordinary use.

Using the same notation, we have as before

$$\frac{\cos \delta - \sin \alpha \sin \beta}{\cos \alpha \cos \beta} = \frac{\cos \delta' - \sin \alpha' \sin \beta'}{\cos \alpha' \cos \beta'}.$$

Adding unity to each side of the equation and reducing, we get

$$\frac{\cos \delta + \cos (\alpha + \beta)}{\cos \alpha \cos \beta} = \frac{\cos \delta' + \cos (\alpha' + \beta')}{\cos \alpha' \cos \beta'};$$

OTHER METHODS OF CLEARING THE DISTANCE. 325

or, $\dfrac{\cos^2 \frac{1}{2}(\alpha+\beta) - \sin^2 \frac{1}{2}\delta}{\cos\alpha\cos\beta} = \dfrac{\cos\frac{1}{2}(\alpha'+\beta'+\delta').\cos\frac{1}{2}(\alpha'+\beta'-\delta')}{\cos\alpha'\cos\beta'}$

or, $\sin^2\dfrac{\delta}{2} =$

$\cos^2\dfrac{1}{2}(\alpha+\beta) - \dfrac{\cos\alpha\cos\beta}{\cos\alpha'\cos\beta'}\cos\dfrac{1}{2}(\alpha'+\beta'+\delta').\cos\dfrac{1}{2}(\alpha'+\beta'-\delta')\ldots(4)$,

where $\alpha - \alpha' =$ combined effect of vertical refraction and parallax for the moon;

and $\beta - \beta' =$ combined effect of vertical refraction and parallax for the planet.

To adapt this to logarithmic computation, let

$\sin^2\dfrac{\phi}{2} = \dfrac{\cos\alpha\cos\beta}{\cos\alpha'\cos\beta'}\cos\dfrac{1}{2}(\alpha'+\beta'+\delta').\cos\dfrac{1}{2}(\alpha'+\beta'-\delta')\ldots\ldots (5)$,

$\therefore \sin^2\dfrac{\delta}{2} = \cos^2\dfrac{1}{2}(\alpha+\beta) - \sin^2\dfrac{\phi}{2}$

$= \dfrac{1}{2}\{1+\cos(\alpha+\beta)\} - \dfrac{1}{2}(1-\cos\phi)$

$= \dfrac{1}{2}\{\cos(\alpha+\beta)+\cos\phi\}$

$= \cos\dfrac{1}{2}(\alpha+\beta+\phi).\cos\dfrac{1}{2}(\alpha+\beta-\phi)$,

or $\sin\dfrac{\delta}{2} = \sqrt{\cos\dfrac{1}{2}(\alpha+\beta+\phi).\cos(\alpha+\beta-\phi)}\ldots\ldots (6)$.

36. We may also deduce another expression for the *cleared distance* involving only versed sines of angles, which has been much used.

Thus, recurring to the fundamental equation,

$\dfrac{\cos\delta - \sin\alpha\sin\beta}{\cos\alpha\cos\beta} = \dfrac{\cos\delta' - \sin\alpha'\sin\beta'}{\cos\alpha'\cos\beta'}$,

we have, by subtracting unity from each side and reducing,

$\dfrac{\cos\delta - \cos(\alpha-\beta)}{\cos\alpha\cos\beta} = \dfrac{\cos\delta' - \cos(\alpha'-\beta')}{\cos\alpha'\cos\beta'}$, or $\cos \delta = \cos(\alpha - \beta) + \dfrac{\cos\alpha \cos\beta}{\cos\alpha' \cos\beta'} \{\cos\delta' - \cos(\alpha' - \beta')\}$

$= \left(\text{if} \quad \cos\theta = \dfrac{1}{2} \cdot \dfrac{\cos\alpha \cos\beta}{\cos\alpha' \cos\beta'}\right)$

$\cos(\alpha - \beta) + 2\cos\theta \{\cos\delta' - \cos(\alpha' - \beta')\}$

$= \cos(\alpha - \beta) + \cos(\theta + \delta') + \cos(\theta - \delta')$

$\qquad - \cos(\theta + \alpha' - \beta') - \cos(\theta - \alpha' + \beta'),$

or, since cosine $= 1 -$ versine,

$1 - \text{versin}\,\delta = 1 - \text{versin}\,(\alpha - \beta)$

$\qquad + 1 - \text{versin}\,(\theta + \delta') + 1 - \text{versin}\,(\theta - \delta')$

$\qquad - 1 + \text{versin}\,(\theta + \alpha' - \beta') - 1 + \text{versin}\,(\theta - \alpha' + \beta'),$

or $\text{versin}\,\delta = \text{versin}\,(\alpha - \beta) + \text{versin}\,(\theta + \delta') + \text{versin}\,(\theta - \delta')$

$\qquad - \text{versin}\,(\theta + \alpha' - \beta') - \text{versin}\,(\theta - \alpha' + \beta').$

37. *Method by observations of Eclipses of the Sun and Moon, and of Occultations of stars by the Moon.*

Since the inclination of the orbit of the moon to that of the earth is small, its mean value being about $5°.9'$, it is plain that if, at a conjunction, the moon should be very near the node of her orbit, she will be interposed wholly or in part between the sun and the earth, or an *eclipse of the sun* will take place; if, on the contrary, she be near her node at opposition, the earth will be interposed between her and the sun, and, the sun's light being prevented from falling on her, her surface presented to the earth will be unilluminated wholly or in part, and an *eclipse* of the moon will take place.

Since this latter obscuration of the moon by the earth's shadow takes place for inhabitants of every part of the earth's surface at the same instant of absolute time, eclipses of the moon would afford good means of determining the longitude by observations of the beginning and the ending of the eclipse in different places, but the entrance of the earth's shadow on the surface of the moon is a phenomenon too vague and indistinct to be capable of being observed with much accuracy, and, in addition, eclipses occur so seldom that practically this method is not of much use.

38. On the contrary, the times of the beginning and end of a solar eclipse, and of an occultation of a star by the moon, are capable of being observed with great accuracy, and though, on account of the moon's parallax, the computations of both these phenomena are intricate and troublesome, yet every advantage is taken of them whenever they occur, both for determination of longitude, and for the correction of the relative places of the sun and moon. The whole theory is therefore of so much importance, and enters so much into the operations of fixed Observatories, that it is desirable to devote a chapter to the subject.

CHAPTER XI.

ON ECLIPSES OF THE SUN AND MOON; AND ON OCCULTATIONS OF STARS OR PLANETS BY THE MOON.

---

1. IF the moon moved in the ecliptic, then at every conjunction with the sun she would be interposed in a direct line between that body and the earth, or an eclipse of the sun would take place; and, at every opposition or time of full moon, the earth would be interposed in a straight line between her and the sun, or an eclipse of the moon would take place. The same effects will manifestly take place, if, at the times of conjunction and opposition, the moon be in one of the nodes of her orbit, that is, if at that time she be crossing the plane of the ecliptic. Eclipses of the sun and moon depend therefore on the distance of the moon from the node at conjunctions and oppositions, both for the possibility of their occurrence, and for their magnitude and duration when they do occur.

2. *On Eclipses of the Moon.*

Let ab, cd be tangents to the sun and earth (S and T) in any plane passing through their centres and on the same sides of them; ad, cb, tangents on opposite sides of them in the same plane. Then, if this plane be supposed to revolve round ST as an axis, and the tangents be produced beyond T, two sets of conical surfaces will be generated representing the shadow cast by the earth, and, if the moon while passing opposition in her orbit $M_1 M_2 M_3 M_4$, be so near the ecliptic as to come within either of these cones, an eclipse will take place.

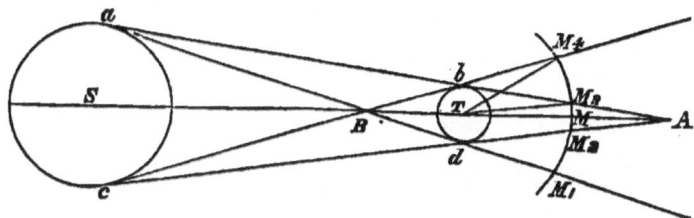

Let now ab, cd be produced till they meet the axis ST produced in A. Then it is evident that within the cone aAc, no light whatever can fall, and if the moon in passing from M_2 to M_3 should be altogether within it, the eclipse will be total, while on the contrary if only part of her surface should be within it, the eclipse will be partial.

It is equally plain that within the portions of the conical surfaces formed by ad and cd produced on the one side of STA, and by cb and ab produced on the other side, that is, within the spaces $M_1 dM_2$ and $M_3 bM_4$ a portion of the sun's light can enter, continually decreasing from M_1, where the whole disk of the sun is visible, to M_2 where no portion of it is visible. These spaces are called the *penumbræ* in contradistinction to the space included within the cone aAc which is called the *umbra*; and while the moon is in the former her surface as viewed from the earth is only obscured, but not rendered invisible; while, during her progress through the *umbra*, a portion or the whole of her surface is rendered invisible, as far as the direct incidence of the sun's rays is concerned.

3. The magnitude and duration of an eclipse of the moon will therefore be seen to depend, first, on the distance of the moon from the ecliptic while passing through the shadow; and, secondly, on the angular breadth of the shadow at the distance of the moon, as seen from the earth. To determine the latter, let S and s be the angular semi-diameters of the sun and moon, and Π and P their horizontal parallaxes for the time of observation.

Then the angular radius of the shadow as seen from the earth

$$= \angle M_sTM = TM_sb - TAb$$
$$= TM_sb - STa + Tab$$
$$= P - S + \Pi.$$

And the angular radius of the penumbra

$$= \angle M_4TM$$
$$= TBM_4 + TM_4B$$
$$= TM_4B + STa + BaT$$
$$= P + S + \Pi.$$

The length of the shadow, or TA,

$$= \frac{\text{earth's radius}}{\sin bAT}$$
$$= \frac{\text{earth's radius}}{\sin (aTS - Tab)}$$
$$= \frac{\text{earth's radius}}{\sin (S - \Pi)}.$$

4. The least values of P, S, and Π are about

$$53'.56'''\cdot 0, \quad 15'.46'''\cdot 0, \text{ and } 8''\cdot 8.$$

The greatest values are about

$$61'.22'''\cdot 0, \quad 16'.18'''\cdot 2, \text{ and } 9'''\cdot 1.$$

And the mean values are about

$$57'.14'''\cdot 0, \quad 16'.2'''\cdot 0, \text{ and } 8'''\cdot 9.$$

Hence the least value of the radius of the shadow at the distance of the moon is $37'.46'''\cdot 6$, the greatest value is $45'.45'''\cdot 1$, and the mean value is $41'.20''\cdot 9$.

And the corresponding values of the radius of the penumbra are $69'.50'''\cdot 8$, $77'.49'''\cdot 3$, and $73'.24'''\cdot 9$.

LUNAR ECLIPTIC LIMIT.

The mean length of the shadow beyond the earth is

$$\frac{\text{earth's radius}}{\sin 15'.53''\cdot 1}$$

$$= \frac{\text{earth's radius}}{953\cdot 1 \times \sin 1''}$$

$$= 216\cdot 4 \times \text{earth's radius}$$

$$= 3\cdot 6 \times \text{mean distance of the moon from the earth, nearly.}$$

5. *On the Lunar Ecliptic Limit.* For the purpose of predicting future eclipses, it is desirable, by inspection of the positions and motions of the sun and moon, to be assured whether an eclipse is possible, so as to avoid the trouble of unnecessary calculations. Now an eclipse cannot take place except the moon be near her node at the time of opposition in longitude or right ascension, and therefore the chief point of inquiry is, what is the limiting distance from the node, within which an eclipse *must* under all circumstances take place.

Imagine then that at the time when the moon is passing through her node at N, the centre of the shadow is at S' on the

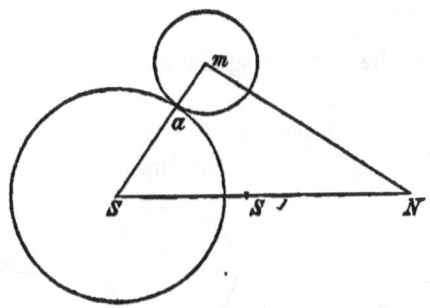

ecliptic NS. Let Nm be a small portion of her orbit considered as a straight line, and, on overtaking the shadow, let her limb just touch its circumference at a, the centre of the shadow being at S. Then if we take for Sa and ma their greatest values, namely, $45'.45''\cdot 1$ and $16'.45''\cdot 0$, $Sm = 62'.30''\cdot 1 = 3750''\cdot 1$; and, the angle at N being the mean inclination, whose value is $5°.9'$,

$$SN = \frac{3750''\cdot 1}{\sin 5°.9'}$$
$$= 41777''$$
$$= 11°.36'.17''.$$

And this is the limiting value of the distance of her node from her position at opposition which will allow an eclipse to be possible, and is usually called the *Lunar Ecliptic Limit*.

Cor. In the time in which the centre of the moon has gone from N to m, and in which therefore her longitude has increased by NS very nearly, the shadow has advanced from S' to S, and these spaces are proportional to the horary mean motions of the moon and sun, or as $32'.56''\cdot 5$ to $2'.27''\cdot 9$. Hence we should find $SS' = 52'.6''$, and $NS' = 10°.44'.11''$.

Therefore to determine at any opposition of the moon, when she is near her node, whether an eclipse is possible, we may take the longitude of the node and the longitude of the sun for the time when the moon has this longitude. The difference, neglecting 180°, must not be so great as $10°.44'.11''$, if an eclipse be possible. Of course all the suppositions which have been made are only approximately true, for the moon's appulse at a is not the true opposition in longitude, nor is S the position of the moon referred to the ecliptic, but a more correct investigation is quite unnecessary.

6. To find the time, magnitude, and duration of a lunar eclipse.

Let Nn be a small portion of the ecliptic and MN of the lunar orbit, considered as straight lines; t and m the positions

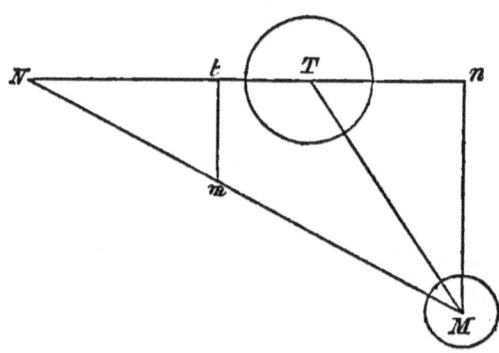

of the centres of the earth's shadow and of the moon at opposition; T and M the positions at time τ before opposition (the moon moving towards the node at N);

λ the moon's latitude at opposition, and g the horary motion in latitude;

m and n the horary motions of the moon and the centre of the earth's shadow (or of the sun) in longitude;

c the distance of the centres of the sun and shadow at time t before opposition.

Then $\quad tT = n\tau$, and $tn = m\tau$;

$$Tn = (m-n)\tau, \text{ and } Mn = \lambda + g\tau;$$

$$\therefore (\lambda + g\tau)^2 + (m-n)^2 \tau^2 = c^2;$$

or, if we put $m - n = m'$ = relative horary motion in longitude of sun and moon,

$$(\lambda + g\tau)^2 + m'^2 \tau^2 = c^2,$$

which will become, if we put $\tan \theta = \dfrac{g}{m'}$,

$$g^2 \tau^2 + 2\lambda g \sin^2 \theta . \tau = (c^2 - \lambda^2) \sin^2 \theta,$$

θ being evidently the inclination of the relative orbit of the moon to the ecliptic.

Solving this equation, we get

$$\tau = \frac{1}{g} (-\lambda \sin^2 \theta \pm \sqrt{c^2 - \lambda^2 \cos^2 \theta} . \sin \theta),$$

in which expression the double sign denotes the times of entering upon and passing out of corresponding phases; and the times of the different phases of the eclipse will be determined by assigning proper values to c.

Let τ' and τ'' be the two values of τ given by the quadratic; so that

$$\tau' = \frac{1}{g} (-\lambda \sin^2 \theta - \sqrt{c^2 - \lambda^2 \cos^2 \theta} . \sin \theta),$$

and $\quad \tau'' = \dfrac{1}{g} (-\lambda \sin^2 \theta + \sqrt{c^2 - \lambda^2 \cos^2 \theta} . \sin \theta).$

These values can be equal only if $c^2 - \lambda^2 \cos^2 \theta = 0$, or if $c = \lambda \cos \theta$.

This corresponds to the least distance of the centres of the moon and centre of the shadow, or to the middle of the eclipse.

If $c =$ radius of penumbra $\pm$ moon's semidiameter
$$= P + S + \Pi \pm s,$$
we get the times from opposition of the first and last contacts with the penumbra, and the first and last instants of total immersion in it.

Finally, if $c = P - S + \Pi \pm s$, we get the times of the corresponding phases of immersion in the shadow.

The magnitude of the eclipse will be determined by the portion of the moon's diameter which is rendered invisible at the middle of the eclipse, and this will manifestly be (since $\lambda \cos \theta$ is equal to the distance of the centres of the moon and the shadow at the middle of the eclipse),

moon's semi-diameter $- (\lambda \cos \theta -$ semi-diameter of shadow)
$$= s - S + P + \Pi - \lambda \cos \theta;$$

or, if as usual, the diameter be supposed to be divided into 12 equal parts or *digits*, the number of digits eclipsed will be

$$\frac{6}{s}(s - S + P + \Pi - \lambda \cos \theta).$$

•. COR. All that has been said above with respect to the motions of the sun and moon in longitude and latitude will apply to right-ascensions and declinations, excepting that the motion in R.A. must be multiplied by the cosine of half the sum of the declinations of the centres of the moon and shadow, and that the motion of the shadow in declination (or that of the sun) must be taken into the account, that is, g will be the relative motion of the moon and shadow in declination.

7. EXAMPLE. We will take the Lunar Eclipse which happened on June 1, 1863.

The elements given in the *Nautical Almanac* (which can be easily calculated from the data in pages I., III., and V. of the month of June) are the following:

CALCULATION OF ECLIPSE OF 1863, JUNE 1.

Greenwich mean time of opposition in R.A., June 1, $11^h.24^m.22^s.8$,

$$☽ \text{ R.A.} \quad 16^h.37^m.17^s.74$$
$$☽ \text{ decl.} \quad -21°.43'.47''.6$$
$$☉ \text{ decl.} +22°. \ 5'.41''.3$$
$$\therefore \text{ decl. of shadow} -22°. \ 5'.41''.3;$$

and therefore difference of declinations $(=\lambda)$

$$= +0°.21'.53''.7 \text{ (moon north of shadow)},$$
$$☽ \text{ hourly motion in R.A. } (m) \quad 40'. \ 8''.4$$
$$☉ \quad\quad\quad\quad\quad\quad\quad\quad (n) \quad 2'.33''.3$$
$$\therefore m' = (m-n).\cos \text{decl.} = 34'.52''.4$$
$$☽ \text{ hourly motion in decl.} -1'.49''.6$$
$$☉ \quad\quad\quad\quad\quad\quad\quad\quad + \quad 20''.2$$
$$\therefore \text{ shadow} \quad\quad\quad\quad\quad\quad - \quad 20''.2;$$

and therefore $g = -1'.29''.4$ (motion southwards),

$$☽ \text{ equat. hor. parallax } 60'.41''.0 = P$$
$$☉ \quad\quad\quad\quad\quad\quad\quad 8''.8 = \Pi$$
$$☽ \text{ true semi-diameter } 16'.33''.8 = s$$
$$☉ \quad\quad\quad\quad\quad\quad\quad 15'.48''.1 = S.$$

Then $\tan \theta = \dfrac{g}{m'} = -\dfrac{89.4}{2092.4}$

$$= -.04273,$$

and $\theta = 357°.33'$,

$$\cos \theta = 0.99909,$$
$$\lambda = +21'.53''.7,$$
$$\therefore \lambda \cos \theta = +21'.52''.5.$$

Semi-diameter of shadow $= P - S + \Pi$

$$= 45'.1''.7 \text{ (nearly the maximum value).}$$

Semi-diameter of penumbra $= P + S + \Pi$
$$= 76'.37''\cdot 9,$$
$$\lambda \sin^2 \theta = + 2'''\cdot 4.$$

We will, for the sake of economy of space, content ourselves with determining the times of first and last contact with the shadow.

For this we shall have
$$c = P - S + \Pi + s$$
$$= 45'.1''\cdot 7 + 16'.33'''\cdot 8$$
$$= 61'.35'''\cdot 5.$$

And, to compute the value of $\sqrt{c^2 - \lambda^2 \cos^2 \phi}$, we must use a subsidiary angle ϕ, such that
$$\frac{\lambda}{c} \cos \theta = \cos \phi,$$
and $\therefore \sqrt{c^2 - \lambda^2 \cos^2 \theta} = c \sin \phi.$

Thus,
Log $(\lambda \cos \theta) =$	3·11810
Ar. co. log $c =$	6·43233
Sum $=$ log cos $\phi =$	9·55043
Log sin $\phi =$	9·97072
Log $c =$	3·56767
Log sin $\theta = -$	8·63091
Sum $=$ Log $\{\sqrt{c^2 - \lambda^2 \cos^2 \theta} \cdot \sin \theta\} = -$	2·16930

$$\sqrt{c^2 - \lambda^2 \cos^2 \theta} \cdot \sin \theta = -\quad 147'''\cdot 7$$
and $\qquad - \lambda \sin^2 \theta = -\quad 2\cdot 4;$

$$\therefore \tau' = + \frac{145\cdot 3}{g} = - \frac{145\cdot 3}{89\cdot 4} = -1^h\cdot 6253$$
$$= -1^h.37^m.31^s\cdot 1,$$

and $\qquad \tau'' = - \dfrac{150\cdot 1}{g} = + \dfrac{150\cdot 1}{89\cdot 4} = + 1^h\cdot 6790$

$$= 1^h.40^m.44^s\cdot 4.$$

Hence, the time of first contact with shadow

$$= 11^h. 24^m. 22^s\cdot 8 - 1^h. 37^m. 31^s\cdot 1$$
$$= 9^h. 46^m. 51^s\cdot 7,$$

and the time of last contact with shadow

$$= 11^h. 24^m. 22^s\cdot 8 + 1^h. 40^m. 44^s\cdot 4$$
$$= 13^h. 5^m. 7^s\cdot 2,$$

agreeing within a minute with the times given in the *Nautical Almanac*.

The magnitude of the eclipse is (in digits)

$$\frac{6}{s} \{s - S + P + \Pi - \lambda \cos \theta\},$$

$$= \frac{238 \cdot 2}{16 \cdot 563} = 14 \cdot 3814$$

$$= \text{(in diameters of the moon) } 1 \cdot 1985.$$

For the middle of the eclipse

$$\tau' = \tau'' = -\frac{\lambda \sin^2 \theta}{g}$$

$$= + \frac{2^{h} \cdot 4}{89 \cdot 4} = + 0^h \cdot 0268$$

$$= + 1^m. 36^s \cdot 5.$$

Therefore the time of the middle of the eclipse was

$$11^h. 24^m. 22^s\cdot 8 + 1^m. 36^s\cdot 5$$
$$= 11^h. 25^m. 59^s\cdot 3.$$

8. Before leaving the subject of lunar eclipses, it is necessary to remark that the diameter of the shadow, as determined by observations of various instances, is always larger than that determined from theory. The theory supposes that the cones of the umbra and the penumbra are formed by rays drawn from the sun's surface, accurately touching the earth's surface. This probably is not the case, as it is likely that many of the rays which graze the surface will be stopped or absorbed by the earth's

atmosphere. This would be equivalent to increasing the earth's diameter or the moon's horizontal parallax, and it is found in fact necessary, for the purpose of reconciling the observations with the theory, to increase the parallax by about one-sixtieth part. If this be done in the preceding example, the magnitude of the eclipse will be found to be 1·231.

Another effect, probably due to our atmosphere, is the dull red coloured light visible on the surface of the moon, while she is totally immersed in the shadow and should therefore be invisible. The solar rays, in passing through the atmosphere, are bent inwards, so as to form a cone of faint light interior to the cone which forms the mathematical shadow, and, in some cases, the effect observed is much more striking than in others. It was particularly observable during the eclipse of June 1, 1863, which has been chosen as an example of calculation, the moon being distinctly visible during the whole of the eclipse, though she was for more than an hour totally immersed in the shadow.

9. *On Eclipses of the Sun.*

An eclipse of the sun is a phenomenon perfectly analogous to an eclipse of the moon, and if we interchange, in the figure on page 329, the positions of the earth and moon, many of the formulæ already derived may be rendered applicable.

A different mode of treatment is however necessary, because it is required to determine, not only the general circumstances of the eclipse, but the parts of the earth's surface at which an eclipse will take place, and to furnish the data for its calculation at each particular place, the apparent positions of the sun and moon being different at each on account of the effects of parallax. We will first give one or two general propositions.

10. Let, as before, $abdc$ be a section of the cone enveloping the surfaces of the sun and earth, and let M be the position of the moon as it is about to enter within the cone, when a portion of the light of the sun will be hindered from reaching the earth. This determines what is called the *beginning of the eclipse generally on the earth.*

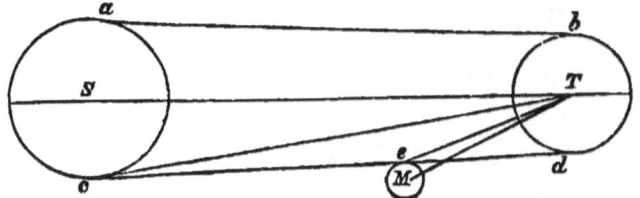

Draw tangents Tc, Te, to the sun and moon, and join TM.

Then, the angular distance of the sun and moon as seen from the centre of the earth at commencement

$$= STM$$
$$= STc + cTe + eTM$$
$$= STc + Tcd - Tce + eTM$$
$$= S + P - \Pi + s,$$

(using the same notation as before).

And the angular semidiameter of the section of the conical surface at the distance of the moon

$$= STe$$
$$= STc + cTe$$
$$= S + P - \Pi.$$

11. *To find the length of the moon's shadow.*

Let S, M, and T, in the same straight line, be the centres of the sun, moon, and earth; aAc, a section of the conical surface enveloping the sun and moon, A being either within the earth's surface, or at a very small distance from it, as is plain from the fact that the angular diameters of the sun and moon, as seen from the earth, are very nearly equal.

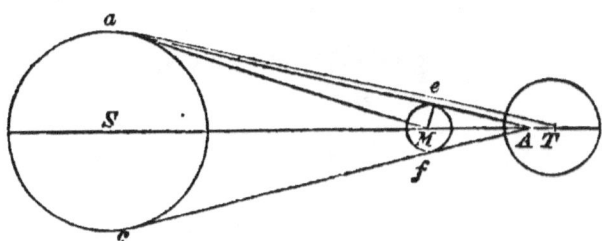

Then length of shadow MA

$$= \frac{Me}{\sin MAa} = \frac{\text{moon's semid}^r}{\sin (SMa - Mae)}$$

$$= \frac{\text{earth's semid}^r. \times \cdot 2729}{\sin (SMa - Mae)},$$

the fraction $\cdot 2729$ being the value of $\dfrac{\text{moon's semid}^r.}{\text{earth's semid}^r.}$ according to the best modern determinations; it is in fact the value of $\dfrac{\text{moon's angular semid}^r.}{\text{moon's mean hor}^l.\text{ parallax}}$.

Now $\quad \angle SMa = \dfrac{Aa}{Ma} \angle SAa$ nearly

$$= \frac{ST''}{MS} \times \angle SAa \text{ very nearly}.$$

$$= \frac{ST}{MS} . S \text{ nearly}$$

and $\quad \angle Mae = \dfrac{Me}{Ma}$

$$= \frac{\text{earth's semid}^r. \times \cdot 2729}{Ma}$$

$$= \frac{SA}{MS} . \frac{\text{earth's semid}^r. \times \cdot 2729}{SA} \text{ very nearly}$$

$$= \frac{ST}{MS} \times \Pi \times \cdot 2729 \text{ nearly};$$

$\therefore \angle MAa = \dfrac{ST}{MS} \{S - \Pi \times \cdot 2729\}$

$$= \frac{ST}{ST - MT} \{S - \Pi \times \cdot 2729\}$$

$$= \frac{\frac{1}{\Pi}}{\frac{1}{\Pi} - \frac{1}{P}} . \{S - \Pi \times \cdot 2729\}$$

$$= \frac{P}{P - \Pi} \{S - \Pi \times \cdot 2729\}$$

$$= \theta, \text{ suppose.}$$

ANNULAR AND TOTAL ECLIPSES. 341

Hence, length of shadow

$$= \frac{\text{earth's semid}^r. \times \cdot 2729}{\sin \theta}.$$

Cor. Since θ is a very small angle, we may put for $\sin \theta$, $\theta \times \sin 1''$. Then the length of shadow will be

$$\frac{\text{earth's semid}^r. \times (P - \Pi) \times \cdot 2729}{P(S - \Pi \times \cdot 2729) \times \sin 1''}$$

$$= \frac{\text{earth's semid}^r. \times \left(1 - \dfrac{\Pi}{P}\right) \times \cdot 2729}{(S - \Pi \times \cdot 2729) \times \sin 1''}$$

$$= \frac{\text{earth's semid}^r. \times \cdot 2729}{S \times \sin 1''} \left\{ 1 - \frac{\Pi}{P} + \frac{\Pi \times \cdot 2729}{S} \right\}$$

very nearly.

Taking then the greatest value of S and the least value of P, namely $978''$ and $3236''$, and, for the value of Π, $9'' \cdot 0$, we shall find,

least length of shadow = earth's semid^r. $\times 57 \cdot 54$.

Similarly, taking the least value of S and the greatest value of P, namely $946''$ and $3682''$, we shall find,

greatest length of shadow = earth's semid^r. $\times 59 \cdot 60$.

Now the moon's distance from the earth varies from about 64 semidiameters of the earth at extreme apogee to 56 semidiameters at nearest perigee. It will therefore sometimes happen that the apex of the conical shadow will not reach the earth, and that sometimes it will pass beyond it. In the former case, if we produce the sheets of the cone to intersect the earth's surface, they will cut off a circular space, at the centre of which the observer, being in the moon's penumbra, will see only an annulus or narrow ring of the surface of the sun. This is called an annular eclipse. If, on the contrary, the apex of the cone lie

342 CALCULATION OF AN ECLIPSE FOR ANY PLACE.

beyond the earth it will, in its passage across the earth's surface, intersect it and cut off circular portions within which no light from the sun can come to the observer. This is a total eclipse.

12. *Calculation of a Solar Eclipse for a particular place*.*

The first thing to be done is to find, for any given time, the moon's apparent hour-angle or right ascension, and apparent declination, in terms of her geocentric hour-angle and geocentric declination.

Let ϕ' = the geocentric latitude of the place,

α = geocentric R.A. of moon's centre at sidereal time t,

h = geocentric hour-angle west, so that $h = t - \alpha$,

Δ = moon's geocentric N.P.D.

r = distance of centres of earth and moon in terms of earth's equatorial radius,

ρ = the earth's radius for the observer's position.

Then refer the moon to rectangular axes of co-ordinates, the equator being the plane of xy; the axis of x in the intersection of the meridian and equator, positive towards the south; that of y at right angles to it, positive towards the west; and that of z parallel to the earth's axis, positive towards the North pole.

Take also another set of rectangular axes, x', y', z', parallel to these and passing through the observer's position.

Then it is plain that if h' and Δ' be the moon's apparent hour-angle and N.P.D., and r' the distance of the observer from the centre of the moon, we shall have the following equations:

$x = r \sin\Delta \cos h, \quad x' = r' \sin\Delta' \cos h', \quad x - x' = \rho \cos\phi',$

$y = r \sin\Delta \sin h, \quad y' = r' \sin\Delta' \sin h', \quad y - y' = 0,$

$z = r \cos\Delta, \quad z' = r' \cos\Delta', \quad z - z' = \rho \sin\phi';$

* See Woolhouse's Article on Eclipses, in *Appendix to N. A. for* 1836.

$$\therefore r' \sin \Delta' \cos h' = r \sin \Delta \cos h - \rho \cos \phi',$$
$$r' \sin \Delta' \sin h' = r \sin \Delta \sin h$$
$$r' \cos \Delta' \quad = r \cos \Delta \quad - \rho \sin \phi'.$$

Also $r = \dfrac{1}{\sin P}$ (P being the moon's horizontal equatorial parallax);

$$\therefore \cot h' = \cot h - \frac{\rho \sin P}{\sin \Delta \sin h} \cot \phi',$$

and
$$\cot \Delta' = \sin h' \left\{ \frac{\dfrac{\cos \Delta}{\sin P} - \rho \sin \phi'}{\dfrac{\sin \Delta \sin h}{\sin P}} \right\}$$

$$= \left(1 - \frac{\rho \sin P \sin \phi'}{\cos \Delta}\right) \cdot \frac{\sin h'}{\sin h} \cot \Delta,$$

or
$$\cot h - \cot h' = \frac{\rho \sin P \cos \phi'}{\sin \Delta \sin h} \quad \ldots\ldots\ldots\ldots(1),$$

and
$$\frac{\cot \Delta}{\sin h} - \frac{\cot \Delta'}{\sin h'} = \frac{\rho \sin P \sin \phi'}{\sin \Delta \sin h} \quad \ldots\ldots\ldots (2),$$

which equations serve for determining immediately the apparent from the geocentric hour-angle and N.P.D.

The calculations would however be rather troublesome, requiring seven-figure logarithms, and it is better to find expressions for $\delta h = h' - h$, and $\delta \Delta = \Delta' - \Delta$.

Multiply (1) by $\sin h' \sin h$,

$$\therefore \sin(h' - h) = \sin \delta h = \frac{\rho \sin P \cos \phi'}{\sin \Delta} \sin h' \ldots\ldots\ldots(3)$$

$$= \frac{\rho \sin P \cos \phi'}{\sin \Delta} \{\sin h \cos \delta h + \cos h \sin \delta h\};$$

$$\therefore \tan \delta h = \frac{\rho \sin P \cos \phi'}{\sin \Delta} \{\sin h + \cos h \tan \delta h\},$$

or $\quad \tan \delta h = \dfrac{\dfrac{\rho \sin P \cos \phi'}{\sin \Delta} \sin h}{1 - \dfrac{\rho \sin P \cos \phi'}{\sin \Delta} \cos h}$ ....(4).

Again from (2), $\dfrac{\cot \Delta}{\sin h} - \dfrac{\cot \Delta'}{\sin h'}$

$= \dfrac{\cot \Delta - \cot \Delta'}{\sin h} + \left(\dfrac{1}{\sin h} - \dfrac{1}{\sin h'} \right) \cot \Delta'$

$= \dfrac{\sin (\Delta' - \Delta)}{\sin h \sin \Delta \sin \Delta'} + \dfrac{2 \sin \dfrac{\delta h}{2} \cos \left(h + \dfrac{\delta h}{2} \right)}{\sin h \sin h'} \cdot \cot \Delta'$

$= \dfrac{\rho \sin P \sin \phi'}{\sin \Delta \sin h}$;

but $\quad \sin \dfrac{\delta h}{2} = \dfrac{\sin \delta h}{2 \cos \dfrac{\delta h}{2}} = \dfrac{\rho \sin P \cos \phi'}{\sin \Delta} \cdot \dfrac{\sin h'}{2 \cos \dfrac{\delta h}{2}}$, from (3);

$\therefore \dfrac{\sin \delta \Delta}{\sin h \sin \Delta \sin \Delta'}$

$= \dfrac{\rho \sin P \sin \phi'}{\sin \Delta \sin h} - \dfrac{\rho \sin P \cos \phi' \cot \Delta'}{\sin h \sin \Delta} \cdot \dfrac{\cos \left(h + \dfrac{\delta h}{2} \right)}{\cos \dfrac{\delta h}{2}}$;

$\therefore \sin \delta \Delta = \rho \sin P \left\{ \sin \phi' \sin \Delta' - \cos \phi' \cos \Delta' \cdot \dfrac{\cos \left(h + \dfrac{\delta h}{2} \right)}{\cos \dfrac{\delta h}{2}} \right\}$...($\alpha$),

$= \rho \sin P \sin \phi' (\sin \Delta \cos \delta \Delta + \cos \Delta \sin \delta \Delta)$

$\quad - \rho \sin P \cos \phi' \dfrac{\cos \left(h + \dfrac{\delta h}{2} \right)}{\cos \dfrac{\delta h}{2}} (\cos \Delta \cos \delta \Delta - \sin \Delta \sin \delta \Delta)$;

APPARENT HOUR-ANGLE AND N.P.D.

$$\therefore \tan \delta\Delta = \frac{\rho \sin P \left\{ \sin \phi' \sin \Delta - \cos \phi' \cos \Delta \cdot \dfrac{\cos \left(h + \dfrac{\delta h}{2} \right)}{\cos \dfrac{\delta h}{2}} \right\}}{1 - \rho \sin P \left\{ \sin \phi' \cos \Delta + \cos \phi' \sin \Delta \cdot \dfrac{\cos \left(h + \dfrac{\delta h}{2} \right)}{\cos \dfrac{\delta h}{2}} \right\}}$$

$$= \frac{\rho \sin P \sin \phi' \sin \Delta \left\{ 1 - \dfrac{\cot \Delta}{\tan \phi'} \cdot \dfrac{\cos \left(h + \dfrac{\delta h}{2} \right)}{\cos \dfrac{\delta h}{2}} \right\}}{1 - \rho \sin P \sin \phi' \cos \Delta \left\{ 1 + \dfrac{\tan \Delta}{\tan \phi'} \cdot \dfrac{\cos \left(h + \dfrac{\delta h}{2} \right)}{\cos \dfrac{\delta h}{2}} \right\}} \quad \ldots\ldots\ldots\ldots (5)$$

$$= \frac{\rho \sin P \sin \phi' \sin \Delta \left\{ 1 - \dfrac{\cot \Delta}{\tan \phi'} \cdot \dfrac{\cos \dfrac{h'+h}{2}}{\cos \dfrac{h'-h}{2}} \right\}}{1 - \rho \sin P \sin \phi' \cos \Delta \left\{ 1 + \dfrac{\tan \Delta}{\tan \phi'} \cdot \dfrac{\cos \dfrac{h'+h}{2}}{\cos \dfrac{h'-h}{2}} \right\}}.$$

To prepare (5) for easy calculation, let

$$\cot \phi' \frac{\cos \left(h + \dfrac{\delta h}{2} \right)}{\cos \dfrac{\delta h}{2}} = \tan \psi, \text{ and } \frac{\rho P \sin \phi'}{\cos \psi} = Q.$$

Then $\delta\Delta = \dfrac{Q \sin \Delta \cos \psi \, (1 - \cot \Delta \tan \psi)}{1 - Q \sin 1'' \cos \Delta \cos \psi \, (1 + \tan \Delta \tan \psi)}$

$$= \frac{Q \sin (\Delta - \psi)}{1 - Q \sin 1'' \cos (\Delta - \psi)} \quad \ldots\ldots\ldots\ldots\ldots\ldots (\beta).$$

346   GEOCENTRIC IN TERMS OF APP. QUANTITIES.

and, from (4), $\delta h = \dfrac{\dfrac{\rho P \cos \phi'}{\sin \Delta} \sin h}{1 - \dfrac{\rho \sin P \cos \phi'}{\sin \Delta} \cos h}$ .... (γ);

or thus, if $\dfrac{\rho \sin P \cos \phi'}{\sin \Delta} = \mu,$

$$\delta h = \mu \sin h + \frac{1}{2} \mu^2 \sin 2h + \&c.$$

NOTE. We have, for tan δh and tan $\delta \Delta$, put δh sin 1" and $\delta \Delta$ sin 1", and for sin P we have put P sin 1". More correctly we might use $\delta h \left(\dfrac{\tan \delta h}{\delta h}\right)$, $\delta \Delta \left(\dfrac{\tan \delta \Delta}{\delta \Delta}\right)$, and $P \left(\dfrac{\sin P}{P}\right)$. (See page 183.) But, if five-figure logarithms be used, it will be sufficient to subtract 2 from the last figure of the logarithm of δh, and 1 from the last figure of the logarithm of $\delta \Delta$, when the computations are completed.

13. We can also express δh in terms of h' and Δ'.

Thus $\delta h = Q' \dfrac{\sin h'}{\sin \Delta},$

where $Q' = \rho P \cos \phi',$

or $\delta h = Q' \dfrac{\sin h'}{\sin (\Delta' - \delta \Delta)}$

$= Q' \dfrac{\sin h'}{\sin \Delta' (1 - \cot \Delta' \cdot \delta \Delta)}$ very nearly,

$= Q' \dfrac{\sin h'}{\sin \Delta'} \cdot \dfrac{1}{1 - \cot \Delta' \times \rho \sin P \{\sin \phi' \sin \Delta' - \cos \phi' \cos \Delta' \cos h'\}}$

with sufficient accuracy,

$= Q' \dfrac{\sin h'}{\sin \Delta'} \cdot \dfrac{1}{1 - Q'' \cos \Delta' (1 - \cot \phi' \cot \Delta' \cos h')},$

where $Q'' = \rho \sin P \cdot \sin \phi'.$

APPLICATION OF THE FORMULÆ.

EXAMPLE. For the reappearance of δ Cancri at the limb of the moon, observed at Greenwich, 1860, March 4, we find the following data:

$$h' = 22°. 30'. 34''{\cdot}3$$
$$\Delta' = 71°. 20'. 7''$$
$$P = 3636''{\cdot}37$$
$$\phi' = 51°. 17'. 26''$$
$$\text{Log}\,\rho = 9{\cdot}99911$$

∴ Log ρ = 9·99911
Log P = 3·56066
Log cos φ' = 9·79614
Sum = Log Q' = 3·35591

9·99911
3·56066
Log sin φ' = 9·89227
Log sin 1'' = 4·68557
Sum = Log Q'' = 8·13761

Log cot Δ' = 9·52865
Log cot φ' = 9·90386
Log cos h' = 9·96557
Sum (log α) = 9·39808
α = 0·250082
1 − α = 0·749918
Log = 9·87501
Log Q'' = 8·13761
Log cos Δ' = 9·50519
Sum = log β = 7·51781
β = 0·003295

1 − β = 0·996705
Log = 9·99856
Ar. co. = 0·00144
Log sin h' = 9·58301
Log cosec Δ' = 0·02347
Log Q' = 3·35591
Sum = log (δh) = 2·96383
δh = 920''·08
= 15'.20''·08
$\dfrac{\delta h}{2}$ = 7'.40''·04
$h + \dfrac{\delta h}{2}$ = 22°.22'.54'''·3

We have also

$$\sin \delta\Delta = \rho \sin P \left\{ \sin \phi' \sin \Delta' - \cos \phi' \cos \Delta' \frac{\cos\left(h + \dfrac{\delta h}{2}\right)}{\cos \dfrac{\delta h}{2}} \right\},$$

348   *APPLICATION OF THE FORMULÆ.*

or
$$\delta\Delta = \rho P \sin\phi' \frac{\sin(\Delta' - \psi)}{\cos\psi},$$

where
$$\tan\psi = \cot\phi' \frac{\cos\left(h + \frac{\delta h}{2}\right)}{\cos\frac{\delta h}{2}}.$$

Then

$\text{Log}\cos\left(h + \frac{\delta h}{2}\right) = 9{\cdot}96598$ $\text{Log}\sin(\Delta' - \psi) = 9{\cdot}75638$

$\text{Ar. co. log}\cos\frac{\delta h}{2} = 0{\cdot}00000$ $\text{Log}\sec\psi = 0{\cdot}09505$

$\text{Log}\cot\phi' = 9{\cdot}90386$ $\text{Log}(\rho P\sin\phi') = 3{\cdot}45204$

$\text{Sum} = \text{Log}\tan\psi = 9{\cdot}86984$ $\text{Sum} = \text{Log}\,\delta\Delta = 3{\cdot}30347$

$\psi = 36°.32'.23''$ $\delta\Delta = 2011''{\cdot}3$

$\Delta' = 71.20.7$ $= 33'.31''{\cdot}3$

$\Delta' - \psi = 34.47.44$

Using now the geocentric values

$$h = 22°.15'.14''{\cdot}2,$$
and
$$\Delta = 70°.46'.36'',$$

we will, for a test of the degree of accuracy of the formulæ, find, by means of (4) and (5), the values of h' and Δ'.

The formulæ are

$$\delta h = \frac{\dfrac{\rho P \cos\phi'}{\sin\Delta}\sin h}{1 - \dfrac{\rho \sin P \cos\phi'}{\sin\Delta}\cos h},$$

and
$$\delta\Delta = \frac{Q\sin(\Delta - \psi)}{1 - Q\sin 1''\cos(\Delta - \psi)},$$

where ψ has been already computed, and $= 36°.32'.23''$; and $\therefore \Delta - \psi = 34°.14'.13''$; and $Q = \dfrac{\rho P \sin\phi'}{\cos\psi}.$

AUGMENTATION OF MOON'S SEMIDIAMETER. 349

We have then,

$\text{Log}\,(\rho P \cos \phi') = 3\cdot35591$ \quad $\text{Log}\,(\rho \sin P \sin \phi') = 8\cdot13761$
$\text{Log cosec}\,\Delta = 0\cdot02492$ \quad $\text{Log sec}\,\psi = 0\cdot09505$
$\text{Log}\cos h = 9\cdot96639$ \quad $\text{Log}\cos(\Delta - \psi) = 9\cdot91736$
$\text{Log sin}\,1'' = 4\cdot68557$

$\text{Sum} = \log \alpha' = 8\cdot03279$ \quad $\text{Sum} = \text{Log}\,\beta' = 8\cdot15002$

$\alpha' = 0\cdot010784$ \quad $\beta' = 0\cdot014126$

$1 - \alpha' = 0\cdot989216$ \quad $1 - \beta' = 0\cdot985874$

$\text{Log}\,(1 - \alpha') = 9\cdot99529$ \quad $\text{Log}\,(1 - \beta') = 9\cdot99382$

$\text{Ar. co.} = 0\cdot00471$ \quad $\text{Ar. co.} = 0\cdot00618$

$\text{Log}\left(\dfrac{\rho P \cos \phi'}{\sin \Delta}\right) = 3\cdot38083$ \quad $\text{Log}\,Q = 3\cdot54709$

$\text{Log sin}\,h = 9\cdot57831$ \quad $\text{Log sin}\,(\Delta - \psi) = 9\cdot75021$

$\text{Sum} = \text{Log}\,\delta h = 2\cdot96385$ \quad $\text{Sum} = \text{Log}\,\delta\Delta = 3\cdot30348$

$\delta h = 920''\cdot12$ \quad $\delta\Delta = 2011\cdot3$
$ = 15'.20''\cdot12$ \quad $ = 33'.31''\cdot3$

The values of δh and $\delta\Delta$, as calculated in the *Greenwich Observations*, are

$15'.20''\cdot08$ and $33'.31''\cdot19$.

If six-figure logarithms were used, we could secure accuracy to the hundredth of a second.

14. To find the value of the *augmented semidiameter* of the moon.

The angular semidiameter of the moon will be larger at the observer's position than at the centre of the earth in the proportion of r to r', or rather the sines of the semidiameters will be in that proportion. If then s' and s be the apparent and geocentric semidiameters,

$$\frac{\sin s'}{\sin s} = \frac{r}{r'}.$$

Let, in the accompanying figure, PZ be as usual the geocentric colatitude, and M and M' the geocentric and apparent positions of the moon; z and z' the corresponding zenith-distances.

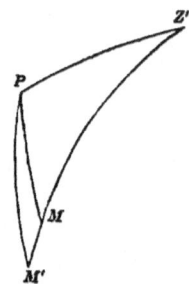

Now, if we imagine a perpendicular to be drawn from the moon to the earth's radius at the observer's position (produced), its length will evidently be expressed both by $r' \sin z'$ and by $r \sin z$;

$$\therefore r' \sin z' = r \sin z,$$

or
$$\frac{\sin s'}{\sin s} = \frac{r}{r'}$$

$$= \frac{\sin z'}{\sin z}.$$

Now
$$\frac{\sin z'}{\sin z} = \frac{\sin (z + \delta z)}{\sin z}$$

$$= \cos \delta z + \cot z \sin \delta z$$

$$= (\text{since } \delta z \text{ is the parallax in Z.D.})$$

$$\cos \delta z + \rho \sin P \cot z \sin (z + \delta z);$$

$$\therefore \sin (z + \delta z) = \frac{\sin z \cos \delta z}{1 - \rho \sin P \cos z},$$

or
$$\frac{\sin s'}{\sin s} = \frac{\cos \delta z}{1 - \rho \sin P \cos z},$$

and
$$\sin s' = \sin s \times \frac{\cos \delta z}{1 - \rho \sin P \cos z}.$$

This expression is rigorously correct, but we may, without sensible error, put $\cos \delta z = 1$,

and then
$$\sin s' = \frac{\sin s}{1 - \rho \sin P \cos z},$$

or
$$s' = \frac{s}{1 - \rho \sin P \cos z},$$

with scarcely sensible error.

TIMES OF FIRST AND LAST CONTACT. 351

Cor. It is also evident that

$$\frac{\sin s'}{\sin s} = \frac{\sin z'}{\sin z} = \frac{\sin \Delta'}{\sin \Delta} \cdot \frac{\sin h'}{\sin h}.$$

Note. A table of corrections for *Augmentation of Moon's Semidiameter* is given in Loomis's *Astronomy* (Table XIII. page 378).

15. From the preceding formulæ we are now enabled to deduce from the geocentric R.A., N.P.D., and semi-diameters of the moon (interpolated from the *Nautical Almanac* for a series of equidistant times at short intervals) the corresponding apparent R.A., N.P.D., and semi-diameters. We might also, by application of the effect of the sun's parallax in R.A. and N.P.D., deduce the apparent R.A. and N.P.D. of the sun. But, as the *relative* motions of the sun and moon are all which are required, it will be sufficient to use the difference of the horizontal parallaxes of the sun and moon instead of the moon's horizontal parallax in the preceding expressions, and afterwards to disregard the solar parallax, the hour-angles and declinations of the two bodies being of course nearly equal. Thus, if

$$P' = \rho \sin (P - \Pi),$$

we must use $\sin P'$ instead of $\rho \sin P$ in the formulæ.

Having then calculated at short intervals a series of apparent positions of the sun and moon (at intervals of half an hour for example, and then by interpolation for every five minutes), the apparent relative orbit of the moon will be traced out, and the contact of limbs will take place when the apparent distance of the centres of the sun and moon is equal to the sum or difference of their apparent semi-diameters. For a distance equal to the sum of their semi-diameters we shall have the commencement or the ending of the eclipse; and, for a distance equal to their difference, we shall have (for places where the eclipse is total or annular) a total beginning or ending, if s' be greater than S, and an annular beginning or ending if s' be less than S.

Let now T be the time nearest to the first or last contact of limbs for which the series of apparent R.A. and N.P.D. has been computed, and let the time of contact be $T + t$, t being a small fraction of the intervals used for computation; at the time $T+t$, let the difference of R.A. of centres of sun and moon be a, and the difference of N.P.D. be d. Then, if c be the sum of semi-diameters, it can be easily shewn, as at page 267, that $c^2 = d^2 + \sin \Delta \sin D \cdot a^2$, with sufficient accuracy, Δ and D being the approximate N.P.D.'s of the centres of the sun and moon for time $T+t$.

Now by differencing the series of computed values of a and d, these quantities can be expressed (as in the case of the transit of Venus, page 269) in the forms

$$a = m + m't + m''t^2,$$
and
$$d = n + n't + n''t^2,$$

and therefore we shall have an equation of the form

$$c^2 = e + ft + gt^2 + ht^3,$$

and, as before,

$$t = -\frac{f}{2g} \pm \sqrt{\left(\frac{f}{2g}\right)^2 + k} \ldots\ldots\ldots (6),$$

where
$$k = \frac{c^2}{g} - \frac{e}{g} - \frac{h}{g}t^3,$$

and the term involving t^3 will be neglected in the first approximation.

If c represent the *difference* of the semi-diameters, the two values of t will give the times of beginning and ending of the total or annular eclipse for places on the central line of the shadow, and, if c represent the *sum* of the semi-diameters, the two values will give the times of first and last contact of the limbs of the sun and moon. But it is safe to use only that value which is very near to the middle epoch of the interpolation, and to deduce another value for the other phase of the eclipse.

16. *To find the positions of the points of first and last contact on the sun's limb.*

For the two values of t deduced from the solution of the quadratic, we can calculate the values of Δ and D; and then, if

DIFFERENT CLASSES OF ECLIPSE-OBSERVATIONS. 353

ψ be the angle made in each case with D, or with the declination-circle passing through the centre of the sun, and

$2\sigma = c + \Delta + D$, we shall have

$$\cos \frac{\psi}{2} = \sqrt{\frac{\sin \sigma \sin (\sigma - \Delta)}{\sin D \sin c}}$$

$$= \sqrt{\frac{c + D - \Delta}{2c}} \cdot \sqrt{\frac{\sin \sigma}{\sin D}} \text{ very nearly.}$$

17. During the progress of a solar eclipse an opportunity is offered for determining the difference of the errors of the tabular places of the sun and moon, and the errors of their assumed semi-diameters, by observations made with an equatorial. The classes of observations which can be made are the following:

(1) Transits of the limbs of the sun and moon observed with an unchanged position of the polar axis, giving the correct difference of the R.A.'s of the limbs, to be compared with the tabular differences, involving the errors of tabular semi-diameters and errors of tabular R.A. of the centres of the sun and moon.

(2) Differences of N.P.D. of the limbs, giving similar comparisons for N.P.D.

(3) Differences of N.P.D. of cusps.

(4) Differences of R.A. of cusps.

We will take these cases in their order.

(1) *Differences of R.A. of limbs of the sun and moon.*

Let α (in arc) and Δ be the tabular apparent R.A. and N.P.D. of the centre of the moon at time of transit of limb over mean of wires; A and D those of the centre of the sun at time of transit of sun's limb.

Then $\alpha \mp \dfrac{s'}{\sin \Delta}$ and $A \mp \dfrac{S}{\sin D}$ will be the R.A.'s of the first or second limb of the moon and sun. The sidereal interval of transit will therefore be

$$A - \alpha \mp \frac{S}{\sin D} \pm \frac{s'}{\sin \Delta},$$

M. A.

and the variation of this expression will be

$$dA - da \mp \frac{dS}{\sin D} \pm \frac{ds'}{\sin \Delta}$$
$$\pm \frac{S \cos D}{\sin^2 D} dD \mp \frac{s' \cos \Delta}{\sin^2 \Delta} d\Delta \ldots\ldots\ldots (7).$$

The observed difference of R.A. of limbs must then be equated to the tabular difference plus the errors of elements as given above.

(2) *Difference of* N.P.D. *of limbs.*

In this case the observed difference must be equated to the tabular difference plus

$$dD - d\Delta \pm dS \mp ds' \ldots\ldots\ldots\ldots\ldots\ldots (8).$$

(3) *Difference of* N.P.D. *of cusps.*

Let a be the excess of the R.A. of the moon above that of the sun; a_c and a'_c the difference of R.A. of a cusp and of each centre, so that $a_c + a'_c = a$.

Then, if Δ_c be the N.P.D. of a cusp, we shall have, as at page 267, the following equations:

$$a_c^2 = \frac{S^2 - (D - \Delta_c)^2}{\sin D \sin \Delta_c}$$

$$a'^2_c = \frac{s'^2 - (\Delta - \Delta_c)^2}{\sin \Delta \sin \Delta_c},$$

and $\qquad a_c + a'_c = a,$

which are easily solved by a tentative method, which can be readily applied, because, in the course of the observations, the difference of N.P.D. of the cusps and limbs can be observed at short intervals if necessary, and approximate values of Δ_c will therefore be known.

Thus, assuming a value of Δ_c, we can compute, for a given time, the values of a_c and a'_c, and the sum of these ought to be equal to a. The difference will shew how great is the error of the assumption, and we must then repeat the process with a new value. A skilful computer will get the correct value in three or four approximations.

DIRECT METHOD FOR N.P.D. OF CUSPS.

The values of Δ_e and a_e may however be found, without much trouble, by a direct computation.

Thus, the same notation remaining,
let $\qquad D - \Delta = d$, and $D - \Delta_e = Z$;
$$\therefore \Delta - \Delta_e = Z - d,$$
and we have the two equations
$$S^2 = Z^2 + \sin D \sin \Delta_e a_e^2,$$
$$s'^2 = (Z - d)^2 + \sin \Delta \sin \Delta_e (a - a_e)^2.$$

Subtracting these equations, and neglecting the small term $(\sin D - \sin \Delta) \sin \Delta_e . a_e^2$, we have
$$2Zd - d^2 + 2 \sin \Delta \sin \Delta_e a . a_e - \sin \Delta \sin \Delta_e a^2 = S^2 - s'^2,$$
or, if $\qquad a \sin \Delta \sin \Delta_e = a',$
and $\qquad \frac{1}{2}(S^2 - s'^2 + d^2 + aa') = \alpha,$
$$Zd + a'a_e = \alpha;$$
$$\therefore a_e^2 = \frac{a}{a'}(S^2 - Z^2) = \frac{a^2}{a'^2} - \frac{2ad}{a'^2}.Z + \frac{d^2}{a'^2}.Z^2;$$
$$\therefore Z^2 - \frac{2\alpha d}{d^2 + aa'}.Z = \frac{aa'S^2 - \alpha^2}{d^2 + aa'}.$$

Let now $\qquad \frac{aa'}{d^2} = \tan^2 \theta;$
$$\therefore Z^2 - \frac{2\alpha}{d}\cos^2\theta . Z = \frac{aa'S^2 - \alpha^2}{d^2}.\cos^2\theta,$$
and $\qquad Z = \frac{\alpha}{d}\cos^2\theta \pm \frac{\cos\theta}{d}\sqrt{aa'S^2 - \alpha^2 \sin^2\theta}$
$$= \frac{\alpha}{d}\cos^2\theta \pm \frac{\sin\theta}{d}\sqrt{d^2 S^2 - \alpha^2 \cos^2\theta}$$
$$= S\cos(\theta \mp \phi),$$
where $\qquad \cos\phi = \frac{\alpha \cos\theta}{Sd}.$

Also $\qquad a_e = \frac{\alpha}{a'} - \frac{d}{a'}Z$
$$= \frac{Sa}{d}.\frac{\sin(\theta \mp \phi)}{\tan \theta}.$$

The omitted quantity $(\sin D - \sin \Delta) \sin \Delta_e \cdot a_e^2$ may then be calculated with the value of a_e, and substituted in the equation, and the operations may be repeated, a corrected value of Δ_e being used in the computation of a'.

To obtain the errors of the elements, we must differentiate the equations on page 354; thus we shall have, (considering Δ_e, Δ, and D' in the denominators to be constant, as their variations will not sensibly affect the result,)

$$da = da_e + da'_e$$

$$= \frac{da_e}{d\Delta_e} d\Delta_e + \frac{da_e}{dD} dD + \frac{da_e}{dS} dS$$

$$+ \frac{da'_e}{d\Delta_e} d\Delta_e + \frac{da'_e}{d\Delta} d\Delta + \frac{da'_e}{ds'} ds',$$

where
$$\frac{da_e}{d\Delta_e} = \frac{D - \Delta_e}{a_e \sin D \sin \Delta_e} = Q \text{ suppose}$$

$$\frac{da'_e}{d\Delta_e} = \frac{\Delta - \Delta_e}{a'_e \sin \Delta \sin \Delta_e} = q \ \ldots\ldots$$

$$\frac{da_e}{dD} = -\frac{D - \Delta_e}{a_e \sin D \sin \Delta} = -Q$$

$$\frac{da'_e}{d\Delta} = -\frac{\Delta - \Delta_e}{a'_e \sin \Delta \sin \Delta} = -q$$

$$\frac{da_e}{dS} = \frac{S}{a_e \sin D \sin \Delta_e}$$

$$\frac{da'_e}{ds'} = \frac{s'}{a'_e \sin \Delta \sin \Delta_e}.$$

Hence, we shall have

$$da = (Q + q) d\Delta_e - Q\, dD - q\, d\Delta$$

$$+ \frac{S}{a_e \sin D \sin \Delta_e} dS + \frac{s'}{a'_e \sin \Delta \sin \Delta_e} ds',$$

or $d\Delta_e = \dfrac{da}{Q+q} + \dfrac{Q}{Q+q} dD + \dfrac{q}{Q+q} d\Delta - \dfrac{1}{Q+q} \cdot \dfrac{S}{a_e \sin D \sin \Delta_e} dS$

$\qquad - \dfrac{1}{Q+q} \cdot \dfrac{s'}{a'_e \sin \Delta \sin \Delta_e} ds' \ \ldots\ldots\ldots$ (9).

And the quantities Q and q admit of easy calculation.

(4) *Difference of* R.A. *of cusps.*

Let α and A be the R.A.'s of the centres of the moon and sun, and α_c that of the cusp.

Then we have

$$d\alpha_c = d\alpha_c - dA = - Q\, dD + Q\, d\Delta_c$$

$$+ \frac{S}{a_c \sin D \sin \Delta_c} . dS,$$

and $\quad d\alpha'_c = d\alpha - d\alpha_c = - q\, d\Delta + q\, d\Delta_c$

$$+ \frac{s'}{a'_c \sin \Delta \sin \Delta_c} ds';$$

therefore, eliminating $d\Delta_c$, we get

$$(Q + q)\, d\alpha_c - q\, dA - Q\, d\alpha = Qq\, (d\Delta - dD)$$

$$+ \frac{qS}{a_c \sin D \sin \Delta_c} . dS$$

$$- \frac{Qs'}{a'_c \sin \Delta \sin \Delta} . ds',$$

or $\quad d\alpha_c = \frac{q}{Q+q} dA + \frac{Q}{Q+q} d\alpha + \frac{Qq}{Q+q} (d\Delta - dD)$

$$+ \frac{qS}{a_c \sin D \sin \Delta_c (Q+q)} . dS$$

$$- \frac{Qs'}{a'_c \sin \Delta \sin \Delta_c (Q+q)} . ds' \ldots\ldots (10).$$

18. For an example of the calculation of an eclipse during which observations of all the classes here discussed were made, the reader may consult the Greenwich *Observations* of 1860 for a very instructive example.

In this instance, however, the apparent places of the moon have been deduced in a different way from that which has been given at page 342, namely, by a method, which has been in use at Greenwich for the reduction of observations made with the altazimuth during several years, called the method of *normal-centric co-ordinates*. The object is to avoid the change from the astronomical to the geocentric zenith in the calculation parallax, and this is effected by taking, as the origin of co-ordinates, not the centre of the earth, but the point where the earth's normal at the place of observation meets the polar axis. Of course the moon is rather more distant from this point than from the earth's centre, and therefore a small correction is necessary to the horizontal parallax, and the geocentric semi-diameter; as also to the geocentric N.P.D., the correction to the latter being the angle made by lines drawn from the moon to the centre and to the foot of the normal.

Without going into details we may state the value of the quantities concerned and the corrections required; γ being as usual the astronomical colatitude.

Distance of centre from foot of normal

$$= \frac{e^2}{\sqrt{1-e^2+\tan^2\gamma}} = \alpha \text{ (suppose)}.$$

Correction to N.P.D. (subtractive)

$$= \frac{1}{\text{moon's distance}} \times \alpha \sin \text{N.P.D.}$$

$$= \alpha \sin P \sin \text{N.P.D.}$$

Correction-factor to hor. equat. parallax

$$= \frac{\text{normal-centric radius}}{\text{earth's semi-major axis}} \times \frac{\text{distance from centre}}{\text{dist. from foot of normal}}$$

$$= \frac{1 - \alpha \sin P \cos \text{N.P.D.}}{\sqrt{1 - e^2 \cos^2 \gamma}}.$$

Correction-factor for semi-diameter

$$= 1 - \alpha \sin P \cos \text{N.P.D.}$$

The student will have no difficulty in investigating the expressions here given. The normal-centric correction having been applied to N.P.D., the normal-centric zenith-distance and azimuth can be computed, and the normal-centric parallax having been added to the zenith-distance, these can again be converted into apparent R.A. and N.P.D. referred to the observer's position.

VARIATION OF MOON'S PARALLAX. 359

This method was used at Greenwich for deducing the apparent R.A. and N.P.D. of the moon for the solar eclipse of 1860, July 18, before referred to.

19. *Variation of Moon's Parallax in Hour-angle and N.P.D.*

Since the amount of the parallax depends on the zenith-distance, it is plain that it will vary very rapidly with change of hour-angle, and, in certain cases, expressions for its rate of change at any distance from the meridian are very useful and necessary.

Expanding δh, we get

$$\tan \delta h = \delta h'' \sin 1'' \text{ (very nearly)} = \frac{\rho \sin P \cos \phi'}{\sin \Delta} \sin h$$

$$+ \frac{1}{2} \frac{\rho^2 \sin^2 P \cos^2 \phi'}{\sin^2 \Delta} \sin 2h + \&c.$$

And, differentiating with respect to h,

$$\frac{d(\delta h)}{dt} = \frac{\rho \sin P \cos \phi'}{\sin \Delta} \cos h \frac{dh}{dt}$$

$$+ \frac{\rho^2 \sin^2 P \cos^2 \phi'}{\sin^2 \Delta} \cos 2h \frac{dh}{dt} + \&c.,$$

if one second be taken as the unit of time, then $\frac{dh}{dt}$ will be the change of moon's hour-angle in 1^s, and will be equal to $(15'' - m) \sin 1''$, where $m =$ motion in R.A. in one second;

$$\therefore d(\delta h) = (15'' - m) \, \delta t \left\{ \frac{\rho \sin P \cos l}{\sin \Delta} \cos h \right.$$

$$\left. + \frac{\rho^2 \sin^2 P \cos^2 \phi'}{\sin^2 \Delta} \cos 2h + \&c. \right\} \text{ very nearly.}$$

Again, taking equation (5) and expanding, we get (if we put $\rho \sin P = R'$),

$$\tan \delta \Delta = \delta \Delta \sin 1''$$

$$= R' \sin \Delta \sin \phi' \left\{ 1 - \frac{\cot \Delta}{\tan \phi'} \left(\cos h - \frac{1}{2} \sin h \cdot \delta h \right) \right\}$$

$$\times \left\{ 1 + R' \sin \phi' \cos \Delta \left(1 + \frac{\tan \Delta}{\tan \phi'} \cos h \right) \right\}$$

$$= \text{(substituting for } \delta h \text{ its approximate value } \frac{\rho \sin P \cos \phi'}{\sin \Delta} \sin h),$$

$$R' \sin \Delta \sin \phi' \{1 - \frac{\cot \Delta}{\tan \phi'} \cos h + \frac{R'}{2} \frac{\cos \Delta}{\sin^2 \Delta} \cdot \frac{\cos^2 \phi'}{\sin \phi'} \sin^2 h\}$$

$$\times \{1 + R' \sin \phi' \cos \Delta + R' \sin \Delta \cos \phi' \cos h\}$$

$$= R' \sin \Delta \sin \phi' \times \begin{cases} 1 - \frac{\cot \Delta}{\tan \phi'} \cos h + \frac{R'}{2} \frac{\cos \Delta}{\sin^2 \Delta} \cdot \frac{\cos^2 \phi'}{\sin \phi} \sin^2 h \\ + R' \sin \phi' \cos \Delta - R' \frac{\cos^2 \Delta \cos \phi'}{\sin \Delta} \cos h \\ + R' \sin \Delta \cos \phi' \cos h - R' \frac{\cos \Delta \cos^2 \phi'}{\sin \phi'} \cos^2 h \end{cases},$$

and, differentiating with respect to h, and collecting terms, we have

$$\frac{d(d\Delta)}{dh} \sin 1''$$

$$= R' \sin \Delta \sin \phi' \frac{dh}{dt} \left\{ \left(\frac{\cot \Delta}{\tan \phi'} + R' \frac{\cos^2 \Delta \cos \phi'}{\sin \Delta} \right) \sin h \right.$$

$$\left. + R' \frac{\cos \Delta \cos^2 \phi'}{\sin \phi'} \left(1 + \frac{1}{2 \sin^2 \Delta}\right) \sin 2h \right\}$$

$$= \frac{dh}{dt} \{(\rho \sin P \cos \phi' \cos \Delta + \rho^2 \sin^2 P \sin \phi' \cos \phi' \cos 2\Delta) \sin h$$

$$+ \rho^2 \sin^2 P \cos^2 \phi' \cot \Delta \left(\frac{1}{2} + \sin^2 \Delta\right) \sin 2h\},$$

and, if we take, as before, one second as the unit of time,

$$d(\delta \Delta) = (15'' - m) \times \{(\rho \sin P \cos \phi' \cos \Delta$$

$$+ \rho^2 \sin^2 P \sin \phi' \cos \phi' \cos 2\Delta) \sin h$$

$$+ \rho^2 \sin^2 P \cos^2 \phi' \cot \Delta \left(\frac{1}{2} + \sin^2 \Delta\right) \sin 2h\}.$$

20. *On Occultations of Stars by the Moon.*

An occultation of a star may be treated as a particular case of an eclipse of the sun, the only difference being that the star has neither proper motion, parallax, nor sensible diameter. Since however the position of the star, when the immersion or emersion takes place, may be considered as a point of the limb of the moon, the application of the parallax in hour-angle and N.P.D. (properly corrected) to the hour-angle and N.P.D. of the star will give the geocentric position of the point of the limb which was in contact, and the equation (6) on page 352 will determine the time of immersion or emersion, if we make c equal to the *geocentric* semi-diameter of the moon, as interpolated from the *Nautical Almanac* for a time tolerably close to that of immersion.

For this idea, which simplifies greatly the calculation of occultations, we are indebted to Carlini, who first proposed his method in the *Milan Ephemeris* for 1809.

21. The geocentric position of the point on the moon's limb, of which the apparent position is defined by the R.A. and N.P.D. of the star, can be found by the use of formulæ (γ) and (α) (pages 346 and 344), of which an example has been already given, and no other method can excel this in simplicity or accuracy. Since however many students may have occasion to study the indirect method of finding the position of the "Corresponding Point," which has been so long in use at Greenwich, it is desirable to give a short explanation of this method.

In the first place, the horizontal equatorial parallax which has been computed for the moon's centre must be corrected for the point of the limb at which the occultation takes place. For the investigation of this correction which, at the maximum, amounts only to $0''\cdot 16$, the student may consult any of the volumes of the *Greenwich Observations* from 1843 to 1845, where he will find also the correction tabulated. We will call the corrected parallax P' to distinguish it from P.

Then from equation (3), page 343, we get

$$\sin (h' - h) = \frac{\rho \sin P' \cos \phi'}{\sin \Delta} \sin h',$$

where h represents the geocentric west hour-angle of the corresponding point, and Δ the geocentric N.P.D.

This is put into the shape, seconds of $\dfrac{(h' - h)}{2}$

$$= \frac{h' - h}{\sin (h' - h)} \times \frac{\cos \phi' \sin h'}{2 \sin \Delta} \cdot \frac{\rho \sin P'}{P'} \times \text{seconds of } P'.$$

Again, formula (2), page 343, gives

$$\frac{\cot \Delta}{\sin h} - \frac{\cot \Delta'}{\sin h'} = \frac{\rho \sin P' \sin \phi'}{\sin \Delta \sin h},$$

or $\qquad \cos \Delta \sin \Delta' \sin h' - \cos \Delta' \sin \Delta \sin h$

$$= \rho \sin P' \sin \phi' \sin \Delta' \sin h',$$

which may be put under the form

$$\tfrac{1}{2} \{\sin (\Delta' - \Delta) (\sin h' + \sin h) + \sin (\Delta' + \Delta) (\sin h' - \sin h)\}$$
$$= \rho \sin P' \sin \phi' \sin \Delta' \sin h',$$

whence $\quad \sin (\Delta' - \Delta) = \dfrac{2\rho \sin P' \sin \phi' \sin \Delta' \sin h'}{\sin h' + \sin h}$

$$- \frac{\sin (\Delta' + \Delta)(\sin h' - \sin h)}{\sin h' + \sin h}$$

$$= \frac{\rho \sin P' \sin \phi' \sin \Delta' \sin h'}{\sin \dfrac{h'+h}{2} \cos \dfrac{h'-h}{2}} - \cot \left(\frac{h'+h}{2}\right) \tan \left(\frac{h'-h}{2}\right) \sin (\Delta' + \Delta).$$

Putting $F = \dfrac{1}{2} \rho \cos \phi' \sin h' \times \text{seconds of } P'$,

and $\qquad G = \rho \sin \phi' \sin \Delta' \sin h' \times \text{seconds of } P'.$

Seconds of $\dfrac{h'-h}{2} = F \operatorname{cosec} \Delta \dfrac{h'-h}{\sin(h'-h)} \cdot \dfrac{\sin P'}{P'}$ ....(11),

and seconds of $\Delta' - \Delta$

$$= G \sec \dfrac{h'-h}{2} \operatorname{cosec} \dfrac{h'+h}{2} \cdot \dfrac{\sin P'}{P'} \cdot \dfrac{\Delta' - \Delta}{\sin(\Delta' - \Delta)}$$

$$- \sin(\Delta' + \Delta) \cot \dfrac{h'+h}{2} \cdot \dfrac{\tan \dfrac{h'-h}{2}}{\dfrac{h'-h}{2}} \cdot \dfrac{\Delta' - \Delta}{\sin(\Delta' - \Delta)}$$

$$\times \text{seconds in } \dfrac{h'-h}{2} \text{.................(12)}.$$

Formulæ (11) and (12) are then put into a logarithmic form and solved by successive approximation, the convergence being very rapid.

22. Taking now the known equation

$$c^2 = d^2 + \sin \Delta \sin D \cdot a^2,$$

where $c =$ geocentric distance between moon's centre and corresponding point,

$a =$ difference of R.A. of point and centre,

and $d =$ difference of N.P.D., D and Δ being the absolute N.P.D.'s; we solve it by assuming

$$\tan^2 \psi = \dfrac{a^2}{d^2} \sin D \sin \Delta,$$

and therefore $\quad c = d \sec \psi.$

Now, c being the computed value of the distance of the corresponding point from the moon's centre, and s the tabular geocentric semi-diameter, let $c + \delta c$ and $s + \delta s$ be their true values. Then we shall have to satisfy the equation

$$s + \delta s = c + \delta c,$$

or $s - c + \delta s = \delta c,$

but, since $\quad c^2 = d^2 + \sin \Delta \sin D \cdot a^2,$

we get, by differentiating all the quantities,

$$\delta c = \frac{d}{c}\delta d + \frac{a^2}{2c}(\sin\Delta\cos D\,\delta D + \cos\Delta\sin D\,\delta\Delta) + \sin\Delta\sin D \cdot \frac{a}{c}\delta a$$

$$= \frac{d}{c}(\delta\Delta - \delta D) + \frac{a^2}{2c}(\sin\Delta\cos D\,\delta D + \cos\Delta\sin D\,\delta\Delta)$$

$$+ \sin\Delta\sin D \cdot \frac{a}{c}\delta a$$

= (without sensible error, since a^2 is a very small quantity, and Δ and D are so nearly equal),

$$\frac{d}{c}(\delta\Delta - \delta D) + \frac{a^2}{4c}\sin(\Delta + D)(\delta\Delta + \delta D) + \sin\Delta\sin D \cdot \frac{a}{c}\delta a$$

$$= \left\{\frac{d}{c} + \frac{a^2}{4c}\sin(\Delta + D)\right\}\delta\Delta + \left\{\frac{d}{c} - \frac{a^2}{4c}\sin(\Delta + D)\right\}\delta D$$

$$+ \sin\Delta\sin D \cdot \frac{a}{c}\delta a;$$

or, if D be greater than Δ,

$$= \left\{\frac{d}{c} + \frac{a^2}{4c}\sin(\Delta + D)\right\}\delta D + \left\{\frac{d}{c} - \frac{a^2}{4c}\sin(\Delta + D)\right\}\delta\Delta$$

$$+ \sin\Delta\sin D \cdot \frac{a}{c}\delta a$$

$$= \alpha\delta D + \beta\delta\Delta + \gamma\delta a \text{ suppose} \ldots\ldots\ldots (13).$$

We shall now have to substitute in this equation the values of δD, $\delta\Delta$, and of $\delta a\,(= \delta\alpha - \delta A)$, where A is the R.A. and D the N.P.D. of the corresponding point.

Thus, commencing with the star, if the R.A. and N.P.D. be increased by e and f, the R.A. and N.P.D. of the corresponding point will be increased sensibly by the same quantities.

Also, if the horizontal parallax be increased by $\frac{1}{n}$ th part, the effect of parallax on the R.A. and N.P.D. of the corresponding point will be increased in the same proportion, that is, the R.A. will be increased or lessened by $\frac{h'-h}{n}$ accordingly as the

EQUATION BETWEEN THE ERRORS OF ELEMENTS. 365

hour-angle is west or east, and the N.P.D. will be lessened by $\frac{\Delta' - \Delta}{n}$.

Again, if δt be the error of the observed time of immersion or emersion, or of the time for which the position and parallax of the moon has been calculated from the ephemeris, then, by the change of hour-angle of corresponding point in this time, the parallax, and therefore the position of corresponding point, will be altered by the quantities formulated in page 359, and at the same time the variation of R.A. and N.P.D. of the moon's centre in δt will be $+ m'\delta t$ and $\pm n'\delta t$, where m' and n' represent the motions in a second of time.

From these considerations it will be easily seen, x and y being the tabular errors of R.A. and N.P.D. of the moon's centre, that

$$\text{moon's corrected R.A.} = \alpha + x + m'\delta t,$$
$$\text{N.P.D.} = \Delta + y + n'\delta t;$$

geocentric R.A. of corresponding point $= A + e +$ correction for change of parallax in $\delta t \pm$ correction for increase of parallax;

and geocentric N.P.D. of corresponding point $= D + f +$ parallax-corrections;

$$\therefore \delta\alpha = x + m'\delta t, \quad \delta\Delta = y + m'\delta t,$$
$$\delta A = e + \text{parallax-corrections},$$
$$\delta D = f + \text{parallax-corrections},$$

and the student will find no difficulty in forming equation (13) on page 363, in any particular case, remembering that a is always to be esteemed positive in taking the difference between α and A.

23. *On the application of observations of Solar Eclipses or of Occultations of Stars by the Moon, to the correction of Geographical Longitudes approximately known.*

An intelligent traveller furnished with a portable-transit, a chronometer, and a sextant, will never find any difficulty in finding an approximate longitude of the station he is visiting, either by the method of moon-culminating stars, or of lunar distances, or of the time of moon's greatest altitude. If in addition to this he be fortunate enough, in an unknown region, to observe the local time of the beginning or ending of a solar eclipse, or of the immersion or emersion of some star occulted by the moon, he will, if he have also got a tolerably correct value of the latitude by some of the processes explained in the last chapter, be able, as soon as he has time to make the requisite calculations, to obtain a much closer approximation to the true longitude.

The method of doing this is almost obvious from the investigation of Article 21. Thus, having assumed a longitude, he will compute the Greenwich mean time of the observation (which we will suppose to be that of an occultation of a star) and will, by interpolation from the data of the *Nautical Almanac*, find the values of geocentric R.A. and N.P.D. of moon's centre and of the equatorial horizontal parallax and semi-diameter; and will also take out from the *Nautical Almanac* (*Elements of Occultations*) the R.A. and N.P.D. of the star, or of the apparent point of the moon's limb where the occultation took place.

The difference between the sidereal local time of the observation (reduced to arc and called the *R.A. of the zenith*) and the R.A. of the star will give the value of h', and he will then proceed to calculate the values of $h'-h$ and $D'-D$, and thus obtain the value of h, and therefore of A (= sidereal time of observation − western hour-angle) and D, that is, of the geocentric R.A. and N.P.D. of the point corresponding to that at which the contact with the limb took place. The difference of R.A. (a) and N.P.D. (d) of the moon's centre and this point are connected by the equation

$$c^2 = d^2 + \sin \Delta \sin D \cdot a^2,$$

and c must be calculated by the formula

$$c = d \sec \psi,$$

where $$\tan^2 \psi = \frac{a^2}{d^2} \sin D \sin \Delta.$$

The coefficients of $\delta\Delta$, δD, (which may be assumed to be equal, the term multiplied by a^2 being omitted) and δa must then be calculated, and the equation (13) formed, or the expression for δc in terms of the errors of Δ, D, and a.

This value of δc must then be equated to

$$s - c + \delta s,$$

and the final equation must be formed, by substituting for δa, $\delta a - \delta A$; and finding the values of δa, δA, $\delta \Delta$, and δD, according to the precepts of Article 22.

We shall thus arrive at an equation of the form

$$s - c + \delta s = Ee + Ef - Gx - Hy \pm I\delta t \pm K\delta P.$$

Now, the places of the stars are so well known at present, at least such as are usually occulted by the moon, that we are always sure of finding a place for a star so correct as to enable us to put $e = 0$ and $f = 0$; Hansen's Tables are also so correct that we may put $x = 0$, $y = 0$, and $\delta P = 0$.

Hence our equation becomes

$$s - c + \delta s = I\delta t,$$

or, if we put also $\delta s = 0$,

$$\delta t = \frac{s - c}{I}.$$

Now, if the observation of the time of immersion or emersion be supposed correct, δt will arise simply from error of assumed longitude, and its magnitude will be proportional to the difference of s and c. If then, on a first assumption of longitude, the calculated value of c result greatly larger or smaller than that of s, a new assumption must be made, by the use of the approximate correction $\delta t = \frac{s - c}{I}$, and the calculations must be repeated two or three times, if necessary, with the successively corrected values.

24. If the time of first or last contact in a *solar eclipse* be the basis of calculation, then the relative parallax and the relative motion of the sun and moon must be used, and the parallax must be applied to the moon. The augmentation of moon's semi-diameter must also be applied. In this case c will

368   BESSEL'S METHOD.

be equal to the sum or difference of the semi-diameters of the sun and moon. For the details of the process *See a paper by Professor Challis in the Supplement to the Nautical Almanac for 1854.*

25. *Bessel's method of treating Occultations.*

Though the method previously given leaves very little to be desired in the combination of perfect accuracy with simplicity of calculation, yet the subject would not be complete without some explanation of Bessel's theory, which is superior to all others in symmetry and elegance, and can be applied better to finding the longitude of an unknown station.

If we conceive a cylinder to envelope the moon, of which the axis is the line joining the centre of the moon and the star, then when the occultation of the star is observed at any point of the earth's surface, that point must be in the surface of the cylinder produced to meet the earth, and, as the star is at an infinite distance, all observers situated in the curve in which the cylinder intersects the earth's surface will see the occultation at the same moment of absolute time.

Using Bessel's notation, let now π be the horizontal equatorial parallax of the moon; α and δ the R.A. and declination of her centre; a and d those of the star; μ the R.A. of the zenith (sidereal time of observation multiplied by 15); and for the system of co-ordinates let the earth's centre be the origin; the axis of z parallel to the line joining the centre of the moon and the star, that of x in the equator, and having the R.A. $90° + \alpha$; and that of y having R.A. a and declination $90° + d$.

Let now ξ and η be the co-ordinates of the observer's position (or of one of the points where the cylinder intersects the earth's surface), and x and y of the centre of the moon; then the distance of the centre of the moon from the origin will be $\frac{1}{\sin \pi}$, if the earth's equatorial radius be taken as the unit of linear measure, and it can be easily shewn that

$$\xi = \rho \cos \phi' \sin (\mu - a) \quad \ldots\ldots\ldots\ldots\ldots\ldots\ldots\ldots (14),$$

and $\quad \eta = \rho \{\sin \phi' \cos d - \cos \phi' \sin d \cos (\mu - a)\} \ldots \ldots (15)$.

Also
$$x = \frac{1}{\sin \pi} \{\cos \delta \sin (\alpha - a)\} \ldots \ldots \ldots \ldots \ldots \ldots (16),$$

and $\quad y = \dfrac{1}{\sin \pi} \{\sin \delta \cos d - \cos \delta \sin d \cos (\alpha - a)\} \ldots (17)$;

and, since the plane of xy is perpendicular to the axis of the cylinder which envelopes the moon, it is plain that if we call the moon's semi-diameter k (in Bessel's notation l),

$$k^2 = (x - \xi)^2 + (y - \eta)^2 \ldots \ldots \ldots \ldots \ldots (18).$$

Since $\alpha - a$ is a very small angle, and δ is nearly equal to d, it will be more convenient to write equation (17) in the form

$$y = \frac{1}{\sin \pi} \{\sin (\delta - d) \cos^2 \tfrac{1}{2}(\alpha - a) + \sin (\delta + d) \sin^2 \tfrac{1}{2}(\alpha - a)\} \ldots (19).$$

Also for k we may put the value previously used, namely $0 \cdot 2729$, which is that assumed by Hansen as derived from the Greenwich Observations (*Table de la Lune*, page 39).

In the use of these equations for the determination of longitude, μ is known from the sidereal time of observation, and therefore the values of ξ and η can be immediately calculated.

For the calculation of x and y, let t be the local mean solar time of the observation, and $t - \omega$ the corresponding mean time on the first meridian (Greenwich for example) for which the places of the moon are calculated in the Ephemeris which is used. Thus ω is the *east* longitude of the place of observation. Let also τ be a time arbitrarily chosen, yet differing so little from $t - \omega$, that, during the interval $t - \omega - \tau$, the moon's motion may be supposed uniform, and x and y may be represented with sufficient accuracy by the expressions

$$x = x_0 + n(t - \omega - \tau) \sin N + dx,$$
$$y = y_0 + n(t - \omega - \tau) \cos N + dy,$$

where $n \sin N$ and $n \cos N$ represent the changes of x and y for the unit of time in which t, ω, τ are expressed, and are obtained by differencing three or four values of x and y calculated at short intervals on each side of the time $t - \omega - \tau$; and dx and dy are the tabular errors of x and y, depending on $d\alpha$, $d\delta$, da, $d(d)$, and $d\pi$.

Substituting these values in equation (18), and attributing an error dk to k, we get

$$(k + dk)^2 = \{x_0 - \xi + n(t - \omega - \tau) \sin N + dx\}^2$$
$$+ \{y_0 - \eta + n(t - \omega - \tau) \cos N + dy\}^2.$$

And, putting for $x_0 - \xi$ and $y_0 - \eta$, $m \sin M$ and $m \cos M$, and developing, (neglecting k^2)

$$k^2 + 2k \cdot dk = n^2(t - \omega - \tau)^2 + 2nm(t - \omega - \tau) \cos(M - N)$$
$$+ 2n(t - \omega - \tau)(\sin N \, dx + \cos N \, dy)$$
$$+ (m \sin M + dx)^2 + (m \cos M + dy)^2$$
$$= n(t - \omega - \tau) + m \cos(M - N) + (\sin N \, dx + \cos N \, dy)^2$$
$$+ m^2 \sin^2(M - N) + 2m\{\sin M - \cos(M - N) \sin N\} dx$$
$$+ 2m\{\cos M - \cos(M - N) \cos N\} dy,$$

and, if we put λ for $\sin N \, dx + \cos N \, dy$,

and λ' for $- \cos N \, dx + \sin N \, dy$,

we shall have very approximately

$$k^2 + 2k \, dk = \{n(t - \omega - \tau) + \lambda + m \cos(M - N)\}^2$$
$$+ \{m \sin(M - N) - \lambda'\}^2.$$

Lastly, let $\sin \psi = \dfrac{m}{k} \sin(M - N)$;

$$\therefore 1 + \frac{2dk}{k} - \left(\sin \psi - \frac{\lambda'}{k}\right)^2 = \left\{\frac{n}{k}(t - \omega - \tau) + \frac{\lambda}{k} + \frac{m}{k}\cos(M - N)\right\}^2,$$

or
$$\frac{n}{k}(t-\omega-\tau)+\frac{\lambda}{k}+\frac{m}{k}\cos(M-N)$$

$$=\pm\sqrt{\cos^2\psi+2\frac{\lambda'}{k}\sin\psi+\frac{2dk}{k}}$$

$$=\pm\{\cos\psi+\frac{\lambda'}{k}\tan\psi+\frac{dk}{k}\sec\psi\};$$

$$\therefore\ t-\omega-\tau=-\frac{m}{n}\cos(M-N)-\frac{\lambda}{n}$$

$$\pm\left\{\frac{k}{n}\cos\psi+\frac{\lambda'}{n}\tan\psi+\frac{dk}{n}\sec\psi\right\},$$

from which ω, or the longitude, can be found immediately.

[For a method essentially the same as that of Bessel the reader may consult a paper by Captain A. R. Clarke, R.E., in Vol. XXIX. of the *Memoirs of the R. A. S*].

APPENDIX.

ON THE ANNUAL PARALLAX OF THE FIXED STARS.

1. By inadvertence this subject was not treated of in its proper place, which would have been either at the end of the Chapter on Parallax, or of that on Aberration.

The stars are all situated at distances from the earth so immense that the angle which the earth's radius subtends at any one of them is immeasurably small, but it is not so certain that the radius of the earth's *orbit* does not subtend a measurable angle at some of them, and indeed it is certain by the measures of Bessel and other Astronomers, that this angle is measurable in the case of 61 Cygni. This displacement in the star's position is called Annual Parallax, and we will proceed to investigate its laws.

2. The maximum parallax or constant of parallax is analogous to the horizontal parallax of the sun, moon, and planets;

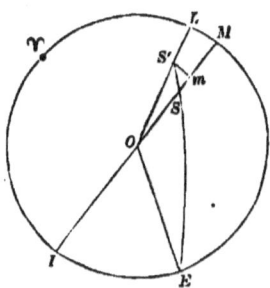

ANNUAL PARALLAX.

that is, it is the angle which would be subtended at the star by the radius of the earth's orbit, supposing the star to be situated in the pole of the ecliptic. We will denote this by ϕ. Let ΥIE be the ecliptic and E the position of the earth, the sun being the centre of the circle. Then, just as in the case of planetary parallax, if S be the true position of a star, and S' its apparent position as affected by parallax ($S'SE$ being the arc of a great circle),

$$SS' = \phi \sin SE,$$

and, if O be the centre of the circle, or the projection of the pole of the ecliptic, and great circles $OS'L$ and OSM be drawn, the angle LOM is the parallax in longitude. Draw now $S'm$ perpendicular to OM.

Then parallax in longitude = angle IOM

$$= \frac{S'm}{\cos S'L} = \phi \frac{\sin ISE \sin SE}{\cos SL} \text{ nearly}$$

$$= \phi \frac{\sin IE}{\cos SL}$$

$$= \phi \frac{\sin (\text{earth's longitude} - \text{star's longitude} + 180°)}{\cos SL}$$

$$= \phi \frac{\sin (\odot - l)}{\cos \lambda},$$

if l and λ be the longitude and latitude of the star, and $\odot$ the sun's longitude as usual.

Again the parallax in latitude

$$= Sm = - SS' \cos ISE$$

$$= - \phi \sin SE \cos ISE$$

$$= - \phi \sin SE \cos SEI \cos IE$$

$$= - \phi \sin IS \cos IE$$

$$= - \phi \sin (180° - \lambda) \cos (\odot - l)$$

$$= - \phi \sin \lambda \cos (\odot - l).$$

FORMULA FOR γ DRACONIS.

Now aberration in longitude

$$= -20''\cdot 45 \frac{\cos(\odot - l)}{\cos \lambda},$$

and aberration in latitude

$$= -20''\cdot 45 \sin \lambda \sin(\odot - l).$$

If then we denote by α and β the aberrations taken out for the value $90° + \odot$, we shall have

aberration in longitude, $\quad \alpha = + 20''\cdot 45 \dfrac{\sin(\odot - l)}{\cos \lambda},$

.... latitude, $\quad \beta = -20''\cdot 45 \sin \lambda \cos(\odot - l);$

that is, parallax in longitude $= \dfrac{\alpha \phi}{20''\cdot 45},$

and parallax in latitude $= \dfrac{\beta \phi}{20''\cdot 45}.$

In the same way it can be shewn that we may find the parallax in R.A. and N.P.D. by substituting in the corresponding aberration formulæ $90° + \odot$ for $\odot$.

EXAMPLE. Find the parallax-factor in N.P.D. for γ Draconis, for which the mean R.A. for 1863, Jan. 1 is $17^h.53^m.25^s\cdot 53$, and the N.P.D. is $38°.29'.37''\cdot 64$.

The aberration-factor in N.P.D. is

$\cos \omega \cos \odot (\tan \omega \sin \Delta - \sin \alpha \cos \Delta) + \sin \odot \cos \alpha \cos \Delta$

$= + \cos \odot (\sin \omega \sin \Delta - \cos \omega \sin \alpha \cos \Delta)$

$\quad + \sin \odot \cos \alpha \cos \Delta,$

where $\qquad \omega = 23°.27'\cdot 3.$

Hence
$$\begin{aligned}
\text{Log sin } \omega &= 9\cdot 59993 \\
\text{Log sin } \Delta &= 9\cdot 79409 \\
\hline
\text{Sum} &= 9\cdot 39402 \\
\hline
\text{1st Number} &+ 0\cdot 24775 \\
\text{2nd Number} &+ 0\cdot 71772 \\
\hline
&+ 0\cdot 96547 \\
\hline
\end{aligned}$$

FORMULA FOR γ DRACONIS.

$-\text{Log} \cos \omega = -9.96255 \qquad \text{Log} \cos \alpha = -8.45765$
$\text{Log} \sin \alpha = -9.99982 \qquad \text{Log} \cos \Delta = 9.89358$
$\text{Log} \cos \Delta = 9.89358 \qquad \text{Sum} = -8.35123$
$\text{Sum} + 9.85595 \qquad \text{Number} = -0.02245$
$\text{2nd Number} + 0.71772$

therefore aberration-factor

$$= 0.96547 \cos \odot - 0.02245 \sin \odot.$$

Let now $\quad A \sin \phi = 0.96547,$
and $\quad\quad\quad A \cos \phi = -0.02245;$

$$\therefore A = \sqrt{(0.9655)^2 + (0.0225)^2}$$
$$= .9658,$$

and $\quad\quad\quad \cot \phi = -\dfrac{0.02245}{0.96547} = -0.02325;$

$$\therefore \phi = 91°.20'.$$

Hence aberration-factor $= + 0.9658 \sin (\odot + 91°.20'),$
and, if we increase $\odot$ by $90°,$
parallax-factor for N.P.D.

$$= -0.9658 \sin (\odot + 1°.20'),$$

and parallax-factor for N.Z.D.

$$= + 0.9658 \sin (\odot + 1°.20').$$

(See *Mem. R. A. S.*, Vol. XXIX., page 185).

3. Several attempts have been made to determine the parallax of some of the brightest fixed stars by means of meridian observations of N.P.D., but with very questionable success. The observations require to be of first-rate excellence to give any chance of success, and the uncertainty of refraction, unless (as in the case of γ Draconis observed at Greenwich) the zenith-

distance be very small, will produce uncertainty enough to prevent the detection of so small a quantity as the parallax. The observations of α Centauri made by Professor Henderson and Sir T. Maclear at the Cape of Good Hope, seem however to prove a parallax of about 1" for that star, and M. Peters of Altona, in a most valuable paper on annual parallax, printed in the *Astronomische Nachrichten*, has discussed his meridian observations of five other stars, Groombridge, 1830, ι Ursæ Majoris, Arcturus, Polaris, and Capella, to which he assigns very small parallaxes, varying from one-fifth of a second of space to half a tenth of a second. The only positive result however which is deducible from such very small quantities is the proof of the almost immeasurable distances of the stars in question, and the necessity of seeking for the parallaxes by some other more effectual method.

4. Now such a method was applied by Bessel in the case of 61 Cygni, by the use of the celebrated Heliometer at Konigsberg.

A heliometer differs in nothing from an equatorially mounted telescope, excepting in having a *divided* object-glass. The glass is cut through its centre, each half glass being fastened into a separate cell, and the cell is made capable of moving laterally by being attached to a sliding-plate moved by screws acted upon by rods which are within reach of the observer. Each half glass produces a separate image of the object which is viewed, (excepting in the case when the optical centres of the two coincide, or at the zero of measurement,) and the angular distance of the two images is proportional to the distance by which the centre of one half glass has been moved past the centre of the other. This distance is read off in parts of a scale attached to the sliding-plate, and the value of the scale can be determined in angular measure by taking transits of the two images corresponding to different readings of the scale, over a system of wires in the eye-piece, or by some other equivalent method.

5. It will be readily seen that a heliometer enables an astronomer to measure with great accuracy moderate angular

distances, such as the distance between the components of a double star, or the diameter of a planet, and it is by this means that it is so useful in the investigation of annual parallax. It can be easily proved as in the case of the aberration-curve (page 151) that, if a star has sensible parallax, it will appear to describe in the course of a year an ellipse about its mean place, and that therefore if it be in the neighbourhood of a star of which the parallax is insensible, it will alternately approach to and recede from this latter star. Now 61 Cygni is a double star of which the components are of about the 5th and 6th magnitudes, and 18" apart, and Bessel, using for his point of reference the middle point of the space between the two stars, measured the distances of two small stars (a) and (b), one of which lay nearly in the direction of the line joining the stars, and the other at right angles to this direction, the distances being about 462" and 706" from the principal star.

It would be easy to prove that the maxima and minima of parallax in distance in the direction of these stars would be separated by an interval of about half a year, and in fact the formulæ expressing the parallactic effects are the following:

Parallax in distance of (a) from 61 Cygni is

$$\phi \times 0{\cdot}909 \sin (\odot - 9^\circ.7'),$$

Parallax in distance of (b) from 61 Cygni is

$$\phi \times 0{\cdot}894 \cos (\odot - 24^\circ.45'),$$

that is, they involve, the one the sine, and the other the cosine of nearly the same arcs. (See *Mem. of R. A. S.*, Vol. XII., page 46.)

If then the screw by which the measures were made should be differently affected by temperature at different seasons of the year, so that, on this account, an effect might be produced on the measures having an annual period and therefore similar to parallax, it would be impossible that the fluctuations in the measures with reference to *both* the stars should be confounded with parallax, if they had their origin in temperature; and if, on the contrary, the fluctuations should have their maxima and minima in both cases in conformity with the formulæ representing the parallax, and should agree in giving nearly the same value of the constant, there would remain very little doubt of the certainty of the result. Now this severe test was perfectly well answered, and the parallax assigned to 61 Cygni by Bessel was $0''\cdot369$. Mr Johnson, with the still more excellent heliometer of Oxford, has verified this value, the mean of his results being $0''\cdot402$.

We are then confident that we know within tolerable limits of accuracy the distance from the sun of one star in the heavens, but with regard to all other stars to which a measurable parallax has been assigned, we may still reserve our opinion. Even with regard to α Centauri, it is most desirable that the parallax of $1''$ attributed to it by Mr Henderson and Sir T. Maclear should be substantiated by differential measures of its position with regard to some neighbouring star.

On Third Differences of Functions, and Differences of a still higher order.

6. The method of interpolation by second differences has been explained at page 315, but, in many cases which occur in Astronomy, third differences, or even fourth differences, would be necessary to give results with the required degree of accuracy.

We will proceed to explain the method to be pursued when third differences are required.

Let $\delta = a + bt + ct^2 + dt^3,$

and let $\delta_{-2}, \delta_{-1}, \delta_0, \delta_{+1}, \delta_{+2}$ be the values of δ corresponding to the values of $t, -2, -1, 0, +1,$ and $+2$; then, as before,

	1st Diff.	2nd Diff.	3rd Diff.
$\delta_{-2} = a - 2b + 4c - 8d$			
	$b - 3c + 7d$		
$\delta_{-1} = a - b + c - d$		$+2c - 6d$	
	$b - c + d$		$+6d$
$\delta_0 = a$		$+2c$	$+6d$
	$b + c + d$		
$\delta_{+1} = a + b + c + d$		$+2c + 6d$	
	$b + 3c + 7d$		
$\delta_{+2} = a + 2b + 4c + 8d$			

THIRD AND FOURTH DIFFERENCES. 379

And, if Σ_1, Σ_2, and Σ_3 be the sums of the 1st, 2nd, and 3rd differences respectively, it is plain that

$$d = \frac{1}{12}\Sigma_3, \quad c = \frac{1}{6}\Sigma_2, \quad b = \frac{1}{4}\Sigma_1 - 4d.$$

7. The student will have no difficulty in finding by *fourth* differences the values of b, c, d, and e, in the equation

$$\delta = a + bt + ct^2 + dt^3 + et^4,$$

if a higher order than the third is necessary.

It would be found for example that, if seven consecutive values of the function were taken, corresponding to the values of t, -3, -2, -1, 0, $+1$, $+2$, and $+3$, and the differences be taken to the fourth order (Σ_4 being their sum),

$$e = \frac{1}{72}\Sigma_4, \quad d = \frac{1}{24}\Sigma_3, \quad c = \frac{1}{10}\Sigma_2 - 13e, \text{ and } b = \frac{1}{6}\Sigma_1 - 9d.$$

If only five consecutive values of the function be taken, and Δ_4 be the 4th difference,

$$e = \frac{1}{24}\Delta_4, \quad d = \frac{1}{12}\Sigma_3, \quad c = \frac{1}{6}\Sigma_2 - 5e,$$

and

$$b = \frac{1}{4}\Sigma_1 - 4d.$$

COR. By a process of approximation similar to that used at page 323, it may be shewn that

$$t = \frac{x}{b} - \frac{c}{b} \cdot \frac{x^2}{b^2} + \left(\frac{2c^2}{b^2} - \frac{d}{b}\right)\frac{x^3}{b^3} - \left(\frac{5c^3}{b^3} - \frac{5cd}{b^2} + \frac{e}{b}\right)\frac{x^4}{b^4}$$

$$+ \left(\frac{14c^4}{b^4} - \frac{21c^2d}{b^3} + \frac{6ce}{b^2} - \frac{3d^2}{b^2}\right)\frac{x^5}{b^5}.$$

EXAMPLES AND PROBLEMS.

1. What is meant by the *mean of the wires* of a Transit-instrument? The intervals in time between the transits of a star across five successive wires being $10^s, 11^s, 9^s, 10^s$; find the time of transit across the mean of the wires: the time of transit across the 1st wire being $9^h.20^m$.

2. If the western pivot of a transit-instrument be a'' higher and β'' more to the north than the eastern, a star is unaffected whose N.P.D. is

$$= \text{co-latitude} + \tan^{-1}\left(\frac{\tan \alpha}{\tan \beta}\right).$$

3. Prove that in the interval between the sun's transit and culmination, his centre describes an hour-angle whose sine equals $\dfrac{m \sin (l - \delta)}{\cos l \cos \delta}$ very nearly; l being the latitude of the place, δ the declination of sun's centre, and m the ratio of the apparent motion of the sun's centre in declination and right ascension.

4. If t be the interval (in arc) of the passage of a star whose N.P.D. Δ is small, between the middle wire of a transit telescope, supposed in the meridian, and any other wire, and if a be the equatorial interval between the wires, shew that it will be determined by

$$\tan a = \frac{\sin \Delta \sin t}{1 - 2\sin^2 \Delta \sin^2 \frac{t}{2}}.$$

EXAMPLES AND PROBLEMS.

5. A transit instrument being fixed so that its plane of motion coincides with the prime vertical, the time of transit of a known star is noted as it passes this line on each side of the meridian; calculate the latitude of the place of observation.

6. Shew that in the course of any day the highest point of the ecliptic describes in the sky about the highest point of the equator an oval which may be defined by the intersection with a sphere of a cone of the 4th order.

7. Find when the inclination of the ecliptic to the horizon increases fastest.

8. Express the latitude and longitude of a star in terms of its observed altitude and azimuth, the observations being made at a given place, when the first point of Aries was on the meridian.

9. The number of seconds occupied by the sun in rising on a given day and at a given place, may nearly be represented by
$$\frac{132}{\sqrt{\cos{(l+\delta)}\cos{(l-\delta)}}},$$
l being the latitude, and δ the sun's declination.

10. At a place in latitude l, a wall of height h has an azimuth of $a°$ to the east of south; shew that at the time of the equinox, the wall casts no shadow at a time denoted by $\frac{1}{15}\tan^{-1}(\sin l \tan a)$ hours before noon: and that at noon the breadth of the shadow is $= h \tan l \sin a$.

11. At a place in the arctic zone the sun will remain above the horizon at the summer solstice for $\frac{365}{\pi}\cos^{-1}\left(\frac{\cos l}{\sin \omega}\right)$ days, neglecting the excentricity of the earth's orbit, l and ω being the latitude of the place and the obliquity of the ecliptic.

12. Three stars A, B, C, are very nearly in a great circle, the angle ABC being $180° - \beta$, where β is small: if t be the time which elapses between the great circles AB and BC being vertical, γ the co-latitude; then
$$t = \frac{\sin z}{\cos A \sin \gamma} \cdot \frac{\beta}{15},$$
where z is the zenith distance and A the azimuth of B.

EXAMPLES AND PROBLEMS.

13. Shew that when the sun rises in the N.E., at a place in latitude l, the time of sunrise is $\dfrac{1}{30}\cos^{-1}(-\sin^2 l)$.

14. Shew that the time at which the sun is south-east may be determined by means of the expression

$$\frac{1}{15}\{\phi - \sin^{-1}(\tan \delta \cos l \cos \phi)\},$$

where δ is the sun's north declination, l is the latitude of the place, and $\tan \phi = \sin l$.

15. Given the latitude of a place, find the time of the year when a given star rises at a given hour.

16. On a given day, in a given latitude, the sun being in the meridian, determine geometrically the angle at which a rod of given length must be inclined to the horizon, that its shadow may be the greatest possible.

17. The altitudes of two stars as they pass the prime vertical are observed, and the difference of their R.A.'s. is known; find the latitude of the place.

18. In a given latitude, find the altitude of the sun on the day of the equinox, at 9 in the morning.

19. If P be the pole of the heavens, Z the zenith, and S a given star, find when the angle ZSP increases fastest.

20. At what hour, in a given latitude, will the vertical circle passing through a known star cut the equator at a given angle?

21. In any latitude find when the time of rising of the sun's disk bears the greatest ratio to the time of its crossing the meridian.

22. Determine when the sum of the zenith distances of two known stars in a given latitude is a maximum.

23. The times of the sun's rising and setting being calculated for a given place, what correction is necessary to make them serve for another place not far distant from it?

EXAMPLES AND PROBLEMS.

24. Supposing the sun to remain above the horizon a given number of days, find the latitude.

25. Find the azimuth of two known stars which are seen at the same instant in one vertical plane.

26. If a body fall to the earth in the time t'', the deviation to the east of the point from which it fell will be $\frac{1}{2} g a t^3 \cos l$; where l is the latitude, and a the angle described by the earth in $1''$.

27. In a given latitude a vertical rod is placed at a given distance from an east and west wall, so as to cast a portion of its shadow upon it; find the equation to the extremity of the shadow traced upon the wall on a given day.

28. If D be the apparent diameter of the sun, θ the altitude of its centre, and s_1, and s_2 the respective lengths of the pure shadow and penumbra, cast by a vertical rod upon a horizontal plane, prove that

$$\frac{s_1}{s_2} = \frac{1}{2}\left(\frac{\sin 2\theta}{\sin D} - 1\right).$$

29. Determine the position of the place nearest to the north pole, at which the sun rises on a given day at the same instant as at Greenwich. If y, z, be the zeniths of the place and of Greenwich, and yzx a quadrant of a great circle on the celestial sphere, the projection of the locus of x on the horizon of z is an arc of an ellipse, whose excentricity = cosine of latitude of Greenwich.

30. The altitudes of a star when it crosses the meridian of a place and the prime vertical are a, a'; shew that, if δ be the declination of the star and l the latitude of the place,

$$\cot \delta = \sec a \operatorname{cosec} a' - \tan a,$$
$$\cot l = \tan a - \sec a \sin a'.$$

31. Shew that the time of sunset is earliest some days before, and the time of sunrise latest some days after, the shortest day.

32. If l, δ be a star's latitude and declination, its distance (d) from the sun, at the moment of his crossing the equator, may be found from the equation

$$\sin^2 d \sin^2 \omega = \sin^2 l - 2 \cos \omega \sin l \sin \delta + \sin^2 \delta.$$

33. At a place on the equator the lengths of the shadows at noon of a vertical rod are h and h', towards the north and south respectively, on successive days: determine approximately the time of the vernal equinox.

34. What is the latitude of a place at which, at the time of an equinox, a star is on the horizon when the sun rises, and on the prime vertical when it sets? Shew that when the sun and this star are on the meridian of any place at the same time, the declination of the sun and star being δ', δ respectively,

$$\tan \delta' = \tan \delta \tan \omega,$$

(ω being the obliquity).

35. Explain the reason why a ship in sailing round the world counts one day too much or too little accordingly as she starts eastward or westward.

Supposing that the ship in sailing touches successively at various places, where will the loss or gain of a day first begin to appear?

36. On January 1st, 1856, the equation of time was $+3^m.36^s.04$ at apparent noon, and on January 2nd, 1856, the equation of time was $+4^m.48^s.0$ at apparent noon. What was the *apparent time at mean noon* on January 1st?

37. If x be the time (expressed in angle) that the clock is before the sun when the sun's mean longitude is l—due to the obliquity of the ecliptic (ω) alone—shew that

$$\tan x = - \frac{\sin^2 \frac{\omega}{2} \sin 2l}{\cos^2 \frac{\omega}{2} + \sin^2 \frac{\omega}{2} \cos 2l}.$$

38. If the obliquity were small and $=n°$, the maximum value of the equation of time would be very nearly $\frac{\pi}{3}n^2$ seconds of time.

39. A style projects from the vertex of an upright cone; trace the hour-lines on the surface of the cone: and find the time of day during which the dial will serve.

40. Shew that if the hour-angle of a body at any instant, and the mean time, be known, its R.A. may be determined.

41. The time of the sun's rising and setting on Nov. 1st are found from the tables to be $6^h.56^m$, and $4^h.32^m$: find approximately the equation of time.

42. If the sun's distance below the horizon when *twilight* ends be $18°$, its duration at the equator is

$$\frac{12}{\pi}\sin^{-1}\left(\frac{\sin\frac{\pi}{10}}{\cos\delta}\right) \text{ hours.}$$

43. Why is the mean duration of twilight shorter at the equator than elsewhere, and when is its duration there shortest?

44. Assuming that the angular displacement of a star, due to refraction, may be expressed in a series, ascending by odd powers of the tangent of the star's apparent zenith-distance, explain how the coefficients of such a series may be determined.

45. Prove that if c be the sun's depression below the horizon when twilight ceases at a place whose latitude is λ, and the angle at the sun made by great circles through the zenith and the pole be S at that time, and S' at sunset, the duration T of twilight is given by the equation

$$\sin^2\frac{T}{2} = \frac{1 - \cos c \cos(S' - S)}{2\cos^2\lambda}.$$

46. From the observed altitudes and azimuths of two stars near the zenith their distance from one another is found. Find the correction to be applied to this distance in consequence of refraction.

47. At what time of the year will the aberration in declination of a star whose right ascension is 90°, vanish?

What was Bradley's object in observing γ *Draconis*, when he discovered *aberration;* and why did he select that particular star for observation?

48. In consequence of the aberration of light, every star appears to describe an ellipse in the heavens, of which the true place of the star is the centre. Prove this, and find the axes of the ellipse.

49. State how the sun, planets, and fixed stars are affected by aberration; and shew that the part of the aberration arising from the motion of the planet varies as $\dfrac{\cos SPT}{\sqrt{SP}}$, S being the sun, T the earth, and P the planet.

50. If, at a place between the tropics, z be the zenith distance of a known star, when the ecliptic comes upon the zenith of the place of observation, and θ the longitude of the earth, when the corresponding aberration in zenith distance vanishes, prove that θ is determined by the equation,

$$\cot(\theta - \lambda) = \frac{\sin^2 \beta \cos z}{\sqrt{\sin(z+\beta)\sin(z-\beta)}},$$

when λ and β are the longitude and latitude of the star.

51. Determine the positions of all stars such that when the aberration either in right-ascension or declination vanishes, the other shall be a maximum.

52. If $z =$ true zenith distance of a planet, $p =$ its actual parallax in zenith distance, and $P =$ horizontal parallax; then

$$\tan\left(\frac{z}{2} + p\right) = \tan\frac{z}{2} \tan\left(\frac{\pi}{4} + \frac{P}{2}\right).$$

53. If $S =$ surface of a portion of the earth $ABCD$, AB being an arc of the equator, and AC, BD two arcs of circles of latitude; also if $AB = c$, $AC = a$, $BD = b$, then will

$$\tan\frac{S}{2} = \frac{\sin\dfrac{a+b}{2}}{\cos\dfrac{a-b}{2}} \tan\frac{c}{2}.$$

EXAMPLES AND PROBLEMS. 387

54. Having given the latitudes of two places on the earth's surface, one of which is N.E. of the other, find the difference of their longitudes and their distance from each other, considering the earth a sphere.

55. If λ, λ' be the latitudes of two stations on the same meridian, prove that the length of the arc included between them is

$$b(\lambda' - \lambda)\left\{1 + \frac{e}{2} - \frac{3e}{2}\cos(\lambda' + \lambda)\frac{\sin(\lambda' - \lambda)}{\lambda' - \lambda}\right\},$$

where $$e = \frac{a-b}{a}.$$

56. The angle of depression of the sun's upper limb at setting is observed, from a certain position upon the mast of a ship, to be δ; the same observation is made soon afterwards from a position upon the mast h feet higher, when the depression is found to be δ'; the ship is supposed stationary: prove that the earth's radius $= \dfrac{h}{\delta' - \delta} \cdot \dfrac{\cos^2 \delta}{\sin \delta}$, approximately.

57. Given the precession in R.A. of a star, find the corresponding change in the angle of position.

58. Explain the method by which the accurate values of the elements of a planet's orbit may be found, when approximate values of those elements are known.

59. Shew that the time occupied by the sun in passing through the rth sign of the zodiac, reckoning Aries the 1st, is approximately,

$$M\left\{1 + \frac{24e \sin 15°}{\pi}\cos(B + 15° - r \times 30°)\right\},$$

where M is the twelfth part of the year, B the angular distance of the solar perigee from the autumnal equinox, and e the excentricity of the earth's orbit.

60. If u be the excentric anomaly of a planet's orbit, and x, y, z the co-ordinates of its place at a given time, referred to

any rectangular planes passing through the sun's centre, then the co-ordinates may be expressed as follows:

$$x = A \sin(u+\alpha) + B, \qquad y = A' \sin(u+\alpha') + B',$$
$$z = A'' \sin(u+\alpha'') + B'',$$

where A, α, B, &c. are constants.

61. If α be the angle of elongation of an inferior planet, when observed to be stationary, from another planet, shew that $\cot \alpha = \sqrt{n^2 + n}$; where n is the ratio of the distance of the superior planet from the sun to that of the inferior; the orbits of the planets being supposed circular, and in the same plane.

62. Assuming the sun's motion in longitude to be uniform, shew that if α, β, be the horary increments in right ascension and declination (expressed in solar measure), and α', β' the horary variations of α and β, then

$$\alpha' = 2\alpha\beta \tan \delta, \qquad \beta' = -\frac{\alpha^2}{2} \sin 2\delta.$$

63. When a planet is stationary shew that its elongation from the sun is $\tan^{-1} \dfrac{n}{\sqrt{1+n}}$, where n is the ratio of the radius of its orbit to that of the earth.

64. If the longitudes of a planet in three different points of its orbit be a, b, c; and its latitudes α, β, γ; then will

$$\tan \beta \sin(c-a) = \tan \alpha \sin(c-b) + \tan \gamma \sin(b-a).$$

65. If the sun's longitude $= c$, and the obliquity of the ecliptic $= \omega$, then will the equation of time arising from the obliquity of the ecliptic

$$= \tan^2 \frac{\phi}{2} \sin 2c - \frac{1}{2} \tan^4 \frac{\phi}{2} \sin 4c + \frac{1}{3} \tan^6 \frac{\phi}{2} \sin 6c - \ldots$$

66. Find the perihelion distance of the comet, moving in the plane of the ecliptic, that remains the longest time within the earth's orbit.

EXAMPLES AND PROBLEMS.

67. What must be the relation of the distances from the sun of a superior and inferior planet, that their synodic revolutions may be equal?

68. Compare the portion of the surface of the earth illuminated by the sun in perigee, with that illuminated in apogee, taking into account the magnitude of the sun.

69. Given three distances of a planet from the sun, and the corresponding arguments of latitude, to find the place of the perihelion, and the true anomaly at the first observation.

70. Two planets, P_1, P_2, revolve in circular orbits at the distances r_1, r_2 from the sun, and when they appear stationary to one another, the cotangent of P's elongation seen from $P_1 = \frac{1}{2} \tan \theta$; shew that

$$\frac{r_1}{r_2} = \frac{1}{2} \tan \frac{\theta}{2} \tan \theta.$$

71. If l be the latitude of a place between the tropics, α and δ the sun's right ascension and declination; the times when the ecliptic is vertical are determined by the equation

$$h = \alpha + \sin^{-1}(\sin \alpha \tan l \cot \delta).$$

72. When that part (E) of the equation of time, which arises from the obliquity of the ecliptic (ω), is a maximum,

$$\sin E = \tan^2 \frac{\omega}{2}.$$

73. When Venus was very near conjunction it was observed that the bright visible crescent, instead of being a semicircle, was $240°$ of a circle; hence calculate the horizontal refraction produced by the planet's atmosphere.

74. Given the position of the moon's nodes and the inclination of her orbit to the ecliptic, to find when her latitude and declination are equal.

75. At a given hour on a given night the moon is observed to rise in the east point; determine the longitude of the node of her orbit, supposing its inclination to the ecliptic known.

76. A ship leaves London at noon on a certain day, and arrives at New Orleans (90° west longitude) at noon local time on the 30th day afterwards—what is the actual time of passage?

77. If two survey-stations upon the earth are mutually visible, their difference of longitude may be determined by reciprocal observations of azimuth.

78. If the latitude of a place be determined by observing the altitude of the sun at 6 o'clock, and the tabulated declination be affected by a small error, find the corresponding error in the latitude.

79. Given the time of sunrise and the altitude of the sun when due east on the same day, to find the latitude of the place, and the declination of the sun.

80. Having given the contemporaneous altitudes of the sun and a known star, on a given day, and also the angular distance between them; find the latitude of the place and the hour of day.

81. A known circumpolar star reaches its maximum azimuth at two different places at the same instant: having given the values of the maximum azimuth at the two places, find their latitudes, and the difference of longitude.

82. Determine the latitude of the place of observation from the times of the rising of two known stars.

83. Given the latitudes of two places, and their difference of longitude; determine the inclination of their horizons, and the day of the year on which the sun sets to both places at the same instant.

84. Find the latitude from observing the angular distance of the extreme points of the horizon in which the sun appears at rising in the course of a year; and, if α, β denote the distances of those points from the point in which the sun rises when the declination is δ, prove that sine of the obliquity

$$= \sin \delta \, \frac{\sin \frac{1}{2}(\alpha + \beta)}{\sin \frac{1}{2}(\alpha - \beta)}.$$

85. The zenith distances of a star (α, β) in the same vertical plane are observed; the interval between the two observations expressed in angle being h. Shew that the latitude l of the place and the declination δ of the star are given by the equations

$$\cos \delta \sin \frac{h}{2} = \sin \frac{\beta + \alpha}{2},$$

$$\sin l \cos \frac{\beta - \alpha}{2} = \sin \delta \cos \frac{\beta + \alpha}{2}.$$

86. The earth is touched by two equal conical surfaces, the planes of whose bases coincide with that of the equator; and its surface appears projected upon them, to an eye placed in its centre. Shew that by a proper assumption of the form of the cones, the earth's surface may be thus projected on a plane circle.

87. Assuming $13°$ and $1°$ as the diurnal angular motions of the moon and sun about the earth, $\frac{1}{60}$ as the sine of moon's horizontal parallax, shew that the duration of a central solar eclipse very nearly $= \frac{4(\alpha + \beta)}{2 - \cos l \sin \theta}$ hours: and the duration of totality or annularity (as the case may be) $= \frac{4(\alpha - \beta)}{2 - \cos l \sin \theta}$ hours: where α and β are the angular diameters of the sun and moon in parts of a degree, l the latitude of the place of observation, θ the inclination of the central line at that place to the meridian.

88. Is it possible for a central eclipse to be total at one place and annular at another?

89. If ϵ and ϵ' be the semi-vertical angles of the earth's umbra and penumbra, S the sun's apparent diameter, then

$$2 \tan S = \tan \epsilon + \tan \epsilon'.$$

90. Investigate an equation for determining the times of the year most advantageous for determining the parallax of a given fixed star by observations of its distance from a neigh-

bouring star. If at one of these times u be the difference of the longitudes of the sun and star, λ the latitude of the latter, δ the angular distance between the two stars, and α the change of position of the line joining them in the course of half a year, shew that the parallax of the greater star

$$= \alpha \sin \delta \sqrt{1 + \cos^2 u \cot^2 \lambda}.$$

91. In what positions has a star (1) no aberration; (2) none in longitude; (3) a negative aberration in longitude only?

www.ingramcontent.com/pod-product-compliance
Lightning Source LLC
Chambersburg PA
CBHW051244300426
44114CB00011B/878